Advances in Immigrant Family Research

Series Editor
Susan S. Chuang
University of Guelph
Guelph, ON, Canada

More information about this series at http://www.springer.com/series/8807

Susan S. Chuang • Roy Moodley
Uwe P. Gielen • Saadia Akram-Pall
Editors

Asian Families in Canada and the United States

Implications for Mental Health and Well-Being

Springer

Editors
Susan S. Chuang
University of Guelph
Guelph, ON, Canada

Roy Moodley
University of Toronto
Toronto, ON, Canada

Uwe P. Gielen
St. Francis College
Brooklyn, NY, USA

Saadia Akram-Pall
Private Practice
Toronto, ON, Canada

ISSN 2625-364X ISSN 2625-3666 (electronic)
Advances in Immigrant Family Research
ISBN 978-3-030-56450-6 ISBN 978-3-030-56452-0 (eBook)
https://doi.org/10.1007/978-3-030-56452-0

This Springer imprint is published by the registered company Springer Nature Switzerland AG
The registered company address is: Gewerbestrasse 11, 6330 Cham, Switzerland

To my parents who immigrated from Taiwan shortly after getting married, who struggled to make a new life in Canada for my three brothers and me, and to my extended family in the United States.

– Susan S. Chuang

I would like to dedicate this volume to Elaine P. Congress who for many years has served as an advocate on behalf of immigrants and refugees.

– Uwe P. Gielen

To all the people and communities that are discussed in this volume, and especially to the many refugees and asylum seekers who are hoping to escape from war, persecution, and oppression.

– Susan S. Chuang, Roy Moodley,
Uwe P. Gielen, and Saadia Akram-Pall

Contents

About the Editors

Susan S. Chuang, PhD, is an Associate Professor at the University of Guelph, Canada. Her research focuses on fathering, parenting, and parent-child relationships of young children among immigrant and ethnic families in various sociocultural contexts (Asian: Canada, China, Hong Kong, Taiwan; Latino/a: Paraguay, the United States; Black: Jamaica). Her second line of research examines families and immigration, collaborating with national organizations in Canada. She conducts numerous volunteer workshops for the local communities that focus on various topics (e.g., parenting, education, child/youth development, employment). She also is the Series Editor for Springer's Advances in Immigrant Family Research. She has organized six international conferences on immigrant and ethnic minority families.

Roy Moodley, PhD, is an Associate Professor in clinical and counseling psychology at the University of Toronto, Canada. Dr. Moodley is also the Director of the Centre for Diversity in Counselling and Psychotherapy. His research interests include critical multicultural counseling and psychotherapy, race and culture in psychoanalysis, global south psychologies, traditional healing, and mix-race relations.

Uwe P. Gielen, PhD, grew up as a displaced person/refugee in Germany. He is the Founder and Executive Director of the Institute for International and Cross-Cultural Psychology at St. Francis College, New York City, USA. His work focuses on cross-cultural and international psychology, Chinese American immigrant adolescents and young adults, international family psychology, and moral development. His more than 190 publications include 30 edited, coedited, and coauthored volumes and nine special journal issues. He has lectured in 34 countries and has served as President of the Society for Cross-Cultural Research, the International Council of Psychologists, and the International Psychology Division 52 of the American Psychological Association.

Saadia Akram-Pall, EdD, is a registered psychologist with the College of Psychologists of Ontario and operates her private practice in the Greater Toronto Areas (GTA), Canada, as well as works within the nonprofit, community-based sector. She has more than 25 years of experience delivering psychological services and professional development trainings to a wide variety of diverse and multicultural populations. She has published in journals as well as authored a book entitled *Abnormal Psychology*, with A-One Publisher (Lahore, Pakistan).

About the Authors

Ahmed Afzal, PhD, is an Assistant Professor of Anthropology at California State University, Fullerton, USA. He is the author of *Lone Star Muslims: Transnational Lives and the South Asian Experience in Texas* (NYU Press, 2015). His research focuses on globalization, urbanism, and everyday life; gender and sexuality cross-culturally; Urdu-language Pakistani television dramas and Indian cinema; anthropology of digital media; and new immigrant experiences in the United States with special geographical interests in contemporary Pakistan and the United States.

Florette Cohen, PhD, is a social psychologist at the College of Staten Island, CUNY, USA. Her interests are centered around the psychology of prejudice and social identity with a focus on anti-Semitism. She has authored or coauthored several empirical studies of anti-Semitism.

Kieu Anh Do, PhD, is an Assistant Professor in the Department of Human Ecology at the University of Maryland Eastern Shore, USA. Her research focuses on family resilience, culture, and mental health.

Denise Farrelly, EdD, is an Assistant Professor of Childhood Education at Kingsborough Community College, USA. Her research is centered on best practices in the development of cultural competence and professional identity within teacher education. Prior to joining Kingsborough's faculty, she worked with early childhood and elementary students as a classroom teacher and literacy consultant in culturally and linguistically diverse classrooms in New York City public schools.

Julie Hakim-Larson, PhD, is a Professor of Child Clinical Psychology at the University of Windsor, Canada. Her research interests include Arab ethnic identity and mental health, culture, and emotional development. She has coedited a book on biopsychosocial perspectives on Arab Americans (2014, Springer) and has written a textbook on emotional development (2018, Palgrave Macmillan).

Yang Hu, PhD, is a Senior Lecturer in the Department of Sociology at Lancaster University, UK. His research focuses on gender, family, and intimate relationships in a global context. He authored, *Chinese-British Intermarriage: Disentangling Gender and Ethnicity* (2016, Palgrave Macmillan). His research interests include gender inequality in household financial organization, perceptions of gendered housework division in cross-national contexts, the role of artificial intelligence in the (re)production of labor market gender and ethnic inequality, and transnational families and family migration.

Ching-Yu Huang, PhD, is a Lecturer (Assistant Professor) in Developmental Psychology at Keele University, UK. She is involved in various research projects in the area of cross-cultural psychology, applied forensic psychology, domestic violence, bullying, parenting, acculturation, and children's social and emotional development. Her research work adopts multidisciplinary, multi-method design and has strong applications for psychological, forensic, educational, and social-work practices.

Jessica J. Jeong, PhD (candidate), is a doctoral candidate in the Clinical-Developmental Psychology at York University, Canada, and a Korean-Canadian scholar whose research/clinical interests include building a stronger sense of belonging and cohesion in our communities.

Bobbie Kabuto, PhD, is a Professor at Queens College, City University of New York, USA, and Chairperson of the Elementary and Early Childhood Education Department. She is the 2019 Recipient of the United Kingdom Literacy Association (UKLA)/Wiley Research in Literacy Education Award. Her research interests include biliteracy and socially constructed identities. She works with families to examine how schooling discourses frame reading and writing identities and how or why families support or challenge these identities in the home.

Daniel Kaplin, PhD, is an Assistant Professor of Psychology and Director of the Forum on Migration at St. Francis College, USA. His research explores cross-cultural psychology, immigration, religion/spirituality, and prescriptive authority for psychologists. He has received many awards and recognition for his work, including NYSPA's prestigious Diversity Award.

Abdul Khaleque, PhD, is an Adjunct Professor in the Department of Human Development and Family Sciences, and a Senior Scientist in the Ronald and Nancy Rohner Center for the Study of Interpersonal Acceptance and Rejection at the University of Connecticut, USA. His areas of research include cross-cultural parenting and lifespan development, and interpersonal acceptance and psychological adjustment of children and adults. His book (2018) entitled *Intimate Relationship Across the Lifespan: Formation, Development, Enrichment, and Maintenance* (ABC-CLIO/Praeger Publications) won two IPPY awards in 2019.

Ann H. Kim, PhD, is an Associate Professor of Sociology at York University and FacultyAssociate of the York Centre for Asian Research, Canada. She is coeditor of

KoreanImmigrants in Canada (University of Toronto Press, 2012), and *Outward and UpwardMobilities: International Studies in Canada, Their Families, and Structuring Institutions* (University of Toronto Press, 2019).

Xuan Li, PhD, is an Assistant Professor of Psychology at NYU Shanghai, China, and is an affiliated member of NYU-ECNU Institute for Social Development, and Department of Applied Psychology, NYU Steinhardt School of Culture, Education, and Human Development, USA. Her research focuses on fatherhood, parent-child interactions and relationships, and children and adolescents' socioemotional development in contemporary Chinese societies.

Jonathan Palumbo, PhD (candidate), is a doctoral student at Pace University, USA. He is completing a clinical internship at Hamilton-Madison House, providing individual and group psychotherapy to an ethnically and culturally diverse clientele. Previously, at Staten Island University Hospital, he conducted neuropsychological assessments and psychotherapy in an inpatient and outpatient setting with cognitively, medically, and physically involved individuals.

Kristen Parente, PhD (candidate), is a doctoral student in the School/Clinical Psychology program at Kean University, USA, and the current President of APA Division 12 Section 10. Her research interests include marginalized groups, specifically in the childhood and adolescent population. She is also an active member of state-level psychological associations.

Shawna A. Scott, PhD, is a registered doctoral psychologist who provides assessment and treatment services to children and youth in Regina, Canada, through the Saskatchewan Health Authority. Her research focuses on emotion-related parenting and maternal values in ethnically diverse families living in Canada.

Uma A. Segal, PhD, is the Curators' Distinguished Professor of the School of Social Work at the University of Missouri–St. Louis, USA. Her specialization is immigrant and refugee integration in a global perspective. As Editor-in-Chief of the *Journal of Immigrant & Refugee Studies* from 2004 to 2012, she redirected it toward an international, interdisciplinary focus in exploring human migration.

Spencer B. Talbot, BA, is a master's student at the University of Guelph, Canada. His research interests focus on areas of family well-being, family communication, fathering, and parental roles in families. He has volunteered at a psychological treatment center, assisted a number of parenting workshops, as well as engaged in the community through the Guelph Minor Hockey Association.

Tracy S. Tiemeier, PhD, is an Associate Professor of Theological Studies at Loyola Marymount University, Los Angeles, USA. She is the author of numerous articles and essays on gender in Asian and Asian American theology and (inter) religious contexts. She is coeditor of *Interreligious Friendship After* Nostra Aetate (Palgrave Macmillan, 2015).

Yan Ruth Xia, PhD, is a Professor in the Department of Child, Youth and Family Studies at the University of Nebraska–Lincoln, USA. She conducts research on immigrant youth behavior and mental health, parent-adolescent communication and relationship, and Asian immigrant families.

Xiaolin (Charline) Xie, PhD, is a Professor of Family and Child Studies at Northern Illinois University, USA. Her research interests include Asian American family strengths, and faith and resiliency of Asian Americans' seniors.

Chapter 1
The Complexities of Asian Families from Around the World: Creating New Lives in Canada and the United States

Susan S. Chuang and Uwe P. Gielen

Abstract As of 2020, Asian immigrants constitute Canada's leading group of immigrants as well as the second largest group in the United States. Migration from Asia's 48 countries and three special territories to the New World has helped to transform both Canada and the United States into multicultural nations in which West and East are meeting each other in creative, challenging, and historically unprecedented ways. This volume will provide the reader with a better appreciation of how diverse Asian traditions can be. Thus, the purpose of the chapters is to portray and analyze Asian American and Asian Canadian immigrant families in an integrated yet nuanced fashion, while paying special attention to their mental health and well-being.

Keywords Canada · United States · Asian families · Defining Asian · Mental health · Well-being · Immigrant families

Throughout a major part of the history of both Canada and the United States, immigrants from Asia were considered unwelcomed until the 1960s when both countries significantly revised their immigration laws (Cohn, 2015; Li, 2000). Currently, Asian immigrants constitute Canada's leading group of immigrants as well as the second largest group in the United States (Statistics Canada, 2017; U.S. Census Bureau, 2018). Immigration is a lifelong process that profoundly influences the identities and well-being of the immigrants themselves as well as their children, grandchildren, and other family members. At the same time, migration from Asia's

S. S. Chuang (✉)
University of Guelph, Guelph, ON, Canada
e-mail: schuang@uoguelph.ca

U. P. Gielen
St. Francis College, Brooklyn, NY, USA
e-mail: ugielen@sfc.edu

S. S. Chuang et al. (eds.), *Asian Families in Canada and the United States*, Advances in Immigrant Family Research,
https://doi.org/10.1007/978-3-030-56452-0_1

48 countries and three special territories to the New World has helped to transform both Canada and the United States into multicultural nations in which West and East are meeting each other in creative, challenging, and historically unprecedented ways.

For this volume, we are classifying and focusing on Asian immigrants whose family background connects them to Asian countries ranging from Japan in the East to the Levant in the West. Specifically, this volume examines Asian immigrant families' psychological, emotional, social well-being, and challenges Asian immigrant families while placing them in broader historical and sociocultural contexts. It is addressed to members of the highly diverse Asian immigrant communitiesy in North America, together with counselors, community workers, educators, social workers, students, and interested individuals who wish to better understand and support these immigrant families.

This volume provides the reader with a better appreciation of how diverse Asian traditions can be. Thus, the purpose of the chapters is to portray and analyze Asian American and Asian Canadian immigrant families in an integrated yet nuanced fashion, while paying special attention to their mental health and well-being. This attempt is very challenging since Asian families and individuals have been arriving from numerous culturally diverse countries and regions within countries that collectively make up about 59.8% of the world's population as of 2020 (Worldometer, n.d.).

Following generally accepted geographic conventions, the volume includes families whose ancestry can be traced to East Asia, Southeast Asia, South Asia, Central Asia, and West Asia (Middle East). In contrast, most U.S.-American books on Asian Americans pay extensive attention to persons with East, South and Southeast Asian backgrounds, but often ignore those with ancestors from Asia's Central and Western regions. Moreover, their contents tend to be restricted to the U.S. only, with little mention of Asian Canadians or other host countries. For example, psychological research does not encompass the global population as Arnett (2008) illustrated in his content analyses of six premier APA journals. He reported that most of the psychological research is American-dominated (Cole, 2006), with American researchers restricting their attention to the U.S. population which only makes up less than 5% of the global population, and ignoring more than 95% of the population. Moreover, the samples in the studies were over two thirds Americans, and the majority were of European backgrounds (60% to 88% across these journals). In contrast, the studies on Asians comprised only 3% (see Arnett, 2008; also see Henrich, Heine, & Norenzayan, 2010).

Even when attention has focused on immigrant Asian families or even broader, ethnic minority families, the exploration of various ethnicities *within* a broader ethnic group like Asians, has been limited. Rather, many books on Asian Americans/ Canadians have been dominated by a relative emphasis on families of East Asian origin, with minimal attention given to other Asian groups such as South, Southeast, West Asian families (Fong, 2007; Kitano & Daniels, 2000; Min, 2005; Russell, Crockett, & Chao, 2010; Trinh, Rho, Lu, & Sanders, 2009).

To address this gap in the current literature, we used an interdisciplinary approach so that the reader can gain an appreciation for both the great diversity as well as the common trends and shared characteristics of the numerous cultural traditions subsumed under the label "Asian." More generally, the chapters analyze ecological and structural aspects, the intertwining of cultural values, norms, social roles, and psychological processes, the nature of intergenerational relations, gender roles, the families' participation in educational, economic, and religious institutions, factors supporting or undermining the mental health of family members, and the broader societal contexts in which their lives are embedded. Some chapters attempt to interweave a discussion of selected common trends and shared characteristics with the contradictions and opportunities that emerge in the context of cultural diversity, ethnic traditions, social class differences, intergenerational processes, and bicultural conceptions of gender roles.

Other important considerations include new immigrant expectations, tacit as well as acknowledged psychological vulnerabilities, and resilience and coping skills that have supported the mental health of family members. In brief, we hope the reader will gain an appreciation of the history and personal narratives of immigrant Asian families in Canada and the United States.

This volume includes four sections: (a) history, religion, and culture; (b) specific countries and regions of origin; (c) counselling and therapy for mental health and well-being; and (d) methodological considerations. It is important to contextualize Asian families in Canada and the United States to gain a broader perspective on the complexities and nuances of the various Asian groups by location and region. Thus, in Part I: History, Religion, and Culture, Gielen, Chuang, Moodley, and Talbot's chapter entitled, *Comparing and Contrasting Asian Families in Canada and the United States* (Chap. 2), provides an historical account of the immigration policies in Canada and the U.S.. However, they first discuss an often overlooked or not well-understood aspect of this topic – the social construction of the label, "Asian." They explore how the label has been defined and operationalized via categories for Census data which has had significant implications for not only researchers but also for various political and policy agendas. Gielen and his colleagues also discuss the similarities and differences among Asian subgroups and between Asian Canadians and Asian Americans to stress the importance of contextualizing both the country of origin as well as the host country.

To further the debate on the importance of culture and context, Tiemeier discusses religion in her chapter entitled, *Asian Families: Religion, Spirituality, and Worldviews* (Chap. 3). As religion, spiritualities and worldviews are integral to the lives of Asian families and communities, Tiemeier discusses 12 religions and the roles that gender, sexuality, and family play in religion. This chapter is essential for mental health professionals to gain greater insights into the dynamics and functioning of families in the context of various religious traditions, their fluidity of change and transformation within and among subethnic groups that are often embedded in the everyday lives of Asian individuals.

The next three sections, Parts II – IV, include eight chapters that focus on specific Asian immigrant groups. There are four chapters that discuss immigrants from East Asian countries and regions, including Mainland China, Hong Kong, and Taiwan, Japan, and Korea (Chaps. 4, 5, 6, and 7). Three chapters explore South

Asian immigrant families from Bangladesh, India, and Pakistan (Chaps. 8, 9, and 10), while one chapter discusses West Asian families from the Levant. The chapters discuss a variety of topics, including various interdisciplinary and ecological approaches conducive to a balanced and integrated consideration of psychological, social, economic, and cultural factors influencing the nature and functioning of Asian families in Canada and the United States. Specifically, general emphasis is placed on the analysis of family structural aspects, the intertwining of cultural values, norms, social roles, and psychological processes, the nature of intergenerational relations, gender roles, factors supporting or undermining the mental health of family members, their participation in educational, economic, and religious institutions, and the broader societal contexts that help shape their lives.

Mental Health and Well-being of Asian Immigrants

Many members of immigrant Asian families will do best in terms of their physical and mental health if they are able to integrate the strengths of their original Asian cultures with the positive opportunities offered by their new North American environments. In this context, some research studies with Asian (and Latin American) immigrants have pointed to the so-called immigrant paradox. The surprising results of these studies indicate that recent immigrants engage in more adaptive behaviors and possess better physical and mental health than their U.S.-born ethnic peers. They are less likely to: be anxious and depressed, be involved in antisocial behavior, depend on alcohol consumption, get involved in risky behaviors, engage in early sexual relations, and drop out of high school (Nguyen, 2011; Takeuchi et al., 2007). This suggests that remaining integrated in a relatively conservative Asian immigrant culture helps many adolescents as well as adults to keep on the straight and narrow path. In contrast, endorsing a melting pot ideology does not seem to be an optimal strategy for Asian immigrants nor may it be for their host countries.

As should be clear from these brief comparisons, the backgrounds and fates of Asian immigrants and their families can vary enormously. However, even the luckier ones among them must cope with stress-inducing situations while adjusting to new forms of thinking, feeling, striving, and behaving. At the same time, the U.S. and Canada need their presence since their native populations are now aging due to their low birthrates. Decades into the twenty-first century, there are even more immigrants who live in the U.S. than anywhere else, yet anti-immigration sentiments have (again) become an important part of the country's political landscape.

In Canada and Australia, the percentage of residents who were born overseas is even higher than that in the U.S.. In all three countries, Asian immigrants have been increasing at a rapid rate, thus reflecting the global rise of Asia together with the emergence of new multicultural and multiracial worlds in North America (Frey, 2018) and elsewhere. The migration of Asians to North America, Europe, and

Australia is an important part of the rise of migration across much of the world (Adler & Gielen, 2003).

At the individual level, migration relies on the personal initiative of those venturing to create psychologically and culturally complex forms of family life far away from their original Asian homelands. The migration context forces most of them to leave behind at least some family-of-origin members, together with childhood friends, ingrained ways of doing things, speaking effortlessly the language that everyone around them speaks, and so much more. At the same time, a good number of immigrants may have to confront disappointments, dashed hopes, or perhaps a sense of rootlessness and feelings of disorientation in their new country. Their counselors, therapists, social workers, teachers, immigration attorneys, and other advocates must always be aware of such possibilities. At the same time, they need to make immigrant children, youths, and adults feel that they are welcome in their new country to which they can contribute so much.

Thus, Part III: Counseling and Therapy for Mental Health and Well-being includes two chapters that explicitly discuss the importance of counseling and therapy for Asian families. Specifically, in Chap. 12 entitled, *Asian-Origin Families in Canada and the United States: Challenges and Resilience*, Do and her colleagues critically explore the challenges of racism, discrimination, stereotypes, aging, as well as domestic and interpersonal violence. Immigration issues such as acculturation and intergenerational relationships as they relate to conflicts and stress are placed into the context provided by various Asian subethnic groups. Importantly, they also stress the strengths and resilience of Asian immigrant families.

Complementing this chapter is Kaplin et al.'s chapter entitled, *Providing Therapy with Asian Immigrant Families: A Review of Prominent Issues and Treatment Considerations* (Chap. 13). The researchers address various common family-related issues among Asian families, with specific attention to the sub-ethnic groups (i.e., East, South, West Asian families). Bridging research and applied practice, they offer a detailed and culturally sensitive 15-item assessment instrument for counselors and therapists as a guideline to better understand the unique cultural nuances and dynamics in Asian families. The key issues that are addressed include: (a) acculturative stress; (b) anti-immigration rhetoric; (c) differences in the experiences of refugees and asylum seekers relative to orderly migration; (d) stereotypes; (e) war-based conflict; (f) mental health stigma; (g) intimate partner violence; (h) physical punishment; and (i) other forms of abuse, neglect, and maltreatment. Attention is also given to intervention programs that have supporting evidence of their effectiveness in families.

Lastly, how researchers define and operationalize their constructs and perspectives on Asian families is reflected in their utilization of methodologies. To illustrate the varying ways that researchers have defined and explored Asian families, Chuang, Li, Huang, and Hu's chapter entitled, *Critically Assessing the Methodological Challenges of Exploring Chinese Immigrant Fathers* (Chap. 14), provides an in-depth exploration of the challenges confronting research on Chinese immigrant fathers. Unfortunately, Chinese fathers have been neglected in the field, although a better understanding of this group would considerably enrich the fatherhood scholarship.

The overall goal of the edited book is to help inform and guide researchers and more importantly, practitioners, of how to enhance the lives of Asian immigrant members in their communities to become fully participating members in their host societies. Counselors have a very important mission, and this holds especially true at a time when re-awakened anti-immigrant feelings in the U.S. and Europe threaten to overwhelm too many native people's feelings of empathy and compassion. In addition, it behooves professionals to correct commonly encountered misperceptions of Asian and other immigrants among the general public. By pointing to the many contributions they have been making, and can still make, to their new home countries, counselors are also indirectly contributing to the mental health and happiness of struggling immigrants, their families and children, and grandchildren.

References

Adler, L. L., & Gielen, U. P. (Eds.). (2003). *Migration: Immigration and emigration in international perspective*. Praeger.

Arnett, J. J. (2008). The neglected 95%: Why American psychology needs to become less American. *American Psychologist, 63*, 602–614. https://doi.org/10.1037/0003-066X.63.7.602

Cohn, D. (2015). *How U.S. immigration laws and rules have changed through history*. Pew Research Center. https://www.pewresearch.org/fact-tank/2015/09/30/how-u-s-immigration-laws-and-rules-have-changed-through-history/

Cole, M. (2006). Internationalism in psychology: We need it now more than ever. *American Psychologist, 61*, 224–235. https://doi.org/10.1037/0003-066X.61.8.904

Fong, T. P. (2007). *The Contemporary Asian American experience: Beyond the model minority* (3rd ed.). Pearson.

Frey, W. H. (2018). *Diversity explosion: How new racial demographics are remaking America* (rev. ed.). Brookings Institution Press.

Henrich, J., Heine, S. J., & Norenzayan, A. (2010). Beyond WEIRD: Towards a broad-based behavioral science. *Behavioral and Brain Sciences, 33*, 111–135. https://doi.org/10.1017/S0140525X10000725

Kitano, H. H. L., & Daniels, R. (2000). *Asian Americans: Emerging minorities* (3rd ed.). Pearson.

Li, P. S. (2000). *Cultural diversity in Canada: The social construction of racial differences*. Department of Justice Canada. https://www.justice.gc.ca/eng/rp-pr/csj-sjc/jsp-sjp/rp02_8-dr02_8/index.html

Min, P. G. (Ed.). (2005). *Asian Americans: Contemporary trends and issues* (2nd ed.). Pine Forge Press.

Nguyen, H. (2011). Asians and the immigrant paradox. In F. T. L. Leong, L. Juang, D. B. Qin, & H. E. Fitzgerald (Eds.), *Asian American and Pacific Islander children and mental health* (Vol. 1, pp. 1–22). Praeger.

Russell, S. T., Crockett, L. J., & Chao, R. K. (2010). *Asian American parenting and parent-adolescent relationships*. Springer.

Statistics Canada. (2017). *Immigration and ethnocultural diversity: Key results from the 2016 Census*.https://www150.statcan.gc.ca/n1/daily-quotidien/171025/dq171025b-eng.htm

Takeuchi, D., Zane, N., Hong, S., Chae, D., Gong, F., Gee, G., … Alegria, M. (2007). Immigration-related factors and mental disorders among Asian Americans. *American Journal of Mental Health, 97*(1), 84–90. https://doi.org/10.2105/AJPH.2006.088401

Trinh, N., Rho, Y. C., Lu, F. G., & Sanders, K. M. (2009). *Handbook of mental health and acculturation in Asian American families*. Humana Press.

U.S. Census Bureau. (2018). *Selected population profile in the United States*. https://data.census.gov/cedsci/table?q=S0201&tid=ACSSPP1Y2018.S0201

Worldometer. (n.d.). *Asian population*. https://www.worldometers.info/world-population/asia-population/

Part I
History, Religion, and Culture

Chapter 2
Comparing and Contrasting Asian Families in Canada and the United States

Uwe P. Gielen, Susan S. Chuang, Roy Moodley, and Spencer B. Talbot

Abstract During the last half century, immigration from Asian countries to Canada and the United States has increased dramatically. Thus, researchers need to better understand the complexities of Asian families in the respective countries. Although Canada and the U.S. share the world's longest undefended border as well as some similarities in their respective histories, the two societies differ in many significant ways. Thus, the purpose of the chapter is to explore Asian families in Canada and the United States. Specifically, we first discuss the conceptualization of the term "Asian" and how countries have defined and operationalized the ethnic term. A brief historical account is also provided, along with a discussion about the issues of labeling individuals. Next, we focus on the immigration policies and demographics of Asian immigrants in the respective countries, bringing some attention to the similarities and differences between them. We further examine the top three largest Asian groups, Chinese, Indian, and Filipino/a immigrants to illustrate the uniqueness of the various ethnic groups.

Keywords Canada · United States · Asian families · Immigrant policies · Demographics · Asian American · Asian Canadian

U. P. Gielen (✉)
St. Francis College, Brooklyn, NY, USA
e-mail: ugielen@sfc.edu

S. S. Chuang
University of Guelph, Guelph, ON, Canada
e-mail: schuang@uoguelph.ca

R. Moodley
University of Toronto, Toronto, ON, Canada
e-mail: roy.moodley@utoronto.ca

S. B. Talbot
University of Guelph, Guelph, ON, Canada
e-mail: stalbo01@uoguelph.ca

S. S. Chuang et al. (eds.), *Asian Families in Canada and the United States*, Advances in Immigrant Family Research,
https://doi.org/10.1007/978-3-030-56452-0_2

During the last half century, immigration from Asian countries to Canada and the United States has increased dramatically. Census figures indicate that 17.7% of all Canadians in 2016 and 6.4% of all U.S.-Americans in 2018 reported Asian ancestry. Asian countries continue to be major source countries to the extent that Asian immigrants are the fastest growing immigrant group of all major "racial-ethnic" groupings in Canada and the U.S.. Moreover, the majority of these Asian immigrants compose of first- and/or second-generation immigrant people (see Table 2.1; Statistics Canada, 2019; U.S. Census Bureau, 2018). Thus, researchers and practitioners need to better understand the complexities of Asian families in the respective countries.

Although Canada and the U.S. share the world's longest undefended border, as well as some similarities in their respective histories, the two societies differ in many significant ways. One major difference concerns their widely differing population sizes: Canadians sometimes joke that living next door to the world's leading global power is like sleeping next to an elephant. Should that elephant decide to turn over, the consequences for the sleeping neighbor could be enormous. Thus, the relationship between Canada and the U.S. is important to further explore the similarities and differences between the two countries. With a specific focus on Asian families, we first discuss the conceptualization of the term "Asian" and how countries have defined and operationalized the ethnic term. A brief historical account is also provided, along with a discussion about the issues of labeling individuals. Next, we focus on the immigration policies and demographics of Asian immigrants in the respective countries, bringing some attention to the similarities and differences between the two countries. We further examine the top three largest Asian groups, Chinese, Indian, and Filipino/as immigrants, to illustrate the uniqueness of the various ethnic groups.

Conceptualizing, Defining, and Operationalizing the Term "Asian"

The comparison of the Asian immigrant population between Canada and the United States is not so straightforward. The countries' historical perspectives on Asian persons and their definitions on this group are considerably different. Thus, a greater understanding of how "Asian" has been operationalized between countries needs to be gained among researchers and practitioners and taken into consideration when discussing Asian families across these two countries (see Table 2.1 for summary).

The first step is to review how each country has conceptualized and defined "Asian," which is then reflected in the Census data. According to Canada's Census, the definition (tabulation) of "Asians" includes persons with origins from West Central Asian and Middle Eastern countries (e.g., Afghanistan, Iran, Israel), South Asian countries (e.g., Bangladesh, Sri Lanka), East and Southeast Asian countries (e.g., China, Japan), and "other" Asian origins countries (Statistics Canada, n.d.). In

Table 2.1 Immigration-related similarities and differences between Canada and the United States

Issue	Canada	United States
Country's population size in 2018	37.1 million	327.2 million
Number and percentage of immigrants born overseas in 2017	7.5 million (21.9%)	44.5 million (13.7%)
Top source continents of immigrants	Africa, East Asia, Europe	Latin America, Asia
Country's definition of "Asian Immigrant"	Includes East, Southeast, South, Central, West Asian immigrants	Includes East, Southeast, South Asian but not Central and West Asian immigrants
Percentage of population with Asian ancestry	17.7% (2016)	6.4% (does not include Central and West Asians) (2018)
Top six Asian groups	Chinese, Indian, Filipino/a, Vietnamese, Pakistani, Iranian	Chinese, Indian, Filipino/a, Vietnamese, Korean, Japanese
Key settlement areas for Asian families	Ontario, British Columbia, Alberta; Metropolitan Toronto, Vancouver, Montreal	West Coast including California, Hawaii; Metropolitan New York, Los Angeles, San Francisco Bay Area, Seattle, Houston, Chicago
Emphases of country's immigration policy	Point system favors well-educated immigrants fluent in English and/or French, less emphasis on family unification, humanitarian considerations	Policy emphasizes family reunion, moderate emphasis on labor/economic needs, declining emphasis on humanitarian considerations
Prevalence of unauthorized immigrants	Unauthorized immigrants not very common	High prevalence among Mexican and Central American immigrants, moderate prevalence among Chinese, Indian, and other Asian immigrants
Most common religious identities of selected Asian immigrant groups	Christians: Philippines, South Korea, Vietnam; Muslims: Pakistan, Bangladesh, West Asia; Hindus: India; Buddhist or unaffiliated: China, Thailand, Vietnam, Cambodia, Laos	Christians: Philippines, South Korea; Muslims: Pakistan, Bangladesh, West Asia; Hindus: India; Buddhist or unaffiliated: China, Thailand, Vietnam, Cambodia, Laos
Examples of racist policies prior to 1960s	Chinese Immigration Act (1885 – Head Tax); Chinese Immigration Act (1923) excludes all Chinese immigrants; Japanese-Canadian Internment (1942–1949) esp. in British Columbia (21,000+ persons)	Chinese Exclusion Act: 1882–1943; Internment of 110,000+ Japanese: 1941ff; Miscegenation laws existed in many U.S. States until 1967

comparison, the U.S. Census definition is more narrow and less inclusive, only encompassing persons with origins from the Far East, Southeast Asia, or the Indian subcontinent (e.g., Cambodia, China, Korea, Pakistan) (U.S. Census Bureau, n.d.).

From geolocation comes "labeling" of ethnic groups which is the starting point for researchers and practitioners to explore ethnic families. However, like the labels given to "the other," the term "Asians" is one that is fraught with tensions, controversies, and complexities. The socio-political and historical contexts and the socioeconomic paradigms within which these definitions are being constructed have frequently changed over time and across space. For example, through the processes and practices of colonialism and imperialism of North American countries, the framing of "the other" has frequently been infused with debatable assumptions, more or less implicit forms of stereotyping, Western conceptions of otherness, and personal and institutional racism (Gilroy, 2000). This phenomenon is typically underpinned by a masculine and patriarchal culture. Because naming "the other" is based on power dynamics, as well as place and context, the terms Asian Americans and Asian Canadians have over a period of time changed their definition and constituency from terms such as Oriental or Mongoloid to Asiatic to Asians.

According to Said (1978), the term, "Oriental," was a negative way in which the West went along with the process of trying to reclaim its identity and self. He maintains, "European culture gained in strength and identity by setting itself off against the Orient as a surrogate and underground self" (Said, 1978, p. 3). Said's analysis of this process was that the Orient was created or, as he called it, 'Orientalized' to establish "a relationship of power, of domination, of varying degrees of a complex hegemony" (1978, p. 5). Moreover, this label became attached with derogatory meaning, while ensuring an "otherness." As Umemoto stated in an interview with NBC News,

> Many of the stereotypes of Orientals and Orientalism were part of the project of imperialist conquest — British, and later, American — in Asia, with the exoticization of the Oriental as well as the creation of threat and fear, as evidenced in the yellow peril movement (Kandil, 2018).

Thus, "Oriental" was changed to "Asian American" in 1968, symbolizing a movement to unite various Asian groups who shared history of immigration, labor exploitation, and racism. This term was self-determined by Asians themselves, not given by "outsiders," and used as a political agenda of equality, anti-racism, and anti-imperialism (Kandil, 2018).

Within the discourse of modern "identity politics," it seems that the panethnic term, Asian, is understood to be too broad and wide, not offering the desired range of diversity in terms of culture, ethnicity, language, and religion. The various groups and communities within the Asian diaspora can, and often do, advocate for more singular concepts and identities defined by country or ethnicity, rather than continent, such as Asian Indians, Bangladeshis, Cambodians, Chinese, Filipino, Hmong, Indonesians, Iranians, Iraqis, Japanese, Koreans, Laotians, Lebanese, Pakistanis, Sri Lankans, Thai, and Vietnamese.

At the same time, broader terms such as Asian immigrants, North Asians, South Asians, East Asians and West Asians (a term currently less often used) have nevertheless become the beacon of hope for academic research projects, social and cultural institutional engagements, Asian American and Asian Canadian academic programs and departments, government organizations, administrative and planning departments, and political control.

Within the Asian diaspora, the terms Asian American or Asian Canadian have been accepted and celebrated to acknowledge the presence of this diverse community as a single unit. This holds true in spite of those contradictions and complications created by notions of culture, religion, race, and ethnicity, and in spite of past wars and present political tensions between various Asian nations.

The term, Asian, creates a boundary or borderline within the broader context of North American multiculturalism. Being Asian is not just about the origins and heritage from the Asian continent, but also about not being a black person as understood by Americans and Canadians (i.e., an African or Caribbean), or a white person of European background, or an indigenous American/Canadian, or a Latinx person from south of the U.S. – Mexican border. This identity then, based on a shared immigration history, urban demography and historical culture, asserts itself in the struggle for rights and privileges, and for social and economic justice. According to Nguyen, Shibusawa, and Chen (2012), it allows this ethnic group to unite under one broader term to provide greater social power to raise attention to past struggles and to fight social discrimination and racism (see also Takaki, 1993).

An important event that launched the creation of the broader Asian American identity occurred in 1968, when students of various ethnic and racial minority backgrounds began a strike at San Francisco State College, California, U.S.. This led to the establishment of the first Asian American Studies Department within the context of a broadly conceived College of Ethnic Studies in 1969 (Whitson, n.d.). Many decades later, it remains the largest department of its kind (San Francisco State University, 2019). Also in Canada, academic programs are involved in tracing the history and formulating the nature of the Asian immigrant experience. In this way, they perform an important service for immigrant students as well as for the larger multicultural society in which they are coming of age. Within the field of psychology, the founding of the Asian American Psychological Association (AAPA) in 1972 helped to establish Asian American Psychology as a promising field of scholarly endeavor and practical importance (Leong, Okazaki, & David, 2007).

Lastly, who is being named and who is doing the labelling have been at the threshold of research as well as mental health policies and practices. For example, even though Asian Americans are the fastest grouping ethnic population in the U.S., their health data are scarce with many health disparities remaining unknown. In Holland and Palaniappan's (2012) review of health studies, they found few studies that examined the leading causes of mortality for Asian communities (Palaniappan, Wang, & Fortmann, 2004; Wild, Laws, Fortmann, Varady, & Byrne, 1995) as few states disaggregated the Asian group from other ethnic groups (Miller, Chu, Hankey, & Ries, 2008). Thus, Asian groups were not investigated as a separate and distinct group. Moreover, many recent survey studies like the Behavioral Risk Factor

Surveillance Survey had omitted a representative sample of Asian American subjects. However, it is data from these types of surveys of social and biological risk factors for disease that are used as the foundation for researchers and policy makers to set the disparities agenda for the country. Even when Asian Americans participated in studies, they were under-sampled, thus their nmbers were often too low to report as a subgroup (see Holland & Palaniapann, 2012).

In the U.S., it was not until President Obama, who signed Executive Order 13515 in 2009 to re-instate President Clinton's Executive Order 13125, that an initiative was established to gain greater knowledge about the health, education, and economic status of Asian American and Pacific Islander communities. President Obama stressed the importance of disaggregating the Asian American subgroup (U.S. White House Office of the Press Secretary, 2009). Based on the Department of Health and Human Services (HHS), the sub-Asian groups on their surveys included: Asian Indian, Chinese, Filipino, Japanese, Korean, Vietnamese, and Other Asian (U.S. Department of Health and Human Services, 2011), which represented the top six largest Asian subgroups in the U.S. in 2010, comprising 97% of the Asian American population (Hoeffel, Rastogi, Kim, & Shahid, 2012).

Immigration Patterns and the Asian Immigrant Populations: Past and Present

An important factor to consider when comparing Asian families in Canada, and the United States is the immigration policies which create demographic differences between these two Asian populations. A closer examination of the demographics of these populations provides greater context for the lived experiences of Asian families (see Table 2.1 for summary). Thus, it is critical to understand the immigration histories of Canada and the United States.

Canada and the United States

Although the two countries have experienced different histories that help shape the ethnic-racial composition of their populations, their overall attitudes toward Asian immigrants have nevertheless evolved in somewhat similar ways over time. Prior to some crucial changes in the immigration laws of both countries during the 1960s–1970s, European immigrants were consistently preferred over "Orientals" and other visibly/racially different immigrants from the non-Western parts of the world. Moreover, the colonial conquerors of those territories that over time would evolve into the independent nations of Canada, the U.S., and Australia, frequently displayed dismissive and brutal attitudes toward native and "racially different" peoples, most of whose lands they had taken away while killing many of them (Ishiguro,

2017). Ideas about White, Anglo-Saxon, and Christian supremacy were frequently voiced and acted upon in all three countries. Such ideas were applied both to Indigenous people and to potential immigrants from non-European countries. Their impact began to weaken after World War II, when many former colonies in Asia and Africa became independent nations and their inhabitants began to celebrate their former days of glory (Betts, 2012).

During the 1850s – 1870s, tens of thousands of male Chinese laborers arrived in the U.S. and British Columbia, Canada, in order to find gold. Soon they were also helping to build America's first Transcontinental Railway, as well as the Canadian Pacific Railway. Generally, they were poorly paid, given the most dangerous jobs, often treated with hostility, and regarded as inferior strangers who were taking away jobs from White laborers (Holland, 2007). Consequently, in the 1880s, both Canada and the U.S. passed a variety of laws designed to halt Chinese immigration. In one form or the other, such laws remained in force until the 1940s. Similarly, there existed much opposition to the immigration of Japanese laborers. Still, after the death of numerous native Hawaiians due to imported diseases, a considerable number of Japanese, Filipino, and other Asian laborers arrived in Hawaii during the 19th and early 20th centuries. This occurred at a time when it was not yet an American state. Later on, following the Japanese attack on Pearl Harbor in 1941, more than 110,000 Japanese Americans, residing largely on the West Coast, were arrested and placed in internment camps away from the Coast. Many of the arrestees were blameless American citizens and long-term residents (Reeves, 2015).

Similarly, more than 21,000 innocent Japanese Canadians ended up in detention camps regardless of citizenship (Government of Canada, 2019). More generally, numerous families of Japanese or partially Japanese origin have lived in North America and Hawaii for a good number of generations and have interbred with other Asians and non-Asians over the course of time. However, the number of recent immigrants from Japan has been relatively low (Kabuto, this volume).

For both countries, the 1960s and 1970s led to crucial changes in their overall immigration policies. Canada and the U.S. had divergent immigration policies due to their motivations and intentions behind these policies such as their geographical locations relative to other countries. Thus, it is important to better understand the historical context of each country.

Canada

In Canada, the historical preference of source countries were individuals from Western Europe, especially Great Britain. Two decades after World War II, Canada continued its preference of White immigrants, hailing from the United Sates, United Kingdom, and other European countries. Between 1954–1967, 60,230 Canadians in professional, technical, managerial, and entrepreneurial occupations immigrated to the U.S.. However, Canada received 33,119 immigrants of similar skilled backgrounds from the U.S. (Li, 2000).

Canada significantly reformed its immigration policy in the late 1960s to become a more economically competitive country, creating a point system which focused on human capital, emphasizing educational and occupational skills (Li, 2000). Thus, in 1967, the implementation of the universal point system, regardless of country of origin or racial background, was Canada's attempt to compete globally for skilled laborers (Li, 1992). In order to identify a person as a skilled worker, the point system favored those who spoke English and/or French, were well educated, had skilled work experience, were not too old, could report a Canadian job offer, and had some past educational or job experience in Canada (Government of Canada, n.d.-b). In 2016, Canada admitted 50.6% of its immigrants for economic reasons (skilled workers and business people), 24.1% for family reasons, 24.1% as refugees or protected persons, and 1.2% for humanitarian reasons (Statistics Canada, 2017b).

With the influx of the immigrant population, multicultural considerations became a part of Canada's self-definition. Specifically, the federal government officially implemented the Multiculturalism policy in 1971 to acknowledge that diversity is fundamental to Canada's identity. Revised in 1988, the Canadian Multiculturalism Act's first policy objective was to recognize and promote cultural and racial diversity of all Canadian individuals (Government of Canada, n.d.-a). Consequently, as of 2016, the population has become increasingly more multi-ethnic and multicultural, with representation of over 250 ethnic groups accounting for 21.9% of the total population, with Asia (including the Middle East) representing the largest source continent (61.5%). Thus, 48.1% of Canada's foreign-born population was born in Asia, as compared to 27.7% who were born in Europe (Statistics Canada, 2017a). The top six Asian groups were Chinese, Indian, Filipino/as, Vietnamese, Pakistani, and Iranian. More broadly, the top three source continents of immigrants include Asia, Africa, and then Europe (see Table 2.1). Due to the geographical location of Canada, it has been estimated that there may be up to 500,000 undocumented/irregular immigrants. For example, from 2017 to 2019, more than 45,000 migrants have entered Canada without proper documentation. Thus, compared to the U.S., undocumented migrants are not common (United Nations, 2019).

United States

Similar to Canada, the historical preference of source countries were individuals from Europe. A 1790 law was the first law for immigrant citizenship to limit the ethnicity of the immigrant – free whites of "good moral character" – who resided in the U.S. for a minimum of 2 years. Immigration laws also followed a quota system that had created unsurmountable barriers against immigration from Asia and Africa.

It was not until October 3, 1965, at a ceremony beneath New York's Statue of Liberty, that U.S. President Lyndon B. Johnson signed the *Immigration and Nationality Act*. Also called the *Hart-Celler Act* after two of its sponsors, it abolished the extant quota system that, since the 1920s, had favored the immigration of northern Europeans over southern Europeans, who were deemed racially inferior.

This landmark *Immigration and Nationality Act* favored family reunification and skilled immigrants. This law limited immigration, creating restrictions on Latin Americans who, prior to the Act, were able to enter fairly easily (Cohn, 2015).

Since the *Immigration and Nationality Act* in 1965, immigrants from source countries located in Asia and Latin America, surpassed those from European countries. Other immigration laws that followed focused on refugees, which included Indochinese refugees who fled war violence in the 1970s, Chinese, Nicaraguans, and Haitians. Other laws focused on unauthorized immigrants, primarily from Latin America, such as the *Immigration Reform and Control Act* in 1986, that granted millions of unauthorized immigrants citizenship (Cohn, 2015).

As of 2017, 13.6% of the population are immigrants as compared to 4.7% in 1970. Although difficult to count precisely, it is estimated that 77% of the immigrants are legally residing in the U.S.. China, with 6% of the immigrant population, is the largest source country, alongside Mexico (6%) (Radford, 2019). More broadly, Asian immigrants account for 31.2% of the immigrant population (U.S. Census Bureau, 2018). The top six Asian groups were Chinese, Indians, Filipino/as, Vietnamese, Koreans, and Japanese. More broadly, the top source continents of immigrants include Latin America and Asia (see Table 2.1).

In contrast to Canada, the U.S. immigration laws prioritize a strong family reunification program. This program places less emphasis on the working skills and advanced educational levels of family members living abroad. In 2017, for example, 43.7% of the 1.10 million legal immigrants in the U.S. were the immediate relatives of U.S. citizens, 19.7% were family sponsored preferences, but only 12% entered the country that year based on employment-based preferences (U.S. Department of Homeland Security, 2017).

Major Asian Immigrant Groups in Canada and the United States

According to the United Nations, 48 countries (plus the territories of Hong Kong, Macao, and Taiwan) are located in Asia. They include the two countries that have by far the world's largest populations, accounting for about 37% of the entire global population. In 2018, China had approximately 1.42 billion people and India was home to about 1.35 billion. It has been estimated that by 2024, India will surpass China's population (Statistics Times, 2018). There is enormous variety of ethnic groups, languages, customs, and belief systems among and within these countries and territories. For example, some 800 languages are spoken in India alone (Segal, this volume). Thus, Asian immigrants to Canada and the U.S. bring with them a greater variety of often highly complex cultures, as compared to immigrants from other large regions, such as Latin America.

Table 2.2 lists 15 of the largest Asian immigrant groups and their estimated population sizes in the U.S., alongside with Canada's respective population sizes. The

Table 2.2 Selected Canadian and U.S.-American populations with full or partial Asian ancestry

Ancestry	Canada (2016 Census)	United States (2015-Pew Research)
Chinese (Taiwanese included)	1,769,195	4,948,000
Indian	1,374,715	3,982,000
Filipino	851,410	3,899,000
Vietnamese	240,615	1,980,000
Korean	198,210	1,822,000
Japanese	121,485	1,411,000
Levantine (Lebanon, Syria, Palestine, Jordan only)	355,670	859,135
Iranian	210,405	600,000–1,000,00
Pakistani	215,560	519,000
Cambodian	38,495	330,000
Hmong (several Southeast Asian countries)	805	299,000
Thai	19,010	295,000
Laotian	24,575	271,000
Bangladeshi	45,940	188,000
Burmese (Myanmar)	9330	168,000

Note: The Canadian numbers are based on the 2016 Canadian Census, and the U.S. numbers rely on Pew Research (2015 – Fact Sheets: Asians [in the U.S.]). The U.S. numbers for Iranian ancestry reflect several conflicting estimates

population estimates rely on Canada's 2016 Census figures and on Pew Research estimates derived from official American figures for 2015. The figures include persons with both full and partial Asian ancestry. Since published estimates for the number of persons in the U.S. with Iranian ancestry differ widely, Table 2.2 includes a range of such estimates. Moreover, the combined estimates for persons with ancestry from the Levant include only those with ancestors from four countries, namely Lebanon, Syria, Palestine, and Jordan.

In many Asian immigrant families, one can encounter intricate and evolving mixtures between the old and the new. This includes a sometimes difficult merging of Asian and Western customs and beliefs, as varied patterns of family life are evolving across the different generations of immigrants (Chuang, 2019). When immigrant children and grandchildren grow up in the New World, they frequently learn English at the expense of their elders' native language. This also means that they are being exposed to new worldviews (Arends-Tóth & van de Vijver, 2004; Chun, 2004). They encounter new gender roles among their peers and in their educational institutions, may choose a marriage partner from another ethnic or racial group, move out of their parents' home when they are becoming college or graduate students, and increasingly live in a North American context. By the third generation, Asian patterns of family life have frequently given way to more egalitarian, peer-oriented, and individualistic North American lifestyles (Costigan & Dokis, 2006).

Many immigrants from Asian countries endorse semi-collectivistic belief systems when compared to the more individualistic convictions predominating in North America (Paik, Rahman, Kula, Saito, & Witenstein, 2017). Since in Islamic countries, collectivistic traditions are often intertwined with powerful religious customs and convictions, this may create public and private tensions when immigrants seek to pursue them in the predominantly Christian or nonreligious social environments in North America (Akram-Pall & Moodley, 2016). More generally, Asian immigrants differ considerably in their respective religious outlooks. For example, not counting the mostly Muslim immigrants from West Asia, the religious affiliations of Asians in 2012 in the U.S. included the following: Christian: 42%; Unaffiliated: 26%; Buddhist: 14%; Hindu: 10%; Muslim: 4%; Other Religions: 3% (Pew Research, 2012). The immigrants' religious beliefs and customs often influence their conceptions of gender roles, which sexual orientations are considered acceptable, their marriage customs, their preferred number of children, childrearing practices, attitudes toward divorce, and the role of grandparents in the family (Akram-Pall & Moodley, 2016).

In both the U.S. and Canada, immigrants with Chinese, Indian, and Filipino ancestry stand out as constituting the three largest groups. Collectively, they include more than 12.8 million persons or 60% of all Asian Americans, and some 3.2 million persons or 65% of all Asian Canadians (U.S. Census Bureau, 2018; Statistics Canada, 2019). At the same time, they represent three quite different cultural traditions based on diverse histories, religions, customs, and identities.

Chinese Immigrants

The Chinese immigrants include persons originally from Mainland China, Taiwan, the former British colony of Hong Kong, ethnically Chinese refugees from Vietnam, persons speaking various dialects/languages, those following a variety of religions or no religion at all, and persons with a broad range of political convictions (Chuang et al., this volume). Neo-Confucianism, an ethical-educational-political philosophy with ancient roots, has influenced most Chinese, South Koreans, and other East Asians. Traditionally, Confucian family life was both hierarchical and patriarchal in nature. It endorsed the importance of education over pleasure, demanded many sacrifices from parents, drew definite boundaries around gender roles, and emphasized the priority of family duties over individualistic strivings for freedom, independence, high self-esteem, and personal fulfillment (Chan, 2013; Chuang, 2009; Paik et al., 2017). The unity of the household took priority over the individual interests of its members.

Many of these traditions have weakened substantially in China, but they have not disappeared altogether. Given that many Chinese immigrants have settled down both in North America's Chinatowns (Gielen & Palumbo, this volume) and in suburban areas (Chuang et al., this volume), various aspects of semi-traditional family life together with other Chinese cultural traditions can be readily observed in the New World. Persons of Han (Chinese) origin represent the largest group of today's Asian immigrants in North America, are culturally related to other East Asian immigrants, and have become influential in the academic world. This volume includes several chapters on Chinese immigrants.

Depending on geolocation, occupations have varied. Specifically, in the U.S., many Taiwanese immigrants tend to hold professional and managerial positions (57.2%), Hong Kong and other Chinese Diasporan immigrants are more varied, with families in both white- and blue-collar statuses, whereas the majority from Mainland China are members of the working class. However, many Chinese Americans have obtained academic success, as seen in the high rates of graduation from colleges and universities (Shinagawa & Kim, 2008). Given this pattern, East Asians exert a strong influence on how the North American public as well as the academic world perceive other Asian immigrants and their traditions. Due to this disproportionate impact, some immigrants from other Asian regions may feel invisible in the Asian American and Asian Canadian communities (Doshi, 1996).

Indian Immigrants

The second largest Asian group, namely Indian immigrants, frequently embrace Hinduism as their religion, while others are Muslims, Sikhs, Jains, Christians, or nonreligious. Hinduism, arguably the world's oldest religious tradition, includes a broad variety of belief systems, and favors distinct ways of life (Tiermeier, this volume). Traditionally, Hinduism was intertwined with the Indian caste system, which emphasizes arranged marriages within a given caste and endorses highly unequal gender roles. In 2020, many Indians in North America favor arranged or semi-arranged marriages (Segal, this volume), and only a small percentage of them get married to partners from other Asian or European backgrounds. In this way, Indian immigrants maintain their ethnic and religious identity. In contrast, Canadianized and Americanized Chinese, Filipina, and Korean women marry Caucasian men quite frequently (Lee & Rodgríguez-García, 2015).

In the U.S., around 72–78% of all immigrants from India have at least a bachelor's degree (Krogstad & Radford, 2018), and they often endorse an entrepreneurial way of life. Their average household incomes are among the highest in North America, surpass those of other Asian groups, and are well ahead of the average incomes of Whites (Budiman, Cilluffo, & Ruiz, 2019). The number of Indian immigrants to North America has rapidly increased in recent years.

Filipino/a Immigrants

Given that the Philippines was a Spanish colony from 1565 to 1898, Filipino immigrants mostly follow Catholic traditions (Tuason, Taylor, Rollings, Harris, & Martin, 2007). Quite a few Filipino/as do not even identify themselves as Asians or Asian Americans. In their conceptions of family life, they tend to resemble Latinos/Latinas more than they resemble other Asian immigrants (Campo, 2016).

When the U.S. took over from Spain as the resident colonial power in 1898, the Philippines became a territory of the U.S.. Soon, the new government introduced American forms of schooling and thinking. While Filipinos were not considered U.S. citizens, they were allowed to migrate to the country until 1934, the year in which the Philippines were granted independence. For many years, Filipino/as constituted the largest group of Asian immigrants in the U.S., although this no longer holds true. English is a main language in Filipino schools, which helps the Filipino migrants to integrate more easily into the host countries. Their strong fluency in English has led to high educational levels, especially in the professional fields of health or science-related professions, especially nursing (Espiritu, 1996; Rumbaut, 2000; Xu & Kwak, 2005; Zhou & Xiong, 2005). Thus, they tend to be middle- and upper-middle-class professionals (Paik, Choe, & Witenstein, 2016; U.S. Census Bureau, 2017; Wolf, 1997). As hospitals and other healthcare systems have employment shortages, many Filipinos are able to immigrate to address these needs (De Castro, Gee, & Takeuchi, 2008).

Various Filipino associations are active in Canada and the U.S. (Government of Canada, 2019). They foster community festivals and civic celebrations such as the annual Philippine Independence Day Parade in Manhattan, newspapers, magazines, and TV and radio stations. These associations and publications help to sustain connections between the relatively dispersed Filipinos who mostly live in ethnically diverse neighborhoods rather than in more homogeneous ethno-burbs and large-scale Filipinotowns (Paik et al., 2017).

Conclusions

Asian immigrants have been coming to North America due to a variety of "push and pull factors." Many of them have been enticed by economic possibilities that they could not find in their respective countries of origin. Such a situation holds true for many immigrants from relatively poor countries, such as the Philippines, Pakistan, and Bangladesh. Others came as refugees to the U.S. or Canada after the Vietnam War, such as numerous Laotians, Hmong, Cambodians, and Vietnamese. As refugees from a war and its troublesome aftermath, they frequently endured much suffering and yet may have felt unprepared to leave their country-of-origin (Tran & Phan, 2012). For them, as well as for the more recent refugees from nations such as Syria, Myanmar (Burma), and Bhutan, adjustment to their new living conditions in

North America can be most difficult. In addition, some groups of refugees arrived with low levels of schooling. For example, many rural Hmong refugees from Vietnam and Laos were illiterate when they arrived in the U.S.. Most of them remained poor, became laborers or housewives, married early, and followed their traditional rural custom of having many children (Her & Buley-Meissner, 2012). It can take the members of such groups several generations before they are fully able to overcome their initial educational, economic, and linguistic disadvantages. Their situation stands in stark contrast to that of many Iranian, Taiwanese, and Indian immigrants, who tend to have urban backgrounds. Most of them are highly educated, well trained, economically secure, and familiar with the modern, globalizing world.

One may compare the troublesome situation of refugees to the easier circumstances facing those who began their careers in North America as foreign students. After receiving a graduate degree from a local university, they may have received an attractive job offer, together with a special permission to remain in the country. Typically, they are fluent in English or French and already understand what it means to live in their newly adopted country. They can look forward to an attractive life in the world of academe, or as information technology specialists in Silicon Valley, or perhaps as managers in Richmond, BC or Monterey, CA, two of North America's most Asian cities. Although many of them will end up leading an upper-middle class life, they nevertheless might encounter a 'bamboo ceiling' (= glass ceiling) when they are applying for an elite position in the business or academic world. That holds true, for instance, for technology companies in the San Francisco Bay Area. Although they hire professionals from Asian backgrounds in large numbers, only occasionally do they promote them to leading executive positions (Gee & Peck, 2017).

Asian families in Canada and the U.S. are uniquely different not only because of the immigration policies they follow in their respective countries but because of the vast diversity within "Asian groups." Researchers and practitioners need to gain greater insights into the complexities and nuances of their sociohistorical backgrounds and lived experiences in their country of origin, their religious and cultural values, and their influence on their lives in Canada and the United States.

References

Akram-Pall, S., & Moodley, R. (2016). "Loss and fear": Acculturation stresses leading to depression in South Asian Muslim immigrants in Toronto. *Canadian Journal of Counselling and Psychotherapy, 50*(3-S), S137–S155. https://cjc-rcc.ucalgary.ca/article/view/61055/pdf

Arends-Tóth, J., & van de Vijver, F. J. R. (2004). Domains and dimensions in acculturation: Implicit theories of Turkish-Dutch. *International Journal of Intercultural Relations, 28*, 19–35. https://doi.org/10.1016/j.ijintrel.2003.09.001

Betts, R. F. (2012). Decolonization: A brief history of the world. In E. Bogaerts & R. Raben (Eds.), *Beyond empire and nation; The decolonization of African and Asian societies, 1930s–1960s* (pp. 23–38). Brill.

Budiman, A., Cilluffo, A., & Ruiz, N. G. (2019). *Key facts about Asian origin groups in the U.S.* Pew Research Center/Factank: News in the Numbers. https://www.pewresearch.org/fact-tank/2019/05/22/key-facts-about-asian-origin-groups-in-the-u-s/

Campo, A. C. (2016). *The Latinos of Asia; How Filipino Americans break the rules of race*. Stanford University Press.

Chan, K. B. (Ed.). (2013). *International handbook of Chinese families*. Springer.

Chuang, S. S. (2019). The complexities of immigration and families: Theoretical perspectives and current issues. In B. H. Fiese, M. Celano, K. Deater-Deckard, E. N. Jouriles, & M. A. Whisman (Eds.), *APA handbooks in psychology. APA handbook of contemporary family psychology: Applications and broad impact of family psychology* (pp. 437–455). American Psychological Association. https://doi.org/10.1037/0000100-027

Chuang, S. S. (2009). Transformation and change: Parenting in Chinese societies. In J. Mancini & K. A. Roberto (Eds.), *Pathways of development: Explorations of change* (pp. 191–206). Lexington Books.

Chun, G. H. (2004). Shifting ethnic identity and consciousness: U.S.-born Chinese American youth in the 1930s and 1950s. In J. Lee & M. Zhou (Eds.), *Asian American youth: Culture, identity and ethnicity* (pp. 113–141). Routledge.

Cohn, D. (2015). *How U.S. immigration laws and rules have changed through history*. Pew Research Center. https://www.pewresearch.org/fact-tank/2015/09/30/how-u-s-immigration-laws-and-rules-have-changed-through-history/

Costigan, C. L., & Dokis, D. P. (2006). Relations between parent-child acculturation differences and adjustment within immigrant Chinese families. *Child Development, 77*, 1252–1267. https://doi.org/10.1111/j.1467-8624.2006.00932.x

Doshi, S. J. (1996). Divided consciousness amidst a new Orientalism: South Asian identity formation on campus. In S. Maira & R. Srikanth (Eds.), *Contours of the heart: South Asians map North America* (pp. 201–213). Asian American Writers' Workshop.

De Castro, A. B., Gee, G. C., & Takeuchi, D. T. (2008). Workplace discrimination and health among Filipinos in the United States. *American Journal of Public Health, 98*(3), 520–526. https://doi.org/10.2105/AJPH.2007.110163

Espiritu, Y. L. (1996). Colonial oppression, labour importation, and group formation: Filipinos in the United States. *Ethnic and Racial Studies, 19*(1), 29–48. https://doi.org/10.1080/01419870.1996.9993897

Gee, B., & Peck, D. (2017). *The illusion of Asian success: Scant progress for minorities in cracking the glass ceiling from 2007–2015*. Ascend. http://www.ascendleadership.org/research.

Gilroy, P. (2000). *Between camps: Race, identity and nationalism at the end of the colour line*. Allen Lane.

Government of Canada. (n.d.-a). *Canadian Multiculturalism Act*. Justice laws website. https://laws-lois.justice.gc.ca/eng/acts/c-18.7/page-1.html

Government of Canada. (n.d.-b). *Comprehensive ranking system (CRS) tool: Skilled immigrants (express entry)*. https://www.cic.gc.ca/english/immigrate/skilled/crs-tool.asp

Government of Canada. (2019). *Events in Asian Canadian history*. https://www.canada.ca/en/canadian-heritage/campaigns/asian-heritage-month/important-events.html

Her, V. K., & Buley-Meissner, M. L. (2012). *Hmong and American: From refugees to citizens*. St. Minnesota Historical Society Press.

Hoeffel, E. M., Rastogi, S., Kim, M. O., & Shahid, H. (2012). *The Asian population: 2010*. 2010 Census Briefs. https://www.census.gov/prod/cen2010/briefs/c2010br-11.pdf

Holland, K. M. (2007). A history of Chinese immigration in the United States and Canada. *American Review of Canadian Studies, 37*(2), 150–160. https://doi.org/10.1080/02722010709481851

Holland, A. T., & Palaniapann, L. P. (2012). Problems with the collection and interpretation of Asian American health data: Omission, aggregation, and extrapolation. *Annals of Epidemiology, 22*(6), 397–405. https://doi.org/10.1016/j.annepidem.2012.04.001

Homeland Security. (2017). *Table 6. Persons obtaining lawful permanent resident status by type and major class of admission: Fiscal years 2016 to 2018.*https://www.dhs.gov/immigration-statistics/yearbook/2018/table6

Ishiguro, L. (2017). Northwestern North America (Canadian West) to 1900. In E. Cavanagh & L. Veracini (Eds.), *The Routledge handbook of the history of settler colonialism* (pp. 125–138). Routledge.

Kandil, C. Y. (2018). After 50 years of "Asian American," advocates say the term is "more essential than ever." *NBC News*. https://www.nbcnews.com/news/asian-america/after-50-years-asian-american-advocates-say-term-more-essential-n875601

Krogstad, J. M., & Radford, J. (2018). *Education levels of U.S. immigrants are on the rise*. Pew Research Center. https://www.pewresearch.org/fact-tank/2018/09/14/education-levels-of-u-s-immigrants-are-on-the-rise/

Lee, J., & Rodgríguez-García, D. (2015). From undesirable to marriageable: Hyper-selectivity and the racial mobility of Asian Americans. *The Annals of the American Academy of Political and Social Science, 662*(1), 79–93. https://doi.org/10.1177/0002716215594626

Leong, F. T. L., Okazaki, S., & David, E. J. R. (2007). History and future of Asian American psychology. In F. T. L. Leong, A. G. Inman, A. Ebreo, L. H. Yang, L. Kinoshita, & M. Fu (Eds.), *Handbook of Asian American psychology* (2nd ed., pp. 11–28). Sage.

Li, P. S. (1992). The economics of brain drain: Recruitment of skilled labour to Canada, 1954-86. In V. Satzewich (Ed.), Deconstructing a nation: Immigration, multiculturalism and racism in '90s Canada (pp. 145–162). Fernwood Publishing

Li, P. S. (2000). *Cultural diversity in Canada: The social construction of racial differences*. Department of Justice Canada. https://www.justice.gc.ca/eng/rp-pr/csj-sjc/jsp-sjp/rp02_8-dr02_8/index.html

Miller, B. A., Chu, K. C., Hankey, B. F., & Ries, L. A. (2008). Cancer incidence and mortality patterns among specific Asian and Pacific Islander populations in the U.S. *Cancer Causes & Control, 19*, 227–256. https://doi.org/10.1007/s10552-007-9088-3

Nguyen, D., Shibusawa, T., & Chen, M. T. (2012). The evolution of community mental health services in Asain Asmerican communities. *Clinical Social Work Journal, 20*, 134–143. https://doi.org/10.1007/s10615-011-0356-z

Paik, S. J., Choe, S. M. M., & Witenstein, M. A. (2016). Filipinos in the U.S.: Historical, social, and educational experiences. *Social and Education History, 5*(2), 134–160. https://doi.org/10.17583/hse.2016.2062

Paik, S. J., Rahman, Z., Kula, S. M., Saito, E., & Witenstein, M. A. (2017). Diverse Asian American families and communities: Culture, structure, and education (Part 1: Why they differ). *Social Community Journal, 27*(2), 35–66.

Palaniappan, L., Wang, Y., & Fortmann, S. P. (2004). Coronary heart disease mortality for six ethnic groups in California, 1990–2000. *Annals of Epidemiology, 14*, 499–506. https://doi.org/10.1016/j.annepidem.2003.12.001

Pew Research Center. (2012). *Asian Americans: A mosaic of faiths*. https://www.pewforum.org/2012/07/19/asian-americans-a-mosaic-of-faiths-religious-affiliation/

Radford, J. (2019). *Key findings about U.S. immigrants*. Factank: News in the Numbers. Pew Research Center. https://www.pewresearch.org/fact-tank/2019/06/17/key-findings-about-u-s-immigrants/

Rumbaut, R. G. (2000). Vietnamese, Laotian, and Cambodian Americans. In M. Zhou & J. V. Gatewood (Eds.), *Contemporary Asian America: A multidisciplinary reader* (pp. 175–206). University Press.

Reeves, R. (2015). *Infamy: The shocking story of the Japanese American internment in World War II*. Henry Holt and Company.

Said, E. W. (1978). *Orientalism*. Routledge & Kegan.

San Francisco State University. (2019). *Asian American Studies Program*. Migration Policy Institute. https://www.migrationpolicy.org/article/asian-immigrants-united-states

Shinagawa, L. H., & Kim, D. Y. (2008). *A snapshot of a portrait of Chinese Americans: Key findings*. Organization of Chinese Americans and the Asian American Studies Program, University of Maryland.

Statistics Canada. (2017a). *Immigration and ethnocultural diversity: Key results from the 2016 Census*. https://www150.statcan.gc.ca/n1/daily-quotidien/171025/dq171025b-eng.htm

Statistics Canada. (2017b). *Distribution (in percentage) of immigrants living in Canada, by admission category and year of immigration, 2016*. https://www.statcan.gc.ca/eng/dai/btd/othervisuals/other007

Statistics Canada. (2019). *Census profile, 2016 Census*. https://www12.statcan.gc.ca/census-recensement/2016/dp-pd/prof/details/page.cfm?Lang=E&Geo1=PR&Code1=01&Geo2=PR&Code2=01&Data=Count&SearchText=Canada&SearchType=Begins&SearchPR=01&B1=Visible%20minority&TABID=1

Statistics Times. (2018). *China vs India by population*. http://statisticstimes.com/demographics/china-vs-india-population.php.

Takaki, R. (1993). Multiculturalism: Battleground or meeting ground? *The Annals of the American Academic of Political and Social Science*, 530, 109–121. https://doi.org/10.1177/0002716293530001008

Tran, T. V., & Phan, P. T. (2012). The changing Vietnamese American family. In R. Wright, C. H. Mindel, T. V. Tran, & R. W. Habenstein (Eds.), *Ethnic families in America: Patterns and variations* (5th ed., pp. 199–224). Pearson.

Tuason, M., Taylor, A. R., Rollings, L., Harris, T., & Martin, C. (2007). On both sides of the hyphen: Exploring the Filipino-American identity. *Journal of Counseling Psychology, 54*(4), 362–372. https://doi.org/10.1037/0022-0167.54.4.362

United Nations. (2019). *World migration report 2020*. https://www.un.org/sites/un2.un.org/files/wmr_2020.pdf

U.S. Census Bureau. (n.d.). *About*. https://www.census.gov/topics/population/race/about.html

U.S. Census Bureau. (2018). *Selected population profile in the United States*. https://data.census.gov/cedsci/table?q=S0201&tid=ACSSPP1Y2018.S0201

U.S. Census Bureau. (2017). *Facts for features: Hispanic heritage month 2017*. www.census.gov/newsroom/facts-for-features/2017/hispanic-heritage.html

U.S. Department of Health and Human Services. (2011). *HHS implementation guidance on data collection standards for race, ethnicity, sex, primary language, and disability status*. https://aspe.hhs.gov/basic-report/hhs-implementation-guidance-data-collection-standards-race-ethnicity-sex-primary-language-and-disability-status

White House Office of the Press Secretary. (2009). *Executive Order 13515 – Asian American and Pacific Islander Community*. The White House. https://obamawhitehouse.archives.gov/the-press-office/executive-order-asian-american-and-pacific-islander-community

Whitson, H. (n.d.). *STRIKE!...Concerning the 1968–69 strike at San Fransisco State College*. http://www.foundsf.org/index.php?title=STRIKE!..._Concerning_the_1968-69_Strike_at_San_Francisco_State_College

Wild, S. H., Laws, A., Fortmann, S. P., Varady, A. N., & Byrne, C. D. (1995). Mortality from coronary heart disease and stroke for six ethnic groups in California, 1985 to 1990. *Annals of Epidemiology, 5*, 432–439. https://doi.org/10.1016/1047-2797(95)00058-5

Wolf, D. L. (1997). Family secrets: Transnational struggles among children of Filipino immigrants. *Sociological Perspectives, 40*(3), 457–482. https://doi.org/10.2307/1389452

Xu, Y., & Kwak, C. (2005). Characteristics of internationally educated nurses in the United States. *Nursing Economics, 23*(5), 233–238. http://search.proquest.com/docview/68845182/

Zhou, M., & Xiong, Y. S. (2005). The multifaceted American experiences of the children of Asian immigrants: Lessons for segmented assimilation. *Ethnic and Racial Studies, 28*(6), 1119–1152. https://doi.org/10.1080/01419870500224455

Chapter 3
Religion, Spirituality, and Worldviews: Implications for Mental Health

Tracy S. Tiemeier

Abstract This chapter introduces Asian religious traditions and draws out some implications for mental health that are important to counselors, mental health professionals, and social workers serving Asian North American families. Special attention is paid to religio-cultural views of gender, sexuality, and family. Hindu, Jain, Buddhist, Sikh, Zoroastrian, Muslim, Baha'i, Confucian, Taoist, Shamanic, Shinto, and Christian traditions are considered.

Keywords Asian American religion · Mental health · Families · Gender · Sexuality

Asian religious traditions have a long history in North America. From its beginnings in the sixteenth century to its current realities, where Asians constitute a large and growing percentage of the immigrant population, Asian immigration brings a rich diversity of religious beliefs and practices (Baker & DeVries, 2010; Mann, Numrich, & Williams, 2008; Pew Research Center, 2012a). The economic success of many Asian North Americans has helped local Asian American religious communities financially and structurally (there has been a veritable boom in temple, gurdwara, and mosque building), even as there is a growing gap between rich and poor among Asian Americans (Coloma, McElhinny, Tungohan, Catungal, & Davidson, 2012; DeVries, Baker, & Overmyer, 2011; Pew Research Center, 2018). In order to facilitate better understanding of and services to Asian North Americans, this chapter provides key information on diverse Asian religions relevant to family and mental health contexts.

It is impossible to present an exhaustive picture of the spiritualities, worldviews, and practices of Asian American religious traditions. From those Asian North American families who have been in Canada and the United States for generations to those who are more recent immigrants, there are wide variances of beliefs and

T. S. Tiemeier (✉)
Loyola Marymount University, Los Angeles, CA, USA
e-mail: Tracy.Tiemeier@lmu.edu

S. S. Chuang et al. (eds.), *Asian Families in Canada and the United States*, Advances in Immigrant Family Research,
https://doi.org/10.1007/978-3-030-56452-0_3

practices. However, since religious traditions and practices are integral to many Asian and Asian American families, researchers have attempted to find ways to develop religious/cultural competencies or to facilitate work with religious communities. One strategy that researchers used was to emphasize the (positive and/or negative) relationship between religion, spirituality, and mental health—in either (or both) research and clinical work (Cashwell & Young, 2011; Koenig, 2018; Loewenthal, 2007). Another common strategy has been to present overviews of religious traditions or of religious views of illness, health, and life cycles (Crisp, 2017; Loue, 2017; Sorajjakool, Carr, & Nam, 2010). While such approaches are important, there is limited understanding in these sources of Asian and Asian American religio-cultural views of gender, sexuality, and family. To address these issues, this chapter offers brief overviews of major Asian religions with a focus on gender, sexuality, and family. Finally, the chapter draws out some important implications from Asian religions for mental health in Asian North American families.

Hindu Spiritualities and Worldviews

Hinduism is a diverse cluster of religious traditions that originates in the Indian subcontinent and spans thousands of years (Flood, 1996). Many Hindu traditions center on devotion to a particular deity or deities, though Hinduism is often understood as an all-encompassing way of life (Flueckiger, 2015). Fifteen percent of the world's population is Hindu, over 1.032 billion people (Pew Research Center, 2012b). The Hindu population in Canada is around 498,000 and 1.79 million in the United States (Chui & Flanders, 2015; Pew Research Center, 2012b).

From a general Hindu perspective, people's identities are constructs formed by our action (karma) over a myriad of lives. All beings have a true self or soul that is united with (or actually is, depending on the tradition) ultimate reality/God/Goddess (Flood, 1996). This principle that the divine is at the core of every being simultaneously downplays the significance of gender, sexuality, and family (because the true self/soul is distinct from physical and social life) as well as affirms the value of persons, families, and society (because the true self/soul is within physical and social life). One's karmic identity is a part of the harmony of the universe. Thus, following one's personal, family, and social path (e.g., performing rituals proper to your place, conforming to gender expectations, marriage, having children, following class and professional obligations) are all important for maintaining personal, social, and cosmic order (Flueckiger, 2015).

The Hindu presumption tends to be that people should get married and have children; in retirement, they can dedicate themselves to purely spiritual pursuits (Courtright, 2006). Women often lead ritual practice in the home (Flueckiger, 2015). Because every person has a place/role in the universe and in society, people who do not fit into a procreative framework must have a legitimate and valued path (Rambachan, 2007). This need can be seen in the Hindu recognition of a third gender (tritiya prakriti) (Lidke, 2003). Third gender persons are recognized legally in Nepal, Pakistan, India, and Bangladesh.

Jain Spiritualities and Worldviews

Jainism is an Indian religious tradition that emphasizes restraint as a path to liberation. Whether ascetics or householders, Jains work to conquer their attachments and devote themselves to the 24 Jinas ("victors") who are Tirthankaras ("bridge builders") across the ocean of birth, death, and rebirth, and into liberation (Vallely, 2010). The global Jain population is difficult to gauge, though estimates range from 4.2 to 12 million (Lee, Matsuoka, Yee, & Nakasone, 2015; Long, 2009). The estimated Jain population in the United States and Canada is 150,000 and 10,000, respectively (The Pluralism Project, n.d.; Wiley, 2004).

While Jain philosophy is somewhat similar to the Hindu concept of a lower self that is a construct of karma, it generally deemphasizes the role of social order and instead emphasizes the liberation found in renunciation of social conventions and materiality. Although the soul is infinite, it is entangled in, and obscured by, karmic matter. Jain values and vows, observed fully by monks and partially by householders, structure Jain practices. The three values are non-violence, non-absolutism, and non-attachment. The five vows of Jain practice are non-violence, truthfulness, non-stealing, chastity, and non-attachment. Through right faith, right knowledge, and right conduct, the soul is liberated (Long, 2009; Vallely, 2010).

In theory, gender distinction goes against a Jain spirituality of renunciation. However, karma does condition the mind and life of a person (Peach, 2002). Thus, women are sometimes seen as naturally more attached to the world since it is in their nature to care for children (Kelting, 2009). If monks and nuns renounce family, sex, and gender/sexual identity, householders uphold but restrain them (Long, 2009). For Jain householders, sex should not be excessive (Mahajan, Pimple, Palsetia, Dave, & De Sousa, 2013). It is only appropriate within marriage and for the purposes of procreation (Long, 2009; Mahajan et al., 2013). Thus, sex has a relative status in Jainism, as celibacy is largely held up as the ideal—even for householders. While this can lead to negative views of sex, sexuality, and same-sex relationships, this can also lead to more egalitarian views of gender.

Buddhist Spiritualities and Worldviews

Although Buddhism, like Hinduism and Jainism, has its origins on the Indian subcontinent, its adherents live largely outside the Indian subcontinent. The historical Buddha, Siddhartha Gautama, himself was born around the sixth century B.C.E. in modern-day Nepal (Seager, 1999). As of 2010, there were around 488 million Buddhists across the three major branches of Theravada, Mahayana, and Vajrayana

Buddhism (7% of the world population) (Pew Research Center, 2012b). Canada's Buddhist population is around 366,800; the U.S. Buddhist population is about 3.57 million (Chui & Flanders, 2015; Pew Research Center, 2012b). However, a Pew Research study found that only 33% of U.S. Buddhists were of Asian descent (Pew Research Center, 2014).

Buddhism shares Hindu and Jain concepts of karma; it prioritizes (along with Jainism) the spirituality of renunciation (Long, 2009). Four truths ground Buddhist thought: (a) everything suffers, dies, and is impermanent; (b) desire for permanence leads to attachment and suffering; (c) when desire is extinguished (nirvana), there is an end to rebirth and suffering; and (d) the path to this liberation is an eightfold path of right understanding, right thought, right speech, right action, right livelihood, right effort, right mindfulness, right concentration (Amore, 2010). All Buddhists are to follow five general precepts to avoid killing, stealing, sexual misconduct, lying, and intoxication (Amore, 2010).

Although Buddhist thought sometimes privileges the monastic path, householders and other lay people are essential for supporting temples, monks, and nuns (Cole, 2006). As a result, there are strong traditions of Buddhist family life often tied to indigenous practices such as ancestor devotion (Lee & Nadeau, 2014). Even so, sexual desire is sometimes seen as an attachment leading to suffering (Wilson, 2003). Although gender and sexuality are aspects of the impermanent, changing self, Buddhists may assume that this psychic construct is important as the medium of religious life (Cabezón, 1992). Negative karma may be perceived to limit women's spiritual abilities; same-sex sex may be seen as a manifestation of sexual attachment (Cabezón, 1992; Wilson, 2003).

Sikh Spiritualities and Worldviews

Sikhism emerged in the rich spiritual and interreligious context of fifteenth century Punjab (Singh, 2010). Guru Nanak (1469–1539 C.E.), the first of ten Sikh Gurus, emphasized liberation in this life (Mandair, 2010; Singh, 2010). Focused on immediate experience of the divine, Guru Nanak developed a path of mystical spirituality at work in the world (Singh, 2010). There are roughly 455,000 Canadian Sikhs and between 200,000 and 500,000 U.S. Sikhs (Chui & Flanders, 2015; Mandair, 2010; Pew Research Center, 2012c).

Sikh spirituality centers on God (Waheguru), the Creator within the self that is one with all things (Ek Onkar) (Kaur, 2014; Mahajan et al., 2013). Guru Nanak stressed the inner paths of meditation and devotion that brings about union with God and liberation from the karmic cycle. Thus, Sikhs see all humans as equal, and love of God and love of others are front and center in spiritual practice (Kaur, 2014). Thus, every Sikh gurdwara, place of worship, has a langar hall for feeding all people for free, regardless of their background (Singh, 2010). Spiritual life and the life of the householder go together, and so Sikh spirituality embeds devotion and meditation within everyday family life: devotional singing, meditation, and remembrance of the divine name are practiced alongside service and active work for justice (Singh, 2010). Sikhs are called to pray, work, and give.

Sikhism prioritizes family life over celibacy and renunciation (Mandair, 2010). The love of marriage is seen as an analogy for the love of God (Mandair, 2010). Husbands and wives are portrayed as equal partners. Marriage is not only spiritual and not only earthly; it is a sacrament for the pursuit of both spiritual liberation and earthly happiness (Mandair, 2010). While sex is a natural good, it must be restrained and channelled in a (usually heterosexual) marriage (Mandair, 2010). Sexual desire, or lust, is seen as a vice. Without restraint in marriage, sexual desire can go out of control and tempt the person away from God (Mandair, 2010).

Zoroastrian Spiritualities and Worldviews

Although there are few Zoroastrians in the Americas today, "Zoroastrianism" refers to communities, beliefs, and practices that span millennia and have far-reaching religious and cultural impact (Rose, 2011a). Global population estimates including Iranian and Indian (Parsi and Irani) Zoroastrians are between 124,000 and 190,000 (Gruzder, 2008). The Canadian population is around 6000 (Statistics Canada, 2011), and the U.S. population is about 11,000 (Eduljee, 2005).

Founded by Zoroaster (or Zarathustra), who lived sometime in the second millennium B.C.E. in present day Iran or Afghanistan, Zoroastrianism believes in one God, Ahura Mazda (Ahura, "Being," and Mazda, "Mind") (Rose, 2011b). Angra Mainyu, the destructive spirit, opposes Ahura Mazda. Ahura Mazda eventually will win; the Saoshyant ("one who brings benefit") will bring about a final renovation of the universe and the dead will be resurrected (Rose, 2011a, 2011b). Zoroastrian spirituality sees humans as essential for protecting and preserving the cosmos (Rose, 2011b). Reverence for the natural elements is also central to Zoroastrian spirituality (water and fire purify, and water is the source of wisdom while fire is the medium of wisdom). The three ethical principles of Zoroastrianism are good words, good deeds, and good thoughts (Rose, 2011b).

Marriage and children are important obligations in Zoroastrian communities. Marriage within the Zoroastrian community is also expected and strongly encouraged (Mahajan et al., 2013). Traditionally, conversion to Zoroastrianism is not allowed, and religious communities may not accept the children of Zoroastrian women and non-Zoroastrian men (Mahajan et al., 2013). Children are essential, as children preserve Zoroastrian faith and promote truth and order (Rose, 2011b). Same-sex sex is traditionally discouraged, as it is not seen as procreative. In protecting and preserving creation, the dynamic of pollution and purity pervades life and affects the social and religious dynamics of family life. Personal purification includes mental purification, daily washing, and cleansing after sex (Rose, 2011b). While both men and women share religious responsibilities, purity observances specific to women do restrict them in some ways (for example, during menstruation and after childbirth) (Rose, 2011b).

Muslim Spiritualities and Worldviews

Islam is a large and diverse religion. Globally, there are more than 1.6 billion adherents (Pew Research Center, 2012b). There are over a million Muslims in Canada and over 2.77 million Muslims in the United States (Chui & Flanders, 2015; Pew Research Center, 2012b). Although Islam emerged in the Arabian Peninsula, the majority of Muslims are not Arab; there are large Asian Muslim populations (Hidayatullah, 2003). Most Muslims (85%) are Sunni; the rest identify as Shi'i or Sufi (Hidayatullah, 2003).

Muslims share some common beliefs and practices, such as faith in the one God (Allah), Muhammad (d. 632 C.E.) as God's prophet, and the Qur'an as Word of God (Hussain, 2011). There are five "pillars": shahada (bearing witness), salat (daily prayer), zakat (almsgiving), sawm (fasting), and hajj (pilgrimage) (Hussain, 2011). Oriented on heaven yet enacted in this world, Muslim worldviews see all things unfold according to the divine will. Faith, righteousness, good works, and surrender of the self to the will of the one God are key aspects of Muslim spirituality (Hussain, 2011). There is a coming Day of Judgment when one's deeds will be judged (Hidayatullah, 2003). Like with Zoroastrianism, Muslim spiritualities are simultaneously present and future oriented.

The Qur'an, Hadith (reports of what Muhammad said or allowed), and Shari'a (legal tradition developed from the Qur'an, Hadith, and debate) guide Muslim approaches to gender, sex, sexuality, and family, though there is significant diversity in attitudes and practices. As there is no centralized determinative body in Islam, there are widely divergent views of sex, marriage, women and women's roles, and practices such as veiling (Hidayatullah, 2003). The Qur'an presumes a mutuality and complementarity of men and women (Al-Hibri & El Habti, 2006). Complementary spheres of life mean that women often have their own distinct spiritual and family roles (Al-Hibri & El Habti, 2006). Islam encourages marriage and parenting; married companionship, mutual pleasure, and children are blessings to cherish (Hidayatullah, 2003). Sex should be confined to (usually heterosexual) marriage (Hidayatullah, 2003).

Baha'i Spiritualities and Worldviews

For the Baha'i Faith, the oneness of God and the unity of humanity are central. Historically very close to Islam, Baha'is see themselves as a distinct tradition—even as they understand there to be one dynamic history of religion (Smith, 2008). The founder of the Baha'i Faith, Baha'u'llah (1817–1892), believed he was a messenger of God and the prophetic fulfillment of other religious traditions (Smith, 2008). While many Baha'is are of Iranian origin, the largest population of Baha'i is Indian (Smith, 2008). There are about five million Baha'is globally (Pew Research Center, 2012b). According to the National Household Survey, there are 18,945

Baha'is in Canada (Statistics Canada, 2011). The number of Baha'is in the United States ranges from 84,000 (Kosmin & Keysar, 2001) to 512,864 (The Association of Religion Data Archives, 2010).

Baha'i spirituality stresses unity: the unity of God (one God), the unity of religion (religions have God as their one source), the unity of humanity (all humans in their diversity are created equal), and world peace (Smith, 2008). Without clergy or many rituals, Baha'is focus on daily prayer, fasting, meditation, and work in the world (Smith, 2008). For Baha'is, marriage and the bearing of faithful children are sacred actions, though not required (Smith, 2008). The family is the central place for realizing and promoting the unity of the world (Smith, 2008).

The spiritual unity of marriage is stressed as the foundation of society (Smith, 2008). Baha'u'llah presumes that marriage is between a man and a woman (Reini & Hiebert, 1996). Sex should be restrained and restricted to marriage (Reini & Hiebert, 1996). Since marriage is presumed to be between a man and a woman, and sex must be confined to heterosexual marriage, Baha'is have generally been against same-sex relationships (Reini & Hiebert, 1996). Even so, same-sex sex is not necessarily more problematic than other issues of personal restraint (Reini & Hiebert, 1996). Baha'i teaching calls Baha'is to treat all people with respect, regardless of sexuality (Reini & Hiebert, 1996).

Chinese Spiritualities and Worldviews

Chinese religions emphasize the order and harmony found through the balance of yin and yang (Woo, 2010). Yin (responsiveness and femininity) and yang (activeness and masculinity) are interdependent, dynamic, and fluid (Hsiung, 2007). While women are predominantly yin and men are predominantly yang, everyone is both, and the cultivation of both is important (Hsiung, 2007). While there are exclusive Confucian or Taoist practitioners (estimates range between six and eight million Confucians and 2.5 to 3.5 million Taoists), the vast majority of practitioners are syncretistic (Woo, 2010; Wu, 2013).

For Confucians, human relationships are characterized by yin and yang (wife subordinate to her husband, son subordinate to father, subject subordinate to the ruler) (Ebrey, 2006). As relationships shift, yin-yang dynamics shift: a male subject is yin to the ruler while yang to his wife; a wife is yin to her husband but yang to her children (Hsiung, 2007). Thus, yin and yang are not synonymous with gender or sex. In the end, the path of harmony is in the person's dedication to a life of virtue: benevolence, reciprocity, self-correcting wisdom, righteousness, filial piety, and right language (Ebrey, 2006; Hsiung, 2007). The importance of children (and especially sons) to fulfill social and ritual obligations does lead to male preference and heteronormative beliefs in many Confucian-influenced communities (Hsiung, 2007).

For Taoism, humanity manifests the basic reality of (and is a microcosm of) the cosmos (Yao, 2003). Ch'i is the manifest Tao, expanding and moving as the vital "breath" or energy of creation (Yao, 2003). The manifestation of ch'i splits into yin and yang, which leads to creation but also to dissipation, division, imbalance, and death (Yao, 2003). If one can cultivate ch'i through the balance of yin and yang forces in the body, ch'i will not dissolve and lead to sickness and death (Yao, 2003). Emphasizing balance leads to some discouragement of same-sex relationships as lacking the balance important for health (Hsiung, 2007). However, many other physical, mental, and religious practices are also ways of bringing balance to oneself and in one's relationships.

Shamanic and Shinto Spiritualities and Worldviews

Shamanic practices cross Asia and Asian America and often co-exist with other beliefs and practices—whether they be Buddhist, Confucian, Taoist, Christian, or otherwise. These worldviews emphasize the interpenetration of the material and the spiritual (Gerdner & Xiong, 2015; Kasulis, 2004; Kim, 2003). For example, Hmong shamanism emphasizes harmony between the spiritual and physical worlds, and rituals are important for the maintenance of much of physical life. The person has multiple souls, all of which must be in balance for a healthy life. Sickness occurs when a soul is lost or seized by another, or when there is another unknown spiritual affliction. A shaman diagnoses and fixes the problem (Gerdner & Xiong, 2015).

The Korean worldview similarly intertwines the spiritual and physical. Korean shamans mediate between spiritual and physical worlds, curing illnesses (through exorcisms or other means) and ensuring well-being. Many problems in the physical world arise when evil spirits or spirits of those who died under unfortunate circumstances afflict the living. Shamans must determine the particular spirit and spirit-problem in order to appease and heal both the living and the dead (Kim, 2003).

Shinto spirituality centers on simplicity, nature, and connection. Being in harmony with the kami (spirits) and others ground Shinto life. Disharmony and disconnection from self, others, kami, and the world lead to pollution, which creates problems for people, families, and even the country. Shinto rites focus on purifying the pollution, restoring balance, and fostering connection (Kasulis, 2004).

In Shamanic and Shinto traditions, there is a fundamental link between spirit and matter, the individual and the social. Family is a central consideration, and family obligations continue after death (Earhart, 1996). The importance of family and social order means that more traditional Shinto and Shamanic approaches tend to privilege (heterosexual) marriage and children. While women are prominent as shamans in Shamanism, shamans are sometimes socially marginal figures (Kim, 2003). Concern over the pollution of menstrual blood has led to more restrictions of Shinto women, though there are many miko (female shrine specialists/shamans) and some female priests (Earhart, 1996; Ellwood, 2016; Kasulis, 2004).

Christian Spiritualities and Worldviews

Although Christianity is often described as a "Western" religion, it emerged in the Near Eastern cultural and religious landscape of the first century (C.E.). Early Christians followed trade routes East and established Asian Christian communities (Moffett, 1998). As a result, there are Asian Americans who have been Christians for generations as well as those who have more recently converted, and there is a wide spectrum of belief and practice (Phan, 2003, 2011). There are around 2.2 billion Christians today, with 13% of the Christian population living in Asia and the Pacific (Pew Research Center, 2012b). Thus, the largest religious group of U.S. Asian Americans is Christian (Pew Research Center, 2012a).

While Christian spirituality generally centers on Jesus and the salvation found through his life, death, and resurrection, Asian Christian spirituality and practice have some distinctive features. Asian and Asian American Christians often interrelate faith in Jesus with charismatic experiences of spirits; a narrative Bible-based faith (particularly for Evangelicals and other Protestants); and popular devotional practices to saints and/or Mary, the mother of Jesus (particularly for Orthodox, Catholics, and other "high church" Christians) (Kim, 2003; Phan, 2003). In all these emphases, Asian Christianity and Asian American Christianity tend to find a close relationship between the spiritual and the physical, personal and social (Phan, 2003, 2011).

Although celibacy and ascetical practices are valued in a number of Christian traditions (notably, Catholic and Orthodox denominations), marriage and family nevertheless are quite important for many. There certainly is a notable ambivalence of sex embedded in some New Testament scripture and early Christian thinkers; celibacy was seen as the higher spiritual path. Even so, the biblical commandment to "be fruitful and multiply" was a strong impulse. In contemporary times, many Christian denominations emphasize marriage as a sacred institution. For many of those that argue that a primary purpose of sex/marriage is procreation, heterosexual marriage and children are important. Artificial contraception may be discouraged or even banned. Some traditions subscribe to a gender complementarity and limit women's ritual/sacramental leadership (Cavendish, 2003; DeRogatis, 2003; Johnson & Jordan, 2006).

Asian North American Religions: Implications for Mental Health

Ethnoreligious worldviews, beliefs, and practices operate in both explicit and implicit ways, affecting cultural, familial, social, and psychological dynamics. However, it is impossible to make any definitive conclusions within Asian religious traditions—much less across them—on mental health in Asian American communities. There are, nevertheless, some broad implications that can help mental health professionals researching and working with Asian North American communities.

First, while there is a broad range in terms of Asian American religiosity and observance (and non-observance), the line between the religious and the cultural is fluid. There may be a religious or "sacred" character to cultural values, beliefs, and practices—even for those who are not observant (Pew Research Center, 2012a). Patients and clients themselves may not fully understand the extent to which religious worldviews affect their own self-understanding and life. This deeply embedded nature of the religious in the cultural means that views of mental health, illness, affliction, sexuality, and family are not easily disposed, replaced, dismissed, or medicalized (nor, necessarily, should they be).

Similarly, the line between the spiritual and physical is also fluid. Physical and mental health are therefore often seen as interconnected and fundamentally related to the spiritual (Koenig, 1998, 2018). While some Asian North Americans may draw a direct line between illness, psychological distress, and the spirit-world, others may not, but may still be inclined toward traditional medicines and therapies based in a holistic, non-dual spirit-body cosmology. Even others may believe in the ecstatic power of prayer or ritual practices for facing illness (Gerdner & Xiong, 2015). In all these approaches, the language of psychology and mental health may sound inadequate, incomplete, patronizing, or even problematic. Many are quite open to combined approaches, particularly in urban American cities where holistic medicine and combined therapies are already more broadly accepted. In talking with Asian North American patients and families, therefore, it may help to speak holistically of a mind-body-spirit connection and work with desires for a combined approach to treatment (Wu, 2013).

Even where individual identity is perceived as a construct, one's spirituality is not simply a matter of individuality. Whether the extinction of desire leads to pure compassion (Buddhism); whether faith in the oneness of God leads to the pursuit of social unity and justice (Islam); whether liberation and nonviolence are related intrinsically (Jainism); the personal is social and the spiritual is ethical. Patients, clients, and their families may be unconvinced by approaches to mental health that seem overly individualistic or prioritize the individual over the social. Instead, since the personal and the social go hand and hand, it is important to perceive the individual in an essential web of relationships, to treat the person while including the family (even extended family) as much as possible, and to understand the person's wider reality of spiritual, familial, and social responsibilities.

Many Asian religious traditions view family as fundamentally sacred and a sacred obligation. Even in traditions that tend to prioritize the path of renunciation (like Buddhism and Jainism), householder traditions are essential for the preservation and flourishing of the religious community. The importance of tradition, procreation, family honor, and family order are all of great concern here. Marriage, sex, and children are routinely prioritized; so are sexual restraint, gender complementarity, and heteronormativity. In terms of mental health, this means patients and clients may experience a number of mental health issues related to sex, sexuality, and gender identity. Families may be inclined to perceive these issues as symptoms of children's Westernization that need to be changed, but study of Asian religious traditions demonstrates the diversity and flexibility of Asian religious views (Ellison & Plaskow, 2007). The more that mental health professionals know about Asian traditions of sacred non-procreative desire/pleasure, women's shamanic/ritual power, third genders, and same-sex relationships, the more they can help their patients and clients navigate families, communities, and themselves.

Future Research

Research on Asian North American religions and families is just beginning. Until now, much work has focused on demography, the history of immigration and migration, social scientific studies of congregations and other public aspects of religious life, intergenerational and interethnic issues in Asian American religions, and constructive theological/ethical articulations of Asian religious faith and practice in the Americas. Asian religions and family, particularly with respect to Asian views of sex, sexuality, and gender, have largely been treated outside of the American context. More consideration of the Asian American context specifically is necessary. Popularly accessible Asian American religious resources on complementary approaches to Eastern and Western health care, family life, sex, sexuality, and gender (beyond religious pronouncements or didactic statements) are also lacking.

Conclusion

When working with Asian North American communities, interference (or perceived interference) in family matters is likely to be met with suspicion and hostility. It is essential for mental health professionals to work *with* families and their values. This requires looking for common ground and respecting the religio-cultural values, practices, and beliefs that may be at play. Contemporary media prefers painting a picture of conflict between Asian religious traditions/cultures and Western norms, between superstitious oppression and broad-minded liberalism. Presuming conflict is profoundly unhelpful and deeply problematic. Understanding the diversity, complexity, and fluidity of Asian religious traditions—and respecting the ways in which spirituality is often embedded into people's lives—allows counselors, mental health professionals, and social workers to work more productively with the communities, families, and persons they serve.

References

Al-Hibri, A., & El Habti, R. M. (2006). Islam. In D. S. Browning, M. C. Green, & J. Witte Jr. (Eds.), *Sex, marriage, and family in world religions* (pp. 150–225). Columbia University Press.

Amore, R. C. (2010). Buddhist traditions. In W. G. Oxtoby & R. C. Amore (Eds.), *World religions, Eastern traditions* (3rd ed., pp. 176–252). Oxford University Press.

The Association of Religion Data Archives. (2010). *Most Baha'i nations*. http://www.thearda.com/QL2010/QuickList_40.asp

Baker, D., & DeVries, L. (2010). Introduction. In L. DeVries, D. Baker, & D. Overmyer (Eds.), *Asian religions in British Columbia* (pp. 1–14). UBC Press.

Cabezón, J. I. (Ed.). (1992). *Buddhism, sexuality, and gender*. State University of New York Press.

Cashwell, C. S., & Young, J. S. (Eds.). (2011). *Integrating spirituality and religion into counseling: A guide to competent practice* (2nd ed.). American Counseling Association.

Cavendish, J. C. (2003). The Vatican and the laity: Diverging paths in Catholic understanding of sexuality. In D. W. Machacek & M. M. Wilcox (Eds.), *Sexuality and the world's religions* (pp. 203–229). ABC-CLIO.

Chui, T., & Flanders, J. (2015). *Immigration and ethnocultural diversity in Canada*. https://www12.statcan.gc.ca/nhs-enm/2011/as-sa/99-010-x/99-010-x2011001-eng.cfm#a6

Cole, A. (2006). Buddhism. In D. S. Browning, M. C. Green, & J. Witte Jr. (Eds.), *Sex, marriage, and family in world religions* (pp. 299–366). Columbia University Press.

Coloma, R. S., McElhinny, B., Tungohan, E., Catungal, J. P. C., & Davidson, L. M. (Eds.). (2012). *Filipinos in Canada: Disturbing invisibility*. University of Toronto Press.

Courtright, P. B. (2006). Hinduism. In D. S. Browning, M. C. Green, & J. Witte Jr. (Eds.), *Sex, marriage, and family in world religions* (pp. 226–298). Columbia University Press.

Crisp, B. R. (Ed.). (2017). *The Routledge handbook of religion, spirituality, and social work*. Routledge.

DeRogatis, A. (2003). Varieties of interpretations: Protestantism and sexuality. In D. W. Machacek & M. M. Wilcox (Eds.), *Sexuality and the world's religions* (pp. 231–253). ABC-CLIO.

DeVries, L., Baker, D., & Overmyer, D. (Eds.). (2011). *Asian religions in British Columbia*. University of British Columbia Press.

Earhart, H. B. (1996). *Religion in the Japanese experience: Sources and interpretations* (2nd ed.). Wadsworth Cengage Learning.

Ebrey, P. (2006). Confucianism. In D. S. Browning, M. C. Green, & J. Witte Jr. (Eds.), *Sex, marriage, and family in world religions* (pp. 367–450). Columbia University Press.

Eduljee, K. E. (2005). *Zoroastrian demographics*. http://www.heritageinstitute.com/zoroastrianism/demographics/#worldwide

Ellison, M. M., & Plaskow, J. (Eds.). (2007). *Heterosexism in contemporary world religion: Problem and prospect*. Pilgrim Press.

Ellwood, R. (2016). *Introducing Japanese religions* (2nd ed.). Routledge.

Flood, G. (1996). *An introduction to Hinduism*. Cambridge University Press.

Flueckiger, J. B. (2015). *Everyday Hinduism*. Wiley-Blackwell.

Gerdner, L. A., & Xiong, S. V. (2015). *Demystifying Hmong shamanism: Practice and use by Hmong Americans across the lifespan*. Bauu Press.

Gruzder, D. (2008, December 09). *The last of the Zoroastrians*. Time. http://content.time.com/time/world/article/0,8599,1864931,00.html

Hidayatullah, A. (2003). Islamic conceptions of sexuality. In D. W. Machacek & M. M. Wilcox (Eds.), *Sexuality and the world's religions* (pp. 255–292). ABC-CLIO.

Hsiung, H. (2007). Gender and same-sex relations in Confucianism and Taoism. In M. M. Ellison & J. Plaskow (Eds.), *Heterosexism in contemporary world religion: Problem and prospect* (pp. 99–134). Pilgrim Press.

Hussain, A. (2011). Muslim traditions. In W. G. Oxtoby & A. Hussain (Eds.), *World religions, Western traditions* (3rd ed., pp. 266–320). Oxford University Press.

Johnson, L. T., & Jordan, M. (2006). Christianity. In D. S. Browning, M. C. Green, & J. Witte Jr. (Eds.), *Sex, marriage, and family in world religions* (pp. 77–149). Columbia University Press.

Kaur, M. (Ed.). (2014). *Her name is Kaur: Sikh American women write about love, courage, and faith*. She Writes Press.

Kasulis, T. P. (2004). *Shinto: The way home*. University of Hawai'I Press.

Kelting, M. W. (2009). *Heroic wives: Rituals, stories and the virtues of Jain wifehood*. Oxford University Press.

Kim, C. (2003). *Korean shamanism: The cultural paradox*. Ashgate.

Koenig, H. G. (Ed.). (1998). *Handbook of religion and mental health*. San Diego, CA: Academic.

Koenig, H. G. (2018). *Religion and mental health: Research and clinical applications*. Academic.

Kosmin, B. A., & Keysar, A. (2001). *American religious identification survey*. The Graduate Center of the City University of New York. http://commons.trincoll.edu/aris/surveys/aris-2001/

Lee, J. H. X., & Nadeau, K. (Eds.). (2014). *Asian American identities and practices: Folkloric expressions in everyday life*. Lexington Books.

Lee, J. H. X., Matsuoka, F., Yee, E., & Nakasone, R. (Eds.). (2015). *Asian American religious cultures* (Vol. 2). ABC-CLIO.

Lidke, J. S. (2003). A union of fire and water: Sexuality and spirituality in Hinduism. In D. W. Machacek & M. M. Wilcox (Eds.), *Sexuality and the world's religions* (pp. 101–132). ABC-CLIO.

Loewenthal, K. (2007). *Religion, culture, and mental health*. Cambridge University Press.

Long, J. D. (2009). *Jainism: An introduction*. I. B. Tauris.

Loue, S. (2017). *Handbook of religion and spirituality in social work practice and research*. Springer.

Mahajan, P. T., Pimple, P., Palsetia, D., Dave, N., & De Sousa, A. (2013). Indian religious concepts on sexuality and marriage. *Indian Journal of Psychiatry, 55*(Suppl 2), S256–S262. https://doi.org/10.4103/0019-5545.105547

Mandair, A. (2010). Sikhism. In S. Sorajjakool, M. F. Carr, & J. J. Nam (Eds.), *World religions for healthcare professionals* (pp. 77–94). Routledge.

Mann, G. S., Numrich, P., & Williams, R. (2008). *Buddhists, Hindus, and Sikhs in America: A short history*. (Reprint ed.). Oxford University Press.

Moffett, S. H. (1998). *A history of Christianity in Asia: Beginnings to 1500* (2nd ed.). Orbis Books.

Peach, L. J. (2002). *Women and world religions*. Prentice Hall.

Pew Research Center. (2012a). *Asian Americans: A mosaic of faiths*. http://www.pewforum.org/2012/07/19/asian-americans-a-mosaic-of-faiths-overview/

Pew Research Center. (2012b). *The global religious landscape*. http://www.pewforum.org/2012/12/18/global-religious-landscape-exec/

Pew Research Center. (2012c). *How many U.S. Sikhs?*http://www.pewresearch.org/2012/08/06/ask-the-expert-how-many-us-sikhs/

Pew Research Center. (2014). *U.S. religious landscape study*. http://www.pewforum.org/religious-landscape-study/

Pew Research Center. (2018). *Income inequality in the U.S. is rising most rapidly among Asians*. http://www.pewsocialtrends.org/2018/07/12/income-inequality-in-the-u-s-is-rising-most-rapidly-among-asians/

Phan, P. C. (Ed.). (2011). *Christianities in Asia*. Wiley-Blackwell.

Phan, P. C. (2003). *In our own tongues: Perspectives from Asia on mission and inculturation*. Orbis Books.

The Pluralism Project. (n.d.). *Jain immigration*. http://pluralism.org/religions/jainism/jainism-in-america/jain-immigration/

Rambachan, A. (2007). "There are many branches on the tree of life": The irreconcilability of Hinduism and homophobia. In M. M. Ellison & J. Plaskow (Eds.), *Heterosexism in contemporary world religion: Problem and prospect* (pp. 201–223). The Pilgrim Press.

Reini, R., & Hiebert, D. (Eds.). (1996). *Baha'i writings on homosexuality*. http://bahai-library.com/compilation_reini_homosexuality#vi
Rose, J. (2011a). *Zoroastrianism: An introduction*. I. B. Tauris.
Rose, J. (2011b). *Zoroastrianism: A guide for the perplexed*. Continuum.
Seager, R. H. (1999). *Buddhism in America*. Columbia University Press.
Singh, P. (2010). Sikh traditions. In W. G. Oxtoby & R. C. Amore (Eds.), *World religions, Eastern traditions* (3rd ed., pp. 106–143). Oxford University Press.
Smith, P. (2008). *An introduction to the Baha'i faith*. New York, NY: Cambridge University Press.
Sorajjakool, S., Carr, M. F., & Nam, J. J. (Eds.). (2010). *World religions for healthcare professionals*. Routledge.
Statistics Canada. (2011). *National household survey*. Statistics Canada catalogue no. 99-010-X2011032.
Vallely, A. (2010). Jaina traditions. In W. G. Oxtoby & R. C. Amore (Eds.), *World religions, Eastern traditions* (3rd ed., pp. 144–175). Oxford University Press.
Wiley, K. L. (2004). *Historical dictionary of Jainism*. The Scarecrow Press.
Wilson, L. (2003). Buddhist views on gender and desire. In D. W. Machacek & M. M. Wilcox (Eds.), *Sexuality and the world's religions* (pp. 133–175). ABC-CLIO.
Woo, T. T. (2010). Chinese and Korean traditions. In W. G. Oxtoby & R. C. Amore (Eds.), *World religions, Eastern traditions* (3rd ed., pp. 254–327). Oxford University Press.
Wu, E. S. (2013). *Traditional Chinese medicine in the United States: In search of spiritual meaning and ultimate health*. Lexington Books.
Yao, X. (2003). Harmony of yin and yang: Cosmology and sexuality in Daoism. In D. W. Machacek & M. M. Wilcox (Eds.), *Sexuality and the world's religions* (pp. 65–99). ABC-CLIO.

Part II
Specific Countries and Regions of Origin: East Asia

Chapter 4
Chinese Families from Mainland China, Hong Kong, and Taiwan

Susan S. Chuang, Xuan Li, and Ching-Yu Huang

Abstract To gain greater insights into contemporary Chinese immigrant families in North America, it is imperative to understand the history of Chinese societies. This chapter provides an overview of the immigration history of Chinese families to Canada and the United States and the intracultural diversity in major Chinese societies (Mainland China, Taiwan, and Hong Kong) that have influenced these families in their native countries and abroad. We then explore how their acculturation pathways have impacted their family relationships, parenting practices and beliefs. Next, we describe the traditional values regarding family, interpersonal relations, and gender roles that have influenced Chinese families, and how some of the recent social changes have influenced contemporary immigrant and non-immigrant Chinese families' family lives. We conclude with some practical implications for the mental health and other helping professions to better assist Chinese immigrants to deal with mental health issues and overcome barriers of seeking professional assistance.

Keywords Mainland China · Hong Kong · Taiwan · Immigration · Acculturation · Parenting practices and beliefs · Confucianism · Mental health

Research on ethnic minority families has increased in recent years, especially within the context of immigrant families (Chuang, 2019; Chuang & Costigan, 2018). This may be the result of countries' ethnoprofiles diversifying from increased international migrants worldwide. Of the 258 million migrants in 2017, over 60% of

S. S. Chuang (✉)
University of Guelph, Guelph, ON, Canada
e-mail: schuang@uoguelph.ca

X. Li
New York University Shanghai, Shanghai, China
e-mail: xuanli@nyu.edu

C.-Y. Huang
Keele University, Newcastle, UK

S. S. Chuang et al. (eds.), *Asian Families in Canada and the United States*, Advances in Immigrant Family Research,
https://doi.org/10.1007/978-3-030-56452-0_4

the migrants were from Asia (80 million), and ten million were specifically from Mainland China (United Nations, 2017). Thus, there has been a particular focus on Chinese families, yet the Chinese populations are typically represented as a homogenous entirety (e.g., Chen, 2014; Newland, Coyl, & Chen, 2010; Tu, Chang, & Kao, 2014). Most empirical research on Chinese families either overlook the historical and socio-political contexts of the various Chinese populations (Chuang, Glozman, Green, & Rasmi, 2018; Luo, Tamis-LeMonda, & Song, 2013) or provide only minimal context (Lee, Zhou, Eisenberg, & Wang, 2013; Liu & Guo, 2010). However, Chinese societies present intracultural variations and complexities due to their long and turbulent history, wide geographic extension, and large populations. Such variations still influence contemporary Chinese families, including those who have migrated to Canada and the United Sates.

To better understand the diversity among Chinese societies which, in turn, influence the sociocultural backgrounds of immigrant families, it is important to explore the historical, political, and social changes in major Chinese populations such as Mainland China, Hong Kong, and Taiwan. A greater understanding and appreciation of the shared cultural roots and divergent modern histories will inform scholars and practitioners about complexities of immigrant Chinese families and the implications to parenting, parent-child relationships, mental health, and well-being. Thus, this chapter begins with a brief overview of history of the Chinese immigrants in Canada and the United States, followed by a description of the diverse political, ethnic and linguistic factors affecting major Chinese societies. We then explore the implications of the Chinese families immigrating and adapting to Canada and the United States, with emphasis on the immigration processes and pathways that have impacted family relationships, parenting practices, and beliefs. Thereafter, the traditional values that have influenced family dynamics and relationships, as well as the recent social, political, and economic changes that have transformed contemporary and recent immigrant Chinese families is discussed. We conclude the chapter with some practical implications for the helping professions on how to effectively assist Chinese immigrants to overcome help-seeking barriers regarding mental health issues.

Immigration History of Chinese Families in Canada and the United States

The Chinese, especially those from the south, have a long tradition of international migration. Southeast Asia, in particular, hosts a large proportion of the overseas Chinese. People of Chinese ethnicity make up about 74% of the population of Singapore and are significant and influential minorities of many other countries such as Malaysia (24.6%, as of 2016), Thailand, Brunei, and Indonesia (Department of Statistics Malaysia, 2019; Department of Statistics Singapore, 2018). In recent decades, countries such as Canada and the United States have experienced a significant influx of immigrants from Mainland China, Hong Kong, and Taiwan (Chagnon, 2013; Hooper & Batalova, 2015). Different immigration policies in Canada and the United States may impact how immigrant families function within its particular context. Thus, it is important to understand the immigration policies of the respective countries, placing immigrant Chinese families within the broader sociocultural context of their host countries.

Canada Historically, Canada's immigration population was primarily from Western Europe, especially Great Britain. After the WWII, immigration policies maintained its preference for immigrants from the United States, United Kingdom, and other European countries for two decades (Li, 2003). However, from 1954 to 1967, the increased immigration flow of over 60,000 Canadians in professional, technical, managerial, and entrepreneurial occupations to the United States greatly impacted Canada's economic market, leading to significant revisions of its immigration policies to focus more on human capital (e.g., educational and occupational skills) as the basis of immigrant selection rather than racial or national origin (Li, 1992). Thus, five years after the 1967 immigration law, Canada experienced a large influx of Chinese and other Asian immigrants; admitted almost 740,000 immigrants, with 15% from Asian countries (Li, 2003).

This influx of immigrants prompted the federal government to officially declare a multiculturalism policy in 1971 which acknowledged that diversity was fundamental to Canada's identity. According to the revised Canadian Multiculturalism Act (1988), the first policy objective for Canada was to recognize and promote cultural and racial diversity of all Canadian individuals. Currently, the population has become increasingly more multi-ethnic and multi-cultural with representation of over 250 ethnic groups, with almost 62% of newcomers from Asian countries (Statistics Canada, 2019). In 2011, the visible minorities accounted for almost 20% of the total population. China accounted for over 11% of the source countries between 2010 and 2015, and the lead source country from 2005 to 2015 accounting for 13% of the newcomers (Morency, Malenfant, & MacIsaac, 2017). Also, the visible minority population increased from 16% to over 19%, and the Chinese (including Mainland China, Taiwan, and Hong Kong) accounted for over 21% of the total visible minority group, the second largest group after South Asians at 25% (Statistics Canada, 2013).

United States Canada's patterns of immigration are similar in the United States. Briefly, the earliest recording of foreign-born population census (1850–1930) recorded an increase from 2.2 million to 14.2 million, reflecting a large-scale immigration of families from Europe. In the early 1880s, restrictive immigration policies such as the Chinese Exclusion Act (1882) were created to bar certain groups of immigrants such as prostitutes, workers who were contracted with particular companies for several years, and the Chinese (Martin, 2010). Similar to Canada's change in immigration policies, the U.S. revised its immigration law in 1965, allowing immigrants with families already in the U.S., and granting requests from U.S. requests from U.S. employers for their immigrant employees (Martin, 2013).

Since 1970, there was an immigration flux with immigrants primarily from Latin America and Asia, increasing the population from 9.6 million in 1970 to 14.1 million in 1980 (Gibson & Lennon, 1999). In 2000, over 2.4 million Chinese people lived in the United States. Placed in a broader context, the last decade revealed a foreign-born population increase of 11% from 8% of the total population. The majority of families (86%) emigrated from Latin America and Asia. The Asian population was also the fastest growing population between 2000 and 2010, accounting for about 5% of the total population. Of the Asian population, 23% were Chinese (U.S. Census Bureau, 2012), suggesting that the Chinese population accounted for 1.15% of the entire population of the United States.

The Chinese: Political, Ethnic, and Linguistic Variations and their Implications

Chinese populations, including both the immigrants and those residing in the Greater China area, are often represented as a homogenous entirety (for critical review, see Chuang et al., 2018). However, there exists political, ethnic, linguistic, and sociocultural diversity within and across the major modern Chinese societies. Such diversity has profound implications for the immigration experiences, acculturative processes, and livelihood of Chinese immigrant families, and thus should be taken into consideration by researchers who investigate the family values and practices among Chinese immigrants.

Political Factors

Until 1912, when the last imperial rule was overturned, China ran a pre-industrial feudal economic system following the Confucian philosophy, where most of the population was engaged in agricultural production under the governing literati class. After the founding of the Republic of China in 1912 and the war-torn 1930s and 1940s, the Chinese societies can be generally divided into the following groups: Mainland China under the Communist government (PRC, 1949 – present), Taiwan under the Nationalist government (ROC, 1912 – present), and Hong Kong (under the British rule from 1842 and became a Special Administrative Region of the PRC since 1997 under the "one country, two systems" policy, which ensures its engagement in capitalism and political autonomy). In addition, Macau, which was a Portuguese colony for over four centuries (1557–1999), was turned over to the PRC in 1999 with similar status as Hong Kong.

These political differences among PRC, Hong Kong, and Taiwan, have important implications to the Chinese immigrants' beliefs and behaviors, especially for recent immigrants. The political landscapes of PRC, Hong Kong, and Taiwan, which have fundamentally shaped the socioeconomic development of these three societies over the last decades, have direct and indirect effects on the characteristics of Chinese immigrant families. For example, post-war Taiwan and Hong Kong quickly restored their economies under the capitalist system and steadily rose to leading powers of global trade and finance. Similarly, Taiwan experienced miraculous economic growth during 1950–1988 due to a series of government-lead economic-policy reforms and the introduction of electronic industry, and Hong Kong, after several major shifts, has been functioning as the finance hub of Asia-Pacific. Meanwhile, Mainland China underwent radical socialist movements such as the Land Reform(1950–1953), the Great Leap Forward (1958–1962) and the Cultural Revolution (1966–1976). During this period, the land was redistributed and the economy was nationalized and re-organized into collective agricultural production units in the rural area and state corporates in the cities (Jacka, Kipnis, & Sargeson, 2013). Thus, international contacts and mobility were severed. Mainland China eventually "reformed and opened" in 1979 after years of turmoil and joined the global capitalist market under a socialist government. After nearly four decades of economic privatization and introduction of foreign investment, China has become one of the world's largest economies, with the GDP per capita ranked 73rd in 2016 (United Nations, 2017). Under such circumstances, the emigration of Chinese from Taiwan and Hong Kong began earlier, whereas the arrival of Mainland Chinese in major destination countries such as the United States drastically increased since the 1980s (Hooper & Batalova, 2015).

Not only the general political economies, but also specific policies in the home Chinese societies have long term effects on the family life of Chinese immigrants. All major Chinese societies have implemented fertility policies during the modernization process to ease the stress of the population growth and to cultivate new generations of high-quality citizens. During the 1960s, Taiwan government was promoting a limit of children to two and parents in Hong Kong were similarly encouraged to have two children (Sun, 2001). The strictest family planning policy was implemented by the government of Mainland China, which instituted the "one-child policy" (1978–2015) that restricted married urban couples to having only one child. The new adult-child ratio as a result of the shrinking family size in all major Chinese societies challenged the Confucian teachings of hierarchy and parental power toward a more "child-centered" framework (Chen & Chen, 2010). In Mainland China, specifically, the one-child policy that partially extended the socialist gender ideology of "gender-sameness" led to an unintended empowering effect for the urban daughters (Fong, 2002).

Ethnic Variations

There are considerable ethnic variations within and across the Chinese populations. The vast majority of the contemporary Chinese population, about 92% of Mainland China, 95% of Taiwan, and 94% of Hong Kong, belong to the Han ethnicity. More specifically, in Mainland China, there are 55 officially recognized ethnic minorities, with Zhuang (1.3%), Hui (0.8%), Manchu (0.8%) and Uyghur (0.8%) being the largest minority groups (National Bureau of Statistics of People's Republic of China, 2012). Islam and Tibetan Buddhism are important religions among the Uyghur and Tibetan minorities. Currently, Taiwan officially recognizes 16 aborigine tribes (Council of Indigenous Peoples of Republic of China, 2017), half of which reside in the eastern plain and the other half in mountainous terrains. The aborigines that originally resided in the western plain of Taiwan have been well-acculturated into the Han Chinese culture through inter-marriage with the Han Chinese (Brown, 2004). In contrast, the non-Chinese population in Hong Kong were more likely to be transient employment seekers from other parts of Asia (such as Indonesian and Filipino domestic helpers) rather than historical settlers (Census and Statistics Department of Hong Kong Special Administrative Region, 2017).

Linguistic and Cultural Variations

Even within the Han ethnicity, there are varying linguistic and cultural factors across regions. Alongside Mandarin, which is the primary official language in all major Chinese societies, other dialects and minority languages such as Wu (including Shanghainese), Yue (including Cantonese), Min (including Hokkien) and Hakka were spoken in specific areas in Mainland China and Taiwan. In Hong Kong, English used to be the sole official language during the British colonial period and Cantonese, the principal vernacular. Over time, Hong Kong transitioned to operating a trilingual system of English, Cantonese, and Mandarin (Government of Hong Kong Special Administrative Region, n.d.).

Variations of written scripts also exist across major Chinese societies because of state and nation building through language policies and regulation. Simplified Chinese characters are used in Mainland China, Singapore, and Malaysia as well as among new immigrants from Mainland China. Traditional Chinese characters are used in Taiwan, Hong Kong, Macau (with slight difference) and among overseas Chinese communities with a longer immigration history. It is worth noting that most major dialects such as Wu, Yue, Min, and Hakka are not mutually intelligible with Mandarin, although the gap between traditional and simplified Chinese is smaller (Dong, 2014).

In addition to languages, regional variances in values and beliefs also exist. The coastal provinces in Mainland China, for example, which are economically better developed with greater exposure to global cultural products, endorse traditional family beliefs such as filial piety to a lesser extent than the western, inland provinces (Hu & Scott, 2016). The rice-farming areas (more common in the south) were also believed to be more collectivist than the wheat-farming areas (more common in the north) (Talhelm et al., 2014).

Traditional Values on Parent-Child Relations and Gender Roles

Underlying the vast political, ethnic and linguistic diversities within the Chinese ethnic group, there is a long shared tradition of the Confucian Chinese culture. These traditional cultural beliefs and family processes would be especially visible in the earlier generations who migrated prior to 1949. Confucianism, which has been the dominant belief system in Chinese societies for over 2000 years, focuses on interdependence, social harmony, and sacrificing one's needs for the sake of the group (Ho, 1987). An individual was viewed within social relationships, holding specific family and societal roles with a clear understanding of his/her "proper place," and was required to uphold his or her roles and responsibilities to maintain social order and harmony.

The most fundamental of all the relationships was the family unit. Confucius conceptualized a template that includes specific rules on family hierarchy, intergenerational conduct, lines of authority, and respect for the status of others (Tang, 1992). In this template, the father-son relationship was believed to be the most structurally important relationship in the family system, and served as the prototype of all relationships. Parents are expected to provide their children with love, wisdom, and benevolence (Kim & Park, 2006). In return, children display filial piety by being obedient, respectful, and devoted to their parents (Miller, Wiley, Fung, & Laing, 1997), and by bringing honor to the family name. When children are older, they are expected to provide financial support and care for their parents (Ho, 1996).

Confucian family ethics also prescribe strict gender roles in the family. Fathers as the "master of the family" are responsible for issues that are outside of the household such as breadwinning whereas mothers are responsible for the household and raising of children. As the traditional adage stated, "strict father, warm mother" (Wilson, 1974). Thus, mothers' daily responsibilities were to nurture and supervise their children whereas fathers were a distant figure who taught, directed, and disciplined the children, especially when they are older (Ho, 1987; Wolf, 1970). Boys are preferred over girls as they are expected to continue the family lineage and are therefore given better resources.

However, the traditional gender roles have undergone profound changes since the early twentieth century, when Chinese intellectuals began to critically reflect on the Confucian family beliefs such as the parent-child hierarchy, filial piety, and gender roles (Edwards, 2000; Glosser, 2003). Family life in Mainland China, Taiwan, and Hong Kong took on different evolutionary pathways since the 1950s under the influence of the sociopolitical systems in the respective societies. For example, the Chinese Communist Party explicitly celebrated gender equality including the female right to receive education and to work as part of its political agenda to liberate women from domestic activities and to maximize its human capital to build the new socialist state (Honig, 2000). The socialist gender equality policy, coupled with the One-Child Policy which also advocated for similar resource allocation to sons and daughters, raised female participation in secondary and tertiary education to similar levels as those of the males (Lui & Carpenter, 2005). For example, from 1966 to 1976, 90% of the urban women aged 25–44 years were working, with even higher working rates among rural women (Bauer, Feng, Riley, & Zhao, 1992), which means that most children grow up with two breadwinning parents. In Taiwan and Hong Kong, girls attained parity in educational attainment around the 1980s (Tsai, Gates, & Chiu, 1994). Thus, recent Chinese immigrants, especially Mainland Chinese immigrants who migrated after 1960 and Taiwanese or Hong Kong immigrants who migrated after the 1980s, may endorse more egalitarian gender-role beliefs.

Cultural Adaptation and Acculturation

With the increasing Chinese population in Canada and the United States, researchers have great opportunities to systematically and comprehensively examine family functioning and relationships among immigrant Chinese families (Chuang, 2019). As a result of the immigration process, all families undergo changes as they leave behind their native country and re-establish themselves in the receiving country (Arends-Tóth & van de Vijver, 2006). Such processes of cultural and psychological changes that individuals encounter when they are in contact with a new culture is called acculturation (Berry, Kim, Power, Young, & Bujaki, 1989). When there are substantial differences between the two cultures, these discrepancies may heighten the pressures on immigrant families to adopt the customs and values of the new country (Costigan & Dokis, 2006). Specifically, immigrants bring with them their cultural values, beliefs, and behaviors from their country of origin, and engage and negotiate a new sociocultural terrain. With the complexities of the acculturative process, each individual acculturates at a different rate, facing his/her own challenges and barriers.

Acculturation Processes and Parent-Child Discrepancies

The immigration experiences are magnified and even more complex when one considers immigration within the family context. For immigrant Chinese parents, their parenting practices and beliefs are influenced by their immigrant context, traditional parenting customs, acculturative experiences, as well as potential influences from the host culture. These interactions with socialization agents in the dominant society may differ from their own ideas about optimal developmental outcomes and desired characteristics in their children, and thus, may promote differing goals and use different child-rearing strategies (Bornstein & Cote, 2004). Thus, parents then negotiate between the two "cultural" worlds (Bornstein & Lansford, 2010).

From the parents' perspective, it is important to consider their life stage and take a developmental ecological orientation. Specifically, parents have matured in their ethnic culture, and thus have the unique challenges of negotiating between the westernized culture and their heritage Asian culture as they parent in a bicultural context (Cheah, Leung, & Zhuo, 2013; Huang, & Lamb, 2015). Moreover, many parents face challenges in learning the new language and culture, which may result in less willingness to adapt to the new norms and customs (Phinney, Ong, & Madden, 2000). However, as Costigan and Koryzma (2011) reported, Chinese mothers and fathers who were more involved in the Canadian culture had greater feelings of parenting efficacy, which led to better psychological adjustment and positive parenting practices (e.g., warmth, reasoning). In contrast, children and youth may have limited or no exposure to their ethnic culture and face different adaptation challenges than their parents (Wang, Kim, Anderson, Chen, & Yan, 2012; Zhou, 1997). Thus, immigrant parents experience their own adaptation challenges as they simultaneously must socialize their children to be successful in the new sociocultural environment (Costigan & Koryzma, 2011; Szapocznik & Kurtines, 1993).

As parents strive to transmit their ethnic culture to their children, their children face the task of interpreting and deriving meaning of their parents' teachings of their ethnic culture in a new culture (Costigan & Dokis, 2006; Kwak, 2003). Children are also more likely to have intensive exposure to the new culture at school and with peers (Chen & Chen, 2010; Costigan, Su, & Hua, 2009; Wang et al., 2012). With their psychological needs of social acceptance and inclusion, and to academically excel, children may adapt more quickly to the values and customs of the new culture than their parents (Chuang & Moreno, 2011).

Researchers have explored immigrant Chinese parents' and their children's discrepant levels of acculturation. When parents and their children have greater acculturation disparities and intergenerational stress, this may lead to higher levels of parent-child conflicts and negative communication (Dinh, Sarason, & Sarason, 1994). There may be greater parent-child discrepancies in some domains of life compared to other domains (Costigan & Dokis, 2006). To address these variations, researchers focused on private and public domains of acculturation. The private domain refers to the socioemotional and value-related aspects of psychological and interpersonal acculturation such as ethnic identity and parenting practices. The public domain refers to the functional and utilitarian aspects of acculturation such as schooling and language use (Arends-Tóth & van de Vijver, 2004). Comparing Mainland Chinese Canadian children's and parents' acculturation levels, Costigan and Dokis (2006) found that the discrepancy was not associated with poorer adjustment for the public domain of acculturation. However, discrepancies between parents (especially with mothers) and children in their engagement of their ethnic culture, an aspect of the private domain, were predictive of the children's adjustment, such as higher levels of conflict intensity, depression, and lower levels of achievement motivation. Moreover, immigrant Chinese parents stated that children were growing up too quickly in America (e.g., becoming more independent at an earlier age) and perceived this accelerated developmental tempo as challenging their parenting; and such a fast pace of change also impacted the amounts of time they spent with their children and their children's ties to their cultural heritage (Chun, 2004).

The examination of acculturation and Chinese fathering remains limited (Chance, Costigan, & Leadbeater, 2013; Chuang & Zhu, 2018). In comparing Chinese fathers from Mainland China and Canada, Chuang and Zhu (2018) reported that regardless of country, fathers were actively involved with their young children, including caring for and playing with them. Interestingly, native fathers were more likely to play with their children than were immigrant fathers, but caring for their children was similar. However, when comparing the proportionate amount of time (i.e., percentage of their available time), the country difference was no longer significant. Country differences were found for accessibility, where immigrant fathers did more household chores than fathers in China. They may be due to the limited social support that immigrant families have access to (e.g., grandparents) and thus, household responsibilities become shared between mothers and fathers.

Comparing mothers and fathers, it is reasonable to argue that Chinese fathers and mothers have different acculturative resources and challenges as men and women. For example, Chance, Costigan, and Leadbeater (2013) found that differential acculturation between Chinese mothers and fathers influenced their child-rearing expectations and the quality of their coparenting relationship such as how much adolescents should assist their families. For these fathers, the Chinese acculturation discrepancies and coparenting were directly related, but not for mothers. As some researchers have revealed, although immigrant (and non-immigrant) fathers are involved in child-rearing, their involvement in decision making is primarily in the context of the joint decision making with the mothers, with few fathers making independent decisions (Chance et al., 2013; Chuang & Su, 2009).

Parenting in Contemporary Immigrant Chinese Families

Contemporary literature on Chinese society and socialization has suggested that parents' beliefs and values are still greatly influenced by Confucian principles, especially regarding parenting practices and parents' conceptions about childhood (Chuang, 2013). Immigrant Chinese parents were found to maintain Chinese traditions and values and were more restrictive and controlling than were Euro-American parents (Luo et al., 2013). However, the child outcomes associated with authoritarian parenting have culturally differed (e.g., negative child outcomes for Caucasian children but positive outcomes for Chinese children). In contrast, the cross-cultural findings on authoritative style are not as straightforward. Some studies found that Chinese parents had lower authoritative scores than Caucasian parents (Liu & Guo, 2010; Su & Hynie, 2011) whereas other researchers found no cultural differences (Pearson & Rao, 2003).

Among the few studies that focused on Chinese and immigrant Chinese fathers, Chuang and Su (2008) examined acculturative influences among fathers in Mainland China and immigrant Chinese fathers in Canada (from Mainland China). Confucianism exerted less influence on Chinese fathers to the extent that, regardless of country of residence, most fathers conceptualized their roles as multi-faceted, including economic provider, caregiver, playmate, and doing household chores (Chuang & Su, 2008; Chuang et al., 2013). Also, immigrant fathers were less authoritarian, more authoritative and, more likely to take their children's interest into consideration when making child care decisions than were fathers residing in Mainland China (Chuang & Su, 2008).

Conceptual and Methodological Issues in Research on Immigrant Chinese Families

While informative, existing research on immigrant Chinese families in North America is not without conceptual and methodological problems. Parenting practices in Chinese and immigrant Chinese families are more complicated than the typical portrayal of immigrant Chinese parents as authoritarian (e.g., Chan, Bowes, & Wyver, 2009; Cheung & McBride-Chang, 2008; Liu & Guo, 2010). Many researchers have addressed this issue by focusing on concepts such as "control" and "parental authority" to further support these claims (Chuang et al., 2018) that derived from Baumrind's (1971) typologies of authoritative (AV) and authoritarian (AN)parenting styles. Briefly, Baumrind's (1971) parenting framework is based on two orthogonal dimensions: demandingness (behavioral control, restrictiveness) and responsiveness (warmth, support). AV parents are described as highly demanding and responsive but also providing positive encouragement to their children's autonomy. These parents are warm, rational, and open to communicating with their children. In contrast, AN parents are also highly demanding but are not responsive to their children's needs. They value respect for authority, obedience without explanation, restrict children's autonomy, and enforce parental authority (Baumrind, 1971).

Yet several reviews offered complicated, inconsistent patterns of parenting (Chuang, 2006, 2019), although such works have seldom been noticed. For example, Taiwanese and Taiwanese-American parents were more controlling than their European-American counterparts, but they also had higher ratings on encouragement of independence than European-American parents (Lin & Fu, 1990). Similarly, Chiu (1987) revealed that Taiwanese-American and Taiwanese mothers had higher scores on the Democratic Attitudes factor (encouraging verbalization, comradeship and sharing, and equalitarianism) than did American mothers. Chuang (2006) also reported that Taiwanese immigrant mothers of young children allowed their children personal freedom and independence on various issues (e.g., choice of clothing, play activities). These findings challenge the Confucian influence on parenting but yet, many researchers continue to perpetuate the Chinese stereotype of parenting. Some only focus on partial findings such as parental control (Chan et al., 2009) or did not report contradictory findings (Lai, Zhang, & Wang, 2010) but then stated that Chinese parents were more authoritarian or restrictive. Others have reversed the findings to further support their claims of Chinese parenting (Liu & Guo, 2010).

One also needs to be careful in explaining the different patterns of change in immigrant families and families in Mainland China, Taiwan, and Hong Kong, which have all gone through significant sociocultural reconfiguration in the last decades. Would such discrepancies be a result of the acculturation process due to the influence of the Canadian culture, or would this also reflect the recent significant social, economic, and cultural changes in Mainland China, Hong Kong, and Taiwan, especially if they were recent immigrants? For example, the transitions in economic and engagement with the competitive global market have influenced Chinese parents and more recent Chinese immigrant parents on how they prepare their children for their future. Rather than promoting traditional Confucian teachings of obedience and filial piety, Chinese parents (in Mainland China, Hong Kong, and Taiwan) reportedly emphasized the values that were more conducive to the new market-oriented climate such as autonomy (Huang & Lamb, 2014), assertiveness, and self-confidence (Chen & Chen, 2010; Chuang & Su, 2009). As a result, Chinese youth were more accepting of the values of individual freedom and liberty (Zhang & Fuligni, 2006). Of the few studies on Chinese fathering, evidence has shown that the sociocultural and political changes have shifted the traditions of fathers as "master of the family" toward more egalitarian parenting roles with mothers (Chuang & Su, 2008, 2009; Chuang, Moreno, & Su, 2013). For example, Chuang and Zhu (2018) found that both Chinese fathers from Mainland China and Canada were actively engaged with their young children, playing with and caring for them. They also had household responsibilities (e.g., cooking, cleaning), and spent considerable amounts of time at home, being accessible to their families (Chuang & Zhu, 2018). As the immigration contexts in both sending and receiving countries continue to evolve, research needs to continue to explore and understand this rapidly-changing group.

Implication for Mental Health and Well-being

Understanding the ethnoprofiles and the country's immigration policies will provide a more nuanced and accurate context for helping professionals to work with Chinese families in different areas. For example, in health care, the "model minority" Chinese immigrants are perceived to experience few social and psychological problems in their adjustment in the United States (Sue & Morishima, 1982). However, research over the the last three decades has revealed that Chinese immigrants do suffer from a range of mental health problems, including anxiety, depression, and suicide (Zhang, Fang, Wu, & Wieczorek, 2013). Moreover, Chinese immigrants, similar to other minority immigrant groups, tend to underutilize mental health services, and when treatment is sought, they terminate prematurely at a much higher rate than nonminority clients (Leong & Lau, 2001).

The underutilization or premature termination of services may be linked to the cultural value and beliefs that such services are shameful. Thus, the avoidance of shame acts as a barrier to the utilization of mental health services and help-seeking process among Chinese immigrants (Tabora & Flaskerud, 1997). Since the family name and "face" are so important to Chinese immigrants, they tend to seek help from family members first to avoid being viewed poorly by others (Webster & Fretz, 1978) and to be more reticent in publicly admitting problems and seeking help.

As Taiwan has not been through the Cultural Revolution brought by the Communist Party, it arguably has retained the most traditional Confucian cultural values, whereas in Mainland China, the majority of Chinese people changed their attitudes and values in many spheres of social life (Schoenhals, 2015). Therefore, the mental health professionals working with different Chinese immigrant subgroups would benefit from gaining greater insight into their clients' native culture which will, in turn, facilitate their treatment.

Family dynamics among Mainland Chinese, Hong Kong, and Taiwanese families also need consideration. For example, with the influence of the one-child policy in Mainland China, parents were more child-centered in the child rearing approach, were less authoritarian, and resources were concentrated on one child (Fong, 2007; Lai et al., 2010). However, parents placed greater emphasis on the importance of academics for their only children as their children were seen as the parents' only source of hope and future dependence (Fong, 2002; Lee, 2012). In contrast, in Hong Kong and Taiwan, without the influence of the one-child policy, parents were more AN in their parenting (Huang, Cheah, Lamb, & Zhou, 2017; Lai et al., 2010). Moreover, some recent studies with Taiwanese parent-child dyads found that although parental-reported and child-perceived parenting were positively correlated, parents tended to report lower scores on authoritarian parenting and higher scores on Chinese parenting than did their children; which had negative effects on children's mental health outcomes (Huang et al., 2019) as well as emotional intelligence (Huang et al., 2017). These potentially differing parenting practices and family structures may alter how the helping professionals interact with and provide services for these families.

In addition, Lau (2010) found a significant association between Chinese American children's problems in school and their parents' use of physical discipline. Given the Confucian cultural imperative on education and parents' significant investment in their children's education, school problems may trigger physical disciplinary encounters when parental reactions involve shame and loss of face. With the higher endorsement of authoritarian parenting and physical discipline in Hong Kong and Taiwanese parents, perhaps service providers need to be more alert about the potential of physical abuse, as parents' endorsement of physical discipline is associated with higher risk of child physical abuse (Maker, Shah, & Agha, 2005).

Conclusion

The shared roots in Confucianism and the unique political, economic, and sociocultural contexts have influenced and transformed the ways of life for Chinese families in and from Mainland China, Taiwan, and Hong Kong. Each society has its own history of international migration and connections with specific destination countries (e.g., Taiwan and the United States), which are important contexts for us to better understand these immigrants. The immigrants from different Chinese societies might also bring with them different values regarding parent-child and gender relations, as well as different sets of resources and cultural heritage. Researchers need to continually challenge existing stereotypes of Chinese families by examining their values, beliefs and how they affect their everyday living. Only by integrating the variations of their complex sociocultural, geopolitical, socioeconomic status, immigrant backgrounds, can we redefine the theoretical and methodological frameworks to better capture the complexities of Chinese families, so that mental health, educational, and other clinical professionals can provide better services to address their needs.

References

Arends-Tóth, J., & van de Vijver, F. J. R. (2004). Domains and dimensions in acculturation: Implicit theories of Turkish-Dutch. *International Journal of Intercultural Relations, 28*, 19–35. https://doi.org/10.1016/j.ijintrel.2003.09.001

Arends-Tóth, J., & van de Vijver, F. J. R. (2006). Issues in the conceptualization and assessment of acculturation. In M. H. Bornstein & L. R. Cote (Eds.), *Acculturation and parent-child relationships* (pp. 33–62). Erlbaum. https://doi.org/10.1111/j.1559-1816.2007.00222.x

Bauer, J., Feng, W., Riley, N. E., & Zhao, X. (1992). Gender inequality in urban China: Education and employment. *Modern China, 18*, 83–103.

Baumrind, D. (1971). Current patterns of parental authority. *Developmental Psychology, 4*, 1–103. https://doi.org/10.1037/h0030372

Berry, J. W., Kim, W., Power, S., Young, M., & Bujaki, M. (1989). Acculturation attitudes in plural societies. *Applied Psychology, 38*, 185–206. https://doi.org/10.1111/j.1464-0597.1989.tb01208.x

Bornstein, M. H., & Cote, L. R. (2004). Mothers' parenting cognitions in cultures of origin, acculturating cultures, and cultures of destination. *Child Development, 75*, 221–235. https://doi.org/10.1111/j.1467-8624.2004.00665.x

Bornstein, M. H., & Lansford, J. E. (2010). Parenting. In M. H. Bornstein (Ed.), *Handbook of cross-cultural developmental science. Part 1: Domains of development across cultures* (pp. 259–278). Psychology Press.

Brown, M. J. (2004). *Is Taiwan Chinese?: The impact of culture, power, and migration on changing identities*. University of California Press.

Canadian Multiculturalism Act. (1988). *Canadian Multiculturalism Act*. http://www.solon.org/Statutes/Canada/English/C/CMA.html

Census and Statistics Department of Hong Kong Special Administrative Region. (2017). *Thematic report: Ethnic minorities*. https://www.bycensus2016.gov.hk/data/16bc-ethnic-minorities.pdf

Chan, S. M., Bowes, J., & Wyver, S. (2009). Chinese parenting in Hong Kong: Links among goals, beliefs and styles. *Early Child Development and Care, 179*, 849–862. https://doi.org/10.1080/03004430701536525

Chance, L. J., Costigan, C. L., & Leadbeater, B. J. (2013). Coparenting in immigrant Chinese Canadian families: The role of discrepancies in acculturation and expectations for adolescent assistance. *Journal of Family Psychology, 27*(6), 905–914. https://doi.org/10.1037/a0034909

Chagnon, J. (2013). *Migration: International, 2011 and 2011*. Component of Statistics Canada Catalogue no. 91-209-W. Ottawa, ON: Statistics Canada.

Cheah, C. S. L., Leung, C. Y. Y., & Zhuo, N. (2013). Understanding 'tiger parenting' through the perceptions of Chinese immigrant mothers: Can Chinese and U.S. parenting co-exist? *Asian American Journal of Psychology, 4*, 30–40. https://doi.org/10.1037/a0031217

Chen, W. W. (2014). The relationship between perceived parenting styles, filial piety, and life satisfaction in Hong Kong. *Journal of Family Psychology, 28*, 308–314.

Chen, X., & Chen, H. (2010). Child's socioemotional functioning and adjustment in the changing Chinese society. In R. K. Silbereisen & X. Chen (Eds.), *Human development: Concepts and results* (pp. 209–226). Sage.

Cheung, C. S., & McBride-Chang, C. (2008). Relations of perceived maternal style, practices, and learning motivation to academic competence in Chinese children. *Merrill-Palmer Quarterly, 54*, 1–22. www.jstor.org/stable/23096077

Chiu, L. H. (1987). Child-rearing attitudes of Chinese, Chinese-American, and Anglo-American mothers. *International Journal of Psychology, 22*, 409–419.

Chuang, S. S. (2006). Taiwanese-Canadian mothers' beliefs about personal freedom for their young children. *Social Development, 15*, 520–536. https://doi.org/10.1111/j.1467-9507.2006.00354.x

Chuang, S. S. (2013). Fathering roles and responsibilities of contemporary Chinese fathers in Canada and China. In S. S. Chuang & C. S. Tamis-LeMonda (Eds.), *Gender roles in immigrant families* (pp. 27–42). Springer.

Chuang, S. S. (2019). The complexities of immigration and families: Theoretical perspectives and current issues. In B. H. Fiese, M. Celano, K. Deater-Deckard, E. N. Jouriles, & M. A. Whisman (Eds.), *APA handbooks in psychology. APA handbook of contemporary family psychology: Applications and board impact of family psychology* (pp. 437–455). American Psychological Association. https://doi.org/10.1037/0000100-027

Chuang, S. S., Glozman, J., Green, D. S., & Rasmi, S. (2018). Family dynamics and relationships in Chinese families: A critical ecological approach. *Journal of Family Theory & Review, 10*, 367–383. https://doi.org/10.1111/jftr.12257

Chuang, S. S., & Moreno, R. P. (Eds.). (2011). *Immigrant children: Change, adaptation, and cultural transformation*. Lexington Books.

Chuang, S. S., Moreno, R. P., & Su, Y. (2013). Moving fathers from the "sidelines": An exploration of contemporary Chinese fathers in Canada and China. In K. B. Chan & N. C. Hung (Eds.), *International handbook of Chinese families* (pp. 343–357). Springer.

Chuang, S. S., & Su, Y. (2008). Transcending Confucian teachings on fathering: A sign of the times or acculturation? In S. S. Chuang & R. P. Moreno (Eds.), *On new shores: Understanding immigrant fathers in North America* (pp. 129–150). Lexington Books.

Chuang, S. S., & Su, Y. (2009). Says who? Decision-making and conflicts among Chinese-Canadian and Mainland Chinese parents of young children. *Sex Roles, 60*(7/8), 527–588. https://doi.org/10.1007/s11199-008-9537-9

Chuang, S. S., & Zhu, M. (2018). Where are you Daddy?: An exploration of father involvement in Chinese families in Canada and Mainland China. In S. S. Chuang & C. L. Costigan (Eds.), *Parental roles and relationships in immigrant families: An international approach* (pp. 11–30). Springer.

Chun, G. H. (2004). Shifting ethnic identity and consciousness: U.S.-born Chinese American youth in the 1930s and 1950s. In J. Lee & M. Zhou (Eds.), *Asian American youth: Culture, identity and ethnicity* (pp. 113–141). Routledge.

Costigan, C. L., & Dokis, D. P. (2006). Relations between parent-child acculturation differences and adjustment within immigrant Chinese families. *Child Development, 77*, 1252–1267. https://doi.org/10.1111/j.1467-8624.2006.00932.x

Costigan, C. L., & Koryzma, C. M. (2011). Acculturation and adjustment among immigrant Chinese parents: Mediating role of parenting efficacy. *Journal of Counseling Psychology, 58*(2), 183. https://doi.org/10.1037/a0021696

Costigan, C., Su, T. F., & Hua, J. M. (2009). Ethnic identity among Chinese Canadian youth: A review of the Canadian literature. *Canadian Psychology/Psychologie Canadienne, 50*(4), 261. https://doi.org/10.1037/a0016880

Council of Indigenous Peoples of Republic of China. (2017). 原住民人口數統計資料 [*Demography of Indigenous peoples*]. http://www.apc.gov.tw/portal/docDetail.html?CID=940F9579765AC6A0&DID=0C3331F0EBD318C2484AF6CD1D5468A9

Department of Statistics Malaysia. (2019). *Population distribution and basic demographic characteristic report 2010*. https://www.dosm.gov.my/v1/index.php?r=column/ctheme&menu_id=L0pheU43NWJwRWVSZklWdzQ4TlhUUT09&bul_id=MDMxdHZjWTk1SjFzTzNkRXYzcVZjdz09

Department of Statistics Singapore. (2018). *Population trends 2018*. https://www.singstat.gov.sg/-/media/files/publications/population/population2018.pdf

Dinh, K. T., Sarason, B. R., & Sarason, I. G. (1994). Parent-child relationships in Vietnamese immigrant families. *Journal of Family Psychology, 8*, 471–488. https://doi.org/10.1037/0893-3200.8.4.471

Dong, H. (2014). Celebration of diversity: Modern Chinese dialects. In H. Dong (Ed.), *A history of the Chinese language* (pp. 152–170). Routledge.

Edwards, L. (2000). Policing the modern woman in republican China. *Modern China, 26*(2), 115–147. https://doi.org/10.1177/009770040002600201

Fong, V. L. (2002). China's one-child policy and the empowerment of urban daughters. *American Anthropologist, 104*, 1098–1109. https://doi.org/10.1525/aa.2002.104.4.1098

Fong, V. L. (2007). Parent-child communication problems and the perceived inadequacies of Chinese only children. *Ethos, 35*(1), 85–127. https://doi.org/10.1525/eth.2007.35.1.85

Gibson, C. J., & Lennon, E. (1999). *Historical census statistics on the foreign-born population of the United States: 1850–1990*. U.S. Bureau of the Census.

Glosser, S. L. (2003). *Chinese visions of family and state* (Vol. 5, pp. 1915–1953). University of California Press.

Government of Hong Kong Special Administrative Region. (n.d.). *Hong Kong – The facts*. https://www.gov.hk/en/about/abouthk/facts.htm

Ho, D. Y. F. (1987). Fatherhood in Chinese culture. In M. E. Lamb (Ed.), *The father's role: Cross-cultural perspectives* (pp. 227–245). Erlbaum.

Ho, D. Y. F. (1996). Filial piety and its psychological consequences. In M. H. Bond (Ed.), *The handbook of Chinese psychology* (pp. 155–165). Oxford University Press.

Honig, E. (2000). Iron girls revisited: Gender and the politics of work in the cultural revolution, 1966-76. In B. Gutwisle & G. Henderson (Eds.), *Re-drawing the boundaries of work, households, and gender* (pp. 97–110). University of California Press.

Hooper, K., & Batalova, J. (2015). Chinese immigrants in the United States. *The Online Journal of the Migration Policy Institute*. https://www.migrationpolicy.org/article/chinese-immigrants-united-states

Hu, Y., & Scott, J. (2016). Family and gender values in China: Generational, geographic, and gender differences. *Journal of Family Issues, 37*(9), 1267–1293. https://doi.org/10.1177/0192513X14528710

Huang, C. Y., Cheah, C. S. L., Lamb, M. E., & Zhou, N. (2017). Associations between parenting styles and children's effortful control within Chinese families in the U.S., the U.K., and Taiwan. *Journal of Cross-Cultural Psychology, 48*, 795–812. https://doi.org/10.1177/0022022117706108

Huang, C. Y., Hsieh, Y. P., Shen, A. C. T., Wei, H. S., Hwa, H. L., & Feng, J. Y. (2019). Relationships between parent-reported parenting, child-perceived parenting and children's mental health in Taiwanese children. *International Journal of Environmental Research and Public Health, 16*(6), 1049. https://doi.org/10.3390/ijerph16061049

Huang, C. Y., & Lamb, M. E. (2014). Are Chinese children more compliant?: Examination of the cultural difference in observed maternal control and child compliance. *Journal of Cross-Cultural Psychology, 45*, 507–533. https://doi.org/10.1177/0022022114555763

Huang, C. Y., & Lamb, M. E. (2015). Acculturation and parenting in first-generation Chinese immigrants in the United Kingdom. *Journal of Cross-Cultural Psychology, 46*, 150–167. https://doi.org/10.1177/0022022114555763

Huang, C. Y., Shen, A. C. T., Hsieh, Y. P., Wei, H. S., Hwa, H. L., & Feng, J. Y. (2017). Cultural perspectives on parenting, emotional intelligence and mental health in Taiwanese children. *International Journal of Emotional Education, 9*(2), 4–16.

Jacka, T., Kipnis, A. B., & Sargenson, S. (2013). Contemporary China: Society and social change. Cambridge University Press.

Kim, U., & Park, Y. S. (2006). The scientific foundation of indigenous and cultural psychology: The transnational approach. In U. Kim, Y. S. Yang, & K. K. Hwang (Eds.), *Indigenous and cultural psychology: Understanding people in context* (pp. 27–48). Springer.

Kwak, K. (2003). Adolescents and their parents: A review of intergenerational family relations for immigrant and nonimmigrant families. *Human Development, 46*, 115–136. https://doi.org/10.1159/000068581

Lai, A. C., Zhang, Z. X., & Wang, W. Z. (2010). Maternal child-rearing practices in Hong Kong and Beijing Chinese families: A comparative study. *International Journal of Psychology, 35*, 60–66. https://doi.org/10.1080/002075900399529

Lau, A. S. (2010). Physical discipline in Chinese American immigrant families: An adaptive culture perspective. *Cultural Diversity and Ethnic Minority Psychology, 16*, 313–322. https://doi.org/10.1037/a0018667

Lee, M. H. (2012). The one-child policy and gender equality in education in China: Evidence from household data. *Journal of Family and Economic Issues, 33*, 41–52. https://doi.org/10.1007/s10834-011-9277-9

Lee, E. H., Zhou, Q., Eisenberg, N., & Wang, Y. (2013). Bidirectional relations between temperament and parenting styles in Chinese children. *International Journal of Behavioral Development, 37*, 57–67. https://doi.org/10.1177/0165025412460795

Leong, F. T. D., & Lau, A. S. L. (2001). Barriers to providing effective mental health services to Asian Americans. *Mental Health Services Research, 3*, 201–214. https://doi.org/10.1023/A:1013177014788

Li, P. S. (1992). The economics of brain drain: Recruitment of skilled labour to Canada, 1954–86. In V. Satzewich (Ed.), *Deconstructing a nation: Immigration, multiculturalism and racism in '90s Canada* (pp. 145–162). Fernwood Publishing.

Li, P. S. (2003). *Cultural diversity in Canada: The social construction of racial difference*. http://www.justice.gc.ca/eng/rp-pr/csj-sjc/jsp-sjp/rp02_8-dr02_8/p3.html

Lin, C. Y., & Fu, V. R. (1990). A comparison of child-rearing practices among Chinese, immigrant Chinese, and Caucasian-American parents. *Child Development, 61*, 429–433.

Lui, J., & Carpenter, M. (2005). Trends and issues of women's education in China. *The Clearing House, 78*, 277–281.

Liu, M., & Guo, F. (2010). Parenting practices and their relevance to child behaviors in Canada and China. *Scandinavian Journal of Psychology, 51*, 489–495. https://doi.org/10.1111/j.1467

Luo, R., Tamis-LeMonda, C. S., & Song, L. (2013). Chinese parents' goals and practices in early childhood. *Early Childhood Research Quarterly, 28*, 843–857. https://doi.org/10.1016/j.ecresq.2013.08.001

Maker, A. H., Shah, P. V., & Agha, Z. (2005). Child physical abuse: Prevalence, characteristics, predictors, and beliefs about parent-child violence in South Asian, Middle Eastern, East Asian, and Latina women in the United States. *Journal of Interpersonal Violence, 20*, 1406–1428. https://doi.org/10.1177/0886260505278713

Martin, S. (2010). *A nation of immigrants*. Cambridge University Press.

Martin, P. (2013). The global challenge of managing migration. *Population Reference Bureau, 68*.

Miller, P. J., Wiley, A., Fung, H., & Liang, C. (1997). Personal storytelling as a medium of socialization in Chinese and American families. *Child Development, 68*, 557–568.

Morency, J. D., Malenfant, E. C., & MacIsaac, S. (2017). *Immigration and diversity: Population projections and its regions, 2011 to 2036*. Statistics Canada.

National Bureau of Statistics of People's Republic of China. (2012). 中国2010年人口普查资料 [*Tabulation on the 2010 Population Census of the People's Republic of China*]. http://www.stats.gov.cn/tjsj/pcsj/rkpc/6rp/indexch.htm

Newland, L. A., Coyl, D. D., & Chen, H. H. (2010). Fathering and attachment in the USA and Taiwan: Contextual predictors and child outcomes. *Early Child Development and Care, 180*, 173–191. https://doi.org/10.1080/03004430903415049

Pearson, E., & Rao, N. (2003). Socialization goals, parenting practices, and peer competence in Chinese and English preschoolers. *Early Child Development and Care, 173*, 131–146. https://doi.org/10.1080/0300443022000022486

Phinney, J. S., Ong, A. D., & Madden, T. (2000). Cultural values and intergenerational value discrepancies. *Child Development, 71*, 528–539. https://doi.org/10.1111/1467-8624.00162

Schoenhals, M. (2015). *China's cultural revolution, 1966–69: Not a dinner party*. Routledge.

Statistics Canada. (2019). *Census profile, 2016 Census*. https://www12.statcan.gc.ca/census-recensement/2016/dp-pd/prof/details/page.cfm?Lang=E&Geo1=PR&Code1=01&Geo2=PR&Code2=01&Data=Count&SearchText=Canada&SearchType=Begins&SearchPR=01&B1=Visible%20minority&TABID=1

Statistics Canada. (2013). *2011 National household survey: Immigration, place of birth, citizenship, ethnic origin, visible minorities, language and religion*. http://www.statcan.gc.ca/daily-quotidien/130508/dq130508b-eng.htm

Su, C., & Hynie, M. (2011). Effects of life stress, social support, and cultural norms on parenting styles among Mainland Chinese, European Canadian, and Chinese Canadian immigrant mothers. *Journal of Cross-Cultural Psychology, 42*, 944–962. https://doi.org/10.1177/0022022110381124

Sue, S., & Morishima, J. K. (1982). *The mental health of Asian Americans: Contemporary issues in identifying and treating mental problems*. Jossey-Bass.

Sun, T.H. (2001, March). *The impacts of a family planning program on contraceptive/fertility behavior in Taiwan*. Paper presented at the Population Association of American, Washington, DC.

Szapocznik, J., & Kurtines, W. M. (1993). Family psychology and cultural diversity: Opportunities for theory, research, and application. *American Psychologist, 48*, 400–407. https://doi.org/10.1037/0003-066X.48.4.400

Tabora, B. L., & Flaskerud, J. H. (1997). Mental health beliefs, practices, and knowledge of Chinese-American immigrant women. *Residential Group Care and Treatment, 18*, 173–189. https://doi.org/10.3109/01612849709012488

Talhelm, T., Zhang, X., Oishi, S., Shimin, C., Duan, D., Lan, X., & Kitayama, S. (2014). Large-scale psychological differences within China explained by rice versus wheat agriculture. *Science, 344*(6184), 603–608. https://doi.org/10.1126/science.1246850

Tang, N. M. (1992). Some psychoanalytic implications of Chinese philosophy and child-rearing practices. *The Psychoanalytic Study of the Child, 47*, 371–389.

Tsai, S. L., Gates, H., & Chiu, H. Y. (1994). Schooling Taiwan's women: Educational attainment in the mid-20th century. *Sociology of Education, 67*, 243–263.

Tu, Y.- C., Chang, J.- C., & Kao, T.- F. (2014). A study on the relationships between maternal gatekeeping and paternal involvement in Taiwan. *Soial and Behavioral Sciences, 122*, 319–328. https://doi.org/10.1016/j.sbspro.2014.01.1347

United Nations. (2017). *International migration report 2017*. New York, NY: Author.

U.S. Census Bureau. (2012). *The Asian population: 2010. 2010 Census briefs*. https://www.census.gov/prod/cen2010/briefs/c2010br-11.pdf

Wang, Y., Kim, S. Y., Anderson, E. R., Chen, A. C. C., & Yan, N. (2012). Parent–child acculturation discrepancy, perceived parental knowledge, peer deviance, and adolescent delinquency in Chinese immigrant families. *Journal of Youth and Adolescence, 41*(7), 907–919. https://doi.org/10.1007/s10964-011-9705-z

Webster, D. W., & Fretz, B. R. (1978). Asian-American, Black and White college student's preference for helping services. *Journal of Counseling Psychology, 25*, 124–130.

Wilson, R. W. (1974). *The moral state: A study of the political socialization of Chinese and American children*. Free Press.

Wolf, M. (1970). Child training and the Chinese family. In M. Freedman (Ed.), *Family and kinship in Chinese societies* (pp. 221–246). Stanford University Press.

Zhang, J., Fang, L., Wu, Y. W. B., & Wieczorek, W. F. (2013). Depression, anxiety, and suicidal ideation among Chinese Americans: A study of immigration-related factors. *The Journal of Nervous and Mental Disease, 201*, 17–22. https://doi.org/10.1097/NMD.0b013e31827ab2e2

Zhang, W., & Fuligni, A. J. (2006). Authority, autonomy, and family relationships among adolescents in urban and rural China. *Journal of Research on Adolescence, 16*, 527–537. https://doi.org/10.1111/j.1532-7795.2006.00506.x

Zhou, M. (1997). Segmented assimilation: Issues, controversies, and recent research on the new second generation. *International Migration Review, 31*, 975–1008.

[illegible]

Chapter 5
Growing Up Between Two Cultures: Young Chinese Americans in New York City

Uwe P. Gielen and Jonathan Palumbo

Abstract This chapter discusses selected themes in the bicultural lives of predominantly working- and lower middle-class Chinese Americans coming of age in New York City, the largest "Chinese city" outside Asia. Findings are partially based on a series of autobiographical essays by, and interviews with, first- and second-generation immigrants. Their self-conceptions and life stories reflect the influence of competing Chinese and American visions of the good life, family relationships, child-rearing strategies, the importance of filial piety (*xiao shun*), gender-based ideologies and body images, and the nature of education. Many of the adolescents and young adults have had to deal with immigration-related challenges such as family separation due to migration, low family incomes, encountering racial-ethnic prejudice and discrimination, and cultural differences between parents and children. The chapter also includes a brief discussion of culturally appropriate mental health services for the Chinese-American community.

Keywords New York Chinatowns · Chinese American adolescents · Autobiographical essays · Cultural childrearing styles · Coping with immigration · Gender roles · Educational achievement · Mental health services · Satellite children

This chapter considers how New York City's Chinese American adolescents and young adults understand their lives and identities in the context of their immigrant families, East Asian and non-Asian friends and peers, schools, colleges, and places of work. Given their bicultural backgrounds, these young people are, to varying extents, influenced by two contrasting cultural approaches to childrearing. These

---

U. P. Gielen (✉)
St. Francis College, Brooklyn, NY, USA
e-mail: ugielen@sfc.edu

J. Palumbo
St. Francis College & Pace University, Brooklyn, NY, USA

S. S. Chuang et al. (eds.), *Asian Families in Canada and the United States*, Advances in Immigrant Family Research,
https://doi.org/10.1007/978-3-030-56452-0_5

reflect competing Chinese and American visions of the good life, its vicissitudes, its recipes for bringing up children, and a variety of prototypical challenges in those children's lives. The interplay between these cultural approaches to childrearing, together with the demands of immigrant life, are of great importance for the life paths and identities of Chinese Americans who may have grown up overseas (first generation immigrants) or in New York (second generation immigrants). To better understand their life paths, the chapter includes discussions of Chinese immigration to New York City; parents' involvement in endless work; satellite children who were born in New York but spent the initial years of their lives with relatives in China; gender roles and gender differences; negative body images; the students' exposure to racial prejudice, discrimination, and violence; and their educational goals and achievements. This is followed by a brief discussion of efforts by mental health experts and community organizations to help New York's Chinese families prosper psychologically and emotionally.

The chapter is partially based on 82 autobiographical essays by, and 72 interviews with, Chinese American adolescents and young adults (Ho & Gielen, 2016). They as well as related research by authors such as Sung (1987) have been used to identify some major preoccupations and themes in the lives of the writers and interviewees. In addition, they provide substantial information about their family backgrounds. A considerable percentage of the respondents' parents and grandparents originally came from rural areas and towns situated in China's southern and coastal regions. Many of them speak little English, have at best a middle school education, and work relentlessly so that their families can survive economically. They fervently hope that their children will succeed educationally, so they can enjoy easier lives than their own ones have been. For such parents, the Big Apple continues its traditional role as the foremost North American entrance place for low-income immigrants who hope their children will succeed in the New World. In addition, the parents include educated and financially better-off professionals, many of whose children attend selective high schools and colleges. Here we pay special attention to working-class and lower middle-class families and their children, including recent immigrants from the Min River Delta of Fujian Province, because less has been written about them than about the children of educated middle-class parents and professionals (Zhao, 2010). Moreover, economic differences between Asian Americans have been increasing considerably in recent decades (Frey, 2018). The Chinese community in New York City includes a greater number of recently arrived, Chinese-only-speaking working-class immigrants than can be found anywhere else in the Western hemisphere. Many of them reside in ethnic enclaves although their middle-class peers are increasingly moving to the city's more multicultural neighborhoods and suburbs. To better understand the context of their lives, we begin by discussing the history and broad contours of Chinese immigrant life in the city.

The Rise of Chinatowns in New York City

A brief overview of the historical developments of Chinatowns in New York City will provide a more comprehensive context for how youth navigate and adapt to their surroundings. The key areas of discussion will focus on the immigration patterns that created Chinatowns, the demographics, family characteristics, predominant language groups and geographic origins of New York's Chinese immigrants, and the creation and rapid expansion of new Chinatowns that occurred after the United States Government passed a revolutionary new immigration law in 1965. In addition, a brief discussion of working conditions and illegal activities in Manhattan Chinatown will be provided.

Migration Patterns and the Expansion and Composition of New York's Chinatowns

The systematic migration of predominantly male Chinese workers from China to the United States and Canada began around 1850, when news about the California Gold Rush reached a country that had been weakened by steep population increases, extensive poverty, the two Opium Wars (1839–1842 and 1856–1860) between Great Britain and China, and the bloody Taiping Rebellion (1850–1864). Arriving by ship on the West Coast, the Chinese laborers hoped to grow wealthy on "Golden Mountain" and return to China with plenty of money in their pockets. However, only some of them succeeded in realizing their plans. Others became agricultural workers or accepted dangerous and underpaid jobs while helping to build the first transcontinental railway.

When in the 1870s an economic crisis hit the United States, extensive anti-Chinese riots broke out which led to the "Chinese Exclusion Act" (in force in various forms between 1882 and 1943). Fearing for their lives, some of the Chinese laborers escaped to places on the East Coast such as New York City, the Vancouver area in western Canada, and sometimes to Mexico. Following the earlier birth of San Francisco's pioneering Chinatown, in the 1870s a small Chinatown began to emerge in Manhattan around southern Mott Street (Hall, 1998; Zhou, 1992). There, the Chinese laborers arriving from the West Coast joined a few dockworkers, sailors, cooks, and stewards, some of whom had escaped from ships that brought tea, porcelain, silk, and other produce from China. The economic basis of this largely male society included hand laundries, shops, restaurants, boarding houses, peddling wares in the streets, and an occasional brothel. By the year 1920, New York City's Chinese population included 5240 males and 553 females, for a total of 5793 persons (Wong, 1985).

Over the next 30 years, Chinatown slowly expanded into a ten-block area south of Canal Street. In 1945, the country had begun to allow some wives of Chinese-American servicemen to join their husbands, and for these and other reasons the lopsided gender ratio in New York and elsewhere began to improve. By 1950, 18,404 Chinese were living in this inward-looking and impoverished ethnic enclave as well as elsewhere in the city. The most dramatic demographic changes, however, occurred after the passing of the country's Immigration and Nationality Act Amendments (also called the Hart-Celler Act) in 1965. Because Chinese and other Asian immigrants were now welcomed, Manhattan's Chinatown began to expand rapidly. With the arrival of more and more women, advanced students, refugees, farmers, and professionals from Hong Kong, Vietnam, Taiwan, Southeast Asia, and after 1979 from PR China, new Chinatowns began to emerge in Queens and Brooklyn. The well-educated Mandarin- and Taiwanese-speaking, middle-class Taiwanese, for instance, felt little kinship with the Taishanese- and Cantonese-speaking working-class inhabitants of Manhattan Chinatown (Chen, 1992; Kwong, 1996; Ng, 1998), and so they began to settle in "Little Asia." Some of them do not even consider themselves to be Chinese. Little Asia refers to the Flushing area in Queens where many Chinese, Koreans, Indians, Bangladeshis and other Asian immigrants reside. During the 1980s–1990s, numerous middle-class immigrants arrived from Hong Kong because they feared the possible economic and political consequences of that city's return to the Chinese motherland in 1997. A number of families resided in Little Asia or Manhattan, while others returned to Hong Kong after a few years (Sussman, 2011). By 2019, at least 240,000 Chinese of diverse geographic and social-class backgrounds lived in Queens, including Flushing, Elmhurst, Corona and some of the eastern areas. Often speaking both Mandarin and English, many of them work either in Manhattan or locally as professionals. In addition, wealthy overseas Chinese have been investing in New York's real estate, trading companies, and financial institutions to safeguard their money. They frequently send their children to North American educational institutions. The children, in turn, often preferred their new life and became immigrants, many of whom ended up in well-to-do neighborhoods.

Beginning in the mid-1970s, many rural and small town inhabitants of the Min River Delta in Fujian Province began to set their sights on New York City. In Manhattan, they mostly settled in the East Broadway and Eldridge Street areas, which prior to their arrival had been mostly populated by persons of Jewish, European, and Hispanic descent. By 2019, the Fuzhounese (also called Fujianese) formed the single largest, linguistically-geographically distinctive group of Chinese immigrants in the city, with former residents of Changle County being especially prominent (Hymowitz, 2014). Unable or unwilling to pay the high rents of Manhattan Chinatown, many moved to much less expensive housing such as Sunset Park around Eighth Avenue in Brooklyn (Guest, 2011). By 2013, this rapidly evolving "Brooklyn Chinatown" included already more inhabitants than the Cantonese-speaking "Old Manhattan Chinatown" and the Fuzhou-Dialect-speaking "New Manhattan Chinatown" taken together (Hum, 2014). Additional Chinatowns can be found in Brooklyn's semi-suburban, multiethnic areas such as Bensonhurst and Sheepshead Bay. Although estimates differ, it is likely that in 2019, at least 220,000 persons of Chinese descent lived in Brooklyn's larger and smaller Chinatowns (see also Hum, 2014).

By the 1980s, New York City had already grown into the largest Chinese immigrant city outside Asia. In 2019, an estimated 650,000–700,000 persons of Chinese descent resided both in the city's nine big and small Chinatowns and in a broad range of multiethnic neighborhoods. The authors' estimate includes multiracial and Taiwanese persons, but may underestimate those who successfully evaded the census takers (Zhao, 2010). The Asian American Federation (2019a, b), in turn, lists 564,636 persons for 2015, plus 10,847 Taiwanese. However, the estimate does not sufficiently take into account the numerous undocumented persons, those who were physically inaccessible for the census takers, and those who were never at home during the day (Chin, 1999; Yoshikawa, 2011; see also below). Seventy percent of the Chinese American population in 2015 were foreign-born, and altogether they made up about 46% of the city's Asian Americans. Another estimated 230,000 persons of Chinese descent live in the adjacent suburban areas that belong to the Greater New York Metropolitan Area. Moreover, numerous Chinese university students from overseas attend the city's educational institutions such as New York University and Columbia University, but they are not considered here.

The city's Chinese Americans are well represented at both the lower and higher ends of the educational and socioeconomic spectra. In 2015, 22% of all Chinese adults in the city had less than a ninth-grade education, whereas 33% had a bachelor's degree or higher. 23.3% of their children experienced poverty (Asian American Federation, 2019a, b). Sixty-one percent reported limited if any proficiency in English, with the older and poorer residents often being unable to make themselves understood in English.

Outsiders rarely realize just how heterogeneous the city's Chinese communities really are. Its members may speak Taishanese, Cantonese, Mandarin, Eastern Min (Fuzhou dialect), Taiwanese, Hakka dialect, Shanghainese, and other highly distinct "dialects" (their spoken versions are more like semi-independent languages), alongside or instead of English. Sub-ethnic tensions, such as those between Cantonese speakers and Eastern Min speakers, are by no means absent. Many immigrants are members of clans and geographically based associations and may either support, oppose or ignore China's present political system. They differ widely in social class, relate in very different ways to their American environment, may have Caucasian spouses or Caucasian adoptive parents, may be barely literate or alternatively have received a doctoral degree from a major university, hold different citizen status even within the same family, and perhaps left China as late as their adulthood years while others have never even visited that country. Having grown up in such diverse ways, they are nevertheless more likely than many other ethnic groups to get involved in entrepreneurial or professional activities, form ethnic-regional social organizations, stay married, and push their children to be educationally successful and upwardly mobile (Hymowitz, 2014; Zhou, 2013).

Working Conditions and Illegal Activities in Chinatown

The Chinatowns of New York are also witnessing many illegal activities. Thus, a considerable number of workers work off the books, are not paid legally required minimum wages by their co-ethnic bosses, and form part of an underground economy (Kwong, 1996). Numerous Fuzhounese as well as other Chinese from places such as Malaysia are smuggled into the country for very high fees by so-called snakeheads (Keefe, 2010), or else they overstay their visitor's visa indefinitely. Not surprisingly, they try to hide from authorities and their true numbers are unknown although they are generally considered to be very high (Chin, 1996, 1999; Finckenauer, 2007; Yoshikawa, 2011). Others are encouraged by certain lawyers to lie to immigration officials in order to be granted political asylum (Semple, Goldstein, & Singer, 2014). Visiting illegal gambling places or houses of prostitution are popular activities for some residents of Chinatown while on Canal Street, immigrants from Wenzhou (Zhejiang Province) and elsewhere are selling fake Rolex watches and Gucci bags that were illegally imported from places such as Hong Kong (Robbins, 2018). In other ways, however, today's Chinatowns are mostly safe places, violent street crime is uncommon, and quite a few of the persons breaking the law are otherwise ordinary residents.

Gang Memberships

From the early 1970s to the mid-1990s, several violent youth gangs such as the Ghost Shadows, the Flying Dragons, and the Vietnamese Born to Kill, fought among each other especially in the Manhattan and Queens Chinatowns. Numerous members were disoriented recent immigrants from places such as Hong Kong, and in their middle to late teenage years. Operating under the control of triads and rival merchants organizations, such as the Hip Sing Tong and the On Leong Tong, they served as enforcers for criminal organizations that controlled the extortion of business owners, gambling activities, heroin trafficking, and places of prostitution (Chin, 1996). Another gang, the Fuk Ching emerged during the mid-1980s (Finckenauer, 2007). It includes Fuzhounese teenagers and young men who have been involved in human smuggling activities. However, while some youth gangs and other law-breaking groups remain active in today's Chinatowns, they are less numerous and far less likely to be involved in the killing of rival gang members when compared to the more violent period between 1975 and 1995. Still, some Chinese immigrant parents fear that their restless son might drop out of his racially divided high school, get involved in a youth gang, join their criminal activities, bring shame upon the family, and thereby nullify his parents' many sacrifices and hopes for him.

Growing Up in a Bicultural World

New York City's Chinese American families live in a demanding bicultural world. The Chinese-only speakers among them are embedded in a mostly Chinese socio-cultural milieu, but nevertheless must adapt to the city's physical, economic, and legal conditions as well as their more Americanized children. In contrast to them, second generation immigrants speaking fluent English often consider themselves to be more American than Chinese. Their parents and grandparents mostly do not. Such identity differences are of great importance because they are involving two contrasting though changing cultural visions that are not easy to reconcile. Table 5.1 depicts some of these contrasting visions, which have been partially derived from large-scale research conducted by Hofstede (2018), Bond (see Hofstede & Minkov, 2010), and Gelfand (2018) on normative differences between countries and societies. Given ongoing cultural changes such as the increasing individualization occurring in Chinese society, the differences between the two countries have increased in complexity and sometimes narrowed, but they have not disappeared.

Table 5.1 Cultural value and religious differences between China and USA

Value dimensions and attitudes toward religion	China	USA
Collectivism vs. individualism (G. Hofstede)	China's collectivistic society favors tightly knit social frameworks, clear rules, social coordination; individuals should subordinate their desires for the common good; the focus should be on "we" rather than the "I"	American society emphasizes individual responsibilities and rights; the focus is on the "I"
Tight vs. loose culture (M. Gelfand)	Its rather tight culture emphasizes powerful social norms and individuals' self-control, but is displaying limited openness	Its loose culture allows for a considerable range of permissible behaviors, but this is also leading to high rates of deviant behaviors
Long-term v. short-term normative orientation (Based on G. Hofstede's interpretation of M. H. Bond's work)	Long-term and pragmatic orientation emphasizes perseverance, common sense, situational approaches to the validity of norms, thrift, educational efforts to prepare for the future	Short-term orientation that is more focused on the present, immediate gratification of needs, selling oneself and one's abilities, and a moralistic emphasis on good vs. evil
Emphasis on power distance and hierarchy (G. Hofstede)	Strong emphasis: Chinese society accepts hierarchical arrangements in which everybody is expected to find a place	Moderate emphasis: American society attempts (within limits) to equalize the distribution of power
Attitudes toward religion	Pragmatic, non-exclusive, may include polytheistic beliefs; many immigrants from PR China are non-religious; communist government is hostile towards religion	Monotheistic religions based on sacred scriptures remain of importance to many families and their conception of ultimate truth

Culture

Chinese society has for many centuries been more collectivistic in nature than American society, which instead has favored a pronounced and intensifying individualism. Collectivistic societies emphasize that individuals should be embedded in social groups, so families attempt to create a "we-identity" rather than an "I-identity" (Bond, 1991). As one of the consequences, Chinese (Xie, 2013) and Chinese American couples have low divorce rates: the overall divorce rate for Chinese Americans is 11% (Pew Research Center, 2017). Because Chinese working-class couples are not necessarily looking for soulmates, they may be willing to enter marriages for mostly practical reasons, as long as the two partners appear to be reasonably compatible (Hung, 2015). In comparison, American society encourages its members to pursue their own dreams, to hold onto their own convictions, and to marry somebody they truly love. Moreover, Chinese society is fairly "tight" rather than "loose" in nature (i.e., it endorses relatively strict social norms together with major sanctions when these norms are violated) (Gelfand, 2018).

Societal Structure

Chinese society has traditionally accepted major power differences between the wealthy and the poor, educated elites and illiterate peasants, teachers and students, parents and children. Although Chairman Mao Zedong attempted to disrupt violently some of these hierarchies in the 1960s and 1970s, many of his efforts were reversed by his successors (Mühlhahn, 2019). In contrast, the American Constitution emphasizes that we are all born equal. Although American society has lived up to this moral claim only in very partial though evolving ways, many Americans attempt to strive for greater equality. This emphasis on equality has influenced present-day relations between parents and their adolescent children to a considerable extent.

Cultural Values

Parents and immigrants arriving in New York during their later teenage years or as adults are likely to be guided by the Chinese values, norms, and customs they had grown up with, and these will at times differ from the ones prevailing in present-day China. In contrast, English-speaking, educated and 1.5 or second generation immigrants from Taiwan and Hong Kong tend to be more influenced by American-Anglo-Saxon values, social norms, and worldviews (Chen, 1992; Jia, 2004). The two value systems are also helping to shape the childrearing practices of Chinese American parents together with the hybrid identities of their children. Table 5.2 compares, in

Table 5.2 Two cultural approaches to childrearing

Selected aspects of childrearing	Traditional Chinese immigrant culture	American mainstream culture
Parental authority and approach to childrearing; importance of family needs	Emphasis on authority of elders, parents; high control of children; less individual privacy; the needs of the family should take priority over individual needs	Considerable emphasis on children's autonomy; more individual privacy; individual needs may take priority over family needs
Filial piety (*xiao shun*)	Confucian emphasis on child's respect, gratitude, and caring for parents as a central moral virtue	Less emphasis on child's obligations and obedience toward parents
Concern for protecting the reputation of self (*mian zi*) and family	Strong cultural emphasis on protecting one's own face and that of the family	Moderate concern for reputation of self and family
Cultural respect for teachers	Pronounced	Uneven
Gender differences	Sons traditionally favored but clear trend toward supporting and pursuing greater gender equality especially among working mothers	Gender equality increasingly emphasized and becoming more explicit
Emotional style and demonstration of affection	Restrained emotional style, many children are not hugged; parental love expressed through parental sacrifices and dedication	Overt displays of affection; parents should consistently express love for their child
Physical punishment of younger children	Common in traditional childrearing	Rather common but discouraged by "childrearing experts"
Emphasis on children's self-esteem and self-reflexivity	Children's self-esteem should be balanced by a realistic assessment of one's abilities; self-reflexivity and self-criticism are encouraged	Parents and teachers should consistently reinforce children's self-esteem rather than encouraging self-criticism
Modesty vs. aelf-assertiveness	Modesty and humility valued; one's achievements should speak for themselves or else be mentioned indirectly	Emphasis on self-assertiveness and individual accomplishments
Individual effort and hard work	Primary emphasis	Moderate emphasis
Self-control and long-term orientation	Strong emphasis on self-control in the service of long-term and moral goals	Moderate emphasis on both since children should also have fun
Emphasis on nemorization in education and while teaching one's child	Memorization necessary to learn Chinese characters and two highly diverse languages	Deemphasized and believed to undermine children's creativity
Emphasis on creativity	Moderate; hard work more important than creativity and innate talent	High

(continued)

Table 5.2 (continued)

Selected aspects of childrearing	Traditional Chinese immigrant culture	American mainstream culture
Should boys become assertive and aggressive if they are attacked or criticized unfairly?	Mostly not	Mostly yes: boys should be assertive rather than "cowardly"
Early dating and expression of sexual impulses	Early dating of girls considered shameful or at least dubious; dating distracts teenagers from pursuing more important educational and long-term goals	Dating by teenage girls considered acceptable; teenage boys may brag about sexual conquests; sexualized peer group cultures common in high schools
Student involvement in sports	Of limited importance since getting top grades in school is more emphasized and admired	Successful football and basketball players are frequently admired while "nerds" are devalued by peers

ideal-typical form, Chinese and mainstream American approaches to raising one's children.

Religion

Traditionally, the Chinese have tended to display pragmatic and nonexclusive attitudes toward religion, while endorsing the veneration of their ancestors. At the same time, China's Communist government has opposed religious practices and beliefs. In a nationwide survey of Asian Americans in the U.S., 26% of all Chinese Americans indicated that they were religiously unaffiliated, 42% said they were Christians, and 14% had a Buddhist identity (Pew Research Center, 2012). For a Christian working-class subgroup of Chinese immigrants in New York, attending church has been serving as a kind of "surrogate family" (Cao, 2005), and a considerable number of Chinese American college students have been joining Christian organizations as well (Hall, 2006). In addition, many of their grandmothers and elders pray in Buddhist, Daoist and Christian places of worship for the success of their grandchildren, children, and other family members (Guest, 2003). Although the majority of our respondents indicated that they were not religious, one can find in today's New York City a broad range of religious and spiritual convictions. They include various Christian, Buddhist, Muslim, and Chinese Folk Religion traditions as well as the spiritual Falun Dafa ("Dharma Wheel Practice") organization, which moved to the city after the Chinese Government outlawed the group in 1999. At the same time, church attendance has declined considerably among younger people in the United States (Jones, 2019).

Familial Structure

Although traditional Chinese culture originally favored a patrilineal and patrilocal kinship system, most Chinese families in New York endorse a neolocal-nuclear system (Wong, 1985). This means that upon marriage, husband and wife move to a new household, which tends to strengthen the bond between them. Moreover, sustained efforts have been underway both in China and elsewhere to increase the status of daughters. Given the prevailing very low birthrates in Taiwan, Hong Kong, and China, most families there have only 1–2 children, who may or may not include a son. Such situations have been undermining the traditional Confucian preference for sons. Harrell and Santos (2017) and Xie (2013), however, argue that despite such cultural changes, strong gender and generational hierarchies persist in today's Chinese societies. Similarly, several of our female interviewees lamented that their Chinese families continue to display the traditional preference for sons (Ho & Gielen, 2016). They were well aware that gender equality has been increasingly emphasized in American families and the wider world of academia, work, and public media.

Family Values

Traditional Chinese families emphasize that their children should show proper behavior from early on in life, and they are encouraged to exert self-control in the service of familial norms. They are also brought up to display perseverance in the service of long-term goals such as educational and economic advancement, together with pragmatic adaptation to shifting situations (Hofstede & Minkov, 2010). Parents frequently lead thrifty lives and make considerable sacrifices so that their children will have it better than they themselves. By way of contrast, American society—and in particular its multicultural New York City variety—tolerates a much broader range of lifestyles by encouraging individuals to express themselves in unique ways. Thus, American norms and convictions allow for a greater emphasis on the present, having fun, emphasizing one's abilities and feelings, yet they also favor evaluating personal and public situations in self-chosen moral terms.

As seen in Table 5.2, traditional forms of Chinese immigrant culture emphasize the authority of parents, elders, and teachers who are supposed to be strict and to instruct and control children, grandchildren and students. The children, in turn, are expected to show respect and gratitude toward their parents and to take care of them in later life in line with the traditional Confucian virtue of filial piety (*xiao shun*). The needs of the overall family are expected to take priority over the individual needs of the parents and the children. Children are also taught that what "happens in the family, stays in the family." They are expected to protect both the reputation of their family as well as their own "face" (*mian zi*). By way of comparison, American mainstream culture encourages parents to grant greater autonomy to their children while considering their needs, preferences, and talents. Some American adolescents lack respect for their teachers while others feel free to discuss various family matters with non-family members.

Parenting

Mainstream American thinking about how best to bring up children is reflected in popular American guides for childrearing (e.g., Faber & Mazlish, 2006). They tend to underline that parents should openly express their love for their children, build up their children's self-esteem, and criticize or punish them only occasionally. The children may be encouraged to mention individual accomplishments in their interactions with others. Mainstream American parents like to believe that in addition to spending some time on their homework, their children are also entitled to enjoy themselves. Similarly, the parents aim to reinforce their children's creativity and unique talents. Thus, they place less emphasis on "mindless" memorization, when compared to Chinese immigrant parents and Chinese teachers in tutorial and Chinese culture schools. Rote learning and sustained effort are required when some immigrant children are taught to remember thousands of Chinese characters in order to understand written Chinese. Quite a few of our respondents, however, disliked the emphasis on memorization and strict discipline in these weekend schools, and so they dropped out of them. While they spoke in Chinese to their parents and grandparents, most second-generation adolescents and young adults could read few if any Chinese characters (Ho & Gielen, 2016).

Parent-Child Relationships

Chinese culture promotes a restrained emotional style in parent-child relationships (Camras, Bakeman, Chen, Norris, & Cain, 2006). For instance, several immigrant adolescents in our sample complained that their parents did not hug them or verbalize their love for them. Many of them had been physically punished in their earlier years. Moreover, the parents often feel that their children's sense of self-esteem should be counter-balanced by expressions and feelings of modesty about their achievements (Du, 2010). They should be able to assess their strengths and limitations in a realistic manner. Such a sense of "realistic humility" and sustained efforts at "self-cultivation" help to restrain excessive displays of assertiveness, but they also contribute to the reputation of Chinese children and adults among their non-Asian peers that they are too reticent, modest, quiet, and unassertive (Zhang, 2010). However, in current Chinese middle-class immigrant families in the U.S., many adolescents favor moderate and flexible rather than high degrees of parental control and strictness (Russell, Crockett, & Chao, 2010). Moreover, Chinese working-class parents often know too little about the American educational worlds of their adolescent children to provide them with detailed guidance.

Education

Chinese children are frequently told that they should focus above all on education, while striving relentlessly so that they will have a chance at entering a prestigious university. To achieve this goal, many Chinese parents enroll their children in tutorial schools, while emphasizing the priority of homework over watching TV, playing video games, relaxing, and other distractions. Tutorial schools play a significant role in the Chinatowns and are one important reason why many Chinese students do quite well in the educational realm (Zhou, 2013). Data indicate that Asian American high school and college students do study harder than all other groups (University of California – San Diego, 2011). However, a good many Fuzhounese parents in the restaurant industry downplay the importance of education for their children because it does not ensure an immediate income (Hung, 2015).

Child Characteristics

Chinese immigrant parents often tell their sons and daughters that physical aggression and excessive assertiveness are inappropriate. If attacked, children should "swallow their anger" and report the attack to their teachers or other authority figures rather than taking things into their own hands. In contrast, American peer group culture and quite a few parents believe that "real" boys should fight back verbally and if necessary physically, should they be attacked. In addition, dating between teenage girls and teenage boys is a common practice in American high schools, whereas Chinese immigrant parents often consider it dubious or shameful if their daughters date that "early." Instead, they tell them that dating interferes with a steady emphasis on educational achievement, which should be of paramount importance to them (Kim & Ward, 2007). While Chinese students tend to be more sexually conservative than many of their non-Asian counterparts, a good number of Chinese teenage girls do date secretly and hide it from their families (Kao & Martyn, 2014). Still, Chinese American women are much less likely to give birth out of wedlock (11% of all births in the year 2010 when compared to 37% for all other racial-ethnic groups) (Pew Research Center, 2013). Chinese parents also downplay the importance of sports activities in their children's lives, whereas such activities play an important role in the lives of many African American, Hispanic, and non-Hispanic Caucasian high school and college students. Consequently, Chinese high school boys may be under peer pressure to develop a masculine identity based on participation in sports and other nonacademic activities (Qin, 2009).

The Impact of Living in an Immigrant Family: Some Examples

To state that somebody grows up in the Big Apple as a person with a Chinese background suggests varying degrees of exposure to the two aforementioned cultural frameworks and forms of childrearing. Typically, they coexist and interact with a broad range of evolving economic conditions and interpersonal situations that immigrant students encounter as they grow up. Together, the students' diverse immigration histories, the predominant economic, educational, and family situations surrounding them, the students' exposure to Chinese and non-Chinese friends and peers, and the two cultural frameworks and forms of childrearing shape the students' complex, evolving, hybrid, and at times contradictory identities and behavior patterns. As an initial example, a brief summary of an interview with a 21-year-old accounting student is provided.

Being Not Fully Chinese but American, I Am Entitled to My Own Opinions: An Interview with Cornelia Yao (Pseudonym)

Growing up first in Chicago Chinatown and subsequently in New York City, Cornelia heard from her immigrant parents about their previous lives in the Taishan region of South China and later on in Hong Kong. Though Cornelia sees herself as an atheist, her family's religious views include Daoism, Buddhism, and Christianity. Her family is not that strict and traditional, and unlike quite a few of her peers, she has never felt the pressure of being expected to only get A's in school. Cornelia feels happy in the United States, and she believes that most of her family members are too. Her Chinese-speaking mother works as a cook in a Chinese restaurant, and her bilingual dad co-owns a metal business with his brother. However, 2 years ago Cornelia's parents got divorced. She admires her mother greatly and also speaks about the love she has for her father, although he does not appear to reciprocate her feelings. She also discusses anger issues that run on her father's side of the family and the abuse in Chinese families that many are not willing to talk about. Though hidden well, Cornelia admits her aunt has been physically abused, while her mother was abused emotionally.

Having attended Madison High School in Brooklyn around 2004, she deplores the violence she saw there and the lack of safety she felt on her way to school. Though she never did experience a physical attack by a bully, she also describes how in middle and high school some of the Chinese boys would get beaten up, held down with a knife or even robbed. Cornelia believes being a victim of such bullying could largely be attributed to the fact they were Chinese, yet she refuses to judge others based on their ethnicity or nationality. Instead, she focuses on the way the bullies were brought up. Moreover, she worries about her brother who was negatively influenced by some of his peers, dropped out of Madison High, and for a while joined a Fuzhounese (Fujianese) group that sold drugs.

Cornelia's three best friends in high school were Chinese, shared the same values, and did not follow the prevailing trends at their school. Thus, Cornelia carefully avoided its sex culture as well as smoking and fighting. Now a college student, she spends most of her days hanging out with her Irish boyfriend, friends and family. Nowadays, Cornelia's boyfriend is her biggest support and her best friend. The two of them have been dating for 2 years and Cornelia hopes to marry him. Both of them still attend college, and while her boyfriend is majoring in sociology, Cornelia hopes to become a registered CPA soon. She dreams of being married at age 24 and having her first child by the time she is 25. However, she is most certain that no matter what path she decides to pursue, she will always look up to her amazing mother, for whom she will always be there.

As holds true for our other interviewees, Cornelia's life reflects complex interactions between individual tendencies, the psychosocial impact of her family, her family's economic circumstances, the conditions at her high school, and an array of Chinese and non-Chinese sociocultural influences. Although she is a happy person, she comes from a broken home. Her brother attended the same troubled high school as she did, yet unlike her he dropped out and joined a drug-dealing gang. This suggests that male and female siblings may behave in very different ways in spite of similar family situations. Her brother left school at least in part because several of his Chinese peers had been demeaned and beaten up by non-Chinese classmates. While Cornelia's parents are working class, she together with quite a few of her Chinese peers has been pursuing an accounting career that will support her entry into the middle class. Her best friends in high school were largely Chinese, but at the same time she hopes to marry her Irish boyfriend whose family she clearly appreciates. Altogether, she has been able to develop an integrated bicultural identity (Berry, Phinney, Sam, & Vedder, 2006). An anxious person, she accomplished this in spite of the racially motivated and scary tensions at her former high school and its neighborhood.

By way of contrast to her positive outlook on life, one may point to Clarence (Pseudonym), a troubled young boy whose Fuzhounese parents had originally been brought into the country by snakeheads. Having to work endless hours in order to pay back the ensuing loans as well as employment problems, they were forced to send the unhappy boy as a satellite child to China for 5 years. Unlike his brother who grew up in New York, he never became attached to his parents but upon his return began to seriously act out. He was, however, to some degree receptive to guidance from his older sister, as she told us in her interview.

Another and more cheerful example concerns Jennifer, who gladdened her originally Taishanese working-class parents when she became the first person in her family to graduate from a MA program. Or perhaps your Chinese family has been living a comfortable middle-class life in Queens and you grow up as their promising only son – but then your upset parents learn accidentally that you are gay, and therefore unlikely to present them with grandchildren. How different such a situation is from that of Julia, an adopted Chinese girl who feels quite at ease when she is joining her fellow Jews in the synagogue of her adoptive parents. She is one of the more than 10,000 girls from China who have been adopted by mostly White and Jewish New Yorkers and tend to reside in places such as Manhattan's Upper Westside (Bowen, 2014). Or else we may remember the 2002 Chinese valedictorian from the infamous but now closed Lafayette High School in Brooklyn, who was beaten unconscious by a non-Asian peer. He and his friends cursed Chinese people while attacking him. The valedictorian was one of quite a few Chinese male and sometimes female immigrant students who over the years were attacked at "Horror High" and subsequently required hospitalization (Kolben, 2003; Rong, 2003). As these examples demonstrate, Chinese American lives can be quite diverse. Nevertheless, there exist certain situations that many of the immigrant youths are likely to encounter.

Five Situations Shaping the Destinies and Identities of Chinese American Children and Youths

Given the broad range of identities among New York's Chinese immigrant children and youths, one may ask what situations and factors are most likely to influence their self-conceptions, behavior patterns, and destinies. In the following, we discuss the impact of five situations and factors that appeared in various autobiographical essays and interviews. Many writers and interviewees discussed the impact of their family's specific immigration situation on their lives, the influence of gender roles on their self-conceptions, their exposure to racial prejudice and discrimination, and their efforts to succeed academically. Some others reflected on the lives of satellite children. While discussing these situations, the students' interpretations would typically reflect their simultaneous exposure to Chinese family life and to mainstream American practices and ideas they had encountered in school, among their peers, and elsewhere.

Theme 1: The Impact of Immigration Status

Many of the writers and interviewees were strongly influenced by the fact that they had been born overseas, how old they were when they arrived in the United States, and the circumstances that brought them as first and 1.5 generation children to New York. Not rarely, serial migration shaped their early lives in which one family member – often the father – arrived first in New York. After he had found a job and established himself financially, and depending on the family's immigration status, mother and children would follow suit in one of the following years. In some other cases, the transnational father would travel regularly between countries and see his children only occasionally. This often meant that they spoke little or no English upon arrival while regarding dad as a sort of semi-stranger known to them mostly via video chats. In this context, the term "1.5 generation" refers to children who are born overseas and arrive in the new country prior to their early teenage years.

Research studies by Jia (2004) and others have found that once they attend school, most of these children switch to English as their preferred language while speaking less than perfect Chinese at home with their parents and other relatives. Because many of them speak their parents' Chinese dialect "like a 7-year-old" and cannot read Chinese, they experience problems when attempting to explain their inner emotions and preoccupations to them. Similar to second generation immigrants, such as Cornelia, they tend to look at themselves as more American than Chinese, may favor a mixture of Chinese and non-Chinese school friends and dates, and watch American mass media and movies rather than soap operas, *kung fu* movies, and news originating in Hong Kong, China or Taiwan. Only rarely can or do they read the Chinese-language newspapers preferred by their parents. In contrast, those immigrating in their middle teenage years or later tend to favor and be more fluent in the Chinese language and mostly embrace a Chinese identity. High discrepancies in parent-child acculturation and in American orientation, however, are related to adolescents' depressive symptoms and more contact with deviant peers (Ho, 2014).

Theme 2: Satellite Children

A considerable number of children especially in the Fuzhounese (Fujianese) community begin their lives as satellite babies and children. Born in New York to poor immigrant parents fighting for economic survival, such children are American citizens given their place of birth, although most of their parents are not (Yoshikawa, 2011). Many parents have been smuggled into the U. S. by snakeheads and need to pay off extensive debts afterwards. Forced to work numerous hours, they may send their baby back to their Chinese hometown a few months after the baby's birth. The baby will be brought up by grandparents, aunts, or other relatives until an approximate age of 4–6 years of age and then returned to New York. There the Chinese-speaking child enters school in a process of reverse migration (Kwong, 2017).

Although we lack systematic longitudinal data on such children, preliminary studies and autobiographical statements suggest that they may find it difficult to replace their original attachments – to their China-based grandmothers or aunts – with new attachments to their own parents, who are experienced as scary semi-strangers (Bohr, Liu, Chen, & Wang, 2018; Bohr & Tse, 2009; Whitfield, 2014). Feeling disconnected, they may be confused and insecure, have a low frustration threshold, turn rebellious and act out, hesitate to confide their fears to their busy parents, and ask themselves whether their parents truly love them since after all they had sent them overseas (Tan, 2015). Furthermore, many of these parents continue to work very long hours and are only partially available to their attention- and love-starved children.

Theme 3: The Impact of Gender Roles and Identities

Gender plays a central role in Chinese American families, as indicated especially by our female respondents. Comparing themselves to their brothers, they describe a broad range of family situations. For instance, a traditional mother may tell her daughter that "education is of no use to you because you will be a housewife and mother later on," or else ask her to clean up the room of Elder Brother, or insist that she but not her brothers must learn how to cook. Some working-class daughters may also be encouraged to enter an economically advantageous marriage and do so in their early years (Hung, 2015).

Traditionally, daughters were trained to become dutiful and devoted spouses as well as exemplary and self-sacrificing mothers. At the same time, Chinese female immigrant students tend to like school more, get better grades, do more homework, and are less likely to drop out than their male peers (Brandon, 1991; Qin, 2006a). Given this context, a number of other female and male interviewees told us that one or both of their parents are making genuine attempts to abandon traditional forms of gender discrimination. Specifically, embracing unequal conceptions of gender roles appears to be most common among members of the older working-class generation who came of age in rural areas, but less so among educated parents who grew up in big, globalized, relatively open and culturally changing cities such as Hong Kong, Guangzhou, Shanghai or Taipei. Moreover, some poor immigrant mothers tell their daughters that they need to be educated and financially independent in case their future husband walks out on them (cf. Louie, 2004, p. 73). Still, girls are kept more at home, are more influenced by family norms, and are supervised more closely so that they will not "get into trouble" (e.g., get pregnant). Boys are granted more independence but sometimes begin to act out and/or develop problems in high school or college (Ho & Gielen, 2016). Parents, however, are reluctant to discuss sexual issues with their sons and daughters (Kim & Ward, 2007).

While Chinese American female adolescents are more likely to be rooted in their ethnic identity than their male peers (Qin, 2009), they also experience more feelings of social anxiety and depression (Ho & Gielen, 2016). In our study, female writers were considerably more likely than male writers and interviewees to mention serious doubts about their body image. For instance, several of them reported that in their earlier years they had wanted to be blond and light-skinned, while having round and blue eyes just like those of their Barbie dolls. In this context, it is interesting to note that skin-whitening creams and facial operations designed to make one's eyes look more striking and Caucasian are quite popular in East Asian countries such as Taiwan, Hong Kong, and South Korea (Tan, 2012). In traditional China, having dark skin was associated with working in the fields, being poor, and having low status. By way of contrast, some male Chinese and Korean Americans complain that they would like to be taller and physically stronger. Many of them believe that non-Asians frequently see them as nerdy, quiet, submissive, socially awkward, small, skinny, and physically weak rather than as physically attractive, sporty and cool guys (Hwang, 2016; see also Chua & Fujino, 1999). Because of that, they may find it difficult to secure dates with white girls who may perceive them as insufficiently masculine. Whereas 30–55% of all new marriages of second and especially third generation Chinese American and Korean American women have been with Caucasian men, Chinese and Korean American men are significantly less likely to be married to Caucasian women. Among Asian newlyweds in 2013, 37% of the women and 16% of the men married outside of their race (Wang, 2015). Moreover, most of our interviewees reported that their parents did not want them to bring home potential African American or Hispanic partners. Although some added to this observation that they themselves did not agree with their parents' racial-ethnic attitudes, intermarriage rates between Chinese and African Americans have traditionally been very low (Le, 2009).

Theme 4: The Impact of Racial Prejudice and Discrimination

Similar to several other studies (e.g., Qin, Han, & Chang, 2011), a considerable number of our interviewees and writers reported that they have experienced racial prejudice and discrimination. They were confronted with racial slurs, derogatory uses of Chinese mock-phrases, and gestures indicating slanted eyes. They also had to listen to stereotypical statements such as "you all look alike," "of course you are good in math," or "why do you have such strange eyes." A few of the male students were beaten by members of other ethnic groups who saw them as weak, nerdy or as "perpetual foreigners" based on their accent and/or appearance. In contrast, quite a few of the female teenagers report that non-Asian men addressed sexual remarks, gestures or invitations toward them, comments that they would only rarely hear in Chinese neighborhoods.

A broad range of studies (Benner et al., 2018) have demonstrated that exposure to racial/ethnic discrimination and prejudice tends to have negative effects on adolescents' mental health and well-being. The effects include internalizing symptoms such as feelings of depression, social anxieties, and lowered self-esteem as well as externalizing behaviors such as acting out, substance abuse, engaging in risky sexual behaviors, and dropping out of school (Benner et al., 2018). Internalizing symptoms are especially common among teenage girls while teenage boys are more likely to drop out of school and to act out.

Negative, racially inspired, and sometimes violent encounters are most likely to occur in poor, racially mixed neighborhoods and schools (Rosenbloom & Way, 2004). Not surprisingly, many Chinese-American students in such schools have negative perceptions of their school environment, do not trust their teachers and blame them for not protecting them, feel fearful, frustrated, and angry about being bullied, and dislike their non-Chinese peers. Many are convinced that neither the adults at home nor those in their school understand them (Zhou & Kim, 2003). In contrast, students attending more selective high schools are much less likely to report dangerous and racially charged encounters. The effects of negative encounters with non-Asian peers appear to be most detrimental to an adolescent's mental health when (s)he is also experiencing serious strains within the family. Moreover, first generation adolescents living in a clearly Chinese environment are better able to cope with negative inter-racial encounters than psychologically more conflicted, second generation students (Zhang, Fang, Wu, & Wieczorek, 2013). Perhaps this is so because they are relying mostly on feedback from the Chinese community rather than believing that as Americans, they should be protected from such violations of cultural ideals and norms. However, New York in the 1980s–1990s was a more violent place both outside and inside the Chinatowns when compared to the decade lasting from 2010 to 2019.

Theme 5: Striving for Academic Excellence

Many Chinese and other Asian students should be, but are not always pleased with their excellent academic performance. For instance, in the school year 2013–2014, Asian students were highly over-represented at New York's free but extremely competitive magnet schools. Admission to these schools is entirely based on a student's performance on the Specialized High School Admission Test. At the famous Stuyvesant High School, 73% of all students were Asians although they made up only 16% of the city's public school population (NYC Department of Education, 2014). Among the Chinese students, about half grew up in poor or quite modest conditions (Qin, Rak, Rana, & Donnellan, 2012). The school admitted less than 5% of all applicants, and within the context of the city it was about as selective as Harvard University has been in a national context. At the Bronx High School of Science, Asians constituted 62% of all students and at the Brooklyn Technical High School it was 61% (NYC Department of Education, 2014). Because African and Hispanic students are vastly underrepresented at these special schools, controversial political efforts during 2017–2019 were seeking to replace the special entrance test with alternative entrance requirements (Wong, 2019). Their readily understandable intent is to ensure more racially and ethnically representative student bodies, but they would do so at the expense of outstanding academic performance.

Relying on phone interviews with male and female persons 25 years and older, Kasinitz, Mollenkopf, Waters, and Holdaway (2008) compared the educational attainment of eight ethnic groups residing in the city. Their study included five ethnic groups of second generation immigrants and three groups whose members had been born in the United States. In the Chinese immigrant group, 73% had received at least a BA, but only 1.1% of them reported that they were high school dropouts. While the phone interviews may have underestimated the percentage of high school dropouts across the various groups, the percentage did nevertheless reach a much higher 22.8% among indigenous Puerto Ricans. The educational performance of the Chinese exceeded that of all other groups including well performing Russian Jewish immigrants and native Whites (see also Hsin & Xie, 2014). This result held true although in New York City, 33.9% of all Chinese immigrants 25 years and older had no high school diploma (they typically grew up overseas), while only 11.7% of them had received a post-graduate degree. Moreover, 25% of the city's Chinese children below the age of 18 grew up in poverty (U.S. Census, 2013 American Community Survey). Reflecting such considerations, Kasinitz et al. summed up their findings by stating that [the Chinese] "children have moved farther than any other group in terms of their distance from their parents' occupation, education levels, and even attitudes" (pp. 16–17). Whether they know it or not, such students are the descendants of the most education-oriented empire in history with its unique Imperial Examination System. That system enabled the sons of obscure peasants and townspeople to join the small elite of the world's most populous country by surpassing everybody else on a grueling series of examinations (Elman, 2013).

Proceeding to more recent times, students at East Asian high schools have been regularly outperforming high school students from the U.S. and many other countries in the international PISA comparisons (e.g., OECD, PISA, 2015 Results). In addition, Chinese (and Indian) high school students have frequently won top spots in the nation-wide Intel Science Talent Search (now Regeneron Science Talent Search) competition and the United States of America Mathematical Olympiad. In the 2016 Intel Science Talent Search, for instance, 11 of the 40 finalists had parents both of whom had been born in China while 14 had parents from India (Anderson, 2017). Because they are over-represented at many of the Ivy League universities, several of these are in effect requiring higher test scores, grades, and (subjective) interview ratings from their Asian American applicants when compared to those from other racial-ethnic groups (Unz, 2012).

Although many Chinese immigrant parents should be well pleased with their children's excellent educational performance, a good number of the youngsters will pay a price for it when the emotional bond and mutual understanding between them and their educationally, culturally, and linguistically dissimilar parents is growing weaker and more superficial over time. For instance, Qin et al. (2012) compared Chinese American and European American students attending a highly selective magnet school in New York. The Chinese American students reported lower levels of psychological adjustment, less family cohesion, and more family conflict than their European American peers. Moreover, among the often poor or semi-poor Chinese American students, the perceived high levels of family conflict and low levels of family cohesion appeared to be causally related to their lower adjustment level (see also Qin, 2006b, 2008). These and other findings suggest a number of intertwined psychological paradoxes: Many of the students are educational stars but report relatively low levels of contentment and psychological adjustment. Although they see their families as conflictual and not very cohesive, they remain aware of the many sacrifices their parents have been making for them. For some of them, growing up is a lonely experience because they see too little of their parents who are at work. While many 1.5 and second-generation immigrants such as Cornelia are in the process of creating happy and successful lives, others, such as her brother, are struggling to reconcile the conflicting expectations and attitudes of their families and peers. In this context, he and many other Asian American children and adults could profit from readily accessible counseling services.

Mental Health Services for Chinese New Yorkers

Given the demanding and stress-inducing circumstances that surround many Chinese and other Asian American families in New York, their ready access to culturally appropriate mental health services should be considered a major priority. According to the Asian American Federation (2017), Asian American adolescent girls reported the highest rates of depression among the major racial/ethnic groups in the United States, together with disproportionately high suicide rates. Among female Chinese immigrants, Americanized second generation immigrants are more at risk for depressive and anxiety disorders than those born in China (Zhang et al., 2013; see also Sue, Cheng, Saad, & Chu, 2012 for a more general overview of Asian American mental health). Moreover, 40% of all Asian seniors are frequently experiencing depression while also being at considerable risk for attempting suicide. However, few Asian Americans report their own emotional difficulties or those of their children to health experts or school officials because of linguistic difficulties, powerful cultural stigma, lack of pertinent knowledge, and financial considerations (Ho, Yeh, McCabe, & McCabe, 2007; Loo, Tong, & True, 1989). Most of them are quite reluctant to discuss negative immigration experiences, domestic violence, gambling addiction, alcohol and drug abuse, work-related stress, experiences of social isolation, tensions with their children, and serious emotional problems with mental health experts (Wong et al., 2013; Kaplin et al., Chap. 17, this volume). They frequently drop out of psychotherapy (Sue, 1977). Undocumented parents of satellite children are especially reluctant to consult social workers and professional experts (Kwong, 2017).

Many Chinese immigrant parents hope to receive socioemotional support and properly articulated, private advice and guidance from people they know. These may include respected family members, friends, and experienced people with whom they interact in the context of community-based and religious organizations. They often prefer subtle and indirect forms of communication that do not embarrass them and protect their "face." While they may be reluctant to share their emotions with others, they tend to react more positively to goal oriented and purposeful social interchanges. Thus, both parents and their youth are likely to respond constructively to those mental health experts who do not inquire at length about their emotional reactions but rather offer them realistic and practical advice leading to improved social relationships. In addition, the treatment of children and youth is more likely to be successful once counselors and therapists succeed in creating positive relationships with the mostly Chinese-speaking parents and other family members. In this context, they may emphasize that the aim of the treatment is to improve the children's adjustment both at home and at school. This, in turn, would be likely to improve their long-term chances for a successful career.

Research evidence suggests that Asian American clients respond more positively to culturally adapted therapies (Hall, Ibaraki, Huang, Marti, & Stice, 2016), favor neighborhood clinics over mainstream clinics, and improve more when they are treated in such clinics (Griner & Smith, 2006). In addition, some elderly persons are likely to consult traditional Chinese doctors who specialize in herbal medicine, acupuncture, and *qigong* (Lei, Lee, & Askeroth, 2004). They may believe that such doctors can diagnose the physical-mental basis of their problems, together with prescribing the dietary, medicinal, and behavioral changes needed to weaken their impact. Traditional Chinese healing is holistic in nature and emphasizes the strengthening of a person's vital energy called *qi*. Low levels of *qi* are thought to result in somatic symptoms as well as mental weaknesses such as depression. Mental health experts and social workers should consider working together with both modern and traditional doctors and their clients when these are exhibiting serious psychological dysfunctions. Such cooperation works best when the experts and social workers have a working knowledge of the nature of Chinese medicine and are personally familiar with some traditional doctors.

The report of the Asian American Federation (2017) emphasizes that the efforts of New York's Asian community oriented organizations to offer mental health services are chronically underfunded. This makes it difficult for them to provide adequate services to Asian clients. Moreover, Chinese and other Asian communities would benefit from expanded preventive programs that can be integrated into already existing services offered within the community. Such programs should be advertised and explained with the help of ethnic and social media, while gaining the support of educational, mental health, medical, religious, and political community leaders and experts. Examples of such programs include leadership programs for younger people, supportive workshops for parents designed to improve their parenting skills, and social programs for the elderly. Institutions and programs such as the large, nonprofit Hamilton-Madison House and the Mental Health Bridge Program, Charles B. Wang Community Health Center (Nguyen, Shibusawa, & Chen, 2012), both in Manhattan Chinatown, have been employing mental health experts who are supporting behavioral health programs offered in various Chinese dialects. The experts are working together with medical doctors and also train community workers, so that they can recognize serious mental health problems requiring specialized treatment.

A community perspective is also useful when considering the situation of Chinese satellite children (Kwong, 2017). How might it be possible to reduce their numbers over time and to improve their situation within the context of their families and surrounding community? Such efforts should include a combination of much needed psychological research about the practice and its long-term effects, more comprehensive community discussions about the necessity and impact of the practice, the expansion of affordable childcare services, providing skills training to parents, and the investigation of the effectiveness of novel forms of intervention such as art therapy for these children (Tan, 2015). It is clear that mental health experts can play an important role in furthering these goals.

Chinese Immigrant Families in New York City and Elsewhere: A Conclusion

Reflecting the stress-inducing nature of immigration, many of New York's Chinese working-class and lower middle-class families and their children have to deal with various intersecting problems. These include family separations due to migration, low family incomes, overcrowded housing, long hours of work leading to reduced contact between parents and children, major linguistic and cultural differences between parents and children, experiences of racial-ethnic discrimination and prejudice, and identity conflicts. Economic and migration-related family stress can induce increased parental tensions, depression, and anger. These, in turn, may lead to more coercive and less supportive forms of parenting which are likely to have a negative impact on children's happiness and school performance (Benner & Kim, 2010).

Although economically privileged professionals and their children tend to enjoy more comfortable lives than their poorer counterparts, they still may have to confront multicultural challenges and psychological tensions both inside and outside their families. The more astonishing then is the educational success of so many–though of course not all–Chinese students, including those living in New York City, the United States, Canada, and elsewhere. At the same time, poverty, prejudice, and discrimination continue to darken the lives of many Chinese youngsters in the metropolis and elsewhere. While the country has made great progress between the passing of the hostile Chinese Exclusion Act in 1882 and today, racial/ethnic equality and fairness remain admirable moral visions that should, but often do not, guide people's behavior.

Although 13–14% of all Chinese Americans in the United States reside in New York City, their situation is neither fully representative for the country as a whole nor for Canada. Take as an example the Los Angeles Metropolitan Area, where the second largest number of Chinese Americans live. According to the 2010 Census, in that year 449,538 Chinese Americans (including 45,808 Taiwanese) resided in Los Angeles County, but only 66,782 of them lived in Los Angeles City itself (20 Years Los Angeles Almanac 1998–2018). Spread out much more than their New York-based peers, quite a few of them did reside in so-called "ethnoburbs" (ethnic suburbs) situated in the San Gabriel Valley (Zhou, 2009a). Compared to New York City, their average income and education levels were considerably higher. Moreover, a greater percentage of them reported Taiwanese backgrounds, were exposed to cosmopolitan ideas, had English-speaking children attending good quality suburban schools, and intermingled with members of other Asian groups. However, they only rarely interacted with recent working-class immigrants from Fujian Province (Zhou, 2009b; Zhou & Kim, 2003).

Altogether, the Chinese in New York City are on average poorer, less well educated, and less proficient in their use of the English language than their peers both in the United States and Canada. In particular, many of the city's recent immigrants are beginning their new lives at the bottom of the economic ladder. They hope that one day in the not-so-distant future, they will be in charge of their own restaurant or shop and perhaps even own a house. Given their linguistic, educational, and cultural handicaps, that is the life that some but not all of them will be able to achieve. Their hopes and ambitions for their children, however, tend to be more wide-ranging.

Although this chapter does not mirror the experiences of the many Chinese professionals and their families in Silicon Valley nor those of certain super-rich Chinese students in Vancouver (Fan, 2016), it does focus on one of the world's foremost global cities. In this capacity, New York remains THE gateway for Chinese immigrants. Increasingly, their daughters and sons are populating the city's schools and universities, such as the 25 institutions making up the very large City University of New York (CUNY) system. For example, in 2017, Asians and Pacific Islanders accounted for an impressive 40.5% of Baruch College's 18,289 undergraduate and graduate students (Baruch College, 2017). Having listened to their parents and peers but also keeping their own practical interests in mind, Chinese students abound in that institution's accounting and business classes both at the undergraduate and graduate levels. They seem to be inspired by a popular Chinese proverb summing up many of their lives: "Remember, a kite raises against, not with the wind."

Although some of these upwardly mobile students may unfortunately encounter a "bamboo ceiling" (= glass ceiling) in their later careers, their academic success will nevertheless gladden the hearts of their parents. Those parents include fathers who are waiters and cooks and mothers who work in nail salons or take care of other people's children in exchange for meager wages. They came to New York with a combination of Chinese and American Dreams in their minds, and it is often their children – not they themselves – who are expected to fulfill those dreams for them. Many tell their children that education is the key to a better life, but because they themselves stand outside New York's educational system and speak limited if any English, they cannot help them in their educational pursuits. Facing these and many other challenges, these youths are pursuing a multiplicity of dreams as they are entering the long and winding road of their adult lives. Our chapter is dedicated to them and the courage so many of them are demonstrating.

References

Anderson, S. (2017, March 17). Children of immigrants are top U.S. high school science performers. *Forbes*, Editors Pick.

Asian American Federation. (2017). *Report on overcoming challenges to mental health services for Asian New Yorkers*. http://aafederation.org/press/pressrelease.asp?prid=367&y=2017

Asian American Federation. (2019a). *Profile of New York City's Chinese Americans*. http://www.federation.org/cic/briefs/2019ch.pdf

Asian American Federation. (2019b). *Profile of New York City's Taiwanese Americans*. http://aafederation.org/cic/briefs/2019tw.pdf

Baruch College. (2017). *Facts and figures*. https://www.baruch.cuny.edu/about/by_the_numbers.html

Benner, A. D., & Kim, S. Y. (2010). Understanding Chinese American adolescents' developmental outcomes: Insights from the family stress model. *Journal of Research on Adolescence, 20*, 1–12. https://doi.org/10.1111/j.1532-7795.2009.00629

Benner, A. D., Wang, Y., Shen, Y., Boyle, A. E., Polk, R., & Cheng, Y.-P. (2018). Racial/ethnic discrimination and well-being during adolescence: A meta-analytic review. *American Psychologist, 73*(7), 855–883. https://doi.org/10.1037/amp0000204

Berry, J. W., Phinney, J. S., Sam, D. L., & Vedder, P. (2006). Immigrant youth: Acculturation, identity, and adaptation. *Applied Psychology: An International Review, 55*(3), 303–332. https://doi.org/10.1111/j.1464-0597.2006.00256

Bohr, Y., Liu, C., Chen, S., & Wang, L. (2018). Satellite babies: Costs and benefits of culturally driven parent-infant separations in North American immigrant families. In M. R. T. de Guzman, J. Brown, & C. P. Edwards (Eds.), *Parenting from afar and the reconfiguration of family across distance* (pp. 304–320). Oxford University Press.

Bohr, Y., & Tse, C. (2009). Satellite babies in transitional families: A study of parents' decision to separate from their infants. *Infant Mental Health Journal, 30*(3), 265–286. https://doi.org/10.1002/imhj.20214

Bond, M. H. (1991). *Beyond the Chinese face: Insights from psychology*. Oxford University Press.

Bowen, J. (2014). *Wish you happy forever: What China's orphans taught me about moving mountains*. New York, NY: Harper Collins.

Brandon, P. R. (1991). Gender differences in young Asian Americans' educational attainments. *Sex Roles, 25*(1–2), 45–61. https://doi.org/10.1007/bf00289316

Camras, L. A., Bakeman, R., Chen, Y., Norris, K., & Cain, T. R. (2006). Culture, ethnicity, and children's facial expressions: A study of European, American, Mainland Chinese, Chinese American, and adopted Chinese girls. *Emotion, 6*(1), 103–114. https://doi.org/10.1037/1528-3542.6.1.103

Cao, N. (2005). The church as a surrogate family for working class immigrant Chinese youth: An ethnography of segmented assimilation. *Sociology of Religion, 66*(2), 183–200. https://doi.org/10.2307/4153085

Chen, H.-S. (1992). *Chinatown no more: Taiwan immigrants in contemporary New York*. Cornell University Press.

Chin, K.-l. (1996). *Chinatown gangs: Extortion, enterprise, and ethnicity*. Oxford University Press.

Chin, K.-l. (1999). *Smuggled Chinese: Clandestine immigration to the United States*. Temple University Press.

Chua, P., & Fujino, D. C. (1999). Negotiating new Asian American masculinities: Attitudes and gender expectations. *The Journal of Men's Studies, 7*, 391–413. https://doi.org/10.3149/jms.0703.391

Du, L. (2010). *Learning to be Chinese American: Community, education, and ethnic identity*. Lexington Books.

Elman, B. A. (2013). *Civil examinations and meritocracy in late Imperial China*. Harvard University Press.

Faber, A., & Mazlish, E. (2006). *How to talk so kids will listen & listen so kids will talk*. William Morrow.

Fan, J. (2016, February 22). The golden generation: Why China's super-rich send their children abroad. *The New Yorker*. https://www.newyorker.com/magazine/2016/02/22/chinas-rich-kids-head-west

Finckenauer, J. O. (2007). *Chinese transnational organized crime: The Fuk Ching*. https://www.ncjrs.gov/pdffiles1/nij/218463.pdf

Frey, W. H. (2018). *Diversity explosion: How new racial demographics are remaking America* (rev. ed.). Brookings Institution Press.

Gelfand, M. (2018). *Rule makers, rule breakers: How tight and loose cultures wire our world*. Scribner.

Griner, D., & Smith, T. B. (2006). Culturally adapted mental health interventions: A meta-analytic review. *Psychotherapy: Theory, Research, Practice, Training, 43*(4), 531–548. https://doi.org/10.1037/0033-3204.43.4.531

Guest, K. (2003). *God in Chinatown: Religion and survival in New York's evolving immigrant community*. New York University Press.

Guest, K. J. (2011). From Mott Street to East Broadway: Fuzhounese immigrants and the revitalization of New York's Chinatown. *Journal of Chinese Overseas, 7*, 24–44. https://doi.org/10.1163/179325411x565399

Hall, B. (1998). *Tea that burns: A family memoir of Chinatown*. Free Press.

Hall, B. (2006). Social and cultural contexts in conversion to Christianity among Chinese American college students. *Sociology of Religion, 67*(2), 131–147. https://doi.org/10.1093/socrel/67.2.131

Hall, G. C. N., Ibaraki, A. Y., Huang, E. R., Marti, C. N., & Stice, E. (2016). A meta-analysis of cultural adaptations of psychological interventions. *Behavior Therapy, 47*, 993–1014. https://doi.org/10.1016/j.beth.2016.09.005

Harrell, S., & Santos, G. (2017). *Transforming patriarchy: Chinese families in the Twenty-First Century*. University of Washington Press.

Ho, G. W. K. (2014). Acculturation and its implications on parenting for Chinese immigrants: A systematic review. *Journal of Transcultural Nursing, 25*(2), 145–158. https://doi.org/10.1177/1043659613515720

Ho, J., & Gielen, U. P. (2016). Chinese American adolescents and emerging adults in New York City: Striving for a place in the sun. In U. P. Gielen & J. L. Roopnarine (Eds.), *Childhood and adolescence: Cross-cultural perspectives and applications* (2nd ed., pp. 347–376). Praeger.

Ho, J., Yeh, M., McCabe, K., & McCabe, R. L. (2007). Parental cultural affiliation and youth mental health service. *Journal of Youth and Adolescence, 36*, 529–542. https://doi.org/10.1007/s10964-006-9114-x

Hofstede, G. (2018). *Hofstede insights: Compare countries*. https://www.hofstede-insights.com/product/compare-countries/

Hofstede, G., & Minkov, M. (2010). Long- versus short-term orientation: New perspectives. *Asia Pacific Business Review, 16*(4), 493–504. https://doi.org/10.1080/13602381003637609

Hsin, A., & Xie, Y. (2014). Explaining Asian Americans' academic advantage over whites. *Proceedings of the National Academy of Sciences of the United States of America., 111*(23), 8416–8421. http://www.pnas.org/content/111/23/8416.full.pdf

Hum, T. (2014). *Making a global immigrant neighborhood: Brooklyn's Sunset Park*. Temple University Press.

Hung, W. T. (2015). Dowries and debts: Fuzhounese youth geographies of fear, resentment, and obligation. *Journal of Asian American Studies, 18*(1), 11–40. https://doi.org/10.1353/jaas.2015.0004

Hwang, S. (2016). *Not man enough: Second-generation Korean-American male youths & masculinity*. http://krieger.jhu.edu/research-opps/wp-content/uploads/sites/86/2015/06/Hwang-Sally.pdf

Hymowitz, K. S. (2014). Brooklyn's Chinese pioneers: Hardworking Fujianese immigrants use the borough as a launching pad to the middle class. *City Journal*, Spring. https://www.city-journal.org/html/brooklyn%E2%80%99s-chinese-pioneers-13640.html

Jia, G. (2004). The acquisition of English and maintenance of first language by immigrant children and adolescents in North America. In U. P. Gielen & J. Roopnarine (Eds.), *Children and adolescence: Cross-cultural perspectives and application* (pp. 350–373). Praeger.

Jones, J. M. (2019). *U.S. church membership down sharply in past two decades*. Gallup. https://news.gallup.com/poll/248837/church-membership-down-sharply-past-two-decades.aspx

Kao, T. S. A., & Martyn, K. K. (2014). Comparing White and Asian American adolescents' perceived parental expectations and their sexual behaviors. *SAGE Open, 4*(2), 2158244014535411. https://doi.org/10.1177/2158244014535411

Kasinitz, P., Mollenkopf, J. H., Waters, M. C., & Holdaway, J. (2008). *Inheriting the city: The children of immigrants come of age*. Harvard University Press and Russell Sage Foundation.

Keefe, P. R. (2010). *The snakehead: An epic tale of the Chinatown underworld and the American dream*. New York, NY: Doubleday.

Kim, J. L., & Ward, L. M. (2007). Silence speaks volumes: Parental sexual communication among Asian American emerging adults. *Journal of Adolescent Research, 22*(1), 3–31. https://doi.org/10.1177/0743558406294916

Kolben, D. (2003, January 1). Lafayette violence makes it horror high. *The Bay Ridge Paper*, 1–7.

Kwong, K. (2017). The developmental impact of reverse-migration separation on low-income Chinese-American children – Provider perspectives. *Open Journal of Social Sciences, 5*, 146–165. https://doi.org/10.4236/jss.2017.55011

Kwong, P. (1996). *The new Chinatown* (rev. ed.). Hill and Wang.

Le, C. N. (2009). *Interracial dating & marriage*. Asian Nation: Asian American history, demographics & issues. www.asian-nation.org/interracial.shtml

Lei, T., Lee, C.-T., & Askeroth, S. (2004). Indigenous Chinese healing: Theories and methods. In U. P. Gielen, J. M. Jefferson, & J. G. Draguns (Eds.), *Handbook of culture, therapy, and healing* (pp. 191–212). Erlbaum.

Loo, C., Tong, B., & True, R. (1989). A bitter bean: Mental health status and attitudes in Chinatown. *Journal of Community Psychology, 17*, 283–296. https://doi.org/10.1002/1520-6629(198910)17:4<283::aid-jcop2290170402>3.0.co;2-c

Louie, V. (2004). *Compelled to excel: Immigration, education, and opportunity among Chinese Americans*. Stanford University Press.

Mühlhahn, K. (2019). *Making China modern: From the great Qing to Xi Jinping*. Harvard University Press.

NYC Department of Education. (2014). *School quality guide 2013–2014*.http://schools.nyc.gov/OA/SchoolReports/2013–14/School_Quality_Guide_2014_HS_K430.pdf

Ng, F. (1998). *The Taiwanese Americans*. Greenwood Press.

Nguyen, D., Shibusawa, T., & Chen, M. T. (2012). The evolution of community mental health services in Asian American communities. *Clinical Social Work Journal, 40*, 134–143. https://doi.org/10.1007/s10615-011-0356-z

OECD, PISA. (2015). *Results*. www.oecd.org/pisa/

Pew Research Center (2012). *Asian Americans: A mosaic of faiths*. https://www.pewforum.org/2012/07/19/asian-americans-a-mosaic-of-faiths-overview/

Pew Research Center (2013). *The Rise of Asian Americans*. http://www.pewsocialtrends.org/2012/06/19/the-rise-of-asian-americans-chinese-in-theu-s/

Pew Research Center (2017, Sept. 8). *Chinese in the U.S. fact sheet*. http://www.pewsocialtrends.org/fact-sheet/asian-americans-chinese-in-the-u-s/

Qin, D. B. (2006a). The role of gender in immigrant children's educational adaptation. *Current Issues in Comparative Education, 9*(1), 8–19. http://www.tc.edu/cice

Qin, D. B. (2006b). Our child doesn't talk to us anymore: Alienation in immigrant Chinese families. *Anthropology and Education Quarterly, 37*, 162–179. https://doi.org/10.1525/aeq.2006.37.2.162

Qin, D. B. (2008). Doing well vs. feeling well: Understanding family dynamics and the psychological adjustment of Chinese immigrant adolescents. *Journal of Youth and Adolescence, 37*, 22–35. https://doi.org/10.1007/s10964-007-9220-4

Qin, D. B. (2009). Being "good" or being "popular": Gender and ethnic identity negotiations of Chinese immigrant adolescents. *Journal of Adolescent Research, 24*(1), 37–66. https://doi.org/10.1177/0743558408326912

Qin, D. B., Han, E.-J., & Chang, T.-F. (2011). Immigration, ecological contexts, and Asian American children's mental health. In F. T. L. Leong, L. Juang, D. B. Qin, & H. E. Fitzgerald (Eds.), *Asian American and Pacific Islander children and mental health* (Vol. 1, pp. 23–46). ABC-CLIO.

Qin, D. B., Rak, E., Rana, M., & Donnellan, B. (2012). Parent-child relations and psychological adjustment among high-achieving Chinese and European American adolescents. *Journal of Adolescence, 35*, 863–873. https://doi.org/10.1016/j.adolescence.2011.12.004

Robbins, L (2018). Investigators seize fake luxury goods worth half a billion dollars. *The New York Times*, August 16. https://www.nytimes.com/2018/08/16/nyregion/fake-luxury-goods-handbags.html

Rong, X. (2003, Jan 7). *Lafayette high student charged with school hate crime*. https://voicesofny.org/2003/01/nycma-voices-48-news-news/

Rosenbloom, S. R., & Way, N. (2004). Experiences of discrimination among African American, Asian American, and Latino adolescents in an urban high school. *Youth & Society, 35*(4), 420–451. https://doi.org/10.1177/0044118x03261479

Russell, S. T., Crockett, L. J., & Chao, R. K. (Eds.). (2010). *Asian American parenting and parent-adolescent relationships*. Springer.

Semple, K., Goldstein, J., & Singer, J. E. (2014, February 7). Asylum fraud in Chinatown: An industry of lies. *New York Times*. https://www.nytimes.com/2014/02/23/nyregion/asylum-fraud-in-chinatown-industry-of-lies.html

Sue, S. (1977). Community mental health services to minority groups: Some optimism, some pessimism. *American Psychologist, 59*, 616–624. https://doi.org/10.1037//0003-066x.32.8.616

Sue, S., Cheng, J. K. Y., Saad, C. S., & Chu, J. P. (2012). Asian American mental health: A call to action. *American Psychologist, 67*(7), 532–544. https://doi.org/10.1037/a0028900

Sung, B. L. (1987). *The adjustment experience of Chinese immigrant children in New York City*. Center for Immigration Studies.

Sussman, N. M. (2011). *Return migration and identity: A global phenomenon*. Hong Kong University Press.

Tan, D. (2012). Who's the fairest of them all. *American Scientist*, Sept. 12, 2012. http://www.asianscientist.com/features/skin-whitening-products-asia2012/

Tan, D. (2015). *Art therapy reduces reverse-migration effects on "satellite babies*." Unpublished Master's thesis, Long Island University, Post Campus. 20 Years Los Angeles Almanac 1998–2010. http://www.laalmanac.com/index.php

University of California – San Diego. (2011). Is there a "tiger mother" effect? Asian students study twice as many hours, analysis finds. *ScienceDaily*. www.sciencedaily.com/releases/2011/05/110505103345.htm.

Unz, R. (2012). *The myth of American meritocracy: How corrupt are Ivy League admissions?* Kindle Edition, Dec. 25, 2012.

Wang, W. (2015). *Interracial marriage: Who is marrying 'out'?* http://www.pewresearch.org/fact-tank/2015/06/12/interracial-marriage-who-is-marrying-out/

Whitfield, N. (2014). *The return of satellite babies: Two studies exploring and responding to the needs of reunited immigrant families*. Unpublished dissertation, York University, Toronto, Canada.

Wong, A. (2019). 4 myths fueling the fight over NYC's exclusive high schools. *The Atlantic*, March 21, 2019.

Wong, B. (1985). Family, kinship, and ethnic identity of the Chinese in New York City, with comparative remarks on the Chinese in Lima, Peru and Manila, Philippines. *Journal of Contemporary Family Studies, 16*(2), 231–254. https://doi.org/10.3138/jcfs.16.2.231

Wong, J. Y. H., Tiwari, A., Fong, D. Y. T., Yuen, K. H., Humphreys, J., & Bullock, L. (2013). Intimate partner violence, depressive symptoms, and immigration status: Does existing advocacy intervention work on abused immigrant women in the Chinese community? *Journal of Interpersonal Violence, 28*(11), 2181–2202. https://doi.org/10.1177/0886260512475311

Xie, Y. (2013). *Gender and family in contemporary China*. Report 13-808, Population Studies Center, University of Michigan.

Yoshikawa, H. (2011). *Immigrants raising children: Undocumented children and their children*. Russell Sage Foundation. https://doi.org/10.5860/choice.49-2391

Zhang, J., Fang, L., Wu, Y.-W. B., & Wieczorek, W. F. (2013). Depression, anxiety, and suicidal ideation among Chinese Americans.: A study of immigration-related factors. *The Journal of Nervous and Mental Disease, 201*(1), 17–22. https://doi.org/10.1097/nmd.0b013e31827ab2e2

Zhang, Q. (2010). Asian Americans beyond the model minority stereotype: The nerdy and the left out. *Journal of International and Intercultural Communication, 3*(1), 20–37. https://doi.org/10.1080/17513050903428109
Zhao, X. (2010). *The new Chinese America: Class, economy, and social hierarchy*. Rutgers University Press.
Zhou, M. (1992). *Chinatown: The socioeconomic potential of an urban enclave*. Temple University Press.
Zhou, M. (2009a). *Contemporary Chinese America. Immigration, ethnicity, and community transformation*. Temple University Press.
Zhou, M. (2009b). Conflict, coping, and reconciliation: Intergenerational relations in Chinese immigrant families. In N. Foner (Ed.), *Across generations: Immigrant families in America* (pp. 21–46). New York University Press.
Zhou, M. (2013). Chinese: Diverse origins and destinies. In N. Foner (Ed.), *One out of three: Immigrant New York in the twenty-first century* (pp. 120–147). Columbia University Press.
Zhou, M., & Kim, R. (2003). A tale of two metropolises: Immigrant Chinese communities in New York and Los Angeles. In D. Halle (Ed.), *Los Angeles and New York in the new millennium* (pp. 124–149). University of Chicago Press.

Chapter 6
Japanese Families in the United States

Bobbie Kabuto

Abstract This chapter will examine Japanese families living in North American, specifically in the United States. This chapter will focus on a discussion of the movement of Japanese families to North America in the later part of the twentieth century due to the globalization of the Japanese economy. After providing a brief history of Japan and discussing trends in marriage and family within Japanese society, this chapter will discuss the impacts that Japanese families' migration to the United States has had on cross-cultural socialization, interracial marriages and children, education, and career choices. The impacts of socialization into multiple ethnic and national groups on identity formation will also be explored. This chapter will conclude with suggestions for further research and implications for educators, counselors, and social workers.

Keywords Japanese families · Cross-cultural socialization · Japanese marriage and children · Japanese education and career choices · Identity

Japan is a society of "old world traditions" and "modernization and globalization." Japan is an archipelago and part of East Asia. It is a society dating back to the first century AD and discovered by Chinese monks, and many Chinese influences are still present in contemporary Japanese society (Rogers, 2005). While there are various regional dialects, Japanese with the standard Tokyo dialect is spoken throughout Japan. The mixture of ancient Chinese kanji is used in conjunction with Japanese hiragana and katakana and the Roman alphabet as the Romanization of Japanese words is becoming increasingly used in Japanese discourse (Rogers, 2005).

Japan is currently an industrialized, free market economy, which has shown mostly decreases, with slight increases, in GDP (Gross Domestic Product) growth in the early part of the twenty-first century. Japan's economy is built on the electronic and automotive industries. With the hit in global markets in 2009, Japan's GDP dropped to a historically low growth rate of −4%. It increased between the

B. Kabuto (✉)
Queens College of the City University of New York, Flushing, NY, USA
e-mail: Bobbie.Kabuto@qc.cuny.edu

S. S. Chuang et al. (eds.), *Asian Families in Canada and the United States*, Advances in Immigrant Family Research,
https://doi.org/10.1007/978-3-030-56452-0_6

years of 2010–2011 to 4.7% and then dropped in 2011 to −0.6% (The Organization of Economic Co-Operation and Development (OECD), 2013).

While Japan is a nation that proudly holds onto tradition, it is also one that is undergoing many ideological struggles related to old and new world ideals with the increasing globalization of its economy. These ideological struggles between that represent tradition and modernization are evolving the ways in which Japanese society is defining family, marriage, gender roles, and education (Makino, 2006; Takahashi, 2013). Reinvention and resistance frame the ways in which Japanese men and women think about marriage, gender equality, social class, and educational and job opportunities. Japanese families are in transition as mothers and fathers redefine their roles and responsibilities in the home and at work, and this redefinition has larger implications on fertility rates in relation to an ageing society and a declining population (Ishii-Kuntz, Makino, Kato, & Tsuchiya, 2004; Ogawa, 2007).

This chapter will discuss the relationships between changes in Japanese society, as part of its globalizing economy, and Japanese migration and families living in North America, specifically in the United States. This chapter is not designed to provide a comprehensive overview of these relationships. Rather, it will present trends and themes for further investigation and research. This chapter will conclude with the implications that an evolving Japanese society has for educators, counselors, and social workers.

Demographics of Japan and Japanese Migration to North America

According to the United Nations Population and Vital Statistics Report (2013), Japan has a population of 128,057,352, with 62,327,737 reported males and 65,729,615 reported females. In 2010, Japan had 1,071,304 reported births (a rate of 8.4) and 1,197,012 reported deaths (a rate of 9.8). Japan has a low infant mortality rate, which the UN reports as 2.2. The life expectancy of Japanese individuals is one of the highest around the world. The life expectancy for men is 80 years, while for women it is 86.9 years. These statistics suggest several natural trends in Japanese society. Even with the low infant mortality rate, Japan's population is declining as the death rate exceeds the birth rate. The United Nations report rates Japan's population growth at −1.4 (The United Nations Population and Vital Statistics Report, 2013). At the same time, Japan's population is not getting younger, but instead is getting older as the life expectancy increases. Finally, with the number of females exceeding the number of males, there are a larger percentage of females not marrying and creating different life courses other than domestic life (Makino, 2006).

Based on the 2010 United States Census, Asian immigration is rapidly increasing (The United States Census Bureau, 2010). Conducted every 10 years, the U.S. Census found that the Asian population increased by 43% between 2000 and 2010. This increase was more than that of other groups. Between those same years, immigration patterns of Japanese individuals showed that there was a decrease in individuals who reported themselves as Japanese as one race (−1.2%), while individuals reporting themselves as Japanese and another race increased by 55.9% and Japanese and another Asian population (i.e., Korean, Filpino) increased by 13.5%. These trends in percentages show changes in the Japanese population living in the United States (The United States Census Bureau, 2010).

While immigration patterns of Japanese-only individuals appear to be decreasing, there are large increases in mixed-race Japanese individuals living in the United States (The United States Census Bureau, 2010). While this may be the case, very little research has been conducted on these groups of individuals. Terminology, socialization patterns, sociocultural and linguistic identities, and language maintenance are critical issues that need further exploration but the current body of research has done little to improve our understandings of Japanese individuals living in counties like the United States.

Japanese Families

According to the United Nations Population and Vital Statistics Report (2013), in 1970, nearly 99% of Japanese men and 95% of Japanese women were married. This percentage decreased for men and women in 2010 when 79% of Japanese men and 88% of women reported to be married. The age of marriage is getting later in Japan. Men tend to marry between the ages of 25 and 34, and women tend to marry between the ages of 25 and 39. The divorce rate is 36% with the highest number of divorces among individuals married between 5 and 9 years or 20 years and more. Japan has a lower percentage of single-parent homes than most Western countries (Makino et al., 2008).

Japanese families tend to be extended families composed of a husband, a wife, children, and grandparents (the parents of generally the husband's family) (Ogawa, 2007). Recently, the extended family organization is becoming less common, while the idea that "Men for work and women for home," or "Man is a bread winner and woman is a consumer" continues to be rooted in Japanese society (Ogawa, 2007). Marriage, traditionally, is an assumed institution that both men and women are expected to enter into so that Japanese society differentiates between "love marriages," or *renai-kekkon*, and arranged marriages, or *omiyai-kekkon* (Takahashi, 2013).

Researchers argue that the nature and composition of Japanese families are changing (Makino et al., 2008). Makino (2006) suggests that there is a declining number of household members, an increasing number of single households, and a declining fertility rate. More Japanese individuals, particularly women, are deciding to forgo marriage and children (Makino, 2006). Researchers suggest that these trends, particularly the declining fertility rate, are related to a gender ideology (Ogawa, 2007; Takahashi, 2013). Recent reporting in the *New York Times* suggests that these trends have persisted in Japan over time (Rich, 2019, 2020).

Makino (2006) argues that women's anxiety over raising children is increasing. Within the ideology of "wife as home-maker" and "husband as breadwinner," women spend more hours in the home with children while husbands spend more hours at work. Ishii-Kuntz et al. (2004) found that men's decreased parental involvement was related to long work hours and time availability, particularly in a country where paternal leave is not as popular as in countries such as the United States, Great Britain, and Sweden, one of the first countries to initiate the leave (Tanaka & Waldfogel, 2007).

The time that Japanese fathers spend on child-rearing activities is lower than other countries like the United States and France. Makino et al. (2008) suggested that 85.9% of child-rearing activities were the responsibility of the mother and 2.5% were conducted by the father. In Sweden, for example, they found that 16% of the child-rearing activities were conducted by the father and 30% were conducted by both. Researchers argue that Japanese mothers are feeling more daily stress and are finding less enjoyment in child-rearing (Raymo, Iwasawa, & Bumpass, 2009).

Researchers credit the shift to late marriage, particularly among educated women, to women desiring economic and professional independence (Raymo & Iwasawa, 2005). Raymo and Iwasawa (2005) generated the "marriage market mismatch hypothesis," which proposes that declines in marriage rates are due to "marriage mismatch," during which educated women are opting to stay in the workforce. At the same time, the numbers of available educated, single men are declining. In addition, with the decline of arranged marriages from 63% in 1955 to 2% in 2002, men and women are looking for their own spouses (Ogawa, 2007). Results from Raymo and Iwasawa's study (2005) study found that one-fourth of declining marriage rates was due to the lack of availability of potential spouses. They concluded that the marriage mismatch was due to an "educational mismatch" between potential marriage partners as women want to be educated and dependent on their spouses for economic stability. Women are attempting to create more desirable life courses during which they can manage both work and family (Kaneko et al., 2008).

This trend is occurring simultaneously with new divorce rates. The number of divorces is steadily increasing in Japan and researchers indicated that the highest rates of divorce are occurring among couples with lower levels of education. Until recently, little has been known about divorce in Japan, partly due to the fact that the idea of divorce is taboo in Japanese society. While in the United States divorce is considered a private matter, in Japan it becomes a public one often leading to social ridicule or isolation among women and negative ramifications within the work setting for men (Raymo, Iwasawa, & Bumpass, 2004).

Japanese families have slightly different views of the roles and relationships of family members than families from Western cultures (Kelsky, 2001). With strong gendered ideologies, Japanese parents tend to take on role specific responsibilities. More equal distribution of family participation is seen as unnecessary in Japanese thought, but is seen as a critical one in Western thought (Kelsky, 2001). Researchers contend that the influences of globalization and Western ideologies are now affecting these gendered ideologies (Takahashi, 2013).

The access to popular culture through movies, television, music, and advertisements and the privileging of English as access to Western principles creates romanticized ideals of the roles of men and women within society and the family (Takahashi, 2013). The following section will further explore the impact of globalization on gendered ideologies in Japanese society.

Economic Globalization and Japanese Migration to North America

Historically, Japan has a strong ethnonational, monolingual identity that privileges a homogenous society. This pre-war ideology, also described as Nihonjinron ideology, continued into the twentieth century and through increased globalization that resulted in the "Bubble Economy" in the 1980's and 1990's. It was during this time that North America experienced an increased shift in Japanese migration (Kamada, 2010). The growing dominance of the Japanese industrialized, free market economy led to a rise in international migration patterns of Japanese individuals as the Japanese economy flourished.

During the time of Japan's growing economy in the 1990s, 258,247 Japanese nationals moved to North America, with Japanese nationals residing largely in the United States, according to the Japan Statistics Bureau of the Ministry of International Affairs and Communications (n.d.). In 2011, the number nearly doubled to 454,828, with the number of Japanese nationals residing in Canada doubling from 21,846 in 1990 to 56,891 in 2011 (Japan Statistics Bureau of the Ministry of International Affairs and Communications, n.d.). These numbers reported by the Statistics Bureau include not only Japanese nationals, but also permanent expatriates and those individuals holding dual citizenship.

One of the major impacts of globalization and the rise in international migration to North America is the positioning of English as a high status language (Kanno, 2008; Takahashi, 2013). Individuals in Japanese society who could speak, read, and write in English held privileged positions in Japan because language was viewed as providing access to international domains (Kanno, 2008). Evidence of the high interest in learning English is the increased numbers of English language schools, or *eikaiwa* schools, and study aboard programs, or *ryugaku*. Tsuda (2000) reported that the English language school industry in Japan reached approximately 1 trillon Yen. The Organization of Economic Co-Operation and Development (OECD), (2013) found that nearly 63,000 Japanese citizens went abroad for a tertiary education in 2010. The United States was the most popular destination followed by the United Kingdom and Australia (Takahashi, 2013).

In addition, international migration patterns have impacted Japanese families, resulting in an increased rate of chiyuzain, a general term used to describe individuals who along with their families moved to other countries for 3–5 years for work purposes (Kamada, 2010). While many chiyuzain families returned back to Japan, some did not–especially the families with children who attended North American universities. Researchers (e.g., Kamada, 2010; Takahashi, 2013) have documented the educational, linguistic, and sociocultural adjustments of children or adolescents who decided to stay in foreign countries, taking on mixed national identities, or returned back to Japan and recaptured their Japanese national identity. Children of chiyuzain families do not feel acculturated into one particular society and lack feelings of belongingness because they are positioned as outsiders within Japanese culture and society to which their parents may belong (Kamada, 2010).

Transnational Generation of Families: Acculturation and Socialization

One of the consequences of the movement of families due to global economic expansion is the creation of transnational Japanese families. These families have unique characteristics and challenges because, as Zhou and Xiong (2007) argued, they can be caught between cultures, beliefs, and ideologies. As a transitional generation, the parental generations tend to hold onto and socialize their children through traditional values and beliefs of their native country that may support and/or contradict the cultural values of the areas in which they live (Zhou & Xiong, 2007).

Consequently, a review of the research suggests that defining a term like Japanese American is complex because these general terms may not address the distinctive characteristics and research needs of individuals across generations. For example, if a first generation mono-racial Japanese American man (generation 1) marries a Caucasian women and they have a biracial child (generation 2), then the intergenerational relationships between generation 1 and generation 2 can be qualitatively different than when a Japanese American mono-racial man marries a Japanese American mono-racial woman (both generation 1) and have a mono-racial Japanese American child (generation 2). Zhou and Xiong (2007) found that second generation children of immigrant families, such as the family in the latter scenario, reported more unequal treatment and identified themselves as "hyphenated" Asian Americans. Perhaps this is the case because second-generation Asian Americans are ambivalent towards prior generations due to cultural differences on how Japanese families view the roles and relationships of family members across generations.

Japanese American Families: Interracial Marriages and Children

With the rise in Japan's global economy and migration patterns to North America, the U.S. has experienced the largest increase in bi/multi-racial Japanese American families due the steady increase in international marriages (Le, 2014; Tsuneyoshi, 2011). According to Tsuneyoshi (2011), in 2008, about 5% of all marriages of Japanese nationals were international marriages as compared to 1965 when the percentage was 0.4%.

Researchers argue that this increase in interracial marriages coincides with the growing global dominance of the English language (Le, 2014; Takahashi, 2013). Japanese men are more likely to have Japanese spouses or other Asian spouses than

Japanese women (Le, 2014). Takahashi (2013) further explored the interracial marriages of Japanese women and found that learning English and the role of language ideologies played a significant role in interracial marriages. Takahashi (2013) argued that learning English is more than a psychological or economic motivation. Rather, it is also about agency and desire to acquire freedom from constraints within one's life course. Takahashi (2013) further argued that Japanese women's "romantic" attachment to English fueled their aspirations to develop relationships with Western men.

Child-Generations of Intermarriages

Identity development of the biracial second generation children has been a topic of interest to researchers, although an under-researched topic. Within the population of Japanese Americans, linguistic, national, and cultural identity formation of the child-generation is often the result of children learning to find belongingness to particular linguistic and cultural communities (Kabuto, 2010; Kanno, 2003). Far less research has been conducted on how parental generations navigate the intersections of "Japanese" and "American" identities and how this navigation influences child-rearing practices and the socialization of their children into North American society.

Of particular interest are the ways in which biracial children are positioned with Japanese terminology, such as *hafuu* (meaning "half") or *daburu* (meaning "double"). Researchers argue that this type of terminology suggests a lack of wholeness in biracial identities that are sitting side-by-side rather than being integrated. (Collins, 2000; Kamada, 2010). In order to combat this arbitrary distinction in one's identity, Kamada (2010) discussed how biracial identities are hybrid identities, which are fluid, flexible, and negotiated. Biracial Japanese American children have the agency to select, explore and situationally use different aspects of their identity to gain access to, and power within, social structures and institutions (Collins, 2000; Kabuto, 2010; Kamada, 2010).

In one of the few studies on the development of biracial identities of children living in the United States, Collins (2000) proposes that biracial identities are undergoing constant changes and evolutions. Collins (2000) found that biracial Japanese American children went through four phases in their developing biracial identities. In phase I, children self-evaluated themselves, questioned who they are and expressed confusion when attempting to fit into a particular ethnic category. In phase II, children attempted to suppress parts of their identity. The process of suppression involved children looking for particular reference groups to belong to. For example, children living in mono-racially white communities attempted to reject their Japanese identity. In phase III, children explored parts of their identity in the attempt to reconcile contradictory and conflicting feelings about who they are as Japanese Americans. While Japanese American children may have previously attempted to reject one part of their identity, they now felt that they were not whole and took action to find feelings of completeness. They traveled to Japan or moved to areas with large multicultural communities. Phase IV was defined as coming to a resolution and accepting their biracial identity.

Children find agency in using their identity to their advantage and acknowledge the shifting boundaries of their identity (Kanno, 2003). Contrarily, very few studies on the phases of identity development have been conducted on second generation mono-racial Japanese children living in North America, such as Japanese adolescents who acculturated into North American society and how they have navigated and developed bicultural, bilingual, and cross-national identities.

Education and Career Pathways

Japan's educational system is composed of both public and private schooling venues, and both receive financial support from the government. Japanese grade school levels are organized into kindergarten (3–6 years old), primary school (6–12 years old) and lower and upper secondary school (12–15 and 15–18 years old) (Kamada, 2010). Upper secondary school is a time for intense university preparation during which students prepare to take a variety of university exams. Unlike universities in countries like the United States and Canada, Japanese universities have their own unique exams required for entrance, and private university exams tend to be more competitive than public university exams (Kamada, 2010).

Parents, who immigrate to North American societies and are socialized into the Japanese educational system model with high levels of competition, place importance and emphasis on formal education, particularly for parents who have hopes of returning back to Japan (Kamada, 2010). Japanese supplementary schools, sometimes called heritage language schools, or hoshuko, have become a venue for Japanese children to receive an education in Japanese language skills in speaking, listening, reading, and writing and Japanese math and history, as well as an education in Japanese values and culture. With the increase in Japanese nationals studying abroad and second generation Japanese returning back to Japan, the Japanese government supported schools furthering rapid in creating quick assimilation of Japanese returnee families into Japanese society (Kanno, 2008).

Kanno (2008) explored Japanese children who returned back to Japan as adolescents for a secondary education. She found that the returnees lacked both English language proficiency and Japanese language proficiency. The former caused adolescents not to fully enter into English dominant social groups, while the latter experienced difficult times in entering into and adjusting to the Japanese university system.

For many Japanese families, returning back to Japan so that their children can have a secondary education is often a top priority. Japan has a tradition of a "designated school" system, in which employers and secondary schools have a close relationship causing employers to select graduates exclusively from certain high schools. At the same time, secondary schools in Japan have a tracking system that regulates students' job applications in relation to academic performance and will provide recommendations on post-secondary career paths. Consequently, Japanese American individuals who do not attend secondary schools or universities in Japan may find it difficult to enter into pathways for highly competitive companies and careers. Furthermore, without a long-term Japanese education, Japanese returnees may not have the language proficiency in speaking, reading, and writing needed for some career pathways, creating unequal job opportunities for Japanese Americans (Kamada, 2010).

Implications for Educators, Social Workers, and Psychologists

There are implications for educators, social workers, and psychologists, particularly on developing further research on how the migration of Japanese families to North America impacts the identities of Japanese families and their educational and career choices.

First, further research that tracks the social and economic trajectories of Japanese American families as they become more acculturated into Western society, particularly after the second generation, is needed. It is critical that educators and researchers continue to monitor and research how institutional structures related to work and school socialize Japanese families into values, beliefs, ideologies and socio-cultural and national identities connected to American society.

Second, further research is needed on the multi-faceted aspects of identity, as a dynamic and changing process, of Japanese families, particularly focusing on interracial families. Familiarity with the phases of identity development will allow professionals to assist children in critical times of need in developing a healthy self-concept (Collins, 2000). Specifically, in developing a healthy self-concept, Japanese Americans, particularly children of Japanese families who immigrated to the U.S., have a desire to find belongingness with other groups. Due to the collectivist nature of the Japanese culture, this process plays an important role in defining their identity (Collins, 2000; Silver, 2002). Providing or developing social support groups for Japanese Americans can assist in the acculturation process and in socializing children into positive self-evaluations of themselves.

Finally, there is limited research that explores Japanese Americans' career choices and their opportunities in the United States. There is a paucity of research on how individuals within Japanese American families navigate the employment system and the types of cultural capital needed to be successful in gaining and maintaining employment, the challenges of language proficiency, and the potential inequalities within the system that deters Japanese American families from finding employment. Further research in this area will assist in educational and career counseling needed for exploring a variety of career pathways.

References

Collins, F. (2000). Biracial Japanese American identity: An evolving process. *Cultural Diversity and Ethnic Minority Psychology, 6*(2), 115–133. https://doi.org/10.1037/1099-9809.6.2.115

Ishii-Kuntz, M., Makino, K., Kato, K., & Tsuchiya, M. (2004). Japanese fathers of preschoolers and their involvement in child care. *Journal of Marriage and Family, 66*(3), 779–791. https://doi.org/10.1111/j.0022-2445.2004.00052.x

Japan Statistics Bureau of the Ministry of International Affairs and Communications. (n.d.). *Population and households*. http://www.stat.go.jp/english/data/nenkan/1431-02.htm

Kabuto, B. (2010). *Becoming biliterate: Identity, ideology, and learning to read and write in two languages*. Routledge.

Kamada, L. (2010). *Hybrid identities and adolescent girls: Being 'half' in Japan*. Multilingual Matters.

Kaneko, R., Sasai, T., Kamano, S., Iwasawa, M., Mita, F., & Moriizumi, R. (2008). Attitudes toward marriage and the family among Japanese singles: Overview of the results of the thirteenth Japanese national fertility survey, singles. *The Japanese Journal of Population, 6*(1), 51–75.

Kanno, Y. (2003). *Bicultural identities: Japanese returnees betwixt two worlds*. Erlbaum.

Kanno, Y. (2008). *Language and education in Japan: Unequal access to bilingualism*. Palgrave Macmillan.

Kelsky, K. (2001). *Women on the verge: Japanese women, western dreams*. Duke University Press.

Le, C.N. (2014). *Interracial dating & marriage: U.S.-Raised Asian Americans*. Asian-Nation: The Landscape of Asian America. http://www.asian-nation.org/interracial2.shtml

Makino, K., Funbashi, K., Watanabe, H., Nakano, H., Sakai, K., & Fujimoto, T. (2008, November). *Japanese families in transition: Results of six-country comparative research*. Paper presented at the National Council on Family Relations. Little Rock, AR.

Makino, K. (2006). What is happening to Japanese families today: Recent family changes in Japan. *Research Monographs*, 99–104.

Ogawa, N. (2007). *The emergence of very low fertility in Japan: Changing mechanisms and policy responses*. Paper presented at the International Symposium on Social Policy in Asia, 9–10 February 2007, Tokyo.

Raymo, J. M., & Iwasawa, M. (2005). Marriage market mismatches in Japan: An alternative view of the relationship between women's education and marriage. *American Sociological Review, 70*(5), 801–822.

Raymo, J. M., Iwasawa, M., & Bumpass, L. (2009). Cohabitation and family formation in Japan. *Demography, 46*(4), 785–803.

Rich, M. (2019, August 3). Craving freedom, Japan's women opt out of marriage. *New York Times*.

Rich, M. (2020, May 16). Stuck at home, men in Japan learn to help. Will it last? *New York Times*.

Rogers, H. (2005). *Writing systems: A linguistic approach*. Blackwell Publishing.

Silver, C. (2002). Japanese and American identities: Values and their transmission in the family. *Sociological Inquiry, 72*(2), 195–219. https://doi.org/10.1111/1475-682X.00013

Takahashi, K. (2013). *Language learning, gender, and desire: Japanese women on the move*. Multilingual Matters.

Tanaka, S., & Waldfogel, J. (2007). Effective of parental leave and work hours on fathers' involvement with their babies: Evidence from the millennium cohort study. *Community, Work and Family, 10*(4), 409–426.

Tsuda, Y. (2000). *Eigoheta no susume*. KK Bestsellers.

Tsuneyoshi, R. (2011). Three frameworks on multicultural Japan: Towards a more inclusive understanding. *Multicultural Education Review, 3*(2), 125–156. https://doi.org/10.1080/23770031.2009.11102886

The Organization of Economic Co-Operation and Development (OECD). (2013). *Education indicators in focus*.

The United Nations Population and Vital Statistics Report. (2013). *Statistical Papers, Series A, Vol. LXV*. http://unstats.un.org/unsd/demographic/products/vitstats/Sets/Series_A_2013.pdf

The United States Census Bureau. (2010). *Asian population*. http://www.census.gov/population/race/data/asian.html

Zhou, M., & Xiong, Y. S. (2007). The multifaceted American experiences of the children of Asian immigrants: Lessons for segmented assimilation. *Ethnic and Racial Studies, 28*(6), 1119–1152. https://doi.org/10.1080/01419870500224455

Chapter 7
Korean Families

Jessica J. Jeong and Ann H. Kim

Abstract This chapter provides a brief overview of the literature on Korean families living in the United States and Canada. According to the 2010 U.S. Census data, there was a 43% increase in the Latino and Asian populations between 2000 and 2010, leading to 14.7 million for the Asian population in 2010 (Hong et al., 2014). Korean Americans ranked as the fifth largest Asian population (Jang et al., 2015; Min, 2013). By 2018, about 1.5 million were Korean Americans (Asian alone category; U.S. Census Bureau, 2018a). There is a smaller but growing Korean population in Canada, with 190,000 residents according to the 2016 Census of Canada. About 150,000 people reported Korean language as their mother tongue and about 70 percent of them (109,000 people) indicated Korean language as language spoken most often at home (Statistics Canada, 2017). Given their substantial presence as an Asian ethnic group in both the United States and in Canada and more importantly, the increasing heterogeneity of the population, this chapter reviews and expands the existing literature on Korean families. Specifically, this chapter examines the diverse characteristics of Koreans in the United States and Canada, and how these factors can be closely linked to supporting the well-being of adults and children in Korean families.

Keywords Korean Canadian · Korean American · Korean families · Family relationship · Family rolves · Ethnic identity · Bicultural · Cultural-ethnic socialization

---

J. J. Jeong (✉) · A. H. Kim
York University, Toronto, ON, Canada
e-mail: jjeong@yorku.ca; annkim@yorku.ca

S. S. Chuang et al. (eds.), *Asian Families in Canada and the United States*, Advances in Immigrant Family Research,
https://doi.org/10.1007/978-3-030-56452-0_7

This chapter examines the diverse social, cultural, and economic characteristics of the Korean population in the United States and Canada, and discusses their implications for the psycho-social well-being of Korean families and implications for informed practice. Although smaller in number than Chinese and Filipino communities in these two countries, the Korean population is a well-established ethnic group with over 100 years of settlement in the U.S. and over 60 years in Canada and there is continued growth through migration. According to the 2010 U.S. Census data, there was a 43 percent increase in the Latino and Asian populations between 2000 and 2010, leading to 14.7 million for the Asian population in 2010 (Hong et al., 2014). Korean Americans ranked as the fifth largest Asian population (Jang et al., 2015; Min, 2013). By 2018, about 1.5 million were Korean Americans (Asian alone category; U.S. Census Bureau, 2018a). There is a smaller Korean population in Canada, with 190,000 residents according to the 2016 Census of Canada but it is one of the fastest growing 'visible minority' groups and the ninth largest immigrant group in the country (Park, 2012). About 150,000 people reported Korean language as their mother tongue and about 70 percent of them (109,000 people) indicated Korean language as the language spoken most often at home (Statistics Canada, 2017).

With the backdrop of their relatively large and growing presence as an Asian ethnic group in both the U.S. and in Canada, and more importantly, of the increasing heterogeneity of the population, this chapter reviews and expands the existing literature on Korean families. In doing so, we attempt to portray the complexity within this particular ethnic group; however, we are cognizant that we are limited by the foci of publish literature, which does not often adequately capture the diversity and dynamism within a given and evolving population. It is important that in such worthy endeavors to understand ethnic groups, we must all be aware of and avoid tendencies to essentialize them and to paint them with a broad brush. With this caveat, we begin this chapter with a brief history of immigration to both countries. Then we provide a profile of families in terms of family migration, family structure, age, and generation, religion, and cultural values, economic integration and educational attainment. In the context of increasing heterogeneity among young Korean families, the remaining sections address how Korean youth negotiate ethnic identity and highlights research on social roles and responsibilities that promotes healthy functioning among Korean Canadian and Korean American families.

Brief Immigration History

The history of migration for Koreans to the U.S. and Canada is often characterized by distinct periods or waves (Lee, 2016). The U.S., compared to Canada, has a much longer history of Korean migration with the first wave arriving in the early 1900s to work at sugar plantations in Hawaii. Since that early period to the 1960s, Korean migration to the U.S. consisted of political refugees from Japanese colonization, students, and military children and wives (Yoon, 2012). The largest migration waves that shaped the Korean-American community took place from the mid-1960s onwards, due to changes in the immigration policy, and the migration flows were composed of predominantly economic and family migrants seeking permanent residency.

Similar to the U.S., military family members and education migrants comprised important groups in the pre-1960 flows of Korean migration to Canada, and this included theology students who studied temporarily in Canada to eventually return and assist Canadian missionaries in Korea (Yoo, 2002; Yoon, 2012). Canada's immigration policy opened doors to non-European permanent migrants in the early 1960s and thus the post-1960 wave is marked by the beginning of permanent migrants from South Korea to Canada (Kim, Noh, & Noh, 2012). And as a testament to the permanent nature of their migration, the majority of immigrants, in both places, have naturalized into citizens (Min & Kim, 2013).

Since the 1960s, Korean migration to the U.S. and Canada has generally been characterized by highly skilled and business migrants, family members, and foreign students, and continuous migration streams along with past waves shape the contemporary Korean population in both places, which can be found in the larger urban centres like Los Angeles, New York, Toronto, and Vancouver (O'Connor & Batalova, 2019; Park, 2012). Emigration from Korea during this new wave of immigration to the U.S. and Canada was initially driven by Korea's unstable economic and political conditions, as well as Korea's bilateral connections with each country (Kim, Yun, Park, & Noh, 2012; Min, 2010). For the most part, immigrants to both the U.S. and Canada were highly educated and sought economic mobility for their children but due to their differences in immigration policies over subsequent decades, Korean migrants to the U.S. tended to be sponsored family members, and in Canada, they were economic and business class migrants. The desire for an improved quality of life and for cultural capital in the form of English language education have motivated more recent middle-class Korean migrants, replacing past motivations related to poorer economic and political conditions in South Korea (Kim, 2015). While they arrive wealthier than their predecessors did, this latest wave of mostly education migrants share their desire for a better life (for a more detailed description of the history of migration; see Min (2013), Joo and Lee (2018) for the U.S., and Kim, Yun, et al. (2012), for Canada).

It is important to note that the focus of this chapter is on families who live in the United States and Canada after migration as a family unit and their experiences as reflected in the literature. The unique migration experiences of other types of Korean families in the United States and Canada has received some research attention but this body of work is not discussed here. Specifically, we are referring to the experiences of transnational families (i.e., families living separately in different countries while maintaining close ties and considering themselves as a family unit, families of international students), and families of North Korean refugees (for a more detailed description of these families' experiences, see Finch and Kim (2012), Jeong, You, and Kwon (2014), for the U.S., and Dorman et al. (2017), Kim, Yun, et al. (2012), Kim and Kwak (2019), for Canada).

A Social, Cultural, and Economic Profile of Korean Families

How families take shape within ethnic communities depends on myriad factors, including migration patterns, social, demographic, and cultural dynamics, as well as educational attainment and economic integration. In this section, we offer a profile of Korean families along these dimensions focusing on family migration, family structure, age, and generation, religion, and cultural values, economic integration and educational attainment.

Where we tend to think of migrants as young unattached adults in search of educational and economic opportunities, overwhelmingly high proportions of Korean immigrants arrived as families with school-aged children (Kim, 2014); and the presence of children creates an incentive to move as parents seek quality of life for their families and social mobility. In 2016, of 160,000 Korean Canadians who had indicated marital status, close to 60 percent of them were married, about 35 percent were never married and not living in common law relationships, and about 4 percent were either divorced or separated (Statistics Canada, 2017). Similarly, in the U.S., close to 60 percent of Asian Americans reported their marital status as married, which was the highest compared to other racial groups (U.S. Census Bureau, 2018b). Specific to Korean families, over two thirds of Korean families were married couples, and about 15 percent of families had children under the age of 18 years living with a single parent (Yu, Choe, & Han, 2002). The lowest divorce or separation status was reported among Koreans, compared to other racial and ethnic groups (Yu et al., 2002).

In terms of age and generation, first-generation Korean immigrants are aging in both countries (Han, Choi, Kim, Lee, & Kim, 2008; Kim, 2014), while, at the same time, second-generation Koreans (i.e., born in the U.S. or Canada) and subsequent generations are increasing in numbers. Specifically, about a third of Korean-Americans were under the age of 25 years (Min & Kim, 2013), representing a large group of children and young adults immersed in multiple cultural contexts, which, in turn, influences their ethnic identities and sense of community, a topic to which we will turn later in the chapter. Such shifts in immigrant generations may be linked to increased rates of interethnic and interracial marriages. For example, interethnic and interracial marriages were more frequently reported among second-generation Korean Americans, particularly among women (Jacobs & Labov, 2002; Kim, 2018), compared to first-generation Koreans.

Despite high rates of ethnic intermarriage, emphasizing and taking pride in one's culture and its traditions – also known as cultural-ethnic socialization – seems to be prevalent among many Asian Americans, regardless of their generational status (Brown & Ling, 2012). This suggests that what Korean Americans find relevant for marriage (i.e., how families are formed), appears to extend beyond ethnicity or cultural-ethnic values and, instead, is closely tied to other social determinants (e.g., gender, socioeconomic status, place of residence and geographic proximity, and social networks) (Lee, 2004). A study examining different aspects of women's interracial marriage indicated that interpersonal similarity (e.g., based on educational and occupational experiences or opportunities) were strong predictors of interracial marriage (Chen & Takeuchi, 2011). Thus, as second and subsequent generation Koreans choose diverse education and work opportunities, they belong to multiple social groups and interethnic and interracial marriages become viable and desirable.

Interethnic and interracial marriages for Korean families is one of the contributing factors to emerging heterogeneity in Korean ethnicity. What it means to be racially and ethnically Korean in the U.S. and Canada is diversifying. One of the fastest growing Korean American populations is biracial/multiracial Koreans (i.e., children of interethnic and interracial marriages that include Korean heritage). They represented 17 percent (about 280,000) of the total Korean American population in 2010. The U.S. Census data reported an 82 percent increase from 2000 to 2010 (Hoeffel, Rastogi, Kim, & Shaid, 2012), and the number is expected to grow because multiracial Korean Americans tend to report higher rates of intermarriage than single-race Korean Americans (Min & Kim, 2013). Mixed-race populations and heterogeneity in Korean ethnicity continue to grow in South Korea as well ("*damunwha*", Kim, 2016), consistent with the emerging trends in the U.S., and Canada. Thus, there is increasing heterogeneity in the lived experiences of Korean families, in terms of how the families are formed and the ways in which Korean ethnicity or identity may be defined by the individuals.

Socio-culturally, local churches are often a centralized place where multiple generations socialize, get exposure to, and practice Korean culture and tradition (Min, 2010), with two thirds of Korean Americans affiliated with Christian churches, for example (Lee, 2019). In Canada, approximately 50 percent were Christian, and the remaining half reported they were either of no religion, Catholic, or Buddhist (Park, 2012). In addition to religious influences, families are shaped by cultural values such as *ga-jok* (family) (Choi, Tan, Yasui, & Hahm, 2016; Kim, 2006).

For many Koreans, the word *Ga-jok* conveys the sentiment of belonging and connection and it carries a strong sense of "we-ness" (*woori*), solidarity, and shared responsibility to one another (Choi & Han, 2008; Yoo, Lee, & Yoo, 2007). This meaning of family relationships is heavily influenced by the historical and sociocultural context for Koreans that emphasizes loyalty, righteousness, respect, trust, and sharing responsibility for the welfare of others (Kim, 2006; Yu et al., 2002). It is believed that the cultural importance of *ga-jok* crystallized in the social climate after the Korean War in the 1950s, which placed many Koreans at risk of experiencing extreme poverty and hardship, and thus compelled nuclear families to unite together and rely on each other for survival (Cheah & Park, 2006), and its continued relevance underscores its intergenerational reproduction. Resilience and adaptation to life stressors and adversity as a collective unit is one of the defining features of Korean families, based on caring relationships among its members, attachment, and exercising flexibility to meet each other's needs (Lee et al., 2004).

The high educational attainment of immigrants, a growing ethnic community, the contemporary nuclear family structure and its concomitant sense of attachment, identity, and duty offered migrating families the class and ethnic capital for certain types of employment. Many first-generation Korean families historically turned to self-employment for their livelihood, such as small business ownership and entrepreneurship, after migration (Kim & Ha, 2010; Thomas & Ong, 2015; Yu et al., 2002). These small businesses ranged from retail (e.g., convenience stores; general merchandising stores; food stores) and clothing/garment businesses (e.g., apparel stores; dry cleaners) to hospitality and service industry (e.g., restaurants; nail salons) (Yang, Colarelli, Han, & Page, 2011). In addition to bank loans, the financial capital to start up the business often came from their own investment and savings, particularly brought from Korea for business migrants (Kim & Ha, 2010), or loans from family members or a close friend (Park, 2010). Korean families who owned small businesses often worked together for very long hours – well over the regular full-time, 40-hour week, which limited their availability for social-cultural integration in the U.S. and Canada. Their overrepresentation in self-employment was possible in part by pooling family labour and resources, which also had the effect of leading to stronger kinship ties and also ties to co-ethnic community members.

Changes to employment trends for Korean families began in the early 2000s (Min, 2013). Self-employment rates decreased among Korean Americans, which was attributed to increasing numbers of second and subsequent-generation Koreans gaining employment opportunities outside of the family business and in other sectors, such as in health care. In a policy report from the IOM Migration Research and Training Centre (Lee, 2016) that was based on the 2014 American Community Survey results, the percentage of Korean Americans who held occupations in the retail trade industry gradually declined from the first generation of immigrants (15 percent) to second and subsequent generations (10 percent). In contrast, for occupations in the professional, scientific, and technical services sector, there was an increase from 9 percent among first-generation Koreans to 14 percent for subsequent generations, and an increase in the health care and social assistance sector as well (from 8 to 13 percent, respectively). Among Korean Canadians, Kim (2010) reported that the three most common occupations were managers from various industries (31 percent), those working in sales and service (24 percent), and professionals in business, finance, and administration (12 percent). Reduced language barriers among recent immigrant families and emerging non-immigrant temporary residents (e.g., international students) also contributed to changes. While small business ownership and entrepreneurship still remain predominant, they now represent the economic experiences of fewer Korean families.

High educational attainment explain recent changes to employment trends. Increasing numbers of second and subsequent-generation Koreans seek employment opportunities outside of family business and in various sectors commensurate with their education. Park (2012) found that in 2006, the majority of Korean Canadian adults over age 25 had one or more combinations of an academic certificate, diploma, or degree, which was four times higher than the general Canadian population in the same age group. Close to 60 percent of first- and second-generation immigrant youth in Canada were attending university in 2006, at a rate that was two times higher than the general population (Sweet, Anisef, Brown, Walters, & Phythian, 2010). About a decade after, in 2016, this pattern was consistent, and the proportion for one or more combinations of an academic certificate, diploma, or degree was 65 percent of Korean Canadians over the age of 15 years (Statistics Canada, 2017), about two thirds of the population. Similar patterns are found in the U.S. Close to 50 percent of the first-generation Korean Americans and 55 percent of the second and subsequent generations of Korean Americans over the age of 25 years had at least a bachelor's degree (Yu et al., 2002), about twice the rate in the general U.S. population. Moreover, according to the 2016 Census Profile, of the 74,000 Korean Canadians who had obtained a university certificate, diploma or degree at the bachelor level or above, about 25 percent of them had a post-graduate education (Statistics Canada, 2017). All of these findings highlight the strong emphasis on education among Korean families in the U.S. and Canada, which, again, is transmitted from generation to generation.

In summary, Koreans in the U.S. and Canada tended to migrate as a nuclear family and maintain a nuclear family structure, they are an aging immigrant population with rising numbers of second and subsequent generations who are interethnic and interracial, and they are kinship-oriented and are influenced by values of respect, trust, and shared responsibility within the family. These characteristics have, in part, also shaped the patterns in employment and educational attainment.

Supporting Korean Families: Ethnic Identity

In light of growing racial and ethnic heterogeneity among young Koreans and families, this first section discusses the factors that may influence the process in which Korean youth negotiate ethnicity and ethnic identity. The focus is on highlighting ethnic identification and cultural-ethnic socialization for Asian Americans, with some studies specific to Korean youth. Then, the findings are integrated to inform practice when supporting ethnic Korean families.

From a psychological perspective, a sense of belonging and feeling connected to family and preferred social groups are critical to the development of identity and individuality, as well as mental well-being. In identity negotiations, bicultural identification was defined as a process in which a person negotiates ethnic identity within the U.S. or Canadian multicultural landscape to achieve a sense of belonging to more than one group (Bulut & Gayman, 2016). Bulut & Gayman's 2016 study with 3271 first-generation Asian and Latino Americans in the U.S. revealed that most of the first-generation Asian Americans were categorized as 'Recent Arrivals' (34 percent) and 'Bicultural' (31 percent). The 'Bicultural' group, which showed strong ties and affinity to both cultures of the U.S. and the ethnic heritage, reported the most adapted mental health functioning, suggesting a potential benefit of maintaining ties to both their new country and the country of origin on individuals' well-being (Bulut & Gayman, 2016). Berry and his colleagues (2006) found a similar pattern in ethnic identification with youth across 13 different countries. Youth who fell in the 'Integration' profile of having high involvement in both their ethnic and national cultures reported the least problems with mental health and school adjustment, compared to youth with other ethnic identification profiles (Berry et al., 2006). With first- and second-generation Korean American youth specifically, the benefit of an 'integrated bicultural identity' with a strong sense of 'being Korean' and ethnic distinction and solidarity in Korean culture (Choi, Tan, et al., 2016) was also documented. It is evident that maintaining ties to one's ethnic heritage and culture, and flexibly integrating those values and cultural practices into one's sense of self, can be beneficial for identity negotiation and individuals' well-being.

However, the dichotomized notion of bicultural identification, as Bulut and Gayman (2016) suggested, may not be encompassing the ethnic identification process often prescribed by Koreans in the U.S. Kim (2010) found that second and subsequent generations of Koreans have begun to create space (e.g., establishing new local churches, as "a self-constructed hybrid third space") that embraced their unique shared identities. At the same time, there is growing recognition of the layering of identities in contrast to a binary perspective, that is, the layering of ethnicity, nationality, race, and panethnicity (Kim, 2018), and the importance of exploring the intersectionality of such identities with gender, sexuality, and social class. Building connections and engaging in dialogues and various social activities through this type of space may have allowed opportunities for healthy cultural-ethnic socialization, as opposed to joining and trying to fit in the pre-existing mainstream or primarily ethnic Korean institutions (Kim, 2010).

Moving away from the dichotomized notion of bicultural identification, when supporting Korean families, helping them to create space for dialogues and engaging in active and intentional process of cultural-ethnic socialization is recommended (Yoon et al., 2017). Cultural-ethnic socialization toward integrated multi-identity may encompass having a right balance of participation in Korean, American/Canadian, and other activities and striving for strong Korean, American/Canadian, and other identities (Choi, Tan, et al., 2016; Kim & Wolpin, 2008; Lee, 2019). Through an active process of cultural-ethnic socialization, parents and practitioners can guide youth to intentionally explore their ethnic heritage and culture and develop a healthy integrated identity. It is worth noting that a high level of perceived discrimination was linked to limited ties to both their ethnic and national cultures (Berry et al., 2006). An active process of cultural-ethnic socialization can provide opportunities to bring attention to explicit and implicit messages related to race and ethnicity that Koreans receive from parents, family members, peers, and in their social contexts. In this process, any negative, stereotypical messages and experiences of perceived discrimination, such as being insulted or feeling unaccepted because of one's race or ethnicity (Berry et al., 2006), can be examined and intervened. Actively making sense of the messages and then negotiating between their multiple social identities may help to developing a healthy integrated one.

An active process of cultural-ethnic socialization will become even more relevant in the future, given on-going trends in interethnic and interracial relationships and contact among different immigrant generations (first, second, and beyond) and different immigrant waves. Such increasing heterogeneity suggests greater variability in how Korean families attempt to preserve, negotiate or re-define values and traditions through cultural-ethnic socialization. Some Korean families, with the determination, capacity, resources, and opportunity, will integrate multiple social identities and different values into their everyday lives while others may struggle to integrate these multiple layers in a meaningful way. For the latter, difficulties in cultural-ethnic socialization can have a particularly detrimental impact on parenting practices and formation of identities for young people (Kim, Knudson-Martin, & Tuttle, 2018; Roopnarine, Krishnakumar, Narine, Logie, & Lape, 2014). Rather than leaving families on their own to struggle between different values and cultural practices, this issue can be recognized and addressed at the community level through coordinated programs of their choice, with ample opportunities for healthy cultural-ethnic socialization and for promoting the family and its members' psychological well-being (Paik, Rahman, Kula, Saito, & Witenstein, 2017). Lastly, cultural-ethnic socialization may be perceived differently for multiracial Koreans, who primarily self-identify as American or Canadian given their place of birth and cultural upbringing, but are also treated as 'others' because of their appearances (Kim et al., 2019). However, the literature in this area is limited. Further research is warranted to explore their unique processes of cultural-ethnic socialization.

In summary, the benefit of 'integrated bicultural identity' is evident for Korean families and their well-being. However, creating space that embraces building connections and engaging in dialogues about shared and layered identities seem more suited for Korean families, as opposed to having to subscribe to the dichotomized notion of bicultural identification. The active and intentional process of cultural-ethnic socialization, which also includes helping people to make sense of the experiences of perceived discrimination and stereotypical messages and to effectively challenge them, is recommended for Korean American and Korean Canadian families.

Supporting Korean Families: Balancing Roles

Focusing on the distinctive cultural values within Korean families, this last section presents literature on roles and responsibilities specifically relevant to Korean families in the U.S. and Canada, in order to inform practice to promote healthy family functioning. We highlight key literature on common roles and responsibilities and then integrate the findings to inform practice when supporting Korean families.

The nuclear family structure and propensity to respond to life events as a collective unit, members within Korean families embody human, cultural, and social capital. It is common then for adult children of Korean families to take on the roles of providing emotional, physical, and financial support for parents when they become older (Choi, Kushner, Mill, & Lai, 2014; Kim, 2014). Accepting a language or cultural brokering role is often the norm and what is expected in being part of an immigrant family. Korean children and young adults often become the advocates and the lens through which their parents navigate the "post-migration world" (Yoo & Kim, 2014). Many Korean parents also make choices and sacrifices in their parenting roles for children, such as relocating to a different city with a better education system and good quality of life (Yoon, 2016) or investing in children's achievement-oriented goals (Cho & Shin, 2008). Being deeply kinship-oriented, a family unit can be a tremendous source of strength and support.

As discussed, when an external social support system is not well established, Korean families rely on their own resources (Bernstein, 2007). Also specific to first-generation families, frequent interactions between family members for the purpose of adjustments and survival in the new country were associated with improved family functioning in the short-term (Rothbaum, Morelli, Pott, & Liu-Constant, 2000). Korean American children who arrived in the U.S. with their parents were less likely to report psychological problems in the short-term than children whose families had separated (Suárez-Orozco, Bang, & Kim, 2010). Cohesive immigrant families that spend more time as a family unit allow each member the opportunity to experience a strong sense of belonging (Chung & Lim, 2014), especially during a time of transition.

An over-reliance on family support and resources alone could, however, lead to social isolation and stress, which may result in an increased level of family conflict (Moon, 2008). Studies on language brokering clearly support this complexity: bilingual Korean children who apply their language skills to advocate and make decisions for their family unit feel both empowered and strained by their imposed roles (Guan, Greenfield, & Orellana, 2014; Kwon, 2014; Shen, Kim, Wang, & Chao, 2014). Moreover, young adults who are second-generation Korean Americans reported that they recognized and often internalized their immigrant parents' hardship and sacrifices while growing up (Kang, Okazaki, Abelmann, Kim-Prieto, & Lan, 2010).

Striving for collective harmony and family goals at the expense of individuality can pose an intricate challenge. For Korean families, parents' relationship as a couple may be less prioritized over their parenting responsibilities or commitment to ensure the well-being of children and the family as a whole (Kim, 2013). Given the strong feeling of connectedness ("we-ness") and shared responsibility within many Korean families, how one member of the family behaves is thought to reflect positively or negatively on other family members and the family as a whole. One family member failing to meet expectations, for instance, can induce a feeling of shame among the whole family, as if the other members see it as a failure on their parts (Castillo & Phoummarath, 2006; Kim, Omizo, & Salvador, 1996).

Taken together, for Korean families in the U.S. and Canada, the weight and importance of family relationships requires a healthy balance. It may become a "double-edged sword" when various family roles are in conflict with other important personal values (Park, Butcher, & Maas, 2004), such as personal satisfaction, freedom of choice, and individuality, all of which are highly valued in Western culture. At the extreme end of role conflict, an individual's well-being may be sacrificed to keep the family intact, such as not reporting domestic violence, elder abuse, or addictions, to prevent perceived shame brought onto the whole family (Choi, Elkins, & Disney, 2016). Promoting through effective communication the development of individuality and external social networks and support, while family members remain cohesive will likely lead to better long-term outcomes. Also, some families may continue to draw upon the support of their family members and their resources in times of struggle, in addition to or instead of seeking resources from external resources (Park, Turnbull, & Park, 2001). Providing validation to such resourcefulness and strength within the family will be crucial before gradually introducing new strategies and working together with families to determine which available supports would work best for their unique circumstances.

There is a clear need for more research to understand the increasingly nuanced social, cultural, economic, psychological, and environmental factors that intersect and influence Korean families living in the U.S. and Canada. We are only beginning to understand how these factors may be integrated into the personal and social identities of being Korean. A thorough exploration is warranted to examine the intersectionality of these socially constructed identities (Kim et al., 2018; Kwon, 2014; Seaton, Caldwell, Sellers, & Jackson, 2010) for Korean families and their link to well-being. In summary, to inform practice, raising awareness of the kinship-oriented roles and family relationships among Korean families is recommended. Each family will have a unique history and circumstances (Schmidtke, 2012) and just as an integrated bicultural identity is beneficial to the well-being of Koreans, it will be critical to work *together* with Korean families to reflect on how they can be supported in balancing various family roles and other important personal values.

Conclusion

This chapter provided a brief overview of the literature on Korean families in the U.S. and Canada. What it means to be racially and ethnically Korean is rapidly changing in the contemporary period with recent events highlighting racial inequality and microaggressions, and while they share some experiences with other racialized, ethnic, and immigrant groups, Koreans families remain distinct in particular ways. Over time and generations, Koreans in both Canada and the U.S. shift and evolve, and at present, we find some combination of long-term migrants, newcomers, temporary residents (i.e. international students), refugees (i.e. North Koreans) and members of the second and third generations. Both countries share a diversity of Korean people within their borders but differ slightly in their composition. For example, Koreans in the U.S. have a longer history, and there is a greater proportion of native-born Koreans in the U.S. than in Canada.

High levels of education and self-employment along with a growing number of multi-ethnic children through interethnic and interracial unions characterize communities in both places. At the same time, there is evidence that, for some, there are significant issues related to stress and mental well-being particularly among socially isolated families and individuals. Experiences of discrimination are also present leading to different types of coping strategies (Kim, 2018). With the resources available in and external to Korean communities, members established institutions sensitive to Korean culture and language in many urban centres. These ethnic organizations and those external to the community can be effective sources of support. In future, we expect further composition shifts in the Korean population in terms of immigrant generation and multi-ethnic individuals, as well as institutional changes to address emerging issues in both countries.

Acknowledgments The first author acknowledges and expresses gratitude to the members of her Academic Breadth Comprehensive Paper committee for their support on an earlier version of this manuscript.

References

Bernstein, K. (2007). Mental health issues among urban Korean American immigrants. *Journal of Transcultural Nursing, 18*, 175–180. https://doi.org/10.1177/1043659606298610

Berry, J. W., Phinney, J. S., Sam, D. L., & Vedder, P. (2006). Immigrant youth: Acculturation, identity, and adaptation. *Applied Psychology, 55*, 303–332. https://doi.org/10.1111/j.1464-0597.2006.00256.x

Brown, C. M., & Ling, W. (2012). Ethnic-racial socialization has an indirect effect on self-esteem for Asian American emerging adults. *Psychology, 3*, 78–81. https://doi.org/10.4236/psych.2012.31013

Bulut, E., & Gayman, M. D. (2016). Acculturation and self-rated mental health among Latino and Asian immigrants in the United States: A Latent class analysis. *Journal of Immigrant and Minority Health, 18*, 836–849. https://doi.org/10.1007/s10903-015-0258-1

Castillo, L. G., & Phoummarath, M. J. (2006). Culturally-competent school counseling with Asian American adolescents. *Journal of School Counseling, 4*, 1–19.

Cheah, C. S. L., & Park, S. Y. (2006). South Korean mothers' beliefs regarding aggression and social withdrawal in preschoolers. *Early Childhood Research Quarterly, 21*, 61–75. https://doi.org/10.1016/j.ecresq.2006.01.004

Chen, J., & Takeuchi, D. T. (2011). Intermarriage, ethnic identity, and perceived social standing among Asian women in the United States. *Journal of Marriage and Family, 73*, 876–888. https://doi.org/10.1111/j.1741-3737.2011.00853.x

Cho, E. K., & Shin, S. (2008). Survival, adjustment, and acculturation of newly immigrated families with school-age children: Cases of four Korean families. *Diaspora, Indigenous, and Minority Education, 2*, 4–24. https://doi.org/10.1080/15595690701752351

Choi, J., Kushner, K., Mill, J., & Lai, D. (2014). The experience of Korean immigrant women adjusting to Canadian society. *Journal of Cross-Cultural Gerontology, 29*, 277–297. https://doi.org/10.1007/s10823-014-9235-8

Choi, S. C., & Han, G. (2008). Shimcheong psychology: A case of an emotional state for cultural psychology. *International Journal for Dialogical Science, 3*, 205–224. http://ijds.lemoyne.edu/journal/3_1/pdf/IJDS.3.1.15.Choi_Han.pdf

Choi, Y., Tan, K. P. H., Yasui, M., & Hahm, H. C. (2016). Advancing understanding of acculturation for adolescents of Asian immigrants: Person-oriented analysis of acculturation strategy among Korean American Youth. *Journal of Youth and Adolescence, 45*, 1380–1395. https://doi.org/10.1007/s10964-016-0496-0

Choi, Y. J., Elkins, J., & Disney, L. (2016). A literature review of intimate partner violence among immigrant populations: Engaging the faith community. *Aggression and Violence Behavior, 29*, 1–9. https://doi.org/10.1016/j.avb.2016.05.004

Chung, G. H., & Lim, J. Y. (2014). Understanding sense of neighbourhood community in Korean adolescents: Its relation to adolescent well-being and the role of parents. *International Journal of Adolescence and Youth, 19*, 350–365. https://doi.org/10.1080/02673843.2012.747971

Dorman, K., Bozinoff, N., Redditt, V., Kim, E., Glazier, R. H., & Rashid, M. (2017). Health status of North Korean refugees in Toronto: A community based participatory research study. *Journal of Immigrant & Minority Health, 19*, 15–23. https://doi.org/10.1007/s10903-015-0307-9

Finch, J., & Kim, S. K. (2012). Kirŏgi families in the US: Transnational migration and education. *Journal of Ethnic and Migration Studies, 38*, 485–506. https://doi.org/10.1080/1369183X.2012.658548

Guan, S. S. A., Greenfield, P. M., & Orellana, M. F. (2014). Translating into understanding: Language brokering and prosocial development in emerging adults from immigrant families. *Journal of Adolescent Research, 29*, 331–355. https://doi.org/10.1177/0743558413520223

Han, H.-R., Choi, Y. J., Kim, M. T., Lee, J. E., & Kim, K. B. (2008). Experiences and challenges of informal caregiving for Korean immigrants. *Journal of Advanced Nursing, 63*, 517–526. https://doi.org/10.1111/j.1365-2648.2008.04746.x

Hoeffel, E. M., Rastogi, S., Kim, M. O., & Shaid, H. (2012). The Asian Population: 2010. *2010 Census Briefs*. United States Census Bureau, U.S. Department of Commerce. https://www.census.gov/prod/cen2010/briefs/c2010br-11.pdf. Accessed July 21, 2018.

Hong, J. S., Peguero, A. A., Choi, S., Lanesskog, D., Espelage, D. L., & Lee, N. Y. (2014). Social ecology of bullying and peer victimization of Latino and Asian youth in the United States: A review of the literature. *Journal of School Violence, 13*, 315–338. https://doi.org/10.1080/15388220.2013.856013

Jacobs, J. A., & Labov, T. G. (2002). Gender differentials in intermarriage among sixteen race and ethnic groups. *Sociological Forum, 17*, 621–646. https://doi.org/10.1023/A:1021029507937

Jang, Y., Park, N. S., Chiriboga, D. A., Yoon, H., An, S., & Kim, M. T. (2015). Social capital in ethnic communities and mental health: A study of older Korean immigrants. *Journal of Cross-Cultural Gerontology, 30*, 131–141. https://doi.org/10.1007/s10823-015-9258-9

Jeong, Y. J., You, H. K., & Kwon, Y. I. (2014). One family in two countries: Mothers in Korean transnational families. *Ethnic and Racial Studies, 37*, 1546–1564. https://doi.org/10.1080/01419870.2012.758861

Joo, R. M., & Lee, S. S. (Eds.). (2018). *A companion to Korean American studies*. https://doi.org/10.1163/9789004335332

Kang, H., Okazaki, S., Abelmann, N., Kim-Prieto, C., & Lan, S. (2010). Redeeming immigrant parents: How Korean American emerging adults reinterpret their childhood. *Journal of Adolescent Research, 25*, 441–464. https://doi.org/10.1177/0743558410361371

Kim, A. H. (2014). Retiring immigrants: Korean seniors' lives after migration to Canada. In T. R. Klassen & Y. Yang (Eds.), *Korea's retirement predicament: The ageing tiger* (pp. 131–145). Routledge.

Kim, A. H. (2015). Structuring transnationalism: The mothering discourse and the educational project. In G. C. Man & R. Cohen (Eds.), *Engendering transnational voices: Studies in family, work, and identity*. Wilfred Laurier Press.

Kim, A. H. (2018). Korean ethnicity and Asian American panethnicity. In R. M. Joo & S. S. Lee (Eds.), *A companion to Korean American studies* (pp. 333–355). Brill.

Kim, A. H., & Ha, Y. (2010). The economic integration of Koreans in Canada: Self-employment and social integration. *Final Report*. York University.

Kim, A. H., & Kwak, M. J. (2019). *Outward and upward mobilities: International students in Canada, their families, and structuring institutions*. University of Toronto Press.
Kim, A. H., Noh, M. S., & Noh, S. (2012). Introduction: Historical context and contemporary research. In S. Noh, A. H. Kim, & M. S. Noh (Eds.), *Korean immigrants in Canada* (pp. 3–18). University of Toronto Press.
Kim, A. H., Yun, S. H., Park, W., & Noh, S. (2012). Explaining the migration strategy: Comparing transnational and intact migrant families from South Korea to Canada. In P. G. Min (Ed.), *Koreans in North America: Their experiences in the twenty-first century* (pp. 103–119). Lexington Books.
Kim, B. S., Omizo, M. M., & Salvador, D. S. (1996). Culturally relevant counseling services for Korean American children: A systematic approach. *Elementary School Guidance & Counseling, 31*, 64–73. https://www.jstor.org/stable/42869172
Kim, E., & Wolpin, S. (2008). The Korean American family: Adolescents versus parents acculturation to American culture. *Journal of Cultural Diversity, 15*, 108–116. PMID: 19025199, PMCID: PMC2702242.
Kim, H. A. (2016). Biracial identity development: A case of Black-Korean biracial individuals in Korea. *International Journal of Multicultural Education, 18*, 40–57. https://doi.org/10.18251/ijme.v18i3.1193
Kim, K. (2006). Hyo and parenting in Korea. In K. H. Rubin & O. B. Chung (Eds.), *Parenting beliefs, behaviors, and parent-child relations: A cross-cultural perspective* (pp. 207–222). Psychology Press.
Kim, L., Knudson-Martin, C., & Tuttle, A. (2018). Transmission of intergenerational migration legacies in Korean American families: Parenting the third generation. *Contemporary Family Therapy*. Advance online publication. https://doi.org/10.1007/s10591-018-9485-7.
Kim, L., Knudson-Martin, C., & Tuttle, A. (2019). Transmission of intergenerational migration legacies in Korean American families: Parenting the third generation. *Contemporary Family Therapy, 41*, 180–190. https://doi.org/10.1007/s10591-018-9485-7
Kim, S. (2010). *A faith of our own: Second-generation spirituality in Korean American churches*. New Jersey: Rutgers University Press.
Kim, S. (2013). Re-discovering voice: Korean immigrant women in group music therapy. *The Arts in Psychotherapy, 40*, 428–435. https://doi.org/10.1016/j.aip.2013.05.005
Kwon, H. (2014). The hidden injury of class in Korean-American language brokers' lives. *Childhood, 21*, 56–71. https://doi.org/10.1177/0907568213483597
Lee, C. W. (2016). Generational comparisons of socioeconomic characteristics among Korean Americans and policy implications. *IOM MRTC Policy Report Series. No. 2016-04*. Goyang-si, Republic of Korea: IOM Migration Research and Training Centre.
Lee, J. Y. (2019). Living as a non-Christian in a Christian community: Experiences of religious marginalisation amongst young Korean Americans. *Journal of Ethnic and Migration Studies, 45*, 2062–2077. https://doi.org/10.1080/1369183X.2018.1427565
Lee, S. S. (2004). Marriage dilemma: Partner choices and constraints for Korean Americans in New York City. In J. Lee & M. Zhou (Eds.), *Asian American youth: Culture, identity, and ethnicity* (pp. 285–298). Temple University Press.
Lee, I., Lee, E. O., Kim, H. S., Park, Y. S., Song, M., & Park, Y. H. (2004). Concept development of family resilience: A study of Korean families with a chronically ill child. *Journal of Clinical Nursing, 13*, 636–645. https://doi.org/10.1111/j.1365-2702.2004.00845.x
Min, P. G. (2010). *Preserving ethnicity through religion in America: Korean Protestants and Indian Hindus across generations*. New York, NY: NYU Press.
Min, P.G. (2013). *The Korean Community in the United States: Changes in the Twenty-First Century*. Paper presented at the International Conference on Korean Diaspora Studies, Korea University. http://www.koreanamericandatabank.org/data-bank/item/73-korea-university-paper-min-september-28-2013.html
Min, P. G., & Kim, C. (2013). Growth and settlement patterns of Korean Americans. In P. G. Min (Ed.), *Koreans in North America: Their experiences in the twenty-first century* (pp. 35–56). Lexington Books.

Moon, S. S. (2008). Acculturation, social support, and family conflict: Korean–American adolescents' perceptions. *Child and Adolescent Social Work Journal, 25*, 227–240. https://doi.org/10.1007/s10560-008-0123-3

O'Connor, A. & Batalova, J. (2019). Korean immigrants in the United States. *Migration Information Source*. April 10. https://www.migrationpolicy.org/article/korean-immigrants-united-states

Paik, S. J., Rahman, Z., Kula, S. M., Saito, L. E., & Witenstein, M. A. (2017). Ethnic afterschool programs and language schools in diverse Asian American communities: Varying resources, opportunities, and educational experiences. *School Community Journal, 27*, 67–97. http://www.schoolcommunitynetwork.org/SCJ.aspx

Park, J. (2012). A demographic profile of Koreans in Canada. In S. Noh, A. H. Kim, & M. S. Noh (Eds.), *Korean immigrants in Canada* (pp. 72–87). University of Toronto Press.

Park, J., Turnbull, A. P., & Park, H. S. (2001). Quality of partnerships in service provision for Korean American parents of children with disabilities: A qualitative inquiry. *Journal of the Association for Persons with Severe Handicaps, 26*, 158–170. https://doi.org/10.2511/rpsd.26.3.158

Park, K. (2010). Sources and resources of Korean immigrant entrepreneurship. *Critical Sociology, 36*, 891–896. https://doi.org/10.1177/0896920510377263

Park, M., Butcher, H. K., & Maas, M. L. (2004). A thematic analysis of korean family caregivers' experiences in making the decision to place a family member with dementia in a long-term care facility. *Research in Nursing & Health, 27*, 345–356. https://doi.org/10.1002/nur.20031

Rothbaum, F., Morelli, G., Pott, M., & Liu-Constant, Y. (2000). Immigrant-Chinese and euro-American parents' physical closeness with young children: Themes of family relatedness. *Journal of Family Psychology, 14*, 334–348. https://doi.org/10.1037//0893-3200.14.3.334

Roopnarine, J. L., Krishnakumar, A., Narine, L., Logie, C., & Lape, M. E. (2014). Relationships between parenting practices and preschoolers' social skills in African, Indo, and mixed-ethnic families in Trinidad and Tobago: The mediating role of ethnic socialization. *Journal of Cross-Cultural Psychology, 45*, 362–380. https://doi.org/10.1177/0022022113509884

Schmidtke, O. (2012). *Citizenship and multiculturalism in the 21st century: The changing face of social, cultural, and civic inclusion* [PDF document]. Metropolis British Columbia Working Paper Series: http://mbc.metropolis.net/assets/uploads/files/wp/2012/WP12-06.pdf

Seaton, E. K., Caldwell, C. H., Sellers, R. M., & Jackson, J. S. (2010). An intersectional approach for understanding perceived discrimination and psychological well-being among African American and Caribbean Black youth. *Developmental Psychology, 46*, 1372–1379. https://doi.org/10.1037/a0019869

Shen, Y., Kim, S. Y., Wang, Y., & Chao, R. K. (2014). Language brokering and adjustment among Chinese and Korean American adolescents: A moderated mediation model of perceived maternal sacrifice, respect for the mother, and mother–child open communication. *Asian American Journal of Psychology, 5*, 86–95. https://doi.org/10.1037/a0035203

Statistics Canada. (2017). *Canada [Country] and Canada [Country]* (table). *Census Profile*. 2016 Census. Statistics Canada Catalogue no. 98-316-X2016001. Ottawa. Released November 29, 2017. https://www12.statcan.gc.ca/census-recensement/2016/dp-pd/prof/index.cfm?Lang=E. Accessed May 23, 2019.

Suárez-Orozco, C., Bang, H. J., & Kim, H. Y. (2010). I felt like my heart was staying behind: Psychological implications of family separations & reunifications for immigrant youth. *Journal of Adolescent Research, 26*, 222–257. https://doi.org/10.1177/0743558410376830

Sweet, R., Anisef, P., Brown, R., Walters, D., & Phythian, K. (2010). *Post-high school pathways of immigrant youth*. Higher Education Quality Council of Ontario.

Thomas, W. F., & Ong, P. M. (2015). Ethnic mobilization among Korean dry-cleaners. *Ethnic and Racial Studies, 38*, 2108–2122. https://doi.org/10.1080/01419870.2015.1036092

U.S. Census Bureau. (2018a). *Asian alone by selected groups, 2018 American Community Survey 1-year estimates*. https://data.census.gov/cedsci/all?q=korean%20family&hidePreview=false&tid=ACSDT1Y2018.C02015&vintage=2018

U.S. Census Bureau (2018b). *Marital status, American Community Survey 1-year estimates*. https://data.census.gov/cedsci/table?q=S1201&tid=ACSST1Y2018.S1201

Yang, C., Colarelli, S. M., Han, K., & Page, R. (2011). Start-up and hiring practices of immigrant entrepreneurs: An empirical study from an evolutionary psychological perspective. *International Business Review, 20*, 636–645. https://doi.org/10.1016/j.ibusrev.2011.02.016

Yoo, G. J., & Kim, B. W. (2014). *Caring across generations: The linked lives of Korean American families*. NYU Press.

Yoo, Y. J., Lee, I., & Yoo, G. (2007). How strong families encounter social challenges in the Republic of Korea. *Marriage & Family Review, 41*, 195–216. https://doi.org/10.1300/J002v41n01_10

Yoo, Y. S. (2002). Canada and Korea: A shared history. In R. W. L. Guisso & Y. S. Yoo (Eds.), *Canada and Korea: Perspectives 2000* (pp. 9–44). Centre for Korean Studies, University of Toronto.

Yoon, E., Adams, K., Clawson, A., Chang, H., Surya, S., & Jérémie-Brink, G. (2017). East Asian adolescents' ethnic identity development and cultural integration: A qualitative investigation. *Journal of Counseling Psychology, 64*, 65–79. https://doi.org/10.1037/cou0000181

Yoon, H. (2016). Family strategies in a neoliberal world: Korean immigrants in Winnipeg. *GeoJournal, 81*, 243–256. https://doi.org/10.1007/s10708-014-9616-0

Yoon, I.-J. (2012). The Korean diaspora from global perspectives. In S. Noh, A. H. Kim, & M. S. Noh (Eds.), *Korean immigrants in Canada* (pp. 37–52). University of Toronto Press.

Yu, E., Choe, P., & Han, S. (2002). Korean population in the United States, 2000: Demographic characteristics and socio-economic status. *International Journal of Korean Studies, 6*, 71–107. http://icks.org/n/data/ijks/1482456493_add_file_4.pdf

Part III
Specific Countries and Regions of Origin: South Asia

Chapter 8
Bangladeshi Families

Abdul Khaleque

Abstract This paper presents an overview of changing patterns of family relations, family norms and values, and socio-cultural lives of Bangladeshi immigrant families in new socio-cultural settings in the United States and Canada. The paper specifically focuses on a brief immigration history, basic demographic information, acculturation and identity issues, family relations, gender roles and family systems, educational achievement, career development, income, and health and well-being of Bangladeshi families in North America. Ideas and information that are presented may be useful to researchers, professionals, and practitioners who are working on family problems including parent-child conflicts, generation gaps in acculturation, cultural alienation, and cultural adaptation of Bangladeshi families in the United States and Canada.

Keywords Bangladeshi families · Acculturation and ethnic identities · Value systems · Health and well-being

The United States and Canada are two multicultural countries in North America consisting of people of different ethno-cultural groups from many parts of the world. The multicultural ideology of the majority ethnic group of a country constitutes a fundamental element in intergroup relations, and determines the policy options for managing cultural diversity within a society, and also defines the constraints of the acculturation processes for immigrant communities (Berry, 2001). Positive or negative attitudes towards multicultural ideology of the majority ethnic groups can influence acculturation processes, cultural orientations, and cultural adaptions of immigrant communities of a country. A positive attitude implies a combination of positive views on cultural maintenance of ethnic groups and an appreciation of the need for accommodation of diversity in an equitable manner. This ideology emphasizes a balance between unity and diversity within a society (Citrin, Sears, Muste, & Wong, 2001). In this context, this paper focuses on the

A. Khaleque (✉)
University of Connecticut, Storrs, CT, USA
e-mail: Abdul.khaleque@uconn.edu

S. S. Chuang et al. (eds.), *Asian Families in Canada and the United States*, Advances in Immigrant Family Research,
https://doi.org/10.1007/978-3-030-56452-0_8

acculturation problems of a growing ethnic minority in Canada and the United States from Bangladesh.

Most of the Bangladeshi immigrant families in North America are settled in the United States and Canada. Although the Bangladeshi immigrant population currently constitutes only about 0.5% (approximate total number is 277,000) of the US foreign born population (Migration Policy Institute, 2014), and approximately 100,000–110,000 in Canada (Statistics Canada, 2016), they are one of the fastest growing immigrant communities in both the countries. The Bengali ethno-linguistic diaspora in North America are in fact not exclusively represented by the immigrants from Bangladesh, they also include a broader Bengali ethno-linguistic immigrant community originating from the Indian State of West Bengal (current official name is Bengal) and parts of Tripura and Assam (MPI, 2014).

To better understand the Bangladeshi families and communities, the chapter provides a brief history of immigration of the Bengali population in North America including their ethnic and linguistic differences, education and income, religious beliefs, sociocultural traditions and values, marital systems, family forms and family relationships, cultural identity, socialization and acculturation problems.

Brief Immigration History

Bangladesh became an independent country in 1971. Prior to 1971, it was a part of Pakistan, known as East Pakistan. The history of immigration of the Bengali population in the United States goes back to the pre-independent period, but their number was very small. Originally, the Bangladeshis started migrating to the port cities of the United States since 1974. Most of the first immigrants were workers on the various ships and hailed from the Sylhet, Chittagong, and Noakhali regions of Bangladesh. Most of the dock workers came from these three districts of Bangladesh. Immigration from Bangladesh to the United States grew slowly but steadily during the 1970s–1980s (Bald, 2013). Since the 1980s, more than ten thousand Bangladeshi immigrants have entered the United States annually (Yearbook of Immigration Statistics, 2012).

Since the 1960s, the Bengali professionals who came to Canada for higher education, as well as professional training, began to settle down as immigrants in Canada. The migration had increased over the later decades and continuing in the 1980s through the 2010s (Bangladesh High Commission, 2019). As in the United States, the immigration of Bangladeshis to Canada takes place in different categories such as: professionals, skilled workers, political refugees seeking asylum, family members and other relatives of the existing immigrants, diversity visa program (only in the US) etc. (Bangladesh High Commission, 2019).

Ethnic and Linguistic Differences Among Bangladeshi Immigrants

The current population of Bangladesh is about 166 million. Approximately 98% of the total population belongs to the major ethnic group—Bengalis who speak Bangla as their first language. These tribal groups speak different dialects, although most of them can speak Bangla, which is the national language of Bangladesh. Different tribal groups have different cultural entities and lifestyles including languages, food habits, dress patterns, family and marriage systems and religions. They live in different regions of Bangladesh (Khaleque, 2016).

Demographic Information

This section provides a brief account about the growth rates of Bangladeshi population in the United States and Canada, including their concentration in different parts of these two countries; and their education, employment and poverty level. It also contains discussion about the cultural traditions, religious beliefs and practices of this ethnic group.

The United States

Although Bangladeshi Americans constitute less than 1% of the United States' population, they are the third largest among South Asian immigrants in the United States (U.S. Census Report, 2010). Patterns of population growth of South Asian immigrants in the U.S. revealed that while population increases have occurred across all these subgroups from 1990 to 2000, the size of Bangladeshi immigrants has increased dramatically (248%) (U.S. Census Report, 2000, 2010).

Bangladeshi immigrants are concentrated mainly in four States—California, New Jersey, New York, and Texas. The largest number (52%) of Bangladeshis live in New York (Kibria, 2006; Singh, 2003), particularly in New York City, where Bangladeshis were the sixth largest Asian subgroup in the year 2000 (Asian American Federation of New York Census Information Center, 2005). The Bangladeshi community in New York City is spread out in different parts of the city with the highest concentration in the Queens borough. According to Asian American Federation Census Information Center (2013), the total Bangladeshi population in New York City is 50,677. The concentration of Bangladeshi populations in different boroughs of New York City are: Queens (60%), Brooklyn (19%), Bronx (17%), and Manhattan (4%). The Bangladeshi immigrant population growth rate in the US during 2000–2010 is 74% (Foreign-born Bangladeshis).

Canada

As of 2016, there are about 110,000 Bangladeshi immigrants who are living in Canada, and this number is steadily increasing every year (Statistics Canada, 2016). They live primarily in the provinces of Alberta, British Columbia, Ontario, Quebec, and Saskatchewan, with a high concentration in major cities such as Calgary and Edmonton (Alberta), Vancouver (British Columbia), Toronto and Ottawa (Ontario), Montreal (Quebec), and Regina (Saskatchewan). More specifically, the majority of Bangladeshi communities live in the greater Toronto area, Montreal, and Vancouver with the highest number of Bangladeshis (about 100,000) living in the province of Ontario. Prior to 1991, the total number of Bangladeshi immigrants were only 4,325, but by 2006 this number rose to 33,230. Thus, within the period of 15 years (1991–2006), 28,905 Bangladeshis immigrated to Canada (Statistics Canada, 2006). Like many other immigrant communities, Bangladeshi immigrants also prefer to live in big cities for several reasons, such as greater opportunities for education, and support from friends and extended families who are also living in big cities. In addition, Bangladeshi immigrants in Canada and the United States also prefer to live in big cities for greater employment opportunity, and business facilities.

Educational Achievement, Employment, and Career Development

Bangladeshi immigrants, though a small ethnic minority, make significant contributions to the educational and economic development of the United States. Specifically, the educational, professional, and economic attainments of Bangladeshi Americans are sometimes better than that of most other ethnic groups in the U.S., including majority European Americans. For example, about 53% of US-born Bangladeshis are college graduates, whereas about 29% of European Americans are college graduates; 30% of Bangladeshi Americans are employed in professional jobs with median annual incomes of $54,000, whereas about 23% of European Americans are employed in professional jobs with median annual incomes of $53,400. Finally, the percentage of Bangladeshi American families below the Federal poverty level is approximately zero, whereas about 5% of European American families live below the poverty level (U.S. Census Report, 2000).

For Canada, the majority of Bangladeshi families live in the greater Toronto metropolitan area. In one study (Murdie & Ghosh, 2012), although about 51% of Bangladeshi adults living in Toronto had a college education, the average household annual income of the Bangladeshi families was $33,925 (Canadian dollars), which is below the national average household income of Canada. In addition, the number of low-income Bangladesh families in Canada was more than 60%.

Many Bangladeshi Canadians are self-employed. They run medium and small business establishments, such as restaurants, gas stations, groceries, and boutiques, selling clothing and other goods everywhere in Canada. Similarly, a large number of Bangladeshi immigrants run restaurants, grocery stores, gas stations, clothing and fabric stores in all the major cities of the U.S.. Many Bangladeshis work in the transport industries of the United States. For example, about 10% of taxi drivers in New York City are from Bangladesh.

Value Systems

Religion

Islam is the religion of the majority of Bangladeshi immigrants, and a small number of Bangladeshi immigrants follow other religions including Hinduism, Buddhism, and Christianity. Approximately 90% of Bengalis are Muslims, 8% are Hindus, and 2% consist of other religious groups, such as Christians, Buddhists, etc. Similarly, most of the Bangladeshi immigrants in North America are Muslim.

Religion plays an important role in the life of Bangladeshi families. There are mosques in most big cities and many smaller towns in the U.S. and Canada. They usually go to a nearby mosque to attend weekly congregational prayers on Fridays, and two Eid prayers yearly.

Bangladeshi immigrants also participate in and contribute to the larger Islamic community, which includes immigrant communities from other Muslim countries. Although most Bangladeshi immigrants in North America are Muslims, there are also some Hindu immigrant families within the cultural mosaic of Bangladeshi community. Bangladeshi Muslims and Hindus in North America have a well-knit and peaceful relationship. There are a few temples and religious congregations in the United States and Canada operated by Bangladeshi Hindus (Bangladesh High Commission, 2019). Since the number of Bangladeshi Hindus is small, they often have contact with Bengali Hindus from West Bengal and other parts of India. The Bangladeshi community in North America joins in celebrating American and Canadian festivals, such as New Year, Independence Day, and Thanksgiving, and they also celebrate religious holidays (Bangladesh High Commission, 2019).

For Muslim Bangladeshis, the two most important holidays are Eid-ul-Fitr at the end of Ramadan-- the month of fasting, and Eid-ul-Azha---the festival of sacrifice, during Hajj--the pilgrimage to Mecca. For Hindu Bangladeshis, important holidays are Diwali--the festival of lights, celebrating the return home of the lord Rama, and Holi---the festival of colors that welcomes the return of spring. In addition, Hindus perform different types of *pujas (prayers)* in honor of various gods and goddesses. In addition to religious holidays, other noteworthy cultural festivals are Pohela Boisakh (Bengali New Year), Ekushe February (International Mother Language Day), and Bijoy Dibosh (Victory day), the day when Bangladesh was liberated from Pakistani occupation (Bangladesh High Commission, 2019).

Cultural Traditions and Social Services

Culturally, Bangladeshi immigrants in North America are very active, which is evident in their participation in all Bangladeshi national festivities with much enthusiasm and vigor. Like other Asian immigrant communities, Bangladeshi communities in North America are very conscious and active to maintain their cultural heritage including their food habits, traditional costumes, dance and music (New Age, 2018).

Bangladeshi cuisine is very popular among the Bangladeshi communities. There are Bangladeshi restaurants in all the big cities of the United States and Canada. Rice is the staple food or main course for Bangladeshis. They also eat a variety of fish, vegetables, and meats, except pork which is forbidden by Islamic tradition. Bangladeshi cuisine is also famous for a variety of milk-based desserts (Ahsan, 2015).

The traditional costumes of Bangladeshi immigrant males and females are different. Men usually wear pants and shirts, women usually wear *salwar-chamise* (loose pants and a long shirt combination in vibrant colors) or *sari*. For religious reasons, Bangladeshi Muslim women cover their heads. On traditional occasions, such as religious and marriage ceremonies, men tend to wear *pajama* (loose-fitting cotton trousers) and *panjabi* or *korta* (loose-fitting, collarless, and knee-length shirt), and Bangladeshi women mostly wear *sari* (Ahsan, 2015).

Bangladeshi people have a rich cultural tradition of music and dance. This tradition has remained alive among Bangladeshi communities in North America. During holidays and festivals, they organize concerts and perform Bangladeshi dance, song, and drama, and recite Bengali poetry. The major categories of Bengali music include classical music, folk songs, Tagore songs, Nazrul songs, patriotic songs, devotional songs, and modern Bengali songs. Bangladeshi culture also has highly developed forms of dance, including classical dances, *bharata-natya,* folk or indigenous dances such as *baul, manipuri,* and snake dances (New Age, 2018).

South Asian immigrant communities including Bangladeshi communities in North America are also very active in providing welfare services to the needy members of their respective communities under various associations. While each group has its own distinctive trajectory, there are many ways that South Asians (including Indian, Bangladeshi, Pakistani, and others) come together to address common concerns. Additionally, there are a couple of South Asian advocacy groups in the United States and Canada that provide legal services, resources and information to those facing racial profiling and discrimination in employment and housing (Kibria, 2006).

Collectivistic Versus Individualistic Values

Results of several studies showed that first generation immigrants tend to be more strongly oriented toward their heritage culture than second generation immigrants (Cauce & Domenech-Rodríguez, 2002; Khaleque, Malik, & Rohner, 2015; Khaleque, Rohner, Nahar, & Sharif, 2008). An important factor that may contribute to the differences in the level of cultural orientations between first and second generations immigrants is the difference in cultural values between the two generations. Cultural values, such as individualism and collectivism, are likely to have differential effects on cultural orientations of different generations of immigrants (Schwartz, Montgomery, & Briones, 2006). The first generation (i.e., the parents) were generally born and brought up in the Oriental society with collectivistic cultural norms and values, which emphasize the well-being of the family, clan, nation, and religion over the needs of the individual. On the other hand, most of the second generation (i.e., the children) were born and brought in the Western society, which focuses more on the needs of the individual than that of the family, clan, or nation.

Marriage Systems

Traditionally, arranged marriages are a longstanding social custom in Bangladesh. Similarly, arranged marriages are still common among the Bangladeshi immigrant families in North America. In an arranged marriage, the bride/groom is chosen by the family with emphasis on matching socio-economic status, educational level, ethnicity, and religion between the two families. In the process of selection, the prospective couples are often encouraged by their parents to see and talk to each other and exchange photos.

Although arranged marriage is still the predominant custom in Bangladesh, the trend the marriage system is slowly changing among the educated urban elite in Bangladesh and Bangladeshi families in North America. Increasingly, young Bangladeshi second and third generation immigrants tend to make their own marital decisions and want to marry someone whom they like and love. In the case of love marriage, the marital decision is taken by the individual herself/himself, regardless of socio-economic status, education, ethnicity, or religion of the bride or the groom and of their families (Khaleque, 2011).

However, premarital cohabitation is very rare among Bangladeshi immigrant families. Prospective intimate partners often inform their parents about their choice, and request them to organize the social and religious ceremonies. In Islam, a marriage is both religious as well as legal contract between the two parties. Often the wedding is held at community centers, and accompanied by feasting, performance of traditional Bengali songs, and dances (Anderton, 2015).

Ethnic and Racial Intermarriages

Ethnic and racial intermarriages are very few among Bangladeshi communities in North America, especially in arranged marriages compared to love marriages. For the purposes of protecting cultural and religious identity, parents more often than children prefer that their sons and daughters marry Bangladeshis either from

Bangladesh or from North America who are belonging to the same religion. However, young Bangladeshi men and women born and brought up in North America often prefer to get married with someone born and brought up in North America with or without adherence to ethnic and religious identities (Basu, 2013; Ghosh, 2007).

Acculturation and Identity Issues

Acculturation is a process through which individuals change their monocultural identity to a bicultural or multicultural identity as a result of contact with members of other cultural groups (Berry, 2006). Although earlier researchers viewed acculturation as a unidirectional process involving acquisition of the new cultural values accompanied by loss of values of the culture of origin, proponents of the bicultural framework consider acculturation to be a combination of both the old and new cultural values in which almost every aspect of behavior changes, such as dress patterns, food habits, and language (Berry, 2005). In this context, this section focuses on acculturation and ethnic identity development of the Bangladeshi immigrants, especially Bangladeshi American and Canadian youth.

Like other Asian families in North America, traditional family relations and values of Bangladeshi immigrants are gradually changing as a result of acculturation. As the length of residence in North America increases, immigrant parents tend to become warmer and more moderate in behavioral control and discipline. Subsequently, immigrant children tend to become more self-reliant, independent, and biculturally oriented (Khaleque et al., 2008; Kibria, 2006; Kim, Han, & McCubbin, 2007). A study (Khaleque et al., 2008) on the acculturation of Bangladeshi immigrant families in the U.S. showed that mothers were more likely to be uniculturally oriented, compared to fathers (i.e., oriented toward heritage culture). Also, these mothers were more likely to stress the importance of Bangladeshi cultural values over Western cultural values as essential to their lives than did fathers. One major reason for this gender difference in acculturation may be the fact that Bangladeshi mothers are less exposed to members of other ethnic groups than fathers. As many mothers are full time stay-at-home mothers, most fathers are working outside of the home, thus, are more exposed to other cultures. The study also reported that a large number of American-born second and third generation immigrants are going through the process of biculturalism as they adapt to the mainstream American culture, along with their heritage culture (Khaleque et al., 2008).

Focusing on parents and their children, Khaleque and his colleagues (2015) revealed discrepancies between parents and children in acculturation or adaptation to host culture. Children tended to be more biculturally oriented, with greater acceptance of host culture than their parents (Khaleque et al., 2015). Several studies have also shown that discrepancies in parent-child acculturation levels are likely to occur when parents tend to retain traditional values of the heritage culture and acculturate less rapidly to the host culture than do children (Gil, Vega, & Dímas, 1994; Szapocznik, Kurtines, Santisteban, & Rio, 1990).

As found among other ethnic minority immigrant families, intergenerational acculturation gaps between parents and children often lead to increased family conflict, children's alienation, conduct problems, alcohol and substance abuse, maladjustment, and depression (Gonzales, Deardorff, Formoso, Barr, & Barrera Jr, 2006; Gonzales, Knight, Morgan-Lopez, Saenz, & Sirolli, 2002).

Forms of Family Life

Research literature on the effects of acculturation on family structure and relationships in Bangladeshi families in North America, though scanty, indicates that the traditional family relationships and parenting behaviors based on heritage cultural values tend to change gradually for Bangladeshi immigrant families as a result of acculturation and duration of immigration. For example, as the duration of immigration in North America increases, immigrant parents tend to become warmer and more liberal in control and discipline, and immigrant children tend to become more self-reliant and independent (Khaleque et al., 2008; Kibria, 2006). In the light of these and other findings, this section focuses on the changing patterns of family structures, roles, and relationships within parents, and between parents and children---from traditional authoritarian to liberal patterns in Bangladeshi families. Norms, values, structures, and dynamics of Bangladeshi immigrant families in North America are mainly based on a mixture of Islamic and Bangladeshi culture--including cultural traditions of other religious sub-groups such as Hindu, Budish, and other groups, and Western cultural traditions. Generally, the family pattern is joint or extended (multi-generational), where parents, children, and grandparents live together. Characteristically, Bangladeshi families are patriarchal, with fathers being the undisputed head. Fathers usually command respect and loyalty from all family members. Fathers also assume full responsibility for the family's social and economic well-being. Mothers, on the other hand, are typically responsible for the nurturance and social-emotional support of family members. Traditionally, the mothers' primary role is to serve their husbands and other family members, and rear their children. Mothers are often discouraged from working outside the home. In typical Bangladeshi families, there is also a tendency for gender privilege, sons are more highly valued than daughters (Sultana & Khaleque, 2016) because sons are seen as more useful than daughters for enhancing family's power and prestige (Khaleque, Shirin, & Uddin, 2013).

Although such gender role divisions are changing in the Bangladeshi families in North America, first generation immigrant women still tend to adhere more closely to the traditional South Asian oriental model, than to the mainstream North American model. However, like other Asian families in North America, traditional family values, parenting roles and behaviors are gradually changing for Bangladeshi immigrant families as a result of acculturation. For example, in recent years increasingly more Bangladeshi women in Bangladesh as well as in North America are achieving higher education and finding employment outside the home (Sultana & Khaleque, 2016).

In Bangladeshi families, there is also a tendency for strict parental control and harsh discipline of children. Like other Asian families, grandparents play important roles in family matters in joint or extended families of Bangladeshi immigrant communities. But many grandparents do not like to live permanently with their immigrant adult offspring in North America, or leave their ancestral home in their country of origin for good for a variety of reasons such as: language problems, too much dependence on adult offspring, lack of friends or relatives of similar age to spend time within a new country, difficulties in performing religious activities as there are no mosques and temples in many small towns in North America, cold temperature in Canada and Northern United Sates during winter, etc.

Socialization Practices

Bangladeshi immigrants parents in North America, especially more mothers than fathers, intend to raise their children with Bangladeshi cultural values (Khaleque et al., 2008). Moreover, like traditional South Asian families, there is strict parental control and restrictive discipline for adolescents, especially for adolescent girls compared to adolescent boys among Bangladeshi immigrant families (Khaleque et al., 2015; Malik, 2012). Parents discourage their adolescent children and young adult offspring from engaging in boyfriend-girlfriend relationships. Autonomy for dating or going out of the home at night with a boyfriend or a girlfriend is restricted for adolescents or young adults, especially for daughters. This sort of restriction sometimes creates parent-child conflicts and family problems in Asian families including Bangladeshi families in North American (Afroz, 2013). Afroz (2013) argued that gender discrimination in parental control is a major stressor for immigrant females in their parent-adolescent relationships. Moreover, immigrant adolescents regardless of gender, often face cultural barriers, bullying, and discrimination in their school environment when they strictly follow rituals, customs and values of their heritage culture. Thus they often experience two conflicting pressures and acculturation conflicts. For example, they experience pressure from parents for observing heritage culture and pressure from peers in school for following the cultural values of the host country. This often leads to cultural alienation and marginalization of Bangladeshi immigrant adolescents and emerging adults (Afroz, 2013).

Health and Well-Being of Bangladeshi Immigrants

One major problem about health information of the Bangladeshi immigrants is that most largescale national health surveys in the United States and Canada have reported aggregated data which did not distinguish between Asian subgroups by countries. Although the epidemiological information available on the Bangladeshi immigrants in North America is sparse (Ghosh, 2010), this section discuses health and well-being problems of Bangladeshi immigrants based on available research evidence.

In the 1960s and 1970s, South Asian immigrants from the Indian subcontinent, including Bangladesh, India, and Pakistan, to the United States and Canada were largely educated professionals, but the demographics have changed in recent years. Since the 1980s, many working class and low income South Asians including Bangladeshi have migrated to the United States and Canada, forming dense communities of low income urban immigrants (Joshi, 2006). Members of these new communities are facing major social and economic challenges and significant health disparities compared to the mainstream population of the United States and Canada.

The major health problems include high rates of obesity, cardiovascular disease and related syndromes including hypertension, depression, hypercholesterolemia, and diabetes, especially for women (Misra et al., 2010). Another issue is the historically low participation rates of South Asian immigrants in health surveys (Patel, Rajpathak, & Karasz, 2012).

Findings of a community-based health needs assessment survey among women in a Bangladeshi population living in New York City showed that over 50% of the women reported poor health, 37% screened positive for the risk of depression, only 35% had engaged in physical activity over the past month, 60% reported never having received a pap smear, 74% were either overweight or obese, and the prevalence of type 2 diabetes and hypertension were 15% and 37% respectively (Patel et al., 2012).

Based on the poor health behaviors and high prevalence of cardiovascular risk factors observed in this group, there is the need for early health promotion and prevention interventions. Some studies reported relationships between cardiovascular disease, tobacco use, and domestic violence among South Asian Americans (Misra et al., 2010; Mohanty, Woolhandler, Himmelstein, & Bor, 2005). A study on elderly Canadian immigrants from Bangladesh showed that cultural, religious, and language differences contributed to in making the new community environment difficult for them. In addition, lack of financial resources and community networks also increased their sense of alienation, isolation, and depression (Hossen, 2012).

Health Behaviors of Bangladeshi Immigrants

Physical activity or exercise has been found to be extremely low among the Bangladeshi immigrants, especially among women. Only 35.1% of women reported engaging at least once in any leisure time physical activity or exercise on average in a month. When compared to other racial/ethnic groups, Bangladeshi women had a much lower rate of physical activity than any other racial/ethnic group (Patel et al., 2012). A study found that nearly 20% of excess mortality among South Asians due to diabetes and cardiovascular disease was explained by physical inactivity

(Williams, Stamatakis, Chandola, & Hamer, 2011). It suggests the need for early intervention in this immigrant group for preventing diabetes and cardiovascular disease.

Implications for Mental Health and Well-Being

Despite limited empirical evidence on health problems of the Bangladeshi immigrants in North America, the studies discussed in this paper provide some valuable information about the health and well-being problems of the Bangladeshi immigrants in North America, including poor health behaviors and high prevalence of diabetes, depression, and cardiovascular risk factors observed in this group. There is a need for early intervention to deal with their problems. In addition, the paper focuses on problems that need special attention including language (English) problems, school readiness of young children, guidance for academic achievement and adjustment problems of children and adolescents both in school and the family. Thus, the ideas and information presented in this paper may be useful to professionals and practitioners including counsellors, social workers, psychologists, and therapists who work with Asian immigrant families, especially Bangladeshi families in North America.

Future Research

Influences of multicultural ideology on the cultural orientations and cultural adaptations of Bangladeshi immigrant parents and children in North America should be addressed in future research. Cultural values such as individualism and collectivism are likely to have differential effects on cultural orientations of different generations of Bangladeshi immigrants. For example, the first generation (i.e., the parents) were generally born and brought up with collectivistic cultural norms and values in their country of origin, which emphasize the well-being of the family and broader society over the needs of the individual. On the other hand, most of the second generation (i.e., the children) were born and brought up in North America, which focuses more on the needs of the individual than that of the family and society.

There should be more research on cultural conflicts between different generations of Bangladeshi immigrants. Moreover, immigrant adolescents often face cultural barriers, bullying, and discrimination in their school environment when they strictly follow the values of their heritage culture. They often experience acculturation conflicts. For example, they experience pressure from parents for observing heritage culture and pressure from peers in school for following the cultural values of the host country. This conflict often leads to cultural alienation and marginalization of Bangladeshi immigrant adolescents and emerging adults (Afroz, 2013). But there is scant empirical evidence on parental socialization practices and cultural conflicts of children of Bangladesh immigrant parents. In addition, to better understand the effects of cultural conflicts on cultural adaptation of adolescents and emerging adults, more research should be done on challenges and resilience factors in parent-adolescent relationships in Bangladesh families in North America.

References

Afroz, F. (2013). *Vulnerabilities and strengths in parent-adolescent relationships in Bangladeshi immigrant families in Alberta* (An unpublished master thesis). University of Lethbridge, Lethbridge, AB.

Ahsan, S. (2015). *An inquiry into the identity constructions of the Bangladeshi diaspora in Greater Toronto Area through their social networks.* (Unpublished doctoral dissertation). McGill University, Montreal, Canada.

Anderton, V. (2015). *Marriage, family and tradition in Bangladesh.* https://www.vsointernational.org/news/blog/marriage-family-and-tradition-in-bangladesh

Asian American Federation Census Information Center. (2013). *Profile of New York City's Bangladeshi Americans: 2013 edition.* http://www.aafny.org/cic/briefs/bangladeshi2013.pdf

Asian American Federation of New York Census Information Center. (2005). *Census profile: New York City's Bangladeshi American population.* https://www.aafny.org

Bald, V. (2013). *Bengali Harlem and the lost histories of South Asian America.* Harvard University Press.

Bangladesh High Commission. (2019). *Bangladesh diaspora in Canada.* https://www.bdhcottawa.ca/bilateral-relations/bangladesh-diaspora-in-canada

Basu, M. (2013). *Bengali Harlem: Author documents a lost history of immigration in America.* http://inamerica.blogs.cnn.com/2013/02/15/bengali-harlem-author-documents-a-losthistory-of-immigration-in-america/

Berry, J. W. (2001). A psychology of immigration. *Journal of Social Issues, 57*, 615–631.

Berry, J. W. (2005). Acculturation: Living successfully in two cultures. *International Journal of Intercultural Relations, 29*, 697–712.

Berry, J. W. (2006). Acculturation: A conceptual overview. In M. H. Bornstein & L. B. Cote (Eds.), *Acculturation and parent-child relationships* (pp. 13–30). Erlbaum.

Cauce, A. M., & Domenech-Rodríguez, M. (2002). Latino families: Myths and realities. In J. Contreras, A. Neal-Barnett, & K. Kerns (Eds.), *Latino children and families in the United States: Current research and future directions* (pp. 3–26). Praeger.

Citrin, J., Sears, D. O., Muste, C., & Wong, C. (2001). Multiculturalism in American public opinion. *British Journal of Political Science, 31*, 247–275.

Ghosh, C. (2010). Healthy people and Asian Americans/Pacific islanders: Defining a baseline of information. *American Journal of Public Health, 93*(12), 2093–2098.

Ghosh, S. (2007). Transnational ties and intra-immigrant group settlement experiences: A case study of Indian Bengalis and Bangladeshis in Toronto. *GeoJournal, 68*(2–3), 223–242. http://www.bdhcottawa.ca/

Gil, A. G., Vega, W. A., & Dímas, J. M. (1994). Acculturative stress and personal adjustment among Hispanic adolescent boys. *Journal of Community Psychology, 22*, 43–54.

Gonzales, N. A., Deardorff, J., Formoso, D., Barr, A., & Barrera, M., Jr. (2006). Family mediators of the relation between acculturation and adolescent mental health. *Family Relations, 55*, 318–330.

Gonzales, N. A., Knight, G. P., Morgan-Lopez, A., Saenz, D., & Sirolli, A. (2002). Acculturation and the mental health of Latino youth: An integration and critique of the literature. In J. Contreras, A. Neal-Barnett, & K. Kerns (Eds.), *Latino children and families in the United States: Current research and future directions* (pp. 45–74). Praeger.

Hossen, A. (2012). Social isolation and loneliness among elderly immigrants: The case of South Asian elderly living in Canada. *Journal of International Social Issues, 1*(1), 1–10.
Joshi, K. (2006). New roots in America's sacred ground: Religion, race, and ethnicity in Indian America. Rutgers University Press. http://www.jstor.org/stable/j.ctt5hj671.5
Khaleque, A. (2011). An overview of the effects of divorce on culture and society within Bangladesh. In R. E. Emery (Ed.), *Cultural sociology of divorce: An encyclopedia*. Sage.
Khaleque, A. (2016). Psychometric properties of two bicultural attitude scales: An update. *Psychological Studies, 61*(4), 288–294. https://doi.org/10.1007/s12646-016-0372-8
Khaleque, A., Malik, F., & Rohner, R. P. (2015). Differential acculturation among Pakistani American immigrant parents and children. *Psychological Studies, 60*(4), 401–411. https://doi.org/10.1007/s12646-015-0337-3
Khaleque, A., Rohner, R. P., Nahar, Z., & Sharif, A. H. (2008). Acculturation and perceived parental acceptance-rejection, control, and psychological adjustment of Bangladeshi immigrant children and parents in America. In F. Erkman (Ed.), *Acceptance: The essence of peace* (pp. 225–236). Turkish Psychological Association.
Khaleque, A., Shirin, A., & Uddin, M. K. (2013). Attachment relationships and psychological adjustment of married adults. *Social Indicators Research, 110*, 237–244.
Kibria, N. (2006). South Asian Americans. In R. Gapmin (Ed.), *Asian Americans: Contemporary issues* (pp. 206–227). Sage.
Kim, E., Han, G., & McCubbin, M. A. (2007). Korean American maternal acceptance-rejection, acculturation, and children's social competence. *Family & Community Health, 30*, 833–845.
Malik, F. (2012). Spillover of spous rejection to parental rejection of children: A new line of research in Pakistan and elsewhere. *Interpersonal Acceptance, 6*(2), 1–3.
Migration Policy Institute (MPI). (2014). *Bangladeshi diaspora in the United States*. The Rockefeller Foundation-Aspen Institute Diaspora Program. https://www.migrationpolicy.org/sites/default/files/publications/RAD-Bangladesh.pdf
Misra, R., Patel, T., Kotha, P., Raji, A., Ganda, O., & Banerji, M. (2010). Prevalence of diabetes, metabolic syndrome, and cardiovascular risk factors in US Asian Indians: Results from a national study. *Journal of Diabetic Complications, 24*(3), 145–153.
Mohanty, S. A., Woolhandler, S., Himmelstein, D. U., & Bor, D. H. (2005). Diabetes and cardiovascular disease among Asian Indians in the United States. *Journal of General Internal Medicine, 20*(5), 474–478.
Murdie, R., & Ghosh, S. (2012). Does spatial concentration always mean a lack of integration? Exploring ethnic concentration and integration in Toronto. In G. Bolt, A. S. Ozuerkren, & D. Phillips (Eds.), *Linking integration and residential segregation*. Routledge.
New Age. (2018). *Entertainment*. http://www.newagebd.net/article/39850/nazrul-songs-anddance-presented
Patel, V. V., Rajpathak, S., & Karasz, A. (2012). Bangladeshi immigrants in New York City: A community based health needs assessment of a hard to reach population. *Journal of Immigrant and Minority Health, 14*(5), 767–773. https://doi.org/10.1007/s10903-011-9555-5
Schwartz, S. J., Montgomery, M. J., & Briones, E. (2006). The role of identity in acculturation among immigrant people: Theoretical propositions, empirical questions, and applied recommendations. *Human Development, 49*(1), 1–30.
Singh, J. (2003). *Bangladeshi & Pakistani Americans Asian-Nation: The landscape of Asian America*. http://www.asian-nation.org/bangladeshi-pakistani.shtml
Statistics Canada (2006). *Projections of the diversity of the Canadian population, 2006 to 2031*. https://www.statcan.gc.ca/pub/91-551-x/91-551-x2010001-eng.pd
Statistics Canada. (2012). *Indo-Canadian population*. https://en.wikipedia.org/wiki/Indo-Canadians
Statistics Canada. (2016). *National Household Survey. Statistics Canada Catalogue no. 99-010-X2011028*. https://www.12.statcan.gc.ca

Sultana, S., & Khaleque, A. (2016). Differential effects of perceived maternal and paternal acceptance on male and female adult offspring's psychological adjustment. *Gender Issues, 33*(1), 42–52. https://doi.org/10.1007/s12147-015-9147-0

Szapocznik, J., Kurtines, W., Santisteban, D. A., & Rio, A. T. (1990). Interplay of advances between theory, research, and application in treatment interventions aimed at behavior problem children and adolescents. *Journal of Consulting and Clinical Psychology, 58*, 696–703.

U.S. Bureau of the Census. (2000). *Summary File 1*. U.S. Government Printing Office.

U.S. Bureau of the Census. (2010). *Summary File 1*. U.S. Government Printing Office.

Williams, E. D., Stamatakis, E., Chandola, T., & Hamer, M. (2011). Physical activity behavior and coronary heart disease mortality among South Asian people in the UK: An observational, longitudinal study. *Heart, 97*, 655–659.

Yearbook of Immigration Statistics. (2012). *Supplemental Table 2*. The U.S. Department of Homeland Security. https://www.dhs.gov/immigration-statistics/yearbook/2012

Chapter 9
Indian Families: The Diaspora in the United States and Canada

Uma A. Segal

Abstract The world's largest democracy, India, has a complex, diverse, and sprawling *Diaspora*. This chapter presents a general profile of Indians in the United States and Canada, identifying resources they bring and challenges they face. The integration of migrants is a slow and gradual process, occurring over decades, and requiring a concerted effort on the part of both immigrant and the receiving nation. The chapter proposes that mental health intervention should focus on the nexus of immigrant and host environment to determine ideal routes to integration, assessing the human and social capital of the former and the opportunities provided by the latter.

Keywords Indian · South Asian · India · Migration · Immigration

Introduction

The High Level Committee of the Indian Diaspora (2014) of India's Ministry of External Affairs described the wide spread of the Indian Diaspora around the globe, and its economic impact, quoting Mauritian poet, Vishwamitra Ganga Aashutosh (Chander, 2006):

> No Gold did they find
> Underneath any stone they
> Touched and turned
> yet
> Every stone they touched
> Into solid gold they turned.

India is a top source country for international migrants, and currently one in five migrants living outside their country of birth have their origins in India (Connor, 2017). Yet, surprisingly, the country has one of the world's lowest emigration rates, at 1% of its population (Connor, 2017), although 1% of over one billion people is

U. A. Segal (✉)
University of Missouri – St. Louis, St. Louis, MO, USA
e-mail: umasegal@umsl.edu

S. S. Chuang et al. (eds.), *Asian Families in Canada and the United States*, Advances in Immigrant Family Research,
https://doi.org/10.1007/978-3-030-56452-0_9

sizable. As do most voluntary migrants, they move to improve opportunities and enhance the quality of their lives. Indians have always maintained deep connections to the homeland which have strengthened with increased globalization, the ease of travel, and superior communications technology (Rabbiosi, Gregorič, & Stucchi, 2019). The size of the Indian immigrant population in the United States (U.S.) is large, and the migrants from India to Canada also constitute a substantial share of the total number of immigrants to the country (Agarwal, 2019). As barriers to entry in the U.S. grow, Indians view Canada as a more attractive alternative (Pasricha, 2019).

India is a land of diversity and complexity, and despite the fact that a general "Indian" culture binds them together, in reality, regional differences in worldviews, language, script, arts, food, and customs are pronounced vary significantly. Emigrants have also differed over the years, in ethnicity and in socioeconomic status, and have influenced nations around the world in a variety of ways. However, overall, wherever they have moved, these emigrants have tended to significantly improve the quality of their lives.

Because of immigration policies, the U.S. has drawn the more highly educated and skilled individuals (Segal, 2002). This was not always the case in Canada, which in the early years, attracted agricultural and lumber laborers. In the last few decades, these patterns have changed: Indian immigrants to Canada are increasingly likely to be professionals who come on their own merit, while more immigrants to the U.S. are entering under family reunification and may not have the same level of professional qualifications as the majority of the entrants in the late Twentieth Century (Lo, Li, & Yu, 2017).

Regardless of origins and destinations, or background, Indians have generally managed to establish fairly strong communities in destination countries. Even as the culture is modified by successive destination-country-born Indians, vestiges of the homeland culture and norms endure for generations (Bhatia, 2016; Misir, 2018; Myutel, 2016; Segal, 2016a). This chapter presents an overview of the present-day Indian Diaspora in North America, providing a comparison of the populations in the U.S. and Canada. Unlike migration to several other parts of the world, this migration has been relatively recent, with substantial entry beginning only in the mid-1960s (Lo et al., 2017). The immigrant experience, with the associated factors of human capital and resources for integration, affects adjustment and adaptation in the new environment and must be considered in the delivery of mental health services to this, and all, immigrant populations.

Brief Immigration History

While Indians have been known to migrate for the last two millennia, the transcontinental migration of significant numbers of people from the Indian Subcontinent began with the colonial period and persists to the present time (Charney, 1996; Van Den Boogaart & Emmer, 2012). Almost all major migrations from India have been labor migrations and the impetus to move to the U.S. and Canada was no different but began later around the turn of the Twentieth Century. Most early migrants to both Canada and the U.S. were Sikh men from the province of Punjab in northern India. From agricultural communities and with reputations of strength and fearlessness, these men were ideally suited to join the lumber and forestry business in Vancouver, British Columbia, Canada, and agricultural enterprises in California, USA (Li & Lo, 2012; Segal, 2002).

These relatively parallel migration streams from the Punjab to British Columbia between 1903 and 1908 (Canadian Council for Refugees, 2000) and to California between 1899 and 1920 (Balgopal, 1995) soon experienced the xenophobia that most Asians were facing in both countries. In Canada, the 1908 "Continuous-Journey" legislation prevented entry of those who did not travel directly from their home countries. Since there was no transportation from India that could cover the distance to Canada without a stopover, the legislation effectively curtailed further Indian migration (Rao, 2013). Likewise, in the U.S., the Johnson – Reed Act of 1924 permitted entry on a national origins quota system, allowing entry to 2% of people of each nationality that were counted in the U.S. census of 1890. Since there were so few people from Asia at the time of that census, it closed all Asian immigration (Office of the Historian, n.d.). Immigration policies in both Canada and the U.S. eased after a couple of decades, however, Indian migration was still sparse.

Recognizing the U.S. need for a larger skilled labor force, President Lyndon Johnson passed the Immigration and Nationality Act of 1965, (Hart-Celler Act, INS, Act of 1965, Pub.L. 89–236) which abolished immigration quotas, liberalizing immigration into the country. About the same time, in 1967, Canada moved to the immigration point system that sought to remove prejudice and capriciousness in the selection of immigrants. Points are awarded up to a fixed maximum on a range of categories, and the immigration law eliminated discrimination based on race and class (Citizenship and Immigration Canada, 2006).

As in most nation states, both Canada and the U.S. immigration policies circumscribe the circumstances under which individuals may enter and are based on at least three priority areas, including: (1) to address labor/economic needs, (2) to allow family reunification, and (3) for humanitarian reasons. The U.S. bases immigration opportunities by allocating an annual number of entry visas in these categories (American Immigration Council, 2016). Canada, on the other hand, also identifies these reasons, but eligibility is based on a points system, with a 67-point minimum, that assesses the individuals' ability to adapt in the Canadian socio-economic environment (Government of Canada, 2017). The primary advantage of the U.S. system is that entrants are expected to have employment commitment, host country-based family support, or governmental funding. Nevertheless, this appears to limit entry to those who already have a relationship with the country. On the other hand, the primary advantage of the Canadian system may be that it does not require a connection with Canada; rather it assesses an applicant's human capital to readily acclimatize to country norms. However, due to its immigration policies, Canada may be experiencing what is termed the "brain waste" as highly skilled people enter the country but are unable to find employment commensurate with their qualifications (Bannerjee, Verma, & Zhang, 2019; Brezis, 2019).

Removing discrimination based on nationality, these two laws opened the doors to immigrants, particularly skilled individuals, in a manner heretofore unseen. Skilled migrants arrived in both the U.S. and Canada in record numbers from India beginning in the middle and late 1960s. The flow of Indian migrants has continued steadily, and the size of the Indian population in these two nations, both by immigration and by birth, is substantial.

Ethnic and Linguistic Diversity

India is one nation, but it may well be called the "Indian Union." This union is composed of several cultures, and a myriad of diverse customs, literature, arts, music, and an unparalleled range of landscapes. Several faiths reflect the Indian population, including that which has migrated. While Hinduism is the majority religion (80%), Muslims (13%), Christians (2.3%), Sikhs (1.9%), and others (1.9%) also are free to practice their faiths, and with a population in 2019 of over 1.37 billion (World Population Review, 2019), each religion can boast a strong following in absolute numbers.

There are two official languages in India, Hindi and English, however, there are 21 state recognized official languages. Even more interesting are the findings of the People's Linguistic Survey of India 2013 report that indicate the existence of 780 spoken languages and 86 different scripts in India. Of these 780 languages, 122 are spoken by over 10,000 people (Hindustan Times,2013). Thus, it is possible to interact with several Indians who have nothing apparently in common barring the land of their birth, and although all of the of the ethnic and linguistic diversity found in India may not be proportionately reflected in the *Diaspora*, its profile is much more complex than it appears.

Demographic Information of Indians in the United States and Canada

In 2017, Indians constituted the second largest immigrant group in the U.S. (Zong & Batalova, 2017), moving from the third spot in 2011 (Whatley & Batalova, 2013). In 1960, immigrants in the U.S. numbered 9.7 million; of the 491 thousand Asians, 12.5 thousand were from India. In 2015, the U.S. reported 43.2 million foreign born individuals, 11.6 million from Asia, and of those 2.4 million were from India accounting for almost 6% of the foreign born (Lopez & Radford, 2017). The numbers of new immigrants to the U.S. from India began slowing, declining by 7.5% in 2018 with restrictions imposed by the Trump Administration (Sangani, 2020). As in the U.S., Canada saw the size of this population grow substantially between 1960 and 2016. In 1960, the total immigrant pool was only 104,000, and the number of immigrants from Asia was limited, with less than 150 being admitted from India in a given year. By 2016, the immigrant population in Canada had grown to 7.7 million, with 3.6 million being from Asia. Of these, 1.5 million were from India (Statistics Canada, 2017a). In addition, in what appears to be a reaction to Trump's immigration restrictions, and with increased difficulties in getting permanent resident visas to the U.S., Indian entrants into Canada surged from 39,705 in 2016 to 80,685 in 2019, an increase of 105% (Anderson, 2020).

Overall, the Indian subgroup continues to constitute a sizable portion of the minority population in the two countries; the change since 1960 reflects the liberalized immigration policies in the U.S. (1965) and Canada (1967). Furthermore, since these numbers do not include the large population of second- and third- generation American- and Canadian-born Indians, the ethnic Indian citizenry is, in reality, even larger. With ongoing migration from the Indian subcontinent and birth of the second and subsequent generations, the numbers of Indian-origin people are expected to continue to grow.

Indians, as a group, tend to congregate in certain parts of the country and usually in the more urban areas. In the U.S., about one-half lives in the states of California or New Jersey, and one quarter lives in three metropolitan areas: New York, Chicago, and San Jose/San Francisco (Zong & Batalova, 2017). The majority of Canadian Indians reside in the provinces of Ontario, British Columbia, and Alberta, and over 75% of the Indian population can be found in the metropolitan areas of Toronto, Vancouver, and Montreal (Statistics Canada, 2017a).

In the U.S., while only 60% of the native born is of working age, this age group (18–64 years) constitutes 82% of the Indian population. It also has a higher rate of home ownership and health insurance, and is less likely to live in poverty (Zong & Batalova, 2017). The majority evidences strong English language skills, and over 29% of males and 19% of females born in India are likely to work in information technology and business, respectively (Whatley & Batalova, 2013). Nevertheless, the profile of Indian immigrants to the U.S. has changed substantially in the last two decades. Between 1965 and 1987, the wave that immigrated was highly educated, professional, and distinct from migrants to other nations, and even from other immigrants to the U.S.. Under the family reunification provision of the Immigration and Naturalization Act of 1965 (PL 89–236), these migrants, now U.S. citizens, are able to sponsor relatives or recruit workers who may not be as skilled as the sponsors. The median income of Indians who immigrated between 1987 and 1990 dipped to one-fifth of that of pre-1980 migrants (Balgopal, 1995; Melwani, 1994). Despite this, the median Indian family income in 2015 was $107,00, substantially higher than that of either other immigrants ($51,000) or the native born ($56,000), and many fewer lived below the poverty level – 7% of Indians versus 17% of all foreign-born or 14% of native-born individuals (Zong & Batalova, 2017).

The profile of Indians in Canada has been somewhat different from that in the U.S. and has changed in the last decade. In 2001, a significant segment of this group lived on low incomes or below the poverty line, and even now, only 2.7% is considered to be of high income (Agarwal & Lovell, 2010). Agarwal and Lovell (2010) also found that Canadian Indians are overrepresented in waste management, manufacturing, and transportation industries. However, increasingly the present day immigrants from India are highly skilled, professional, and in their mid-30s (Statistics Canada, 2017a). Changes in the immigration point system in Canada in January 2013 was expected to make it more difficult for Indians to migrate and to curb the "brain waste" that several skilled workers experienced in the first decade of the twenty-first Century (Duttagupta, 2013), such as driving taxis when they had professional degrees in their home countries (Migration News, 2005). However, Prime Minister Justin Trudeau made a major thrust to welcome more professionals from India in 2017 (Bhattacharya, 2016). Overall, Indians who have entered Canada between 2011 and 2016 are now, as are those in the U.S., more highly educated and affluent than the native-born population (Statistics Canada, 2017a).

Although Indians in the U.S. are generally successful and enter the country through legal channels, the Migration Policy Institute reported that between 2011 and 2014 there were approximately 267,000 unauthorized immigrants living in the country (Zong & Batalova, 2017). Moreover, in 2016, 15,000 Indian youth were eligible for the 2012 Deferred Action for Childhood Arrivals (DACA) program, but only about 3700 had applied for it (Zong & Batalova, 2017). There is less information about unauthorized immigration from India to Canada, although some blogs and webpages of immigration lawyers indicate entries by Indians seeking assistance in legalizing their presence in the country.

The assertion that the Indian lifestyle and philosophy is highly centered on the integrity of the family continues to hold true, as Census data indicated few families without a husband present or consisting of cohabiting partners (American Community Survey, 2018; Statistics Canada, 2013). There appears to be no large-scale studies on the Indian population in the U.S. or Canada nor are there representative data on the rates of marriage and/or divorce. Yet, observation suggests that marriage continues to be the preferred choice of lifestyle among Indians, and parents encourage their children (especially women) to marry while they are in their twenties. Most first-generation Indians, regardless of when they come, bring their spouses and children with them or return to India to marry according to family tradition (Segal, 2012a). Further observation suggests that the divorce rate among Indians in America is on the rise. However, no studies have yet focused on these topics and other topics such as the perceptions of marriage longevity, which is prevalent among Indian families.

Acculturation

In many ways, because it has experience with colonization and exposure to the West, India has prepared its middle classes for some aspects of the American society. Most Indians who have migrated to the U.S. and Canada in the last two decades are comfortable with the English language, and with a language, one is exposed to the culture of the native language speakers. However, it would be faulty to assume that acculturation or adaptation is ever easy. Different norms, patterns of behavior, attitudes, and a variety of other less abstract dimensions, such as food, clothing, and entertainment, make adaptation difficult in the best of circumstances. The absence of the traditional support of family, friends, and one's own society, as well as differences in infrastructure, exacerbate difficulties. Nevertheless, most voluntary migrants are highly resilient and develop contexts in which they can survive and even flourish (Segal, 2002; Segal, Elliott, & Mayadas, 2010).

The Indian Diaspora has always been tightly knit, regardless of the country in which its members settle. While Indians in the U.S. have not traditionally developed ethnic enclaves, this is beginning to change; in Canada, there have long been such ethnic communities particularly in Vancouver and Toronto. Regardless of the distribution of place of residence, however, community centers, religious institutions such as temples, health care facilities, have emerged to assist Indians to adapt to their host countries as well as maintain and transmit their cultural heritage. An interesting phenomenon has occurred with the Diaspora, as it does for all migrant groups: the culture maintained by immigrants is that which existed in the home country when the individuals emigrated. Thus, immigrants from India who arrived in North America in the mid-1960s brought with them the Indian culture of that period; those arriving in the 1990s reflect India's culture of those years (Segal, 2002). As a result, immigrants are generally "stuck" or rooted in the culture of their countries that existed when they emigrated, maintaining and guarding patterns of behavior and traditions of that period. When they return to India, they can find that they are misfits in their homeland. With globalization, India's society and its norms have changed, while several emigrants have closely guarded their old traditions, their eating patterns, their clothing, and their expectations of interpersonal relationships. Like many of any country's *Diaspora*, they find that the India they left has changed and is significantly different from the India of the 1960s, 1990s or even the first decade of the 21st Century (Segal, 2016b).

Segal's (1991) seminal article that identified social and cultural differences among Indian immigrants, the second generation U.S. born children, and the majority population continues to be meaningful and relevant. This suggests that researchers and practitioners are still grappling with understanding intergenerational, intercultural, and migration related acculturation issues with the Indian population in the U.S. and Canada (Bornstein & Putnick, 2018; Cionea, Van Gilder, Hoelscher, & Anagondahalli, 2019; Mahapatra & Rai, 2019) and that the extant knowledge on Indian integration is limited. Furthermore, when newcomers enter a country in substantial numbers, they often strain the host country's cultural homogeneity and threaten societal norms (Barni, Cavazza, Russo, Vieno, & Roccato, 2020; Bohman, 2018; Mayadas & Elliott, 1992; Mayadas & Segal, 1989). When native populations believe their norms and values are affected by the newcomers, there can be a nativist backlash, as has been evidenced by the BREXIT vote in the United Kingdom and the rise of the conservatives and far right in the U.S. and Europe. Although Indians in these two nations have generally been professionally successful and well integrated into the workforce, socially they have a tendency to segregate themselves from their American counterparts (Segal, 2002). With the increasing size of the

Indian population and the development of Indian enclaves, xenophobia, of and by, Indians has also become more evident (Segal, 2016a).

Regardless of reasons for emigrating, all immigrants to a new country find adjustment to foreign values, expectations, and environment challenging. Differences in language and culture affect interactions and the development of relationships with native populations, and also interfere in the navigation of institutions and systems in the pursuit of goals, (Mayadas & Elliott, 1992; Ramakrishnan, Barker, Vervoordt, & Zhang, 2018). For those who are phenotypically different, as are those from Asia, assimilation is not possible since they always remain distinguishable and seen as "other" (FitzGerald, Cook-Martín, García, & Arara, 2017; Portes & Zhou, 1993; Wimmer, 2008). Separated from their culture of origin, and not able to truly assimilate into the country of destination, several immigrants who look different experience crises in identity and feelings of isolation and alienation (Baruth & Manning, 2016; Sue, 1973). Such stress results in one of three reactions: (1) close adherence to the values of the culture of origin, (2) over adaptation and rejection of own culture, or (3) integration of aspects of both cultures perceived as most amenable to the development of self-esteem and identity (Sue, 1973). Portes and Zhou (1993) propose an alternative possibility—segmented assimilation—professional integration coupled with social separation that helps maintain the home culture. A study of 105 Indians found that 65% identified themselves as being mostly Indian, 21% preferred a good mix of Indian and American lifestyles, and 7% did not self-identify as Indian (Sodowsky & Carey, 1988).

Traditional Values and Family Life

In many ways, Asian groups are very dissimilar from each other, yet in others, they share several values, expectations, and norms of behavior. At least five beliefs underlie most family relationships: (1) allocentrism, or belief that individuals should subordinate their desires for the larger good (Hofstede, 1980; Segal, Segal, & Niemcyzcki, 1993), (2) patriarchy, or preference for males who are heads of households and decision makers (Mullatti, 1995; Segal, 2002), (3) filial piety, or obedience and respect of younger family members toward elders (Dutt, 1989; Segal, 2002), (4) high expectations of dependency, particularly of females and their offspring (Saran, 1985), and (5) interpersonal control through an inculcation of a sense of obligation and of shame (Chatrathi, 1985; Sue, 1981).

As with other Asian families, the traditional Indian joint family is hierarchical, patriarchal, and patrilineal, has three or more generations living together, and age, gender, and generation circumscribe behavior and relationships. In the joint family, two or more family groups within a generation may also live together when sons bring their wives to reside in the parental home, where unmarried members of families continue to live. Less likely to be evident among Indians in North America, traditional patterns of joint family behavior and role relationships continue to be preferred, even when homes are separated by great distances. Allocentrism and subjugation of personal desires and needs are normative expectations in the traditional Indian family. While such traditions bind and control individuals, they also enhance the integrity of the family providing it with a group identity (Triandis, Bontempo, Villareal, Asai, & Lucca, 1988), which also strengthens and supports it (Segal, 1991, 2012a).

Indians in the U.S. and Canada are now facing a new phenomenon. A large number entered these countries when they were of a working age during the period between the mid-1960s and the 1990s. They left in India their parents who were also, at that time, of working age. Now, unable to monitor and care for their aging parents from afar, several adult children sponsor these parents as their dependents, frequently uprooting them from India against their wishes (Subramaniam, 2019). These aging parents, divorced from the culture and the society with which they are familiar, truly became dependent, subsequently losing their traditional status of authority (Sadarangani & Jun, 2015). In addition, the immigrants of the twentieth Century are now aging themselves, however, having aged in the West, they are highly independent, refusing to live with their children and choosing instead to move into retirement communities. Most continue to maintain independent homes and separate lives, relying on their contemporaries and the friendship networks they have developed over the years. As a group, they have not yet thought about their healthcare and the chronic needs that are correlated with the aging process (Shibusawa & Mui, 2010).

The first generation of immigrants to any country begins life anew and must devote much time, effort, and finances in establishing itself. The second generation is much more influenced by the host culture, and is also not charged with beginning a new life in a new country. Most Indians in the U.S. and Canada have been financially and professionally successful, and their children have not directly experienced major financial and social integration struggles. Furthermore, many new immigrants from India are now entering the U.S. to much more lucrative posts than did Indians in the past. Their remittances support their parents in India, without uprooting them, and they do not require their parents' assistance for child care in the U.S. (Bailey, Hallad, & James, 2018). In Canada, where there is a "point system" for immigration, immigrants may find that they are underemployed, nevertheless, the strength of numbers in the Indian community as well as labor shortages provide opportunities that were not available to the smaller Indian population of the Mid-1960s (Joshi, 2019).

Immigrant Identity and America–Born Offspring

For decades, researchers have explored issues of acculturation, identity, and cross-cultural difficulties within the immigrant families. Acculturation, or the process of learning a new culture and integrating its norms and values into one's perspectives and lifestyle is a function of a number of factors. The closer the host and the immigrant backgrounds, the easier the transition. Thus, the more westernized the Indian immigrant before entry into the Americas, the more readily s/he is acculturated and able to function comfortably in North America. This may, or may not, affect perceptions of self and identity, however, when immigrants return to the home country, regardless of the country from which they hale, they find they are perceived as outsiders by those in their country of origin (Segal, 2016b). They are all substantially and substantively altered by the immigrant experience and must reassess their own identities. Thus, in the West, they are identified as Indians (or Indian Americans/Indian Canadians) and in India, they are seen as Americans.

The experience of the second generation frequently does involve the dilemma of establishing an identity. This is a group that is American, but of Indian origin. Its members may never have been to the home country, but because of phenotypic characteristics, they will always be identified as Indian, even when they do not so self identify (Drouhot & Nee, 2019). Most function well in the majority culture, yet at home, several experience a culture that is distinctly different (Portes & Zhou, 1993; Sinha, 2010).This is probably not unusual for any ethnic minority in any country as it learns to balance the norms of the majority culture with those of its own. While the second generation is economically as well placed as the third generation (Tu, 2010), literature has suggested that the third generation has fewer identity inflicts than does the second, and that, in fact, it is usually quite assimilated into most of the norms of the host culture, although, the phenotypically "different" migrant is always perceived as being foreign regardless of its place of birth (Sandil & Srinivasan, 2018).

The first generation also has few identity conflicts, for though it may have to reassess how it is perceived by others, it is usually clear that it is Indian living in another country (Sinha, 2010). The second generation stands with one foot in each culture and is strongly influenced by the identity of its parents, even as it attempts to forge a new one of its own (Segal, 2002). The effect of the home culture is diluted for members of the third generation that are born into families that may be more American than Indian, and regardless of how others perceive them, they usually perceive themselves as American having left home country norms and traditions behind or having greatly modified and adapted them (Portes & Zhou, 1993; Sinha, 2010).

As second generation individuals stand firmly planted in two different cultures, they may engage in conflicts over a number of issues with their immigrant parents. These disagreements may range from preferences in use of language, daily food, and attire to issues of freedom and curfews, friendship, and dating (Segal, 1991). These differences may persist as these children grow to adulthood and affect decisions about career choice and life partners. Such issues are more difficult perhaps for children whose parents migrated in the Twentieth Century, as there was, in the U.S. and Canada, very little precedence of how to balance host and home country norms (Berry & Hou, 2017). It appears that Westernization has become commonplace in India with increased global communication and has mitigated some of the difficulties in adaptation for new immigrants from India, allowing them to better understand the desires and expectations of the second generation. Hence, although cultural differences between the two groups may still be evident, they may not now appear as dramatic or as insurmountable as they may have felt in the past.

The messages Indian parents give their children may also, inadvertently, be mixed. For example, they are instructed by parents to assume leadership roles in school and speak up, yet at home, they are expected to be docile and obedient. They are told that, in this country, one can be whatever one wants to be, but when they begin selecting a profession, they are directed toward medicine, engineering, or business (Segal, 2012a). Nevertheless, one finds the second generation of Indians selecting careers that may not have been preferred by Indian immigrant parents. While a large number continues to prefer professions in medicine, engineering, law, or business, an increasing number is choosing careers in the fine arts and social sciences. Some individuals in the second generation do allow parents to arrange their marriages, but these arranged marriages are substantially different from those of the past (Segal, 2016a). Usually the young couple, while understanding that the plan is for them to marry, spend some time getting to know each other to determine if they think they will be compatible.

Online dating services are flourishing as young people are seeking and screening their own life partners without parental involvement until they are ready to make a decision. In addition, the frequency of dating and its acceptance by the immigrant generation has risen. The outcome is that partners may be outside the regional group of the family or may be non-Indian. In fact, literature has shown that Asians, including Indians, are proportionately more likely to out-marry than are those of African or Spanish origin (Fryer, 2007). Discussions of dating and sexual restraint that haunted Indian immigrant families two decades ago may be passé with the youth of the Twenty-first Century. The world is becoming more accepting of dating and premarital sex, and norms are changing even in India (Cionea et al., 2019; Spittel, 2018). Indian parents often cope with this reality by sticking their heads in the sand and not acknowledging, even if their children are dating, that they could be sexually involved.

Traditional gender roles are also being modified. The male continues to be the primary wage earner; however, the female is increasingly working outside the home and is also a more equal partner. New immigrants and young people in the second generation are more likely to have a relationship in which both partners contribute to the daily functioning of the home, to child rearing, and to decision making (Yeung, 2013).

Indian parents in the U.S. and Canada are finding that subjects such as dating and sexuality, that have traditionally been considered taboo, must now be faced. Perhaps this is not a change in culture but a generational change worldwide. As one considers issues in the selection of life partners, it is time for Indians in the U.S. and in Canada to also recognize that there is a sizable lesbian, gay, and transgender Indian population (Yue, 2012). Even as the population is coming to terms with interracial marriages, it is beginning to face variations in sexual orientation and/or gender identity. Little academic, and particularly empirical, research has focused on the Indian lesbian, gay, bisexual, and transgendered, and questioning (LGBTQ) populations, perhaps because it is difficult for them to so self identify and the difficulties they may encounter as double or triple minorities in the U.S. and Canada. Indian news is now covering the LGBTQ community in North America (Haniffa, 2019), but social workers and counselors are ill prepared to work with them and their families (Sandil & Srinivasan, 2018).

Implications for Mental Health

The literature on immigrants and the second generation is vast, and mental health practitioners are becoming more knowledgeable about the unique issues facing these families. It is important that service providers move away from placing the responsibility of adaptation solely on the shoulders of the immigrant and the immigrant family. When immigrants choose to enter a new country, they are not truly aware of all the ramifications of the move; it is usually seen as an economic opportunity. Likewise, when a country accepts immigrants, it pays little heed to the reality, as Swiss novelist Max Frisch famously quipped, "We wanted workers, but we got people instead!" It is the joint responsibility of the immigrant and the host country to ensure a smooth integration process.

For voluntary migrants, such as most Indians to the U.S., there may not be many programs or services that are either available or accessible to provide them tools for adaptation. Canada, on the other hand, has purposefully, systematically, and successfully, developed its immigrant integration programs (Griffith, 2017). While, in the U.S., there are numerous organizations that work with refugees and others that provide protective and supportive services for those without the requisite visas, the majority of authorized Indian migrants do not fall into these categories. There are few, if any, orientation programs for voluntary migrants in the U.S., particularly those that are publicly funded, and these migrants usually navigate the new culture, its norms, and its infrastructure on their own. Few programs proactively aim to mitigate the loneliness of new immigrants, to help them to connect with others from their home country, to learn about cultural differences, or to socialize with the host country's natives. While some ethnic groups have developed community centers and programs that can serve this function with their own populations, they are not established for this purpose. Most voluntary immigrants to the U.S. are not prepared for the social and cultural differences between them and the host country, and when they become apparent, immigrants may neither have the tools to cope with them nor know where to turn for assistance (Potocky & Naseh, 2019). In Canada, many programs and services have been found to be very effective in enhancing integration of both voluntary and involuntary migrants in smaller communities, but the actual quality of services provided is generally superior in metropolitan areas where integration is more spotty (Chadwick & Collins, 2015). Reasons for this are unclear, but it appears that opportunities for greater interaction provided by programs in the smaller communities enhances mutual acceptance and integration.

The mental health profession increasingly recognizes the significance of context and the impact of environment on human behavior. Frequently difficulties in adjustment occur at junctions at which the client, whether it is an individual, family, or group, intersects with its environment. This may require that the client changes or the environment change, or both. Keeping this in mind, social workers may need to assess what levels of social work require their attention – the individual and family level, the organizational and community level, and/or the policy and societal level – to help them provide effective intervention services to their clients of Indian origin (Segal, 2012b).

Mental health practitioners working with Indian immigrants and their offspring must become knowledgeable about the immigrant experience as well as get a broad overview of the Indian culture; immigrants are, themselves, a good source for this information. Counselors should also remember that while they are being culturally sensitive and aware of the unique characteristics of particular groups, regardless of culture, human beings share more similarities than evident differences. Focusing too much on dissimilarities may cause one to lose sight of common human needs, erecting barriers to mitigating difficulties. However, as practitioners address issues in working with Indians in the U.S. and Canada, focusing exclusively on immigration related concerns will provide a skewed perspective as are assumptions that all presenting problems are correlated with migration. It is important that in the process of addressing integration into the host culture, universal needs, such as economic security, housing, health, education, general welfare, and family integrity not be overlooked (Segal, 2014).

Future Directions

It is time for the mental health profession to move beyond discussing issues of adaptation, child rearing, dating and marriage, and career choice. It is striking that Segal's 1991 article in still cited frequently in the year 2020. There is little new in the immigration literature that has emerged in recent years, and several of these concerns are similar for all migrants, regardless of country of origin or of destination. It is time to identify what the profession can do, including: (1) prepare existing programs and services to meet the needs of immigrants, (2) provide orientation programs to help new immigrants integrate into the country, and (3) develop opportunities for longer established immigrants to adapt to emerging issues as they care for their aging parents, cope with their own acute and chronic health needs, or plan for their own retirements. It is time to move away from focusing only on child rearing, the academic achievement of children, and parent-child relationships. With the sizable Indian population, one must address problems related to economic security, health and well-being, conjugal violence, aging, retirement, healthcare, and end-of-life issues. Thus, the focus must be on the immigrant lifespan. These emerging concerns have received little research attention. Furthermore, no attention has been directed to lesbian, gay, bisexual, and transgender Indians or to their families, and there have been no outreach efforts to these individuals who are finally beginning to openly express their sexual orientation and/or gender identities.

Still seen as the "Model Minority," Asians are inadvertently precluded from mainstream services in the U.S., as they are not perceived as having significant needs. Thus, ethnic organizations emerge to take care of their own, resulting in the duplication of services and poor use of limited resources. In fact, in many geographic areas, there are neither human nor monetary resources to either start or sustain such services. During the 1960s and the Civil Rights movement, Indians, along with other Asian Americans, received the dubious distinction of being dubbed the "Model Minority," not because of their achievement and success, but because these groups were identified as models for African Americans to emulate as they were seen as being passive, less visible, and unlikely to make waves (Petersen, 1966). Services and programs for Indians in Canada are substantially greater than for those in the U.S. Services in the former are available through Indian organizations as well as Canadian migration services. Li and Lo (2009) provided a systematic comparison of Indian migration to the U.S. and Canada and found, particularly among the skilled workers from India, the services for Indians were lacking in the U.S. while Canada's recognition of the social services needs of these migrants led to the development of integration programs for them in Canada. Perhaps this is based on differences in the implicit perspectives of the two nations toward immigrants. Canada's immigration and immigrant policies are welcoming and inclusive, while those of the U.S. appear to have, under the current administration, moved to policies of enforcement, border security, suspicion of entrants on work visas (Lo et al., 2017). With increasing numbers and visibility in the U.S. and Canada, Indians are experiencing overt xenophobia and the emergence of anti-Indian violence, sometimes precipitated by memories of the terror attacks in the U.S. on September 11, 2001. This is a relatively new occurrence that has received little research attention, however, media reports provide evidence of hate crimes against Indians in both Canada and the U.S. (Ngo, 2017; Statistics Canada, 2017b; Yam, 2018). Future research may focus on emerging issues and differences of Twenty-first Century Indians from those of the Twentieth Century, with changing implications for the education and training of mental health practitioners.

Conclusion

The area of mental health has begun to appreciate the presence and impact of globalization and immigration in the northern hemisphere and to recognize that these also have substantial implications for research, education, and practice (Bhavsar, Zhang, & Bhugra, 2019; Potocky & Naseh, 2019). Workers must be prepared for the growing immigrant population, whether it be from India or from elsewhere. This chapter has presented an overview of the Indian-American and Indian-Canadian populations and has indicated that globalization's infrastructure and existing immigration policies in both the U.S. and Canada will continue to encourage the entry of individuals and families from the Indian subcontinent. The chapter has identified some of the more general characteristics of the Indian immigrant population, particularly in these two nations of North America, and explored some concerns facing it. Now is time to integrate this into raising the awareness and enhancing the training of professionals in mental health as they are being prepared to work with minorities with relatively recent histories in North America.

References

Agarwal, S. C. (2019). Number of Indians acquiring permanent residency in Canada jumps 50% in 2018. *Business Today*. https://www.businesstoday.in/current/policy/indians-acquiring-permanent-residency-in-canada-spike-in-2018/story/362873.html

Agarwal, S. K., & Lovell, A. (2010). *Indian immigrants in Canada: The shades of economic integration*. https://www.poafoundation.org/wp-content/uploads/2014/11/indo-cdn_economic_integration_report.pdf

American Community Survey. (2018). *Families and household characteristics*. https://data.census.gov/cedsci/all?q=Families%20and%20Household%20Characteristics&tid=ACSST1Y2018.S1001

American Immigration Council. (2016). *How the United States Immigration system works*. https://www.americanimmigrationcouncil.org/research/how-united-states-immigration-system-works

Anderson, S. (2020). Indians immigrating to Canada at an astonishing rate. *Forbes*. https://www.forbes.com/sites/stuartanderson/2020/02/03/indians-immigrating-to-canada-at-an-astonishing-rate/#7383e4382b5f

Bailey, A., Hallad, J., & James, K. S. (2018). 'They had to go': Indian older adults' experiences of rationalizing and compensating the absence of migrant children. *Sustainability, 10*, 146. https://doi.org/10.3390/su10061946

Balgopal, P. (1995). Indian Americans. In R. L. Edwards (Ed.), *Encyclopedia of social work* (19th ed., pp. 256–260). Washington, DC: NASW Press.

Bannerjee, R., Verma, A., & Zhang, T. (2019). Brain gain or brain waste? Horizontal, vertical, and full job-education mismatch and wage progression among skilled immigrant men in Canada. *International Migration Review, 53*(3), 646–670. https://doi.org/10.1177/0197918318774501

Barni, D., Cavazza, N., Russo, S., Vieno, A., & Roccato, M. (2020). Intergroup contact and prejudice toward immigrants: A multinational, multilevel test of the moderating role of individual conservative values and cultural embeddedness. *International Journal of Intercultural Relations, 75*, 106–117. https://doi.org/10.1016/j.ijintrel.2020.02.004

Baruth, L. G., & Manning, M. L. (2016). *Counseling the culturally different* (6th ed.). Routledge.

Berry, J. W., & Hou, F. (2017). Acculturation, discrimination and well-being among second generation of immigrants in Canada. *International Journal of Intercultural Relations, 61*, 29–39. https://doi.org/10.1016/j.ijintrel.2017.08.003

Bhatia, P. (2016). The Indian Diaspora in Mauritius. *NewsGram*. https://www.newsgram.com/indian-diaspora-in-mauritius

Bhattacharya, A. (2016). Canada's 2017 immigration plan to benefit Indians. *The Hindustan Times*. https://www.hindustantimes.com/world-news/canada-s-2017-immigration-plan-to-benefit-indians/story-VblWySKIH1vwFoBAGfR9KO.html

Bhavsar, V., Zhang, S., & Bhugra, D. (2019). Conceptualizing globalization for mental health research. *Journal of Social Psychiatry, 65*(2), 87–91. https://doi.org/10.1177/0020764018823806

Bohman, A. (2018). Who's welcome and who's not? Opposition towards immigration in the Nordic Countries, 2002–2014. *Scandinavian Political Studies, 41*(3), 283–306. https://doi.org/10.1111/1467-9477.12120

Bornstein, M. H., & Putnick, D. L. (2018). Parent-adolescent relationships in global perspective. In J. E. Lansford & P. Banati (Eds.), *Handbook of adolescent development research and its impact on global policy* (pp. 107–129). Oxford University Press.

Brezis, E. S. (2019). Should individuals migrate before acquiring education or after? A new model of brain waste vs. brain drain. *The BE Journal of Macroeconomics*. https://econ.biu.ac.il/files/economics/working-papers/2019-03.pdf

Canadian Council for Refugees. (2000). *A hundred years of immigration to Canada 1900–1999*. https://ccrweb.ca/en/hundred-years-immigration-canada-1900-1999

Chadwick, K. A., & Collins, P. A. (2015). Examining the relationship between social support availability, urban center size, and self-perceived mental health of recent immigrants to Canada: A mixed-methods analysis. *Social Science & Medicine, 128*, 220–230. https://www.sciencedirect.com/science/article/pii/S0277953615000623?via%3Dihub

Chander, A. (2006, April). Symposium: A tribute to the work of Kim Barry: The construction of citizenship in an emigration context: Symposium: Homeward Bound. *New York University Law Review, 81*, 60. https://advance.lexis.com/api/document?collection=analytical-materials&id=urn:contentItem:4JPR-F520-02BN-1056-00000-00&context=1516831

Charney, P. (1996). Negotiating roots: Indian migrants in the Lima Valley during the Colonial Period. *Colonial Latin American Historical Review, 5*, 1–20. https://digitalrepository.unm.edu/clahr/vol5/iss1/1

Chatrathi, S. (1985). Growing up in the U.S.: An identity crisis. *India Abroad, 15*, 2.

Citizenship and Immigration Canada. (2006). ARCHIVED – Forging our legacy: Canadian citizenship and immigration, 1900–1977. http://www.cic.gc.ca/english/resources/publications/legacy/chap-6.asp#chap6-5

Cionea, I. A., Van Gilder, B. J., Hoelscher, C. S., & Anagondahalli, D. (2019). A cross-cultural comparison of expectations in romantic relationships: India and the United States. *Journal of International and Intercultural Communication, 12*(4), 289–307. https://www.tandfonline.com/doi/abs/10.1080/17513057.2018.1542019

Connor, P. (2017). *India is a top source and destination for world's migrants*. Pew Research Center. https://www.pewresearch.org/fact-tank/2017/03/03/india-is-a-top-source-and-destination-for-worlds-migrants/

Drouhot, L. G., & Nee, V. (2019). Assimilation and the second generation in Europe and America: Blending and segregating social dynamics between immigrants and natives. *Annual Review of Sociology, 45*. https://doi.org/10.1146/annurev-soc-073117-041335

Dutt, E. (1989). Becoming a 2nd generation. *India Abroad, 20*(2), 16.

Duttagupta, I. (2013). Indian applicants face uncertain future as Canada tightens immigration laws. *Economic Times*. http://articles.economictimes.indiatimes.com/2013-01-20/news/36432613_1_skilled-immigrants-immigration-and-multiculturalism-jason-kenney

FitzGerald, D. S., Cook-Martín, D., García, A. S., & Arara, R. (2017). Can you become one of us? A historical comparison of legal selection of 'assimilable' immigrants in Europe and the Americas. *Journal of Ethnic and Migration Studies, 44*(1), 1–21. https://doi.org/10.1080/1369183X.2017.1313106

Fryer, R. G. (2007). Guess who's been coming to dinner? Trends in interracial marriage over the 20th century. *The Journal of Economic Perspectives, 21*(2), 71–90. https://doi.org/10.1257/jep.21.2.71

Government of Canada. (2017). *Six selection factors – Federal skilled workers (express entry)*. https://www.canada.ca/en/immigration-refugees-citizenship/services/immigrate-canada/express-entry/eligibility/federal-skilled-workers/six-selection-factors-federal-skilled-workers.html

Griffith, A. (2017). Building a mosaic: The evolution of Canada's approach to immigrant integration. Migration Policy Institute. https://www.migrationpolicy.org/article/building-mosaic-evolution-canadas-approach-immigrant-integration

Haniffa, A. (2019). A big, fat Indian-American gay wedding where rituals were rendered gender neutral. *India Abroad*. https://www.indiaabroad.com/indian-americans/a-big-fat-indian-american-gay-wedding-where-rituals-were/article_e0b89c08-a29d-11e9-b81d-abec0b518223.html

High Level Committee of the Indian Diaspora. (2014). *Report of the High Level Committee on the Indian Diaspora*. https://gfmd.org/pfp/ppd/313

Hindustan Times. (2013). People's Linguistic Survey of India. *780 languages spoken in India, 250 died out in last 50 years*. https://www.hindustantimes.com/books/780-languages-spoken-in-india-250-died-out-in-last-50-years/story-Y3by8ooYbXRA77xP2AEWKN.html

Hofstede, G. (1980). *Culture's consequences*. Sage.

Immigration and Nationality Act. (1965). *Public Law 89–236*. https://www.govinfo.gov/content/pkg/STATUTE-79/pdf/STATUTE-79-Pg911.pdf

Joshi, S. (2019, June 23). Canada dreaming: Why Indian professionals are moving in growing numbers, and what it's like to start again. *The Times of India*. https://timesofindia.indiatimes.com/home/sunday-times/canada-dreaming-why-indian-professionals-are-moving-in-growing-numbers-and-what-its-like-to-start-again/articleshow/69908446.cms

Li, W., & Lo, L. (2009). Highly-skilled Indian migrations in Canada and the US: The tale of two immigration systems. *Working Paper 4*. http://lib.jnu.ac.in/sites/default/files/pdf/imds_p/IMDS_Mar_2009_WP_4.pdf

Li, W., & Lo, L. (2012). New geographies of migration? A Canada-U.S. comparison of highly skilled Chinese and Indian migration. *Journal of Asian American Studies, 15*(1), 1–34.

Lo, L., Li, W., & Yu, W. (2017). Highly-skilled migration from China and India to Canada and the United States. *International Migration., 57*(3), 317–333. https://doi.org/10.1111/imig.12388

Lopez, G., & Radford, J. (2017). *Facts on U.S. Immigrants, 2015. Statistical portrait of the foreign-born population in the United States*. Pew Research Center. https://www.pewresearch.org/hispanic/2017/05/03/2015-statistical-information-on-immigrants-in-united-states/

Mahapatra, N., & Rai, A. (2019). Every cloud has a silver lining but… "pathways to seeking formal-help and South-Asian immigrant women survivors of intimate partner violence." *Health Care for Women International*. https://www.tandfonline.com/doi/full/10.1080/07399332.2019.1641502

Mayadas, N. S., & Elliott, D. (1992). Integration and xenophobia: An inherent conflict in international migration. In A. S. Ryan (Ed.), *Social work with immigrants and refugees* (pp. 47–62). Haworth Press.

Mayadas, N. S., & Segal, U. A. (1989). *Asian refugees in the U.S: Issues in resettlement* [unpublished manuscript]. University of Texas-Arlington, Arlington, TX.

Melwani. (1994). Dark side of the moon. *India Today, 60c-60f.*

Migration News. (2005). *Canada: Brain waste, 112*(3). https://migration.ucdavis.edu/mn/more.php?id=3115_0_2_0

Misir, P. (2018). *The Subaltern Indian woman: Domination and social degradation*. Palgrave Macmillan. https://link.springer.com/book/10.1007%2F978-981-10-5166-1

Mullatti, L. (1995). Families in India: Beliefs and realities. *Journal of Comparative Family Studies, 26*(1), 11–26.

Myutel, M. (2016). *Indians and national television in Indonesia: Behind the seen* (Unpublished PhD dissertation). Australian National University. https://openresearch-repository.anu.edu.au/bitstream/1885/113156/1/Myutel%20M%20Thesis%202016.pdf

Ngo, B. (2017). Immigrant education against the backdrop of "Make America Great Again". *Educational Studies, 53*(5), 429–432. https://doi.org/10.1080/00131946.2017.1355800

Office of the Historian. (n.d.). *The Immigration Act of 1924 (The Johnson-Reed Act), Department of State, USA*. http://history.state.gov/milestones/1921-1936/ImmigrationAct

Pasricha, A. (2019, June 15). *Indian immigrants eye Canada as US barriers rise*. https://www.voanews.com/south-central-asia/indian-immigrants-eye-canada-us-barriers-rise

Petersen, W. (1966, January 9). Success story, Japanese-American style. *The New York Times Magazine*, 21.

Portes, A., & Zhou, M. (1993). The new generation: Segmented assimilation and its variants. *AAPSS Annals, 530*, 74–96.

Potocky, M., & Naseh, M. (2019). Best practices for social work with refugees and immigrants, 2nd edition. Columbia University Press.

Rabbiosi, L., Gregorič, A., & Stucchi, T. (2019). Diaspora ownership and homeland firms' internationalization. *Journal of International Management, 25*(3). https://doi.org/10.1016/j.intman.2018.12.002

Ramakrishnan, S., Barker, C. D., Vervoordt, S., & Zhang, A. (2018). Rethinking cross-cultural adaptability using behavioral developmental theory: An analysis of different migrant behaviors. *Behavioral Development, 23*(2), 138–152. https://psycnet.apa.org/fulltext/2017-05868-001.pdf

Rao, A. (2013). The Indian Diaspora – past, present, and future (Part I). *Fair Observer.* https://www.fairobserver.com/region/central_south_asia/indian-diaspora-past-present-and-future-part-i/

Sadarangani, T. R., & Jun, J. (2015). Newly arrived elderly immigrants: A concept analysis of "aging out of place". *Journal of Transcultural Nursing, 26*(2), 110–117. https://doi.org/10.1177/1043659614549074

Sandil, R., & Srinivasan, R. (2018). South Asian American health: Perspectives and recommendations on sociocultural influences. In M. Perera & E. Chang (Eds.), *Biopsychosocial approaches to understanding health in South Asian Americans: Cross-cultural research in health, illness and well-being* (pp. 95–117). Springer.

Sangani, P. (2020). Indian immigration to U.S. down by 7.5%. *The Economic Times*. https://economictimes.indiatimes.com/nri/visa-and-immigration/indian-immigration-to-us-down-7-5/articleshow/73262243.cms?from=mdr

Saran, P. (1985). *The Asian Indian experience in the United States*. Vikas Publishing House, PVT. Ltd.

Segal, M. N., Segal, U. A., & Niemcyzcki, M. A. P. (1993). Value network for cross-national marketing management: A framework for analysis and application. *Journal of Business Research, 27*, 65–84.

Segal, U. A. (1991). Cultural variables in Asian Indian families. *Families in Society, 11*, 233–241.

Segal, U. A. (2002). *A framework for immigration: Asians in the United States*. Columbia University Press.

Segal, U. A. (2012a). The Indian American family. In R. Wright, C. H. Mindel, R. W. Habenstein, & T. V. Tran (Eds.), *Ethnic families in America* (Vol. 5, pp. 288–319). Prentice-Hall.

Segal, U. A. (2012b). Working with immigrants and refugees. In R. Link & L. Healy (Eds.), *Handbook of international social work* (pp. 73–80). Oxford University Press.

Segal, U. A. (2014). Human rights and migration. In K. Libal, M. Berthold, R. Thomas, & L. Healy (Eds.), *Advancing human rights in social work education* (pp. 435–453). Council on Social Work Education.

Segal, U. A. (2016a). South Asian immigrant and refugee children and families. In A. Dettlaff & R. Fong (Eds.), *Immigrant and refugee children and families: Culturally responsive practice* (pp. 191–213). Columbia University Press.

Segal, U. A. (2016b). Opportunities and challenges of return migration. In Q. Xu & L. P. Jordan (Eds.), *Migrant workers: Social identity, occupational challenges and health practice* (pp. 171–190). Nova Science Publishers.

Segal, U. A., Elliott, D., & Mayadas, N. S. (2010). The immigration process. In U. A. Segal, D. Elliott, & N. S. Mayadas (Eds.), *Immigration worldwide* (pp. 3–16). Oxford University Press.

Shibusawa, T., & Mui, A. C. (2010). Health status and health services utilization among older Asian Indian immigrants. *Journal of Immigrant and Minority Health, 12*(4), 527–533.

Sinha, C. B. (2010). Dynamic parenting: Ethnic identity construction in the second-generation Indian American family. *Sociology Dissertations*. https://scholarworks.gsu.edu/cgi/viewcontent.cgi?article=1058&context=sociology_diss

Sodowsky, G. R., & Carey, J. C. (1988). Relationships between acculturation-related demographics and cultural attitudes of an Asian-Indian immigrant group. *Journal of Multicultural Counseling and Development, 16*(3), 117–136.

Spittel, G. (2018). Telemodernities: Television and transforming lives in Asia. *Pacific Affairs, 91*(2), 337–340.

Statistics Canada. (2013). *Immigration and ethnocultural diversity in Canada* (Ministry of Industry, catalogue no. 99-010-X2011001). https://www12.statcan.gc.ca/nhs-enm/2011/as-sa/99-010-x/99-010-x2011001-eng.pdf

Statistics Canada. (2017a). Number and proportion of the population belonging to a visible minority group, Canada, 2001 to 2016. *Focus on Geography Series, 2016 Census*. http://www12.statcan.gc.ca/census-recensement/2016/as-sa/fogs-spg/Facts-can-eng.cfm?Lang=Eng&GK=CAN&GC=01&TOPIC=7

Statistics Canada. (2017b). *Police reported crime, 2016*. https://www150.statcan.gc.ca/n1/daily-quotidien/171128/dq171128d-eng.htm

Subramaniam, M. S. (2019). *Examining the experience of aging out of place in the United States for Asian Indian late-life immigrants and the risk and protective factors within multigenerational Asian Indian families* (Unpublished dissertation). Michigan State University.

Sue, D. W. (1973). Ethnic identity: The impact of two cultures on the psychological development of Asians in America. In S. Sue & N. Wagner (Eds.), *Asian-Americans: Psychological perspectives* (pp. 140–149). Science and Behavior Books.

Sue, D. W. (1981). *Counseling the culturally different*. Wiley.

Triandis, H. C., Bontempo, R., Villareal, M. J., Asai, M., & Lucca, N. (1988). Individualism ands collectivism: Cross-cultural perspectives on self-ingroup relationships. *Journal of Personality and Social Psychology, 19*, 323–338.

Tu, J. (2010). *Explaining the labour market outcomes of first, second and third generation immigrants in Canada*. [Forschungsinstitut zur Zukunft der Arbeit, No. 5128]. http://ftp.iza.org/dp5128.pdf

Van Den Boogaart, E., & Emmer, P. C. (2012). Colonialism and migration: An overview. In P. C. Emmer (Ed.), *Colonialism and migration; indentured labour before and after slavery*. Martinus Nijhoff Publishers.

Whatley, M., & Batalova, J. (2013). Indian immigrants in the United States. *Migration Information Source*. https://www.migrationpolicy.org/article/indian-immigrants-united-states/

Wimmer, A. (2008). The making and unmaking of ethnic boundaries: A multilevel process theory. *American Journal of Sociology, 113*(4), 970–1022.

World Population Review. (2019). *India population 2019*. https://worldpopulationreview.com/countries/india-population/

Yam, K. (2018). Trump invoked in 20 percent of hate crimes against South Asians, Middle Easterners, Report Says. *Huffington Post*. https://www.huffpost.com/entry/saalt-hate-crimes-report_n_5a7390fee4b01ce33eb12ae4

Yeung, W.-J. J. (2013). Asian fatherhood. *Journal of Family Issues, 34*(2), 143–160.

Yue, A. (2012). Queer Asian mobility and homonational modernity: Marriage equality, Indian students in Australia and Malaysian transgender refugees in the media. *Global Media and Communication, 8*(3), 269–287.

Zong, J., & Batalova, J. (2017). *Indian immigrants in the United States*. https://www.migrationpolicy.org/article/indian-immigrants-united-states

Chapter 10
Pakistani Families

Ahmed Afzal

Abstract This chapter provides an overview of Pakistani immigration, adaptation and integration in the United States of America and Canada with a special emphasis on mental health issues. The chapter begins with a brief history of Pakistani immigration to North America as a starting point for situating Pakistani families. I discuss the intertwining of immigration with patterns of population growth, domestic life and settlement in North America. Next, I explore the Pakistani population as a transnational community and examine forms of family life, value systems, socialization practices, and intergenerational relations and conflict. I then provide an overview of gender roles and familial concerns around ethnic and interracial marriages. I also discuss educational expectations and achievements and career patterns found within Pakistani families in North America. Finally, the chapter concludes with a discussion of the implications of these findings for counselors and social workers and identifies areas for particular concern. These concerns include the occurrence of domestic violence and abuse, homophobia and transphobia, Islamophobia and racism, and the uses of traditional homeopathic medicinal and spiritual healing practices.

Keywords Pakistani Americans · Pakistani Canadians · History · Immigration patterns · Family life · Mental health · 9/11 · Domestic violence · LGBTQ Pakistani Americans · Islam · Inter-generational conflict

Although Pakistanis have been coming to North America since the late nineteenth century when the territories that make up present-day Pakistan were a part of British colonial India. The majority of the Pakistani population is made up of new immigrants who arrived in the United States and Canada in the decades following the end of British colonial rule and the simultaneous creation of Pakistan in 1947. The immigration increased in the 1960s and by the 2000s, the number of Pakistanis had grown considerably and represented an internally diverse community. By 2015,

A. Afzal (✉)
California State University Fullerton, Fullerton, CA, USA
e-mail: aafzal@fullerton.edu

S. S. Chuang et al. (eds.), *Asian Families in Canada and the United States*, Advances in Immigrant Family Research,
https://doi.org/10.1007/978-3-030-56452-0_10

Pakistanis in North America represented all major income levels, occupations and professions. The population also represents all major Pakistan ethno-linguistic and religious communities (Afzal, 2015). The presence of Pathan, Punjabi, Sindhi, Kashmiri and Balochi ethno-linguistic groups, and of Ismaili Shia, Sunni, Bohra and Ahmadiya Muslims, as well as Zoroastrian, Christian, Sikh and Hindu Pakistanis exemplifies a microcosm of contemporary Pakistan in North America. In spite of the population growth and the increasing internal diversity of Pakistani populations in North America, there is a relative paucity of research on Pakistanis in North America, especially as it pertains to issues relating to family life and mental health and the stresses associated with being a minority community in highly racialized North American societies. Thus, this chapter is an overview and survey of Pakistani immigrant history, adaptation, and integration in the United States of America and Canada with a special emphasis on family life and issues relating to mental health.

A historical context for Pakistani immigration provides an important starting point for situating Pakistani family and community formations in North America. The chapter, therefore, begins with a brief history of Pakistani immigration to North America, noting the business networks and domestic arrangements that had characterized the public and private lives of Pakistanis in the late-nineteenth and the early twentieth century when Pakistanis first started to travel to North America. This historical context illuminates the similarities between practices of adaptation into North America from over a hundred years ago and during the contemporary period. I also discuss the racialized immigration policies and the legal frameworks in the United States and Canada to demonstrate the intertwining of immigration law with patterns of population growth and settlement in North America. Next, I analyze the acculturation of Pakistanis in the U.S. and Canada. I explore the Pakistani population as a transnational community and also examine forms of family life, value systems, socialization practices, and intergenerational relations and conflict. I then provide an overview of gender roles and familial concerns around ethnic and interracial marriages. I also discuss educational expectations and achievements and career patterns within Pakistani families in North America. Finally, the chapter concludes with a discussion of the implications of these findings for counselors and social workers and identifies areas for particular concern. These concerns include the occurrence of domestic violence and abuse, homophobia and transphobia, Islamophobia and racism, and the uses of traditional homeopathic medicinal and spiritual healing practices.

Immigration History and Demographics

To gain greater insights into Pakistani families, and more specifically, immigrant Pakistani families, a brief history of Pakistani immigration to North America is meaningful in providing insights into the continuities as well as the changes in Pakistani domestic life and arrangements in North America over time. I also relate Pakistani family life to the changes in the U.S. immigration law in 1965 which opened doors for immigration from countries in Asia including Pakistan and allowed opportunities for "family reunification," (i.e., the immigration of family and kin). Salient issues discussed include the growth and internal diversity within the Pakistani population and Pakistani settlement patterns in North America.

Immigration During the Late-Nineteenth and the Early Twentieth Century

Pakistanis have been coming to North America since the late nineteenth century when the territories that constitute present-day Pakistan were a part of British colonial India (Bald, 2015). In the early decades of the twentieth century, racialized immigration policies in the United States and Canada favored European immigration. These policies severely curtailed immigration from Asia including regions that make up present-day Pakistan until the post-World War II period.

In spite of restrictions on immigration and racialized immigration policies, a few thousand South Asian immigrants arrived in North America during this period. Working-class Muslim men from villages in East Bengal (present-day Bangladesh), Kashmir, Punjab, and Khyber Pakhtunkhwa (present-day Pakistan) constituted the majority of the population of South Asian silk peddlers, merchants, sailors, and industrial workers. Having had their livelihood disrupted due to colonization, industrialization and the mechanization of agriculture during British colonial rule in India, these men arrived in the United States and Canada looking for jobs and seeking markets for traditional Indian goods (Bald, 2015).

Business Networks and Domestic Life in North America

Business networks made up of kinfolk in North America were critical to the viability and success of Bengali business operations. Over time, these networks encompassed several states in the Northeast, Midwest, South, and Southwestern United States. Bengali peddlers (i.e., wholesalers who brought goods such as silk cloth from colonial India to sell to retailers and wholesalers in the U.S.) relied on these networks to identify business opportunities, and develop strategies to navigate exclusionary U.S. immigration laws (Bald, 2015).

Business networks in the U.S. extended to domestic life and to living arrangements. Peddlers and the subsequent waves of ex-seamen who jumped ship at port cities created single-sex households, living with other migrant men in dormitories, boardinghouses and apartments in cities such as New York City and New Orleans (Bald, 2015). These single-sex households were multiethnic and multiracial in composition and included migrants from different countries. These domestic arrangements provided the infrastructure and the support necessary to establish and also to expand businesses in other cities. These domestic arrangements also created opportunities for mentorship and companionship. Significantly, these all-male households constituted spaces for sexual intimacies and homosocialities between migrants (Shah, 2011).

Recent historiographies attest to the complexities of the domestic life and experiences of these early immigrants and show the prevalence of intimate relationships and ties with other communities of color, notably African-Americans and Puerto Ricans (Bald, 2015). For example, Bengali peddlers and Indian merchants and ex-seamen became incorporated into multiethnic and multiracial communities such as the Bengali-Puerto Rican and the Bengali-African American communities in Harlem, New York in the 1940s and the 1950s. Similarly, Punjabi farmers who settled in Canada, Washington, Oregon and California and British Columbia provided labor on rural farms, married Mexican women and created a Mexican-Punjabi community (Leonard, 1992; Shah, 2011).

Post-1965 Immigration from Pakistan to the U.S.

Pakistani immigrationline to North America increased following immigration reforms in the United States and Canada following World War II. During the decades following the creation of Pakistan as a sovereign nation-state in 1947, Pakistanis (mostly men) traveled to the United States for higher education. The total number of Pakistanis in the United States between 1947 and 1965 is estimated at approximately 2500 university and graduate students (Najam, 2006).

In the United States, the passage of the U.S. Immigration and Naturalization Act in 1965 abandoned prior legislation that had set the national origins quota system based on the national diversity of the U.S. population in 1890. The 1965 Act replaced the quotas with an annual limit of 170,000 immigrants (subsequently raised to 270,000) for countries outside of the western hemisphere. In the 5 years following the 1965 immigration reforms, over 30% of the total immigrants came from outside of the western hemisphere (Williams, 1988), and Asia became a major source of immigration to the U.S. (Abraham, 2000; Leonard, 1997; Lessinger, 1996; Prashad, 2000; Rangaswamy, 2000). While Asians had constituted less than 4% of total U.S. immigration between 1921 and 1960, Asians comprised 35% of legal immigration from 1971 to 1980, and 42% from 1981 to 1989 (Ong & Liu, 2000). From 1971 to 1989, more than 4 million Asians, primarily from China, India, Pakistan, Korea, the Philippines and Vietnam immigrated to the U.S. (Ong & Liu, 2000).

In the U.S., although the immigration reforms of 1965 had made immigration more available to Asian nationality groups, it was the educated middle-class and the elite men who benefitted the most from these reforms and constituted the majority of the South Asian immigrants (Prashad, 2000). From the mid-1960s until the late 1980s, the majority of Pakistani immigrants to North America were western-educated and trained professionals (Najam, 2006). Physicians and engineers from urban Pakistan featured prominently among the new immigrants (Powell, 2005).

The U.S. Immigration Reform and Control Act of 1986 that granted legal status to undocumented immigrants meeting specific requirements, along with the U.S. Immigration Act of 1990 that increased the numbers for family-based immigration, led to further growth of the Pakistani population in the 1980s and the 1990s. Almost 75% of Pakistanis in the U.S. have immigrated since 1987, and only 10% immigrated prior to 1978 (Najam, 2006).

These immigration laws have contributed to patterns of chain migrations, whereby a first wave of highly skilled white-collar labor is followed by subsequent waves of immigrants that include family members and kin who work primarily in the service industries, especially ethnic businesses (McDaniel & Drever, 2009). These working-class South Asians arrive with varying levels of education, ranging from some high school education to postsecondary degrees, and varying levels of fluency in English. Many find menial and low paying jobs in Pakistani and Indian restaurants, convenience stores, gas stations, and ethnic grocery shops and businesses (Prashad, 2000). A smaller grouping of immigrants consists of political refugees belonging to Pakistani ethno-linguistic communities, religious minority groups and political groups who immigrate to the United States and Canada to escape persecution in Pakistan and reside in exile in North America.

By 2015, Pakistanis in North America came to represent all major income levels, occupations and professions. They also represent all major Pakistan ethno-linguistic and religious communities The presence of Pathan, Punjabi, Sindhi, Kashmiri and Balochi ethno-linguistic groups, and of Ismaili Shia, Sunni, Bohra and Ahmadiya Muslims, as well as Zoroastrian, Christian, Sikh and Hindu Pakistanis exemplifies a microcosm of Pakistan in North America (Afzal, 2015).

Pakistani Immigration to Canada

In Canada, immigration regulations selected for immigrants with advanced education and professional skills. During the 1950s and the 1960s, Pakistani immigrants benefitted from such regulations. In 1976, Prime Minister Pierre Elliot Trudeau revised the Immigration Act, which contributed to an increase in Pakistani immigration to Canada (Magocsi, 1999). Immigration from Pakistan increased further in the 1980s. Much like the post-1965 wave of Pakistani immigrants to the U.S., the majority of Pakistani Canadians were urban, well-educated white-collar professionals (Magocsi, 1999).

The dependents and relatives sponsored for permanent residence and citizenship to Canada in the years after 1990 are characterized by lower levels of education. According to the Canadian census of 2005, approximately 44 per cent of Pakistan-born immigrants fall below the poverty line (Statistics Canada, 2006). Many Pakistani immigrants experience downward economic mobility as Pakistani trained engineers, doctors and PhDs drive taxi cabs or work in service sector industries that provide little financial security or professional growth. A significant number of new immigrants from Pakistan face under- or unemployment (Haider, 2016).

Settlement Patterns

The total number of Pakistanis in the U.S. in 2013 is estimated at 474,784 (Center for American Progress, 2015). The Center for American Progress (2015) suggests that between 2000 and 2013, the Pakistani American population grew faster than the U.S. average. The total number of Pakistanis residing in Canada in 2016 is estimated at 215,560.

In 2013, in terms of state-wide distribution, New York (88, 779), Texas (62,834), California (60,834), Virginia (39,890) and New Jersey (31,958) made up 59.75% of the total Pakistani population, and were home to the largest Pakistani communities in the U.S. (Center for American Progress, 2015, p. 1). Smaller populations can be found in all other U.S. states (Najam, 2006). In terms of cities, the largest settlements of Pakistani immigrants are found in Jersey City, New York City, Chicago, Philadelphia, Los Angeles and Houston, in addition to Washington D.C. (Afzal, 2015). In Canada, the largest concentrations of Pakistanis are in Ontario (149,060), Alberta (29,265), Quebec (13,535), and British Columbia (12,580) and smaller populations in other provinces. Toronto (122,950), Calgary (18,495), Montreal (13,125) and Vancouver (10,825) have the highest percentage share of the Pakistani Canadian population (Statistics Canada, 2016).

The majority of the working class and the working poor reside in primarily working-class multi-ethnic gated communities that are located near places of work. Within walking distance to mosques, Pakistani restaurants, South Asian grocery stores and super markets, barbers shops, travel agencies, and ethnic boutiques, these gated communities were well suited for Pakistani immigrants with limited financial resources or limited access to automobiles to travel long distances especially in car-centered cities such as Houston and Los Angeles (Afzal, 2014, 2015).

Ethnic enclaves with concentrations of Pakistani residences and ethnic businesses include Gerrard Street in Toronto, Park Extension in Montreal, Coney Island Avenue and Jackson Heights in New York City, Artesia in Los Angeles, Hillcroft Avenue and Bissonnet Street in Houston, and Devon Avenue in Chicago. As an example, in Houston, the presence of mosques, Islamic community centers and schools, the offices of Pakistani professionals – doctors, lawyers, real estate brokers and social service workers – and multiplex cinema theatres featuring first-run Indian movies have created a thriving South Asian ethno-religious environment around Hillcroft Avenue, with newer South Asian business and residential concentrations developing further southwest on Bissonnet Street. Most strip malls with Pakistani businesses in Houston and also in Chicago, New York City and Los Angeles are multi-ethnic in composition and reflect the broader racial and ethnic diversity locally (Afzal, 2015).

On the other end of the socio-economic and income spectrum, residential settlement in exclusive and wealthy gated-communities, suburbs and neighborhoods demonstrates the investment Pakistani professionals make in grounding themselves within specific status-laden localities in the United States. Such settlement positions these professionals within the mythology of the American dream, where success is symbolized by home ownership and the white picket fence (Afzal, 2015). The emphasis on home ownership in suburbs dominated by White and Asian Americans indicates appropriations and assertions of the model minority (Shankar, 2008).

Acculturation: Transnational Community Formations and Assimilation

Pakistanis in North America are a transnational community (i.e., a community with affiliations and everyday engagements that transcend the borders of a single country and encompass multiple countries). In this section, I elaborate on the varied transnational affiliations and engagements, and focus on sustained familial, financial/economic, political, religious, cultural and social involvements in the homeland. These engagements complicate our understanding of earlier models of acculturation and assimilation that are predicated on a break from the homeland and instead demonstrate belonging to multiple countries.

Pakistanis are also invested in transnational religious communities that transcend national borders. Religion is a central and significant marker of identity and community for North American Muslim communities such as Pakistanis in the U.S. and Canada. However, this emphasis on religion has placed the spotlight on Pakistanis especially following the attacks of 9/11. This has intensified Islamophobia and racism and contributed to misinterpretations of practices such as veiling among Muslim women. Significantly, Islamophobia and racism are sources of acculturative stress and contribute to mental health problems as demonstrated in a study of Asian Americans including Pakistani Americans (Miller, Yang, Farrell & Lin, 2011).

These transnational engagements have not undermined assimilation into mainstream society in either the U.S. or Canada. Being American and Canadian are vitally important facets of identity, especially for the second- and third-generation Pakistani-Americans and Pakistani-Canadians. Pakistanis are deeply involved in local governance and politics and civic engagements at local and national levels and have forged interethnic and interreligious alliances locally and nationally. Moreover, the presence of Pakistanis in all professions and occupations attests to their assimilation into mainstream North American societies.

Transnational Pakistani Community Formations

As immigrants who trace their ancestral affiliations to regions that make up present-day Pakistan, Pakistani are transmigrants, (i.e., immigrants who maintain and participate in familial and kin-based relationships in their ancestral homeland), with variegated engagements in the homeland (Basch, Blanc-Szanton, & Glick Schiller, 1992). A 2015 survey of 120 Pakistani families from different socio-economic and educational backgrounds in three cities in eastern U.S. found significant levels of investment in Pakistan, especially among the first-generation (Khaleque, Malik, & Rohner, 2015). Transnational engagements in Pakistan include but are not limited to remittances sent to family and kin, charitable donations to construct schools, medical facilities and mosques in their native village or city, involvement in politics in the homeland, and regular visits to Pakistan to visit family and kin (Zaki, 2013).

Cultural Organizations

Pakistanis in North America are not a monolithic transnational community. This is evident from the proliferation of Pakistani cultural organizations. These cultural associations are centered on South Asian ethno-linguistic and regional affiliations (e.g., Punjabi, Sindhi and Pathan) and religious sects (e.g., Sunni, Bohra, Shia, and Ahmadiya). These organizations provide vitally important organizational spaces for Pakistanis to come together and build community along ethno-linguistic, regional and religious sectarian affiliations. Pakistani-American organizations plan the annual Pakistan Day Festival in August that celebrates the creation of Pakistan on August 14, 1947. These organizations also organize religious festivals such as *Eid-ul-Fitr* that marks the end of the month of fasting and *Eid-ul-Azha* that follows the completion of the pilgrimage of Hajj to Mecca. These organizations also advocate for the local Pakistani community especially in cases involving racism, discrimination and hate crimes directed at Pakistani individuals, businesses and property.

Radio

In recent decades, Pakistanis in North America have utilized commercial radio, notably, Urdu language Pakistani radio programs, to build a transnational community. These programs are a transnational space because they connect Pakistanis with their homeland. These programs are produced in cities such as Toronto, Chicago, New York, Houston, and Los Angeles. Pakistani radio programs feature news reports on current affairs, especially issues that impact Pakistanis in the U.S.. The programs air news reports of politics and culture in Pakistan. The programs also provide culturally specific entertainment such as airplays of Indian and Pakistani songs and music, in addition to information about local South Asian businesses and services, and a calendar of local cultural and religious events (Afzal, 2015).

Movies, Television and Sports

Pakistanis constitute a major audience for Indian films and television produced in India, and Urdu-language Pakistani television drama series and films made in Pakistan. This media is available for instant streaming and/or to rent and buy on online platforms such as Netflix, Amazon Prime, YouTube and Dailymotion among others and represent transnational media consumed by Pakistanis in North America. Mainstream movie theaters in cities with significant Pakistani populations also screen first-run Indian and Pakistani films. Satellite television services such as Dish Network also offers packages that consist of Pakistani and Indian television channels that are based in Pakistan and India and are available to audiences in North America. Pakistanis routinely attend and also organize South Asian musical programs and exhibits featuring artists from India (Leonard, 1997). They also participate in cricket matches and basketball leagues that connect the various South Asian nationality groups (Thangaraj, 2015).

Religion and Transnational Community Formation

Religion is a central component of transnational community for many Pakistanis in North America. Ethnographic and historical analyses of South Asians in the U.S. and Canada attest to the importance of religion in constructions of transnational identity and community (Afzal, 2015; Williams, 1988). As an example, Pakistani-Americans and Pakistani immigrants in Houston, a city with one of the largest Pakistani populations of any city in North America, developed religious institutions and infrastructure during the early 1970s when the South Asian Muslim population began to grow locally (Afzal, 2015). Pakistani Americans hold important leadership roles in Muslim student associations on college campuses in the U.S. and Canada. Pakistanis are also actively involved in Islamic schools and community centers in major cities in North America (Williams, 1988). Mosques and Islamic community centers play important roles in connecting Pakistanis with Muslims from other nationality and ethnic groups (D'Alisera, 2004). Muslim summer camps for adolescents and the youth and schools for religious education are increasingly popular forums for socialization within certain segments of the Pakistani populations.

Pakistani Christians worship at churches all over the country. Likewise, Pakistani Hindus worship at Hindu temples and participate in the religious life of Hindu American communities. Equally, Pakistani Sikhs worship at Gurdwaras (Sikh temples) and participate in the religious life of Sikhs from Pakistan and other countries with Sikh populations. Pakistani Zoroastrians, who trace their roots to ninth-century Persia, worship at Fire Temples which can be found in several North American cities with significant Zoroastrian population (Afzal, 2015).

Islamophobia and Racism

Since the terrorist attacks of 9/11, Muslim communities have experienced the rise of Islamophobia and racism, and state surveillance and profiling of Muslims and public spaces associated with Muslims (Center for American Progress, 2015). Doing so has upended investments in, and claims of belonging to mainstream American and

Canadian society. In the U.S., as the American government quickly identified Osama bin Laden as the mastermind behind the 9/11 attacks, Muslim Americans began to draw the sharp attention of law enforcement and intelligence services. Several thousand Muslim men of South Asian and Middle Eastern descent were detained for months without being charged with crimes; many were deported for minor infractions (Afzal, 2015). U.S. government agencies began targeting mosques, as well as South Asian and Middle Eastern charities, community centers and businesses based on the perception that these places propagate and nurture Islamic militancy, terrorism and anti-Americanism. These characterizations of Pakistani immigrants and practices of surveillance and profiling have persisted into the 2010s (Afzal, 2015; Maira, 2009; Rana, 2011).

Pakistanis in Canada have also experienced increased hate crimes centered on Islamophobia and racism, and state and public scrutiny following 9/11. These experiences have contributed to acculturative stress and negatively impacted mental health (Yang & Lin, 2011). The public's inability to distinguish between Islam and perpetrators of 9/11 has contributed to a "negative visibility" (i.e., a visibility that results in alienation from mainstream society and contributes to "otherness") (Jamil, 2014). A study found that working- and middle-class Pakistani and Bangladeshi Muslim immigrants in Montreal had experienced increased levels of scrutiny, suspicion and negative perceptions after 9/11 (Jamil, 2014). The findings also revealed that the personal impact of post 9/11 Islamophobia has been especially severe for working-class Pakistanis and Bangladeshis. Specifically, working class Pakistani men in Montreal reported difficulties in finding employment, accessing health care and social services, and providing financially for their families since 9/11 (Jamil, 2014).

Research also suggests that discrimination is associated with an increase in the use of informal, ethnic and religious services and sources of authority such as religious and ethnic leaders and organizations instead of formal mental health services (Spencer, Chen, Gee, Fabian, & Takeuchi, 2010). A study of Pakistani immigrants in Canada found higher rates of diagnosed stress and anxiety disorders in Pakistani immigrants compared to Canadian-born non-Pakistani populations (Islam, Khanlou, & Tamim, 2014).

Veiling Practices

The veil can refer to a headscarf (hijab), or a face veil (lithma) that women usually wear just under their eyes, or an all-enveloping cloak that covers the body from head to toe (burka). Veiling practices can be found in all major world religions – Judaism, Christianity and Islam. Veiling practices in these religions are typically associated with formal prayer and ritual, where veiling symbolizes the piety, honor, modesty and respectability of the person and their family (Gole, 1996). Other religious interpretations and appropriations of the veil are less literal, characterizing the veil as a metaphysical separation between human beings or the world and God (Glasse, 2001).

In spite of the prevalence of veiling in all major religious communities, veiling practices among Muslim women in particular have dominated public discourse and media scrutiny globally especially in the West. Recent research has problematized reductive interpretations of veiling practices in contemporary Muslim communities that equate the veil solely with female oppression and subordination in patriarchal Muslim societies and cultures (Abu-Lughod, 2002). Reductive understanding of the veil and veiling practices have contributed to hate crimes directed against hijab wearing women following 9/11 (Maira, 2009).

Assimilation and Contested Belonging to Mainstream North American Societies

In spite of deep investments in the homeland and in religious communities, ethnographic research indicates that transnational belonging and assimilation into mainstream societies in North America are concurrent processes. Research indicates that second-generation Pakistanis in Canada and the U.S. are assimilated and integrated in mainstream society (Diamant, 2017; Zaki, 2013) While many first-generation Pakistani Americans continue to speak their native languages at home, the second-generation communicates primarily in English but are bilingual, and code-switch between English and their native language (Afzal, 2015).

At the same time, income and immigration status, educational levels and the extent of family and kin support available are co-related with acculturative stress. Specifically, a study of psychological well-being of Pakistani immigrants in Toronto found that lower levels of social support, low income-status, and jobs with limited upward mobility and growth contribute to higher rates of acculturative stress and reduced mental well-being among Pakistani immigrants (Jibeen & Khalid, 2010).

Forms of Family Life

All forms of family life including single-parent, nuclear, extended, and transnational are found within the Pakistani population in North America. In recent decades, immigration law has enabled opportunities for family reunification through the immigration of family and kin. The immigration of family and kin from Pakistan and elsewhere in the diaspora has contributed to the formation of nuclear and extended families in the cities of settlement. In many extended family households, elderly grandparents often assume household duties and responsibilities of childcare of their grandchildren (Leonard, 1997).

South Asian households that are made up of single men or married men who have immigrated alone and do not have any family locally are also common. These households are similar to the single sex household types established by South Asian male immigrants in the late nineteenth and the early twentieth century (Shah, 2011). In the 2000s and the 2010s, vacancies are advertised through word-of-mouth or hand-written notices on the bulletin boards in South Asian restaurants, barbers shops and grocery stores (Afzal, 2015). For example, a recently arrived Pakistani immigrant might utilize existing contacts to find accommodation in a two-bedroom apartment that is shared by four or more men.

While most of these apartment complexes are managed and owned by non-Pakistanis, management often ignores violations regarding the permissible number of occupants. Occupants negotiate the limited living space by carefully choosing working and sleeping hours in order to accommodate all housemates. Many migrants, especially men, who are away from their families in Pakistan for extended periods, develop living arrangements that are outside of norms around family that have centered on the nuclear and the extended family and produce migrant homosocialities and non-heteronormative social relationships and sexuality that reference their marginality in the racial and classed hierarchies in North American societies (Rana, 2011).

Pakistanis in North America also maintain transnational families that extend to multiple countries (Afzal, 2015). Through innovations in technology, such as FaceTime, Zoom and other video conferencing platforms, Pakistani immigrants play active roles in the everyday life and concerns of their families in the homeland. Specifically, Pakistani immigrants consult with family in Pakistan about a broad range of familial issues and also participate in decision-making on matters that impact the entire family.

Value Systems

While it is difficult to generalize value systems of North American Pakistanis because they represent diverse religious and ethno-linguistic communities and ideologies and beliefs around morality, ethnographic evidence points to the importance placed on family and community. A recent survey of Pakistani families in the United States of America found that many first generation Pakistanis who were born and raised in Pakistan represent a collectivist mindset that emphasizes family and kin over the individual (Khaleque et al., 2015). Another study similarly notes that Pakistani-Americans tend to be family-oriented and community-oriented with strong familial and social connections to families in the homeland and in the United States (Zaki, 2013).

Community Formation in Historical Contexts

In the 1960s and the 1970s, constructions of community among Pakistani immigrants emphasized an inclusive South Asian heritage that included immigrants from all South Asian countries (i.e., Bangladesh, India, Nepal, Maldives, Pakistan and Sri Lanka). South Asian community formations were also inclusive of the different religious communities and included Buddhism, Christianity, Hinduism, Islam, Sikhism, and Zoroastrianism (Afzal, 2015; Leonard, 1997; Williams, 1988).

By the 1990s, the confluence of several factors radicalized community formation and contributed to assertions of difference based on religion and country of ancestral affiliation and transformed terms of belonging. These factors included: dramatic increase in the Pakistani Muslim population; rapid growth of Muslim infrastructure and business enterprises in cities with major Pakistani populations; increasing interactions between Pakistani Muslim immigrants and co-religionists from India, the Gulf States, Asia, Africa and beyond; and, the influence of militaristic and political tensions between India and Pakistan in diasporic communities in cities such as Houston (Afzal, 2015).

Consumption Patterns as Indexes of Religious Value Systems

Since the 1990s, religious value systems have become central in community formations as evidenced by consumption patterns among segments of the Pakistani Muslim population in North America. For example, Pakistani supermarkets sell copies of the Qur'ans, prayer beads, skull caps, rugs, bumper stickers, key chains, posters, framed Qur'anic verses, greeting cards, decorative items, paper models of mosques, and miniature plates with Qur'anic verses (D'Alisera, 2004). Pakistani fashion boutiques carry a wide variety of hijab along with other staple South Asian ethnic clothing and fashion accessories. Pakistani travel agencies routinely organize seminars as part of the "Hajj package" for individuals and families traveling to Mecca in Saudi Arabia for the annual Muslim pilgrimage. Pakistani restaurants serve only halal food, and also maintain cordoned off areas for prayers and separate dining sections for women and families. Many Pakistanis do not eat pork and have a preference for meat products that are halal, i.e., meat that is slaughtered and prepared according to Islamic law. In addition to halal meat and frozen food items, Pakistani supermarkets in cities with large Muslim populations also sell oils and herbal medicines and syrups such as black seed and caraway oil that are mentioned in the Prophet Mohammad's hadiths (sayings) (Afzal, 2015).

Socialization Practices and Intergenerational Relations and Conflict

It is difficult to generalize socialization practices and intergenerational relations and conflict issues given the diversity of experiences and lifestyles found within the Pakistani population in North America. This is primarily due to the internal diversity and the broad range of life experiences that are found in Pakistani communities. In spite of the variety of lived experiences, religion is a significant marker of identity in the lives of the second- and third-generation. This emphasis on religion is aligned with the salience of religion in building community and in shaping value systems discussed in previous sections.

Attesting to the salience of Islam in the lives of the second-generation, a study found that a significant challenge facing second-generation Muslim Americans pertains to perceptions of the differences if not an incompatibility between the values of the broader American and Canadian societies on the one hand, and the religious values and beliefs of Muslim Americans on the other. A study of Muslim youth found that teenage Muslim boys and girls experienced depression and negative effects on their self-esteem as a result of their alienation and discrimination as Muslims in the U.S. and Canada (Zaki, 2013).

Intergenerational Relations and Conflict

In spite of the salience of religion in the life of second- and third-generation Pakistani Americans and Pakistani Canadians, there are tensions between assimilation into mainstream (Euro-American) American and Canadian society and the transmission and retention of Islam and Pakistani culture. A survey of Pakistani American families found that "intergenerational acculturation gaps" contribute to familial conflicts, alcohol and substance abuse, and depression (Khaleque et al., 2015). Physical disciplining or corporal punishment of children by parents is another contentious issue within the Pakistani community. Some parents, especially among first-generation Pakistanis, invoke culture and tradition to legitimate corporal punishment of children by parents and oppose state intervention in this issue. Yet, many first-generation Pakistanis also fear that corporal punishment of children might result in the children's removal from the family and the placement of children in foster care (Leonard, 1997).

Other issues that may cause intergenerational conflict pertain to parental management and control over their children's private life including sexuality and marriage. Specifically, parents may impose curfews, keep track of friendships, and monitor phone calls and social interactions between their adult children and their friends (Leonard, 1997). Double standards such as one set of rules for men and another set of rules for women, extend to dating, premarital sex and "love marriages" with greater openness and flexibility for male children. They are another source of intergenerational conflict.

These issues and concerns hold the potential for sometimes severe mental stress especially for the second generation. Yet, stigma is often attached to mental health problems especially within the first generation. This stigma undermines and prevents clinical intervention (Ta, Holck, & Gee, 2010). Moreover, there appears to be a preference, especially among the first generation, to utilize ethnic, religious and kin networks and sources of authority such as religious leaders, and practices such as praying, reading religious texts, or reaching out to Allah to address mental health issues instead of turning to mental health services (Ashraf, 2016).

Gender Roles and the Family System

Given the wide range of gendered experiences found within the Pakistani population in North America, it is difficult to make generalizations regarding gender and sex roles. In spite of the variety of gendered experiences, Pakistani women's experiences attest to the subordination of women and restrictions on their mobility, as well familial conflicts over rights of women (Dasgupta, 1998). The emergence of progressive women's organizations and South Asian LGBTQIA (Lesbian, Gay, Bisexual, Transgender, Queer/Questioning, Intersex and Asexual) organizations highlight domestic violence, particularly spousal and familial violence and abuse. Homophobia and transphobia within segments of the Pakistani communities in North America extends beyond women and includes sexual minorities such as gay, lesbian, bisexual and transgender women and men and may negatively impact mental health and well-being.

Gendered Experiences: Women's Rights and Labor in the Workforce

A 2013 study found that there were significant differences between men and women over issues such as the right of women to work, right to education, right to choose marriage partners, right to a divorce, and the socialization of children (Zaki, 2013). At the same time, studies also show that there is greater flexibility in terms of sex roles in the family as women acquire more education and pursue careers, and start to play major economic roles within their families (Leonard, 1997). Research points to the significance of family labor in the everyday operations of ethnic business, and especially the importance of women's labor (Yanagisako, 1995). Indeed, women are central to the labor provided in the case of ethnic businesses. There also appears to be an expectation that immigrant wives will participate in the management of family businesses as an extension of their spousal duties that include cooking, cleaning and child rearing (Gupta, 2006). These expectations blur the boundaries between work and home (Dhaliwal, 1998), and also point to structural barriers that limit the possibilities for career advancement, educational opportunities and English language training for working-class and lower-middle class South Asian female immigrants (Shankar, 2008).

South Asian Women's Organizations

Studies of Pakistani-American communities have noted the occurrence of domestic violence especially spousal and familial violence and abuse (Abraham, 2000). A study of South Asians including Pakistani women in the U.S. found that the majority of women included in the study had witnessed or experienced psychological and physical violence in their families (Maker & deRoon-Cassini, 2007). Another study of South Asian immigrant women survivors of partner violence in Canada found that the majority of women drew on social networks and sought professional assistance following domestic violence (Ahmad, Rai, Petrovic, Erickson, & Stewart, 2013). In turn, for these women, recourse to social networks and professional assistance were critically important in their transformation from being a victim to a survivor. Moreover, these women reported an increased sense of autonomy, a more positive outlook, and a greater desire to pursue work opportunities. Such transformations also contributed to a greater sense of belonging to Canada and a desire to contribute to their community.

Since the 1990s, South Asian women's organizations have emerged to provide advocacy for women facing domestic and spousal violence and abuse. These organizations provide support, counseling and legal assistance to South Asian women experiencing domestic and familial violence and abuse (Abraham, 2000; Gupta, 2006). These organizations include: AshaKiran: A Ray of Hope in Alabama; South Asians for Safe Families in Arizona; Maitri, Narika, Sahara and South Asian Network in California; Sneha in Connecticut; Sahara in Florida; Raksha in Georgia; Apna Ghar in Illinois; ASHA – Asian (Women's) Self-Help Association and Counselors Helping Asian Indians (CHAI) in Maryland; Saheli in Massachusetts; Mai Family Services in Michigan; Manavi in New Jersey; the Islamic Center of Long Island, Domestic Harmony Project, Sakhi for South Asian Women and SAATHI in New York; Kiran in North Carolina; Asha: Ray of Hope in Ohio; South Asian Women's Empowerment & Resources Alliance (SAWERA) in Oregon; Asians Against Domestic Abuse, Chetna, Daya and Asian Family Support Services (formerly known as Saheli) in Texas; SAPNA, South Asian Women's Centre, South Asian Community Health Services and South Asian Couple Therapy Project in Toronto; and API Chaya in Seattle (Washington).

South Asian LGBTQIA Organizations

Grassroots South Asian LGBTQIA organizations exist in major cities like Austin, Boston, Chicago, Los Angeles, New York City, San Francisco, Toronto, Vancouver and Washington DC. Organizations include Trikone Tejas in Austin; the Massachusetts Area South Asian Lambda Association (MASALA) in Boston; Sangeet in Chicago, Satrang in Los Angeles; South Asian Lesbian and Gay Association (SALGA) in New York City; Trikone in San Francisco; Khush in Toronto; Sher in Vancouver; and Khush Desi in Washington, D.C.

Importantly, similar organizations are conspicuously absent in Houston, in spite of its large South Asian population. As of 2020, LGBTQIA South Asians in Houston have avoided forming social and civic organizations centered on intersectional religious, ethnic and sexual identities. Rather, Pakistani Muslim American gay men have forged informal social networks comprised of queer Muslim men for friendship, support and community (Afzal, 2014, 2015).

South Asian LGBTQIA individuals report the prevalence of homophobia in their families as well as in segments of the broader Pakistani and Muslim communities in North America (Gupta, 2006). The exclusion of South Asian LGBTQIA organizations from the India Day and the Pakistan Day Parades in New York City is an important example of homophobia within some segments of the South Asian communities. Tensions erupted over the participation of SALGA (South Asian Lesbian and Gay Association) and Sakhi, a progressive women's organization, from marching in the annual India Day Parade. Parade organizers invoked family values, arguing that the inclusion of SALGA and Sakhi at the India Day Parade would send the wrong message to young people watching the parade (Lessinger, 1996). It was only in the year 2001 that the National Federation of Indian Associations reluctantly allowed SALGA and Sakhi to march in the India Day Parade. SALGA continues to be denied permission at the Pakistan Day Parade in New York City (Gupta, 2006).

In spite of homophobia and transphobia within their ethnic and religious communities, gay, lesbian, bisexual and transgender Pakistanis in the U.S. and Canada nonetheless construct a queer identity that incorporates ethnicity and religion. Narratives and biographies of LGBTQIA Muslim activists in Canada and the U.S. in research studies illuminate the importance of Islam and self-identification as Muslims for many gay and bisexual Pakistani men and women in North America (Afzal, 2014, 2015; Kugle, 2014). As the narratives and biographies included in these research studies demonstrate, lesbian, gay, bisexual and transgender Muslims in the United States and Canada do not reject Islam. Rather, they actively engage with Islam by reinterpreting the Qur'an. Others participate in lesbian and gay Muslim groups and seek out LGBTQIA co-religionists in an effort to reconcile their non-heteronormative sexuality with a professed belonging to Islam (Afzal, 2015).

Ethnic and Racial Intermarriages

Given the relative absence of research data on ethnic and racial intermarriages in Pakistani communities in North America, it is difficult to make any definitive claims about this topic. Available literature on the topic points to familial tensions and conflicts regarding dating, "love-marriages" and arranged marriages. Research suggests that among many segments of the Pakistani community, especially in the first-generation, dating and "love marriages" are discouraged and arranged marriage is preferred. Relatedly, pre-marital sex and public expressions of affection between men and women are not condoned in some segments of the Pakistani population (Leonard, 1997).

In some families, intergenerational conflict persists over the role of parents in selecting a partner for marriage versus the freedom to choose one's life partner (Pavri, 2009). At the same time, a study noted a gradual openness and changes in parental attitudes toward marriages outside of the Pakistani community (Zaki, 2013). This study found that while parents are increasingly open to their children marrying outside of the Pakistani community, there is still an expectation that the children will marry within their religious community. Another study similarly found that Pakistani men and women preferred a Muslim or a convert to Islam as their marriage partner regardless of ethnic or racial background (Skerry, 2013). More broadly, a study showed that intermarriage is in fact quite common within Pakistani communities in North America and that the rate of intermarriages will only increase with each successive generation (Moore, 2011). This openness runs counters to concern from some religious leaders and organizations that emphasize in-group marriages as a way to promote the continuity of family, community, religious traditions and control of female sexuality (Leonard, 1997).

As evident from the above studies, an emphasis on religion permeates the issue of ethnic and racial intermarriages. These findings notwithstanding, greater research is required to document the full range of experiences around racial and ethnic intermarriages among the Pakistanis in North America.

Educational Expectations and Achievements and Career Patterns

Similar to other Asian American communities, there is a concerted emphasis on higher education and career achievements by parents in Pakistani families in the U.S. and Canada. An overview of the educational and professional profiles of Pakistani immigrants to North America provides insights into the structural barriers to upward economic mobility in mainstream corporate and private sectors.

As discussed earlier in the chapter, the opening up of immigration from Asia following immigration reforms of 1965 in the U.S. selected for educated, middle-class and elite men. As a result of this Act, the vast majority of post-1965 Pakistani immigrants were male, middle-class and elite, urban professionals such as engineers, physicians, scientists and other skilled workers. Many initially arrived for higher education and planned to return to Pakistan following the completion of their education. However, a significant number applied for a work permit and subsequently, permanent residency and citizenship and chose to build careers and family in North America (Afzal, 2015; Zaki, 2013).

In part due to the growth of the South Asian ethnic economy since the 1990s, many Pakistanis have turned to entrepreneurship and started businesses that cater to a South Asian clientele. Moreover, a significant percentage of Pakistanis, who received their education in Pakistan, have found that their foreign academic and professional credentials have not translated into jobs and careers in their professional fields in the U.S. and Canada. The concentration of Pakistanis in the taxi cab industry in cities such as Toronto, New York City and Washington, D.C. and in the convenience store business in Houston reflects job markets that are marked by an ease of entry (Afzal, 2015). These careers also point to structural barriers to upward economic mobility in the context of a highly racialized North America in which career and educational opportunities are circumscribed by race and ethnicity (Shankar, 2008).

In spite of structural barriers, parents place a high emphasis on academic achievement and career attainment of their children (Leonard, 1997; Shankar, 2008). Medicine, engineering and business administration are especially favored and parents push their children to pursue higher education at elite institutions (Afzal, 2015). However, in spite of a preference for the hard sciences, second and third generation Pakistani Americans and Pakistani Canadians have built successful careers in the arts and music, public service and social work. Nonetheless, the emphasis on higher educational and career expectations can be excessive and is a source of stress for the children who may come to resent their parents (Leonard, 1997).

Implications for Counselors and Social Workers

The overview of Pakistanis in North America in this chapter points to three salient issues that have implications for counselors and social workers who work with Pakistani communities. One, as discussed in this chapter, Pakistanis have forged alliances with other South Asian nationality groups to form community-based organizations that address pressing issues such as domestic violence and the abuse of women, and homophobia and transphobia. It will be important for counselors and social workers to network and collaborate with these organizations to design culturally appropriate practices and strategies in order to effectively intervene in issues impacting Pakistani women and LGBTQIA Pakistanis.

Two, the post-9/11 period has been characterized by the rise of Islamophobia, discrimination, harassment and racism in the U.S. and Canada, as Pakistani immigrants have found themselves at the receiving end of governmental profiling and surveillance on the one hand and hate crimes directed towards them from the general public on the other. Counselors and social workers should work with community elders and leaders to make contact with Pakistanis, especially the undocumented and the working poor who remain the most vulnerable to state regimes of surveillance. Equally, it will be important for counselors to consider the occurrence of post-traumatic stress disorders and anxiety within the Pakistani population due to persistent surveillance and profiling, racism and harassment.

Three, research points to a reluctance if not a stigma attached to seeking out mental health and social services within some segments of the Pakistani population in North America. Rather, a segment of Pakistani population is more open to the use of traditional homeopathic medicine and spiritual healing practices (Zaki, 2013). Counselors and social workers should seek to incorporate such medicinal and healing practices in coming up with effective treatment strategies. Relatedly, counselors and social workers should also consider the variety of sources consulted by Pakistanis for mental health issues. For example, segments of the Pakistani population, especially first generation Pakistani Canadians and Pakistani Americans may prefer to seek counsel from community elders, kin and friends, in addition to religious specialists such as holy men and imams at local mosques (Ashraf, 2016). Counselors and social workers should seek to identity and collaborate with such sources on a case-by-case basis in designing effective mental health treatment.

Conclusions

Certain common themes emerge from the survey of Pakistani families in North America in this chapter. One, it is not accurate to conceptualize the Pakistani experience in either the United States or in Canada as monolithic and Pakistanis as a homogenous community. Indeed, it is difficult to generalize Pakistani families in North America, as familial experiences and individual identities vary by age, gender, sexuality, educational level, socio-economic status, religious affiliation and levels of religiosity, and citizenship status among other markers of identity.

Two, there is an increasing emphasis on religion in mediating assimilation and incorporation into the mainstream society in the U.S. and Canada and in constructing transnational identity and community. This emphasis intersects with Islamophobic state policies and discourses centered on a persistent slippage between Pakistanis and the perpetrators of terrorism. Professed emphasis on religion is a significant mediating lens in constructing a transnational and an American identity. Religion also increasingly shapes consumption patterns, friendship circles, the choice of marriage partner, and family values and life.

Three, in spite of incorporation into mainstream societies in the United States of America and Canada and the salience of religion, Pakistani Americans and Pakistani Canadians are a transnational community with varying levels of involvement and engagements in the homeland. These engagements are varied and include visits to relatives and family in Pakistan, remittances and charitable contributions to organizations and family and kin, and interest in Pakistani politics and nation-building, among others.

Finally, Pakistani women, and gay, lesbian and transgender men and women are especially vulnerable to multiple levels of oppression and violence. There is a relative invisibility of these issues and concerns facing women and LGBTQIA+ in public discourse within broader Pakistani community life. Yet, anecdotal evidence and available research data points to the vulnerabilities and stresses faced by these segments of the Pakistani population in North America.

Future Research

Given the relative paucity of research on Pakistani communities in North America, it will be imperative for future research to more fully address acculturation and socialization practices and the ways these practices vary by gender, sexuality, age, and citizenship and socio-economic status. It will be important to also consider the prevalence of post-traumatic stress disorder among the undocumented and the working class, who are especially vulnerable to profiling and state regimes of surveillance and racial profiling. The issues of domestic violence and abuse among women, and homophobia and transphobia, and HIV occurrence in Pakistani immigrant populations also requires additional research.

References

Abraham, M. (2000). *Speaking the unspeakable: Marital violence among South Asian immigrants in the United States*. New Brunswick, NJ: Rutgers University Press.

Abu-Lughod, L. (2002). Do Muslim women really need saving?: Anthropological reflections on cultural relativism and its others. *American Anthropologist, 104*(3), 783–790. https://doi.org/10.1525/aa.2002.104.3.783

Afzal, A. (2010). From an informal to a transnational Muslim heritage economy: Transformations in the Pakistani ethnic economy in Houston, Texas. *Urban Anthropology, 39*(4), 397–424.

Afzal, A. (2014). "Being gay has been a curse for me": Gay Muslim Americans, narrative and negotiations of belonging in the Muslim ummah. *Journal of Language and Sexuality, Special Issue: Queering Borders: Language, Sexuality and Migration, 3*(1), 60–86. https://doi.org/10.1075/jls.3.1.04afz

Afzal, A. (2015). *Lone star Muslims: Transnational lives and the South Asian experience in Texas*. New York University Press.

Ahmad, F., Rai, N., Petrovic, B., Erickson, P., & Stewart, D. (2013). Resilience and resources among South Asian immigrant women as survivors of partner violence. *Journal of Immigrant Minority Health, 15*, 1057–1064. https://doi.org/10.1007/s10903-013-9836-2

Ashraf, A. K. (2016). *Perceptions of mental health amongst Pakistani-Americans* (Unpublished master's thesis). California State University, San Bernardino, CA.

Bald, V. (2015). *Bengali Harlem and the lost history of South Asian America*. Harvard University Press.

Basch, L., Blanc-Szanton, C., & Glick Schiller, N. (Eds.). (1992). *Towards a transnational perspective on migration: Race, class, ethnicity, and nationalism reconsidered*. Annals of the New York Academy of Sciences.

Center for American Progress. (2015). *Who are Pakistani Americans?* Washington, DC: Center for American Progress.

D'Alisera, J. (2004). *An imagined geography: Sierra Leonean Muslims in America*. University of Pennsylvania Press.

Dasgupta, S. (1998). *A patchwork shawl: Chronicles of South Asian women in America*. Rutgers University Press.

Dhaliwal, S. (1998). Silent contributors: Asian female entrepreneurs and women in business. *Women's Studies International Forum, 21*(5), 463–474.

Diamant, J. (2017). *American Muslims are concerned – but also satisfied with their lives*. Washington, DC: Pew Research Center. http://www.pewresearch.org/fact-tank/2017/07/26/american-muslims-are-concerned-but-also-satisfied-with-their-lives/

Glasse, C. (2001). *The new encyclopedia of Islam*. New York, NY: Altamira Press.

Gole, N. (1996). *The forbidden modern: Civilization and veiling (critical perspectives on women and gender)*. The University of Michigan Press.

Gupta, M. D. (2006). *Unruly immigrants: Rights, activism and transnational South Asian politics in the United States*. Duke University Press.

Haider, M. (2016, November 26). The harsh reality of Pakistanis living in Canada. *Dawn*. https://www.dawn.com/news/1298978

Islam, F., Khanlou, N., & Tamim, H. (2014). South Asian populations in Canada: Migration and mental health. *BMC Psychiatry, 14*, 154–166. https://doi.org/10.1186/1471-244X-14-154

Jamil, U. (2014). The impact of securitization on South Asian Muslims. In P. Bramadat & L. Dawson (Eds.), *Religious radicalization and securitization in Canada and beyond* (pp. 145–163). University of Toronto Press.

Jibeen, T., & Khalid, R. (2010). Predictors of psychological well-being of Pakistani immigrants in Toronto, Canada. *International Journal of Intercultural Relations, 34*, 452–464. https://doi.org/10.1016/j.ijintrel.2010.04.010

Khaleque, A., Malik, F., & Rohner, R. P. (2015). Differential acculturation among Pakistani American immigrant parents and children. *Psychological Studies, 60*(4), 407–411. https://doi.org/10.1007/s12646-015-0337-3

Kugle, S. S. A.-H. (2014). *Living out Islam: Voices of gay, lesbian, and transgender Muslims*. New York University Press.

Leonard, K. (1992). *Making ethnic choices: California's Punjabi Mexican Americans*. Temple University Press.

Leonard, K. (1997). *The South Asian Americans (The New Americans)*. Greenwood Press.

Lessinger, J. (1996). *From the Ganges to the Hudson: Indian immigrants in New York City*. Allyn and Bacon.

Magocsi, P. (1999). *Encyclopedia of Canada's peoples*. Toronto, ON: Multicultural History Society of Ontario.

Maira, S. (2009). *Missing: Youth, citizenship, and empire after 9/11*. Duke University Press.

Maker, A. H., & deRoon-Cassini, T. (2007). Prevalence, perpetrators, and characteristics of witnessing parental violence and adult dating violence in Latina, East Asian, South Asian, and Middle Eastern Women. *Violence and Victims, 22*(5), 632–646. https://doi.org/10.1891/088667007782312122

McDaniel, P., & Drever, A. (2009). Ethnic enclave or international corridor? Immigrant businesses in a new South city. *Southeastern Geographer, 49*(1), 3–23. https://doi.org/10.1353/sgo.0.0040

Miller, M. J., Yang, M., Farrell, J., & Lin, L. (2011). Racial and cultural factors affecting the mental health of Asian Americans. *American Journal of Orthopsychiatry, 81*(4), 4889–4897. https://doi.org/10.1111/2Fj.1939-0025.2011.01118.x

Moore, K. M. (2011). Pakistani immigrants. In R. H. Bayor (Ed.), *Multicultural America: An encyclopedia of the newest Americans* (pp. 1655–1693). Greenwood Press.

Najam, A. (2006). *Portrait of a giving community: Philanthropy by the Pakistani-American Diaspora*. Harvard University Press.
Ong, P., & Liu, J. (2000). U.S. immigration policies and Asian migration. In M. Zhou & J. V. Gatewood (Eds.), *Contemporary Asian America: A multidisciplinary reader* (pp. 155–174). New York University Press.
Pavri, T. (2009, March 29). *Pakistani Americans*. http://www.everyculture.com/multi/Le-Pa/Pakistani-Americans.html#ixzz4fnRyxwop
Powell, J. (2005). *Encyclopedia of North American immigration*. Facts on File.
Prashad, V. (2000). *Karma of brown folk*. Minneapolis, MN: University of Minnesota Press.
Rana, J. (2011). *Terrifying Muslims: Race and labor in the South Asian Diaspora*. Duke University Press.
Rangaswamy, P. (2000). *Namasté America: Indian immigrants in an American metropolis*. Pennsylvania State University Press.
Shah, N. (2011). *Stranger intimacy: Contesting race, sexuality and the law in the North American West*. University of California Press.
Shankar, S. (2008). *Desi Land: Teen culture, class and success in Silicon Valley*. Duke University Press.
Skerry, P. (2013). *Problems of the second generation: To be young, Muslim, and American*. Washington DC: Brookings Institute. https://www.brookings.edu/articles/problems-of-the-second-generation-to-be-young-muslim-and-american/
Spencer, M., Chen, J., Gee, G., Fabian, C., & Takeuchi, D. (2010). Discrimination and mental health-related service use in a national study of Asian Americans. *American Journal of Public Health, 100*(12), 2410–2416. https://doi.org/10.2105/AJPH.2009.176321
Statistics Canada. (2006). *Census of population*. Statistics Canada catalogue no. 97-563-XWE2006002.
Statistics Canada. (2016). *Census of population*. Statistics Canada catalogue no. 98-400-X2016187.
Ta, V., Holck, P., & Gee, G. (2010). Generational status and family cohesion effects on the receipt of mental health services among Asian Americans: Findings from the National Latino and Asian American Study. *American Journal of Public Health, 100*(1), 115–121. https://doi.org/10.2105/AJPH.2009.160762
Thangaraj, S. I. (2015). *Desi hoop dreams: Pickup basketball and the making of Asian American masculinity*. New York University Press.
Williams, R. B. (1988). *Religions of immigrants from India and Pakistan: New threads in the American tapestry*. Cambridge University Press.
Yanagisako, S. (1995). Transforming orientalism: Gender, nationality and class in Asian American studies. In S. J. Yanagisako & C. L. Delaney (Eds.), *Naturalizing power: Essays in feminist cultural analysis* (pp. 275–298). Routledge.
Zaki, K. P. (2013). Pakistanis and Pakistani Americans, 1940-present. In E. R. Barkan (Ed.), *Immigrants in American history: Arrival, adaptation, and integration* (pp. 1181–1192). ABC-CLIO.

Part IV
Specific Countries and Regions of Origin: West Asia

Chapter 11
Arab Families From the Levant (Lebanese, Syrian, Palestinian, Jordanian): Adaptation and Mental Health

Julie Hakim-Larson and Shawna A. Scott

Abstract The region of the Arab Middle East known as the Levant is located on the continent of southwestern Asia and includes the people of Lebanon, Syria, Israel/Palestine, and Jordan. The focus of this chapter is on the immigration of families from this region to the United States and Canada. This chapter provides a summary of the culture and values that the people of these regions bring with them when they immigrate to North America, as well as the currently available demographic patterns of data. Mental health and family vulnerability issues are reviewed given the potential histories of wartime trauma and post-migration acculturative stresses, including prejudice and discrimination experienced by those from the Levant. The implications of adverse life circumstances for adaptation and resilient functioning are highlighted in the context of acculturation issues, preventative interventions, and future research agendas.

Keywords Levant · Arab Americans · Arab Canadians · Acculturation · Mental health · Resilience · Bioecological theory · Prevention · Intervention · Immigration · Families · Trauma

Pre-migration, migration, and post-migration issues are all relevant ones to consider in fostering the overall health and well-being of Arab families in North America whose origins are from the Levant region of the Middle East. The Levant region includes the modern-day countries of Syria, Lebanon, and Israel/Palestine (Mansel, 2010), as well as some regions of western Jordan (BibArch, 2013). The inhabitants of this region have a wide diversity of backgrounds, and Eastern or Levantine Arabic

---

J. Hakim-Larson (✉) · S. A. Scott
University of Windsor, Windsor, ON, Canada
e-mail: hakim@uwindsor.ca; scott1p@uwindsor.ca

S. S. Chuang et al. (eds.), *Asian Families in Canada and the United States*, Advances in Immigrant Family Research,
https://doi.org/10.1007/978-3-030-56452-0_11

is only one of the many languages spoken. The focus of this chapter is on Arab people who speak the Levantine or Eastern Arabic dialect (El-Baz, 1968), a group whose members have been immigrating to North America for more than a century.

We have used a bioecological approach to provide an overview of the microsystems and macrosystems relevant for the adaptation of Levantine Arab families to North American life. Racism, discrimination, and prejudicial attitudes, prevalent historically, have extended into contemporary times. Historically, pre-migration wars and conflicts influenced the immigration patterns to North America; thus, the demographics of five waves of immigration to North America since the late nineteenth century are summarized. Following next are discussions of the stress of acculturation to the United States and Canada and socialization to foster enculturation and preservation of the heritage culture. A presentation of religious and family values is followed by sections that address gender roles, intermarriages, and educational and career achievements. Finally, we consider implications for the mental health and adaptation of families from the Levant and future directions for research and practice.

Bioecological Theory and Levant Families

Taking a bioecological approach to human development (e.g., Bronfenbrenner, 1994; Bronfenbrenner & Morris, 2006), it becomes apparent that sociopolitical issues have direct relevance for the mental health and well-being of immigrant families who may be stressed by both historical memories and ongoing turmoil. For example, Phillips and Lauterbach (2017) highlighted the importance of examining the mental health of American Muslim immigrants, many of whom are from the Levant region, through a transactional model such as Ecological Systems Theory (Bronfenbrenner, 1994). They proposed examining interactions between microsystem and macrosystem variables with respect to racism, mental health, and mental health stigma as experienced by American Muslim immigrants.

Microsystem and Macrosystem Racism

Microsystem racism corresponds to discrimination within settings such as home, school, and the workplace and has been found to be associated with poor mental and physical health. Even though not all Arabs are Muslim (many are Christian, other religious denominations, or no religion) and not all Muslims are Arabs (most Muslims worldwide come from outside the Middle East), the terms 'Arab' and 'Muslim' are often conflated in North America (Suleiman, 1999). Thus, racism and discrimination towards one group often generalizes to the other. This overgeneralization has been especially likely to occur after the tragic events of 9/11, resulting in the two groups often being treated as one monolithic entity (e.g., Cainkar, 2016).

Consistent with the macrosystem generalized racial discrimination, American Muslim immigrants with mental illness tend to be especially prone to mental health stigma and aversive interpersonal interactions (e.g., Phillips & Lauterbach, 2017). Discrimination toward Arab Americans more generally has been linked to increases in their psychological distress (Awad & Amayreh, 2016). In addition, children in U.S. elementary schools have been found to hold stereotypes and prejudicial views about Arab Muslim immigrants as compared to Arabs without clothing that indicates they are Muslim and White families from Ireland (Brown, Ali, Stone, & Jewell, 2017). In the Brown et al. study (2017), children ages 6–11 years in the United States read three vignettes about immigrant families. They found that the children viewed Arab Muslim males as anti-American and perceived Arab Muslim females as more oppressed than the other groups, and this was particularly the case for those who had limited contact with Arab Muslims. When children did not distinguish Arab Muslims and the American in-group, they had a more positive attitude toward Arab Muslims who immigrated to the United States in the vignette.

Macrosystem racism includes ideological and institutional racism and captures the systemic oppression associated with factors such as socio-economic status, resources, and employment, all of which are associated with mental health outcomes (Phillips & Lauterbach, 2017). Scholars have noted that even though Arab Americans tend to be better educated than the general American population, they may nonetheless experience racism, discrimination, social injustices, disparities, and intolerance (Arab American Institute, 2017). While macrosystem racism has a distal influence on Arab immigrants, microsystem racism has more proximal and direct effects on everyday interactions at home, school and work through microaggressions and insults (Phillips & Lauterbach, 2017).

To better understand the contemporary sociopolitical climates for Arab families in Canada and the US where such macrosystem and microsystem racism occurs, a closer examination of the both pre- and post-migration pathways is needed to contextualize Arab families. The insights from sociohistorical landscape for Arab families may assist in finding ways to counteract discrimination and promote social justice and tolerance with the goal of promoting the adaptation and well-being of Arab families from the Levant.

Pre-Migration Influences and Immigration Patterns

The pan-ethnic term, Arab American which includes people from the Levant, is relatively new and arose in the 1970s due to the many socio-political changes and events occurring in the Middle East (Abdelhady, 2014). Arab Americans come from both northern Africa and southwest Asia and thus vary by race, religion, and country-of-origin; the common binding factor is the Arabic language and culture arising from their homelands in one of the 22 Arab League of States that extend from Morocco in the West to the Arabian Peninsula and Persian Gulf in the east (e.g., Samhan, 2001). A broad label given to the region is MENA, which stands for

Middle Eastern and North African and includes the Levant, Arabic speaking countries, and Middle Eastern countries where Arabic is not the official language (e.g., Afghanistan, Iran). Given this heterogeneity, it is important to consider pre-migration influences on the well-being of families by specific country of origin, and region within country, whenever possible.

Taking into consideration sociopolitical history, of interest and concern is the fact that pre-migration individuals originating in the Levant region who are closer to the epicentre of regional conflicts and warfare tend to be impacted more profoundly by the traumatic events. Regions of the Levant have been sought after for their land, oil, water, and the coastline for trade purposes; the ensuing conflicts have thus devastated the region's families and affected their local cultures for centuries (Abi-Hashem, 2006). During the multiple and ongoing wars in the Arab Levant, some people have rebelled and fought while remaining in their homeland, while others have fled and coped by leaving their war-torn country in search of safety, better economic opportunities, and a better life for themselves and their families (e.g., Naff, 1985). Immigration patterns from the Levant and from other Arabic-speaking regions of the Middle East have varied throughout history and include those who came directly to North America from their homelands for economic advancement, those who were attempting to escape wartime adversities, and those who incurred multiple displacements to other countries around the world (e.g., Europe, other countries in the Middle East, Africa) before finally settling in North America (e.g., Abdelhady, 2014; Hodes et al., 2018; Mowafi, 2011).

Arab immigrants have arrived in the United States in four major waves in recent history (Nassar-McMillan, Ajrouch, & Hakim-Larson, 2014) with a fifth wave that is current. In the first wave of Arab immigration to America in the late 19th and early 20th centuries, Arab ethnic communities or enclaves were settled in a variety of locations (e.g., Cedar Rapids, Iowa; Detroit, Michigan); these immigrants supported their families primarily as peddlers or as laborers in industry (e.g., factory workers) (Naff, 1985). This first wave of Arab immigration occurred from the 1870s to the mid-1920s and consisted primarily of families from Greater Syria (Syria, Lebanon, and Palestine) (Haboush & Barakat, 2014). These people were of Semitic origin and descended from the indigenous inhabitants of the region extending back to the Neolithic period (Nydell, 2006). The Levantine people from this initial wave were mostly Christian non-professionals (farmers, peddlers, shopkeepers, and laborers) in search of a better life trying to escape the Ottoman occupation (Suleiman, 1999).

The second wave extended from post-World War II to the mid-1960s and included families from Palestine, Jordan, Egypt, Syria, and Iraq. They were primarily Muslim skilled professionals who were escaping war and civil conflicts in their countries of origin (Abdelhady, 2014). The third wave of immigration extended from the mid-1960s to the early 2000s and included primarily Muslim professional and non-professional immigrants from Palestine, Jordan, Lebanon, Egypt, Iraq, and Syria who were fleeing a series of civil wars and regional conflicts taking place in the Middle East (Suleiman, 1999).

The fourth wave of immigrant professionals and non-professionals has extended from the early 2000s to about 2011. This more recent wave not only included Arab families from the Levant but also those from other regions, such as Iraq and North Africa; their reasons for immigration included political instability and lack of economic opportunities in addition to wars (Haboush & Barakat, 2014). Immigration subsided only temporarily in the immediate aftermath of the September 11, 2001 attacks on the United States (Sue & Sue, 2008). Many immigrants from the Middle East have had extensive exposure to war and political unrest, have limited English language proficiency which affects their opportunities for work or further education, and have had to contend with discrimination in a post 9/11 era that included a number of changes in government policies (Haboush & Barakat, 2014).

A fifth wave of ongoing immigration is currently occurring worldwide. The Syrian civil war has led to historically unprecedented displacement of 13 million people (Connor, 2018). Since the beginning of the Syrian civil war around 2011, Syrians have either been internally displaced (more than 6 million or approximately 50%) or have had to flee; those who have fled their homeland have resettled in the Levant (e.g., Lebanon, Jordan), other countries in the Middle East (e.g., Turkey, Iraq, Egypt), in Europe, or various other countries around the world including Canada and the United States (Connor, 2018), as discussed further next.

Immigration of Syrian Refugees

Although the U.S. and Canada have both accepted some Syrian refugees as a result of the international crisis resulting from the Syrian civil war (ongoing since 2011), their histories and current policies differ. The Pew Research Center (Radford & Connor, 2019) conducted an analysis concerning resettled refugees in 2018 from the United Nations High Commissioner for Refugees and found that while nearly half of the world's refugees in 2018 were from the Middle East, less than 1% of the refugees resettled in the U.S. were from that region; furthermore, in 2018 for the first time Canada resettled more refugees overall than the US. Policy changes in the Trump administration have led to a lower cap placed on the number of Arab refugees allowed into the US as compared to previous years (Radford & Connor, 2019). In addition, the overall number of refugees admitted to the US under the Trump administration progressively declined after 2016 (Krogstad, 2019).

Contrary to the current relatively open immigration policy in Canada, Arabs faced barriers to their admission to Canada and were considered among the undesirable immigrants prior to World War II. It was thought that the influx of Arab immigrants would have a negative impact on Canada's Anglo-Saxon heritage and emphasis on White European culture (Abu-Laban & Abu-Laban, 1999b). These views began to change after World War II, and Canada began to liberalize its immigration policy for Arabs especially after 1967 (Abu-Laban & Abu-Laban, 1999b). A policy of multiculturalism was introduced in Canada in 1972 with the goals to avoid assimilation, increase intergroup harmony, increase intergroup contact and sharing, and encourage the learning of English and French (Berry et al., 2006). From 1990 to 1993, there was a great increase in Arab immigrants arriving in Canada who were fleeing the war in Lebanon (Canadian Arab Institute, 2013). Between January 2015 and May 2016, approximately 25,000 refugees from Syria resettled in Canada (Houle, 2019). Among those who were refugees from Syria, the majority were younger than other groups of refugees, and 85% were couples with their children. Demographic characteristics also differed between government-assisted refugees and privately sponsored refugees. As compared to privately sponsored Syrian refugees, government-assisted Syrian refugees tended to belong to larger families, were younger, had lower levels of education, and less proficiency in English or French. Over half of the refugees admitted into Canada in 2018 were from the Middle East (Radford & Connor, 2019).

Current Demographic Trends

Collecting information about the demographics of people from the Middle East and the Arab Levant has been challenging for researchers because these immigrants and refugees have been classified inconsistently and unreliably throughout history by their assumed race or another shifting category of classification; as a result, Arabs in the U.S. have often been described as an 'invisible' minority (Naber, 2000). Nonetheless, organizations such as the Arab American Institute in Washington, DC, continue to work towards collecting reliable information and estimates regarding Arab ancestry demographics.

The Arab American Institute (2019a) in the US estimates that there are approximately 3.7 million Americans with Arab ancestry. However, there are discrepancies between this estimate and the more conservative estimates arising from the ancestry question methods used by the U.S. Census Bureau, which have resulted in an undercount of the Arab American population. The U.S. Census Bureau (2018) used the results of the American Community Survey and estimated that there are at least 2.1 million Arab Americans in the U.S. Of the total number of Arab Americans in the U.S. in 2018, 496, 962 reported Lebanese ancestry (which is the largest subgroup of Arab ancestry in the U.S.), 192,497 reported a Syrian ancestry; 129,431 reported a Palestinian ancestry; and 95,937 reported a Jordanian ancestry (U.S. Census Bureau, 2018). In the United States currently, the majority of Arab Americans are descendants of the early immigrants who were primarily Christian, while Muslims represent the fastest growing segment of the Arab American community given recent immigration from the primarily Muslim Arab world after 1965 (Arab American Institute, 2019a; Arab American National Museum, 2009).

In the Arab world in general, there is a 'youth bulge' with the majority of people under 25 years of age (Harb, 2016). Arabs in both Canada and in the U.S. also are considered to be a relatively young group. Arab Canadians are considered to be among the visible minorities according to Canada's Employment Equity Act. Among visible minorities, those of Arab ancestry represent the second youngest group, with a median age of 30.2 years, compared to 40.1 years for the entire Canadian population (Statistics Canada, 2011).

According to the results from the 2016 Canadian Census (Statistics Canada, 2016), 219,555 Canadians reported having a Lebanese origin; 44,820 reported having a Palestinian origin; 77,045 reported having a Syrian origin and 14,250 reported having a Jordanian origin. In 2016, Arabic was reported to be spoken by 629,055 Canadians, with 419,890 reporting Arabic as their mother tongue. It is important to take into consideration how countries have defined Arab immigrants. The U.S. Census Bureau's definition of Arab ancestry is quite heterogeneous, as Arabs are described as individuals with ancestry originating from any of the Arabic-speaking countries of the world (de la Cruz & Brittingham, 2003). Unlike Canada, the U.S. does not officially recognize Arab Americans as a visible minority group. Noteworthy is the fact that obtaining accurate data is therefore quite difficult for researchers and practitioners because Arab Americans are counted among people who are designated as White or Caucasian, making them indistinguishable from European Americans in research, unless specific ancestry questions are posed (Samhan, 2014). Such specific ancestry questions are not included on the basic form that is sent to all families in the U.S. Census. There are pros and cons regarding the various potential methods of collecting census ancestry data, an issue that is currently being studied by the U. S. Census Bureau (Samhan, 2014), and is as yet unresolved (Arab American Institute, 2019b).

There has been a 76% increase in the number of people living in the U.S. with an Arab ancestry from 1990 to the 2006–2010 time period (Asi & Beaulieu, 2013). With each successive wave of immigration, there has been an increase in the number of Arab Americans. In addition, given that the first wave of immigration occurred at the turn of the late 19th and early 20th centuries, there are now an unknown number of third, fourth, and even fifth generation Arab Americans, many of whom continue to have informal ties to their ancestry through cultural traditions in their religious institutions and food preparations.

Arab Ethnic Identity: Acculturation and Acculturative Stress

For immigrants and refugees, maintaining an ethnic identity that allows them to retain their heritage culture while acculturating to their host culture is sometimes stressful and may lead to mental health challenges. Like other immigrant families, Arab Americans and Arab Canadians must adapt to their new environment by learning or improving on their use of the language(s) in their host culture and finding new emotional support systems (Nydell, 2006). Immigrants generally have to overcome barriers to their adjustment into the workforce, school systems, their neighborhood, and the legal systems in their new country of residence, all of which is quite stressful and this can be especially the case for younger recent Syrian immigrants, many of whom have parents facing acculturation challenges themselves (Hadfield, Ostrowski, & Ungar, 2017).

The pre-migration stresses for families from the Levant include their exposure to wars and its effects directly or vicariously on themselves, their family members, and their friends and acquaintances (Hadfield et al., 2017). During migration, many developed the status of 'refugee' and had to settle and resettle sometimes in places that were also war-torn geographical regions before eventually arriving in the US (Hakim-Larson, Kamoo, Nassar-McMillan, & Porcerelli, 2007). Another stressor is when the families' preferred settlement location could not accommodate the family and thus, the family had to settle away from their relatives and friends (Hadfield et al., 2017). Exposure to torture and other forms of abuse and suffering before migrating can be cumulatively stressful and add to difficulties in coping and adapting during the post-migration acculturation process (Kira, Amer, & Wrobel, 2014).

For immigrants of Arab ancestry, post-migration acculturative stress is complicated even more by the issue of prejudicial feelings and overt discrimination post 9–11 (Ahmed & Mana, 2017; Awad, 2010; Nassar-McMillan, Lambert, & Hakim-Larson, 2011). To cope with this, children of immigrants may strive toward assimilation; thus, an acculturation gap may exist in which there is a discrepancy in the degree to which parents and their children adopt the values and customs of their new post-migration culture. This gap can lead to intergenerational conflicts and an exacerbation of post-migration difficulties involving ethnocultural identity development (Rasmi, Chuang, & Hennig, 2015).

Acculturation stress may be especially problematic for immigrants and their children who are Muslim due to their visibly noticeable religious dress. Amer (2014) and Awad (2010) found that Arab Americans who are Muslim in contrast to those who are Christian, may be more likely to be the subject of discrimination, and may therefore experience greater levels of acculturative stress. However, having a strong ethnic identity (i.e., identification with the heritage culture) and the support of one's local Muslim community are likely to be protective factors. When Middle Eastern/Arab American adults have high religiosity and low to moderate levels of family connectedness, they are vulnerable to psychological distress associated with ethnic discrimination (Ikizler & Szymanski, 2017). Family connectedness, religious, and cultural factors have complex, and perhaps unique, relations to psychological distress among Middle Eastern/Arab Americans.

At a sociopolitical level, Muslim Arabs residing in North America where Judeo-Christian values and customs are normative, may be viewed with caution and skepticism in their communication and interpersonal interactions with those in the mainstream culture. This type of prejudice likely has implications for their adjustment and ethnic identity development (e.g., Britto, 2008; Britto & Amer, 2007), although additional research is needed to clarify the conditions under which it is likely to occur. Skin color and overt physical features in addition to religious dress, may also affect discrimination experiences and ethnic identity differentially with some individuals of Arab ethnicity self-identifying as being 'White' and others self-identifying as being a 'person of color' (Awad & Amayreh, 2016).

Many Christian immigrants from the Levant were among some of the earliest immigrants to North America, and several generations later remain a large percentage of the Levantine Arab ethnic group in North America. Many of them have adapted in ways that differ from more recent immigrants who tend to more likely be Muslim (Suleiman, 1999). Thus, these religious differences in Arab Americans and Arab Canadians may be due to generational status and historical immigration pattern differences between families from different religious backgrounds (Amer, 2014).

The extent of the support networks and community organizations may be qualitatively different for Arab Americans who are Christian in comparison to those who are Muslim for more than one reason. Arab Christians are religiously and culturally closer to the dominant western society which may give them more options for active participation in their local communities (e.g., they can attend any of a variety of Christian church services). In addition, they have roots that are more likely to go back several generations in North America with some intermarriages outside of the Arab community. Depending on whether an Arab Muslim family has immigrated to a community with many local resources and relevant activities, they may or may not have as many options available for local community supports.

Although there are some differences among Arab religious groups in North America, Khoury (2017) has noted that additional factors such as socioeconomic status (SES) and income also play a role in acculturation and the associated stresses since many individuals show less strict adherence to their respective religions over time. Thus, similarities may outweigh differences. Similarly, hostilities in the Arab world with Israel may not carry over to everyday interactions between those of the Christian, Muslim and Jewish faiths in North America, as perceived similarities in Middle Eastern culture (e.g., food, traditions) and values may outweigh the perceived differences (Khoury, 2017). The possible lessening of perceived differences among those belonging to various religious groups in North America as a function of SES, income, and acculturation status are issues worthy of future study.

Socialization of Beliefs and Values Within the Family: The Enculturation Process

In developing an Arab heritage ethnic identity, immigrants to North America and their children must be socialized into the beliefs and values of their respective Levantine Arab heritage cultures. Dominant Western values in North America include individualism, in which personal privacy, autonomous functioning, equality under the law, and environmental control by humans are emphasized (Nydell, 2006). In contrast, Arab beliefs and values are more collectivistic with clear distinctions assumed between men and women, an emphasis placed on family and social group goals (rather than personal ones), and a belief in fate or destiny (Nydell, 2006). Individualism includes emotional detachment from the social group, an emphasis on the needs and desires of the self, maximizing personal profits and avoiding personal losses, and the understanding that one's viewpoint is independent of that of the group (Triandis, 1994). This individualistic approach may be viewed as 'selfish' and unhealthy by those who come from collectivistic cultures, where top priority is given to the needs and goals of the extended family (Abi-Hashem, 2008). The collective determines what is appropriate to believe and what the norms are for behaviors that are implemented in a cooperative and self-sacrificing way for the good of the group (Triandis, 1994).

In addition to acculturating to the host culture and adapting to individualistic values, Arab immigrants and refugees become enculturated (i.e., socialized) into some of the collectivistic features of their ancestral heritage culture through interactions with their families around religion, food, music, and other cultural traditions that are specific to their gender (Abraham & Shryock, 2010). Group settings such as religious institutions and family gatherings are where such socialization of beliefs and values often takes place.

In the Levant, there are commonalities in religious values. Islam, Christianity, and Judaism have Abraham of the Old Testament as their common ancestor (Esposito, 2003). According to Nydell (2006), some basic religious values and beliefs are shared among the Christian (e.g., Maronite Catholic, Orthodox) and Muslim (e.g., Shiite, Sunni, Druze) sects, such as the belief in a powerful God, God's will or fate, religious piety, and conservative, traditional religious practices. In contrast, Western tolerance of youthful rebellion, use of drugs and alcohol, sexual freedoms, unchaperoned dating and other liberal practices associated with individual choice in the West are often considered unacceptable to those of Arab ethnic background because they are thought to weaken family ties and lead to the adoption of immoral social standards. Other religious values and beliefs are different between the two groups. For example, while Christian Arab Americans uphold the separation of church and state as valued in the West, the traditional Islamic view is that religion should be part of the school curriculum and government policies (Nydell, 2006).

Family values oftentimes coincide with the religious values that are enculturated. A sense of community and responsibility toward family members is common among Arab families. The extended family can include several generations who are emotionally close to each other across generations and within the same generation (Nydell, 2006). Family members tend to live in close proximity to one another (Beitin & Aprahamian, 2014; Hakim-Larson, Nassar-McMillan, & Paterson, 2012), and maintain frequent contact, so that children grow up experiencing the traditions as they are handed down from one generation to the next. This is especially the case because grandparents oftentimes live in the same home with their children and grandchildren (Nydell, 2006). Elders are thus highly respected, and obedience and respect to them is emphasized (Hakim-Larson et al., 2012).

In traditional Arab extended families, patriarchal values are upheld. Arab males are expected to provide and care for elders into their old age and parents are more likely to live with their married sons than with their married daughters (Beitin & Aprahamian, 2014). Often, older Arab American adults in need of extra attention and services will live with younger family members instead of seeking care in a nursing home (Hakim-Larson et al., 2012). Social networks that include extended family are often disrupted however during the immigration process. For example, Salma and Salam (2020) examined health and social factors among older adults that included Arab Muslims residing in Canada. Muslim older adults reported that they excluded themselves from social situations that did not seem welcoming, but many of them were able to increase their social connectivity through volunteering, religious programs, employment, community initiatives, and keeping in contact with family in their countries of origin.

Extended family members and elders are intimately involved in the socialization process (Abdulrahim & Ajrouch, 2014). Important for successive generations of Arabs in North America is the process of enculturation in which the children and grandchildren of older immigrants and extended family members learn about the cultural and religious traditions, behaviours, and values that link them to their Arab ancestry (Hakim-Larson & Menna, 2016). Both the younger and older generations may be proactive in the enculturation process in which they engage in a variety of cultural activities (e.g., Arabic language use and music, food preparation, dances) meant to maintain important ties with the family's culture of origin (Abraham & Shryock, 2010; Hakim-Larson & Menna, 2016; Yoon et al., 2013).

The socialization process for immigrant parents is a challenging one not only because they belong to a different generation, but because they were raised in a completely different culture compared to that of their own children (Abu-Laban & Abu-Laban, 1999a). This process may begin even before the child's birth and extend throughout early child development into adolescence and emerging adulthood. In the U.S., the limited research on parenting and factors affecting childcare in Arab youth is primarily due to the fact that researchers do not have ethnic identifiers for this population in their reported statistics and large-scale surveys (Dallo, Archer, & Misra, 2014).

Dwairy's (2010) cross-cultural research on comparing Western and Eastern cultures on parent-adolescent connectedness found that Arab adolescents (e.g., Levantine Bedouins, Jordanians) were more financially dependent and thus connected to their parents than were adolescents from Western countries (e.g., France, Poland) and from India. These findings demonstrate that there were some clear differences in values and expectations in Western cultures that emphasized independence from parents and Eastern collectivistic values where youth were encouraged to maintain connections to their parents. Furthermore, gender by culture interaction revealed that females in Eastern cultures were more financially dependent on their parents and functionally connected to them in their daily activities than were females in Western cultures.

Gender Roles and the Family System

Traditionally, Arab men hold great authority and are viewed as having more power in family matters than women, but they are also expected to protect women and provide for them (Abudabbeh, 2005; Feather, 2004; Glick & Fiske, 2001; Hakim-Larson et al., 2012). Males, especially the eldest male in the household, hold the greatest decision-making power (Hakim-Larson et al., 2012), and boys are given more freedom than girls prior to marriage (Cainkar & Read, 2014). Arab females, in contrast, are traditionally expected to uphold family honor by remaining chaste and modest, demure in their interactions with men, and by staying with their parents until marriage (Shakir, 1997). Brothers are often permitted to exercise authority over their sisters (Haboush, 2005) and often have more social freedom than their sisters. Thus, girls are carefully monitored while boys experience fewer restrictions (Hakim-Larson et al., 2012).

Given the clash of Western values that emphasize individualism and Eastern values that emphasize collectivism, Arab girls and women have had to balance acculturating to the demands of Western independence while enculturating and learning the values of their heritage cultures. Thus, Arab American females have shown great diversity in how they have actually negotiated their ethnic identities with ensuing inner emotional conflict and outright rebellion toward their families and traditions at times (Shakir, 1997).

Arab cultures are patrilineal, and paternalism is valued such that males are afforded greater privileges than females, who are traditionally viewed as dependent upon their families and men; nonetheless, women yield some power in their homes and as mothers (e.g., Beitin & Aprahamian, 2014; Hakim-Larson et al., 2012). Arab families can be thought of as vertically hierarchical with fathers and senior males holding the most power, followed by mothers and other family elders. Obedience is of great importance and thus, speaking negatively about a parent is seen as inappropriate. However, in immigrant families, a role reversal may occur when children act as a translator for their parents (Hakim-Larson et al., 2012).

Some Arab immigrants may adhere strictly to their cultural traditions and try to prevent family assimilation to the host culture, while others may shift to more egalitarian ideals and foster an ethnic identity that values both the heritage and host cultures. In traditional Arab families, family management is seen as the primary responsibility of women, while women's achievement in education and employment have been of less importance. Among some, however, women's high educational attainment is seen as a collective benefit for the family. As time spent in the U.S. increases, Arab women have participated in the work force at higher rates (Cainkar & Read, 2014). Traditionally, however, women were expected to marry, and their marriages were arranged by their families with emphasis placed on their financial security, status within the community and continuation of the patrilineal line through having children (Nydell, 2006).

Marriage Customs and Intermarriages

Culturally sanctioned marriages for both Christians and Muslims has traditionally meant marriages arranged by the family and by male elders to a partner who was not only of the same specific Arab ethnic background and religion, but from the same village or clan, and biologically related (i.e., endogamous marriage to cousins; Abudabbeh, 1996). Thus, traditionally there was general disapproval for marriage to non-Arabs and to marriage outside of the family's religion among Arab Canadians

(Hayani, 1999). However, in modern Islamic law, a Muslim man is permitted to marry a non-Muslim woman, but a Muslim woman is not allowed to marry a non-Muslim man (Esposito, 2003). In Hanafi law, the non-Muslim woman must be either Jewish or Christian, which is allowed because of the common Abrahamic ancestry (Abudabbeh, 1996).

However, traditional views on marriage partner selection and family involvement in arranging the marriage are being challenged on several fronts in contemporary Arab families. More young people are delaying marriage and objecting to their parents' involvement in their choice of partner; these changes coincide with reforms that are being made with respect to women's roles and rights (Beitin & Aprahamian, 2014), including their education and career achievements.

Educational Expectations, Achievement, and Career Patterns

As both individual and family successes are deeply valued in Arab culture, education and employment are highly regarded (Haboush & Barakat, 2014). Education and job success are a source of family honour, particularly among Arab males (Haboush & Barakat, 2014). It is noteworthy that over 60% of the Arab population in Canada have postsecondary certificates, diplomas or degrees (Mandil, 2019). Similarly, many Arab Americans have obtained a high level of education. Nearly half (49%) of Arab Americans have a bachelor's degree or higher; comparatively, 32% of those from the overall U.S. population fall into this category (Arab American Institute, 2019a). It must be noted, however, that more recent Arab immigrants may not be as well educated as other Arab Americans (Haboush & Barakat, 2014). Encouraging Arab American parents to become involved in their children's education, particularly when parenting a child with a disability, has been recommended (Al Khateeb, Al Hadidi, & Khatib, 2015).

Implications for Mental Health

It is important for health-care professionals to consider the individualized mental health needs of their Arab American and Arab Canadian clients while remaining sensitive to their specific ethnic backgrounds. For immigrant families from the Levant, it is especially important to explore and comprehend family members' pre-migration histories, which may include torture, direct exposure to war atrocities, vicariously experienced exposure to trauma, or dispossession of their homes and property.

The migration experiences to be addressed during the assessment phase of treatment include learning how, when, and where the family members settled even temporarily. Assessment of their post-migration adjustment will need to consider the stresses of adjusting to North American life in a post 9–11 climate of prejudice and discrimination. Key considerations should include the variety of risk factors and protective factors that are potentially linked to the well-being, mental health, and resilience of immigrant families from the Levant, as well as from other regions of the world (Abu-Ras, 2016).

Researchers are now beginning to consider how individual differences in background and perceptions of prejudice and discrimination are linked to psychological outcomes in people with Arab ancestry (e.g., Awad, 2010; Nassar-McMillan et al., 2011). Thus, treatment planning may need to include ways to cope with the broader society's reactions and cautious skepticism during interpersonal encounters. In addition to learning to cope with the ordinary stresses of acculturation such as adapting to a new home, neighborhood, legal, school, and work system, recent immigrants may have to contend with interpersonal micro-aggressions that involve their ethnic background (Abu-Laban & Abu-Laban, 1999b). For individuals with a war-time history, recovery from collective and cumulative traumas requires specialized assessment and treatments by culturally competent therapists and counselors to build their resilience and provide support for the healing process (Kira et al., 2014).

Mental health therapists, school, career, and family/marriage counselors will all need to enhance their level of multicultural competence with clients of Arab ancestry by increasing their basic knowledge from academic sources (e.g., learning about the culture and research evidence for clinical interventions) and by improving their own personal clinical skills (e.g., overcoming personal biases and developing empathy) (Nassar-McMillan, Nour, & Al-Qimlass, 2016). Although not unique to people from the Arab world, the stigma of attaining mental health treatments through direct help-seeking behavior has been noted by several researchers and providers (Bushra, Khadivi, & Frewat-Nikowitz, 2007), and thus working with clients to overcome this stigma is a worthy treatment goal. Bushra et al. (2007) further note that the history of colonization of the Levantine region has had a negative impact on the self-esteem of the indigenous people who may have an internalized idealization of the West accompanied by an internalized self-denigration; thus, they may reject much of their own native culture, language, and customs. Coming from countries where publicly expressing views on politics and world affairs has historically been censored seems to have led some immigrants to North America to take a stance that involves feelings of fear and distrust of any government agency (e.g., community mental health center); this is especially important when considering the therapist-client relationship given that assurances of confidentiality may be met with skepticism (Bushra et al., 2007).

Another possible treatment barrier that has been noted in the literature on Arab immigrants is the cultural belief in fate which may lead some individuals to believe that there is nothing that can be done to alter their life courses (Hakim-Larson et al., 2007). This view is sometimes reflected in a feeling of resignation that future events are possible only 'if God wills it' (insha 'Allah' in Arabic). This accepting approach to life is often an adaptive coping strategy and can be viewed as a potential resource in treatment. However, it can potentially be a barrier to those in treatment who may need to more fully explore and actively confront the impact of their background traumas and losses or address the immediate concerns of their life circumstances

(Bushra et al., 2007). For example, Thabet and Vostanis (2017) found that PTSD symptoms among Palestinians in the Gaza Strip were predicted by avoidance coping strategies (e.g., wishful thinking and escape-avoidance).

In addition to the challenge of overcoming fatalism when it is not adaptive, clinicians need to be alert to some culturally based beliefs. For example, like those from other Mediterranean cultures, some traditional immigrants from the Levant may hold belief in the power of being given the evil eye. Thus, amulets comprised of artistic depictions of eyes or blue beads are common in Arab culture as a means of protection against evil befalling individuals if they are looked upon with envy (Nydell, 2006). For this reason, Nydell (2006) describes the importance of avoiding the impression of feeling envious. Instead, it is considered appropriate to make statements of goodwill or to offer benedictions or blessings regarding the person's good fortune or new possession. In addition to beliefs around the evil eye, some traditional Muslims also may hold a belief in the Jinn, sorcery, or black magic (Khalifa, Hardie, Latif, Jamil, & Walker, 2011).

Although there are many barriers to obtaining and receiving appropriate services, one significant factor is that revealing family secrets and any shameful behavior to outsiders is viewed as having a negative effect on the whole family in Arab collectivistic cultures (Abudabbeh, 1996). Less educated Arab immigrants may be especially prone to the effects of stigma and may somaticize their own symptoms of emotional distress or those of their family members; thus primary health care providers may be the ones to initially provide clinical services rather than a mental health professional (Hakim-Larson et al., 2007). Western diagnostic assessment measures may be inappropriate given that Arab immigrants may express their psychological distress as somatic symptoms (Cho, 2018). Cho (2018) recommended the use of culturally valid assessment tools that consider acculturation status, language, how psychopathology is interpreted within the culture, and religious/cultural values relevant to mental health distress. As well, psychologists need to be mindful that Muslims may deny suicidal ideation as it is forbidden in Islam (Cho, 2018). Health care providers thus need to be especially sensitive to the potential need to make appropriate referrals for mental health services.

Preliminary research evidence supports the use of cognitive behavioral therapy (CBT) with adults in the Arab world and the Arab diaspora. In a recent meta-analysis of nine studies with people of Arab ethnic background, Kayrouz et al. (2018) found support for the efficacy of CBT treatment (delivered face-to-face or remotely) for adults with anxiety, depression, and PTSD. Kira and his colleagues (Kira, Ashby, Omidy, & Lewandowski, 2015) have adapted CBT methods specifically to address some of the complexities involved when the traumas experienced have not only occurred in the past but continue to occur in one form or another later on. The model they propose with preliminary evidence for its effectiveness is called the Current, Continuous, and Cumulative Trauma-Focused Cognitive Behavior Therapy (CCC-TF-CBT). Using a developmental framework that considers the types and frequencies of traumas experienced, Kira et al. (2015) describe the potential utility of eight mechanisms of change when intervening with clients with histories of trauma: (1) safety planning, (2) behavioral skills training such as personal and group-based emotion regulation to address threats, (3) stimulating the will to live and the development of positive dispositional characteristics such as optimism, (4) identity work to enhance the various facets of identity such as personal, social, and role identities as well as collective identity, (5) psychoeducation to help self-awareness and other-awareness, (6) stress inoculation to assist with anticipatory coping, (7) trauma narration to promote processing of emotions by writing about or orally telling the trauma stories, and (8) providing external supports for advocacy, social justice, and reconnection to social groups. There is a clear need for comprehensive services to address the needs of multiply traumatized children, adolescents, and adults with origins from war-torn regions of the world.

Some clinicians who have worked with Arab families have found it helpful to consult with or enlist the aid of the clients' religious cleric (i.e., an imam or a priest) whenever appropriate (Hakim-Larson et al., 2007). It is important to take the time necessary to work on building a sense of trust in the therapeutic relationship. Providing psychoeducation early in the treatment process and making efforts to destigmatize mental illness can be especially helpful in overcoming potential obstacles to psychotherapy (Bushra et al., 2007). Family dynamics, such as intergenerational conflicts, may be addressed through family therapy (Cho, 2018).

Future Research Directions

Currently, mental health professionals in the Arab region are calling for action to promote research, dissemination of findings, and overall mental health awareness (Maalouf et al., 2019). In conducting research on individuals with origins in the Arab world, a non-pathological approach holds promise with special attention given to variables related to collective values and spirituality (Abi-Hashem, 2006). Although Levantine families face many ongoing stresses and challenges to their adaptation, they also have a rich historical legacy that can foster a sense of realistic pride. A major strength and potential resource of families from the Levant is their culturally sanctioned ability to successfully navigate their extensive familial and community social support networks when such supports are available.

The use of social supports as a means of coping has been identified as a potential protective factor among individuals of Arab ethnicity given the importance of the collectivistic social network (Amer, 2014; Amer & Awad, 2016). Some individuals with Arab ethnicity have a locally available extended family and community social support network that they can turn to for assistance, and some members of this network may provide tangible (e.g., information, finances) and intangible (e.g., emotional support) help, while others in the network may actually add to the ongoing everyday stress and hassles (Hakim-Larson et al., 2007). Other individuals may have suffered great losses within their social support network before arriving in North America and thus they may have increased risks when it comes to mental health issues unless a substitute social support network is formed. These issues are worthy of further exploration in future research studies with Arab Americans and Arab Canadians.

Given the importance and significance of the extended family unit for Arab Americans and Arab Canadians, the influence of both past and current socio-political events on interpersonal relationships is worthy of further exploration. It is especially important to conduct research on preventative interventions for trauma in Arab youth who have experienced war and conflict (Hakim-Larson, Nassar-McMillan, & Ajrouch, 2014).

Conclusion

Families from the Levant are facing a number of challenges to their healthy functioning. While some families have extended across several generations and have been settled in North America for over a century, others have only recently immigrated. A comprehensive biopsychosocial ecological model such as that of Bronfenbrenner's (1994) has been applied to families under stress (e.g., Swick & Williams, 2006), and can be helpful in examining the socio-political influences on reasons for immigration, and their impact on the problems encountered by families from the Levant in North America. Such challenges include facing prejudicial attitudes and discrimination in a variably hostile post 9–11 sociopolitical climate at the macrolevel, and microaggressions at the more proximal level in everyday interpersonal interactions. Some research evidence suggests that prejudice and discrimination have influenced Arab families and communities regardless of length of time since immigration (Awad & Amayreh, 2016), although more research is needed to better understand how best to promote resilient functioning in spite of the various risks.

Some risk factors are especially important to consider when assessing the mental health of recent immigrants from the Levant. Risk factors include premigration stressors, such as exposure to wartime traumas, disruptions to attaining normal developmental tasks involving adaptive social relationships and school/work achievements, and multiple displacements both within and outside the country of origin. Post-migration stressors involve the stresses of resettlement and acculturation such as learning a new language, attaining gainful employment, learning new cultural traditions and values, and overcoming prejudices and overt discrimination, including bullying. Variations of cognitive behavior therapy have been found to be especially useful in addressing mental health symptoms and ameliorate risks, although more research is needed to test proposed models. While some individuals are more vulnerable to risks than others, others manage to overcome adversities and achieve resilient outcomes and psychological well-being perhaps due to their own psychological resources (e.g., cognitive and emotional skills) or other tangible resources available to them (e.g., social or financial supports).

Thus, even though individuals may have a history of traumatic experiences, current modifiable resources can be fostered in the effort to prevent or address mental health problems. Adaptation to North American life for immigrants from the Levant is thus likely dependent on several factors. These include the extent to which they have adequate and effective resources, supports, and advocacy at various levels personally, socially, academically or at work. Finally, adaptation depends on obtaining resources through the broader socio-political systems and institutions that immigrants from the Levant encounter in their everyday life.

References

Abdelhady, D. (2014). The sociopolitical history of Arabs in the United States: Assimilation, ethnicity, and global citizenship. In S. C. Nassar-McMillan, K. J. Ajrouch, & J. Hakim-Larson (Eds.), *Biopsychosocial perspectives on Arab Americans: Culture, development and health* (pp. 17–43). Springer.

Abdulrahim, S., & Ajrouch, K. J. (2014). Arab Americans and the aging process. In S. C. Nassar-McMillan, K. J. Ajrouch, & J. Hakim-Larson (Eds.), *Biopsychosocial perspectives on Arab Americans: Culture, development and health* (pp. 107–125). Springer.

Abi-Hashem, N. (2006). The agony, silent grief, and deep frustration of many communities in the Middle East: Challenges for coping and survival. In P. Wong & L. Wong (Eds.), *Handbook of multicultural perspectives on stress and coping* (pp. 457–486). Springer.

Abi-Hashem, N. (2008). Arab Americans: Understanding their challenges, needs, and struggles. In A. J. Marsella, J. L. Johnson, P. Watson, & J. Gryczynski (Eds.), *Ethnocultural perspectives on disaster and trauma: Foundations, issues, and applications* (pp. 115–173). Springer.

Abraham, N., & Shryock, A. (Eds.). (2010). *Arab Detroit: From margin to mainstream*. Wayne State University Press.

Abudabbeh, N. (1996). Arab families. In M. McGoldrick, J. Giordano, & J. K. Pearce (Eds.), *Ethnicity and family therapy* (2nd ed., pp. 333–346). Guilford Press.

Abudabbeh, N. (2005). Arab families: An overview. In M. McGoldrick, J. Giordano, & N. Garcia-Preto (Eds.), *Ethnicity and family therapy* (3rd ed., pp. 423–436). Guilford Press.

Abu-Laban, B., & Abu-Laban, S. M. (1999a). Arab-Canadian youth in immigrant family life. In M. Suleiman (Ed.), *Arabs in America: Building a new future* (pp. 140–153). Temple University Press.

Abu-Laban, S. M., & Abu-Laban, B. (1999b). Teens between: The public and private spheres of Arab-Canadian adolescents. In M. W. Suleiman (Ed.), *Arabs in America: Building a new future* (pp. 113–128). Temple University Press.

Abu-Ras, W. (2016). Psychological well-being: Understanding risk and protective factors. In M. M. Amer & G. H. Awad (Eds.), *Handbook of Arab American psychology* (pp. 175–187). Routledge/Taylor & Francis Group.

Ahmed, S. R., & Mana, M. (2017). Arab Americans in context: A sociocultural ecological perspective for understanding the Arab American experience. In M. A. Bond, I. Serrano-García, C. B. Keys, & M. Shinn (Eds.), *APA handbooks in psychology®. APA handbook of community psychology: Methods for community research and action for diverse groups and issues* (pp. 523–538). American Psychological Association.

Al Khateeb, J. M., Al Hadidi, M. S., & Khatib, A. J. (2015). Addressing the unique needs of Arab American children with disabilities. *Journal of Child and Family Studies, 24*, 2432–2440. https://doi.org/10.1007/s10826-014-0046-x

Amer, M. (2014). Arab American acculturation and ethnic identity across the life span: Sociodemographic correlates and psychological outcomes. In S. C. Nassar-McMillan, K. J. Ajrouch, & J. Hakim-Larson (Eds.), *Biopsychosocial perspectives on Arab Americans: Culture, development and health* (pp. 153–173). Springer.

Amer, M. M., & Awad, G. H. (2016). Research scholarship: Critique of the existing literature and visions for the future. In M. M. Amer & G. H. Awad (Eds.), *Handbook of Arab American psychology* (pp. 414–427). Routledge/Taylor & Francis Group.

Arab American Institute. (2017). *Advocacy road map*. https://www.aaiusa.org/advocacy_road_map

Arab American Institute. (2019a). *Demographics*. https://www.aaiusa.org/demographics

Arab American Institute. (2019b). *Ensuring a fair and accurate count in the 2020 census*. https://d3n8a8pro7vhmx.cloudfront.net/aai/pages/9805/attachments/original/1558040613/2019LD_Census_Issue_Brief.pdf?1558040613

Arab American National Museum. (2009). *Religion*. http://www.arabamericanmuseum.org/umages/IMLS_religion_exhibit/AA_religion.html

Asi, M., & Beaulieu, D. (2013). *Arab households in the United States: 2006–2010. American Community Survey Briefs, U.S. Department of Commerce*. https://www.census.gov/library/publications/2013/acs/acsbr10-20.html

Awad, G. H. (2010). The impact of acculturation and religious identification on perceived discrimination for Arab/Middle Eastern Americans. *Cultural Diversity and Ethnic Minority Psychology, 16*, 59–67. https://doi.org/10.1037/a0016675

Awad, G. H., & Amayreh, W. M. (2016). Discrimination: Heightened prejudice post 9/11 and psychological outcomes. In M. M. Amer & G. H. Awad (Eds.), *Handbook of Arab American psychology* (pp. 63–75). Routledge/Taylor & Francis Group.

Beitin, B. K., & Aprahamian, M. (2014). Family values and traditions. In S. C. Nassar-McMillan, K. J. Ajrouch, & J. Hakim-Larson (Eds.), *Biopsychosocial perspectives on Arab Americans: Culture, development and health* (pp. 67–88). Springer.

Berry, J. W., Westin, C., Virta, E., Vedder, P., Rooney, R., & Sang, D. (2006). Design of the study: Selecting societies of settlement and immigrant groups. In J. W. Berry, J. S. Phinney, D. L. Sam, & P. Vedder (Eds.), *Immigrant youth in cultural transition: Acculturation, identity and adaptation across national contexts* (pp. 15–45). Erlbaum.

BibArch. (2013). The Levant. http://www.bibarch.com/ArchaeologicalSites/index.htm

Britto, P. R. (2008). Who am I? Ethnic identity formation of Arab Muslim children in contemporary U.S. society. *Journal of the American Academy of Child & Adolescent Psychiatry, 47*(8), 853–857. https://doi.org/10.1097/CHI.0b013e3181799fa6

Britto, P. R., & Amer, M. M. (2007). An exploration of cultural identity patterns and the family context among Arab Muslim young adults in America. *Applied Developmental Science, 11*(3), 137–150. https://doi.org/10.1080/10888690701454633

Bronfenbrenner, U. (1994). Ecological models of human development. In *International Encyclopedia of education* (Vol. 3, 2nd ed., pp. 1643–1647). Elsevier.

Bronfenbrenner, U., & Morris, P. A. (2006). The bioecological model of human development. In R. M. Lerner & W. Damon (Eds.), *Handbook of child psychology: Theoretical models of human development* (pp. 793–828). Wiley.

Brown, C. S., Ali, H., Stone, E. A., & Jewell, J. A. (2017). U.S. children's stereotypes and prejudicial attitudes toward Arab Muslims. *Analyses of Social Issues and Public Policy, 17*(1), 60–83. https://doi.org/10.1111/asap.12129

Bushra, A., Khadivi, A., & Frewat-Nikowitz, S. (2007). History, custom, and the twin towers: challenges in adapting psychotherapy to Middle Eastern culture in the United States. In J. C. Muran (Ed.), *Dialogues on difference: Studies of diversity in the therapeutic relationship* (pp. 221–235). American Psychological Association.

Cainkar, L. (2016). Race and racialization: Demographic trends and the process of reckoning social place. In M. M. Amer & G. H. Awad (Eds.), *Handbook of Arab American psychology* (pp. 19–33). Routledge/Taylor & Francis Group.

Cainkar, L., & Read, J. G. (2014). Arab Americans and gender. In S. C. Nassar-McMillan, K. J. Ajrouch, & J. Hakim-Larson (Eds.), *Biopsychosocial perspectives on Arab Americans: Culture, development and health* (pp. 89–105). Springer.

Canadian Arab Institute. (2013). *Arab immigration to Canada hits record high*. https://new.canadianarabinstitute.org/publications/reports/arab-immigration-canada-hits-record-high/

Cho, E. (2018). Ethical considerations for psychologists providing treatment to Arab Americans. *Ethics & Behavior, 28*(5), 347–369. https://doi.org/10.1080/10508422.2018.1435282

Connor, P. (2018, January 29). *Most displaced Syrians are in the Middle East, and about a million are in Europe*. Pew Research Center. http://www.pewresearch.org/fact-tank/2018/01/29/where-displaced-syrians-have-resettled/

Dallo, F. J., Archer, C., & Misra, D. P. (2014). Maternal and child health. In S. C. Nassar-McMillan, K. J. Ajrouch, & J. Hakim-Larson (Eds.), *Biopsychosocial perspectives on Arab Americans: Culture, development and health* (pp. 325–346). Springer.

de la Cruz, G. P., & Brittingham, A. (2003). *The Arab population: 2000. Census 2000 Brief.* U.S. Census Bureau. http://www.census.gov/prod/2003pubs/c2kbr-23.pdf

Dwairy, M. (2010). Adolescents-family connectedness: A first cross-cultural research on parenting and psychological adjustment of children. *Journal of Child and Family Studies, 19*, 8–15. https://doi.org/10.1007/s10826-009-9335-1

El-Baz, F. (1968). *Say it in Arabic (Egyptian dialect)*. Dover.

Esposito, J. L. (Ed.). (2003). *The Oxford dictionary of Islam*. Oxford University Press.

Feather, N. T. (2004). Value correlates of ambivalent attitudes toward gender relations. *Personality and Social Psychology Bulletin, 30*(1), 3–12. https://doi.org/10.1177/0146167203258825

Glick, P., & Fiske, S. T. (2001). An ambivalent alliance: Hostile and benevolent sexism as complementary justifications for gender inequality. *American Psychologist, 56*(2), 109–118. https://doi.org/10.1037/0003-066X.56.2.109

Haboush, K. L. (2005). Lebanese and Syrian families. In M. McGoldrick, J. Giordano, & N. Garcia-Preto (Eds.), *Ethnicity and family therapy* (3rd ed., pp. 468–486). Guilford.

Haboush, K. L., & Barakat, N. (2014). Education and employment among Arab Americans: Pathways to individual identity and community resilience. In S. C. Nassar-McMillan, K. J. Ajrouch, & J. Hakim-Larson (Eds.), *Biopsychosocial perspectives on Arab Americans: Culture, development and health* (pp. 229–255). Springer.

Hadfield, K., Ostrowski, A., & Ungar, M. (2017). What can we expect of the mental health and well-being of Syrian refugee children and adolescents in Canada? *Canadian Psychology/Psychologie Canadienne, 58*(2), 194–201. https://doi.org/10.1037/cap0000102

Hakim-Larson, J., Kamoo, R., Nassar-McMillan, S., & Porcerelli, J. (2007). Counseling Arab and Chaldean American families. *Journal of Mental Health Counseling, 29*, 301–321. https://doi.org/10.17744/mehc.29.4.u5468716955w1023

Hakim-Larson, J., & Menna, R. (2016). Acculturation and enculturation: Ethnic identity socialization processes. In M. M. Amer & G. H. Awad (Eds.), *Handbook of Arab American psychology* (pp. 34–47). Routledge/Taylor & Francis Group.

Hakim-Larson, J., Nassar-McMillan, S., & Paterson, A. D. (2012). Counseling Middle Eastern Americans. In G. McAuliffe (Ed.), *Culturally alert counseling: A comprehensive introduction* (2nd ed.). Sage.

Hakim-Larson, J., Nassar-McMillan, S. C., & Ajrouch, K. J. (2014). Health and well-being in Arab Americans: Prevention strategies using a biopsychosocial approach. In S. C. Nassar-McMillan, K. J. Ajrouch, & J. Hakim-Larson (Eds.), *Biopsychosocial perspectives on Arab Americans: Culture, development and health* (pp. 387–401). Springer.

Harb, C. (2016). The Arab region: Cultures, values, and identity. In M. M. Amer & G. H. Awad (Eds.), *Handbook of Arab American psychology* (pp. 3–18). Routledge/Taylor & Francis Group.

Hayani, I. (1999). Arabs in Canada: Assimilation or integration? In M. W. Suleiman (Ed.), *Arabs in America: Building a new future* (pp. 284–303). Temple University Press.

Hodes, M., Vasquez, M. M., Anagnostopoulos, D., Triantafyllou, K., Abdelhady, D., Weiss, K., … Skokauskas, N. (2018). Refugees in Europe: National overviews from key countries with a special focus on child and adolescent mental health. *European Child & Adolescent Psychiatry, 27*(4), 389–399. https://doi.org/10.1007/s00787-017-1094-8

Houle, R. (2019). *Insights on Canadian Society: Results from the 2016 Census: Syrian refugees who resettled in Canada in 2015 and 2016.* https://www150.statcan.gc.ca/n1/pub/75-006-x/2019001/article/00001-eng.htm

Ikizler, A. S., & Szymanski, D. M. (2017). Discrimination, religious and cultural factors, and Middle Eastern/Arab Americans' psychological distress. *Journal of Clinical Psychology, 74*(7), 1219–1233. https://doi.org/10.1002/jclp.22584

Kayrouz, R., Dear, B. F., Kayrouz, B., Karin, E., Gandy, M., & Titov, N. (2018). Meta-analysis of the efficacy and acceptability of cognitive-behavioural therapy for Arab adult populations experiencing anxiety, depression or post-traumatic stress disorder. *Cognitive Behaviour Therapy, 47*(5), 412–430. https://doi.org/10.1080/16506073.2018.1445124

Khalifa, N., Hardie, T., Latif, S., Jamil, I., & Walker, D. (2011). Beliefs about Jinn, black magic and the evil eye among Muslims: Age, gender and first language influences. *International Journal of Culture and Mental Health, 4*(1), 68–77. https://doi.org/10.1080/17542863.2010.503051

Khoury, B. (2017). Everything you always wanted to know about Arab Americans and their mental health. *PsycCRITIQUES, 62*(6), Article 8. https://cdm15960.contentdm.oclc.org/digital/collection/p15960coll21/id/73278/rec/1

Kira, I. A., Amer, M. M., & Wrobel, N. H. (2014). Arab refuges: Trauma, resilience, and recovery. In S. C. Nassar-McMillan, K. J. Ajrouch, & J. Hakim-Larson (Eds.), *Biopsychosocial perspectives on Arab Americans: Culture, development and health* (pp. 175–195). Springer.

Kira, I. A., Ashby, J. S., Omidy, A. Z., & Lewandowski, L. (2015). Current, continuous, and cumulative trauma-focused cognitive behavior therapy: A new model for trauma counseling. *Journal of Mental Health Counseling, 37*(4), 323–340. https://doi.org/10.17744/mehc.37.4.04

Krogstad, J. M. (2019). *Key facts about refugees to the U.S.* https://www.pewresearch.org/fact-tank/2019/10/07/key-facts-about-refugees-to-the-u-s/

Maalouf, F. T., Alamiri, B., Atweh, S., Becker, A. E., Cheour, M., & Darwish, ...Akl, E. A. (2019). Mental health research in the Arab region: Challenges and call for action. *The Lancet Psychiatry, 6*(11), 961–966. https://doi.org/10.1016/S2215-0366(19)30124-5

Mandil, G. (2019). *Insights into the Arab population in Canada based on the 2016 census data.* Canadian Arab Institute. https://www.canadianarabinstitute.org/research

Mansel, P. (2010). *Levant: Splendour and catastrophe on the Mediterranean*. Yale University Press.

Mowafi, H. (2011). Conflict, displacement and health in the Middle East. *Global Public Health: An International Journal for Research, Policy and Practice, 6*(5), 472–487. https://doi.org/10.1080/17441692.2011.570358

Naber, N. (2000). Ambiguous insiders: An investigation of Arab American invisibility. *Ethnic and Racial Studies, 23*, 37–61. https://doi.org/10.1080/014198700329123

Naff, A. (1985). *Becoming American: The early Arab immigrant experience*. Southern Illinois University Press.

Nassar-McMillan, S., Ajrouch, K. J., & Hakim-Larson, J. (2014). Biopsychosocial perspectives on Arab Americans: An introduction. In S. C. Nassar-McMillan, K. J. Ajrouch, & J. Hakim-Larson (Eds.), *Biopsychosocial perspectives on Arab Americans: Culture, development and health* (pp. 1–9). Springer.

Nassar-McMillan, S., Lambert, R. G., & Hakim-Larson, J. (2011). Discrimination history, backlash fear, and ethnic identity among Arab Americans: Post-9/11 snapshots. *Journal of Multicultural Counseling and Development, 39*, 38–47. https://doi.org/10.1002/j.2161-1912.2011.tb00138.x

Nassar-McMillan, S. C., Nour, M. D., & Al-Qimlass, A. M. (2016). Counseling: Settings, clinical considerations, and counselor cultural competence. In M. M. Amer & G. H. Awad (Eds.), *Handbook of Arab American psychology* (pp. 289–302). Routledge/Taylor & Francis Group.

Nydell, M. K. (2006). *Understanding Arabs: A guide for modern times* (4th ed.). Intercultural Press.

Phillips, D., & Lauterbach, D. (2017). American Muslim immigrant mental health: The role of racism and mental health stigma. *Journal of Muslim Mental Health, 11*, 39–56. https://doi.org/10.3998/jmmh.10381607.0011.103

Radford, J., & Connor, P. (2019, June). *Fact Tank, Pew Research: Canada now leads the world in refugee resettlement, surpassing the U.S.* https://www.pewresearch.org/fact-tank/2019/06/19/canada-now-leads-the-world-in-refugee-resettlement-surpassing-the-u-s/

Rasmi, S., Chuang, S. S., & Hennig, K. (2015). The acculturation gap-distress model: Extensions and application to Arab Canadian families. *Cultural Diversity and Ethnic Minority Psychology, 21*(4), 630–642. https://doi.org/10.1037/cdp0000014

Salma, J., & Salam, B. (2020). "Growing old is not for the weak of heart": Social isolation and loneliness in Muslim immigrant older adults in Canada. *Health & Social Care in the Community, 28*(2), 615–623. https://doi.org/10.1111/hsc.12894

Samhan, H. (2001). *Who are Arab Americans?* (First published in Grolier's Encyclopedia). http://arabvoices.net/docs/whoarearabamericans.pdf

Samhan, H. H. (2014). Intra-ethnic diversity and religion. In S. C. Nassar-McMillan, K. J. Ajrouch, & J. Hakim-Larson (Eds.), *Biopsychosocial perspectives on Arab Americans: Culture, development and health* (pp. 45–65). Springer.

Shakir, E. (1997). *Bint Arab: Arab and Arab American women in the United States*. Praeger.

Statistics Canada. (2011). *Immigration and ethnocultural diversity in Canada*. http://www12.statcan.gc.ca/nhs-enm/2011/as-sa/99-010-x/99-010-x2011001-eng.cfm#a2

Statistics Canada. (2016). *2016 census of population*. Statistics Canada Catalogue number 98–316-X2016001 [Table]. https://www12.statcan.gc.ca/census-recensement/2016/dp-pd/prof/index.cfm?Lang=E

Sue, W. S., & Sue, D. (2008). *Counselling the culturally diverse: Theory and practice* (5th ed.). Wiley.

Suleiman, M. (1999). Introduction: The Arab immigrant experience. In M. Suleiman (Ed.), *Arabs in America: Building a new future* (pp. 1–21). Temple University Press.

Swick, K. J., & Williams, R. D. (2006). An analysis of Bronfenbrenner's bio-ecological perspective for early childhood educators: Implications for working with families experiencing stress. *Early Childhood Education Journal, 33*, 371–378. https://doi.org/10.1007/s10643-006-0078-y

Thabet, A. A., & Vostanis, P. (2017). Relationships between traumatic events, religious coping style, and post-traumatic stress disorder among Palestinians in the Gaza Strip. *Journal of Nursing and Health Studies, 2*(1:2), 1–9. https://doi.org/10.21767/2574-2825.100009

Triandis, H. C. (1994). Major cultural syndromes and emotion. In S. Kitayama & H. R. Markus (Eds.), *Emotion and culture: Empirical studies of mutual influence* (pp. 285–306). American Psychological Association.

U.S. Census Bureau. (2018). *People reporting ancestry 2018 ACS 1-year estimates B04006* [Table]. https://data.census.gov/cedsci/table?q=Ancestry&hidePreview=false&t=Ancestry&tid=ACSDT1Y2018.B04006&vintage=2018

Yoon, E., Chang, C. T., Kim, S., Clawson, A., Cleary, S. E., Hansen, M., … Gomes, A. M. (2013). A meta-analysis of acculturation/enculturation and mental health. *Journal of Counseling Psychology, 60*, 15–30. https://doi.org/10.1037/a0030652

Part V
Counseling and Therapy for Mental Health and Wellbeing

Chapter 12
Asian-Origin Families in Canada and the United States: Challenges and Resilience

Kieu Anh Do, Yan Ruth Xia, and Xiaolin (Charline) Xie

Abstract One out of five Canadians and one out of eight Americans are foreign-born (World Bank, 2020). The United States is home to the largest proportion of the global immigrant population from Asia, and Canada is home to approximately 3.3% of this global immigration flow (United Nations, 2017). This chapter examines key challenges and issues that impact Asian-origin families in these two predominant countries. It provides an overview of demographic characteristics, acculturation, intergenerational relationship, and aging of individuals and families originating from Asia, along with challenges such as racism, discrimination, stereotypes, domestic and interpersonal violence. Our review highlights the needs for future research on Asian subgroups and on Asian Pacific Islanders' families, emphasizing the strengths and resilience of Asian-origin families in Canada and the United States.

Keywords Asian family · Immigration · Canada · United States · Acculturation · Intergenerational relationship · Aging · Racism · Discrimination · Stereotype · Domestic violence

K. A. Do (✉)
University of Maryland Eastern Shore,
Princess Anne, MD, USA
e-mail: kado@umes.edu

Y. R. Xia
University of Nebraska – Lincoln, Lincoln, NE, USA
e-mail: rxia2@unl.edu

X. (Charline) Xie
Northern Illinois University, DeKalb, IL, USA
e-mail: xiaolinx@niu.edu

S. S. Chuang et al. (eds.), *Asian Families in Canada and the United States*,
Advances in Immigrant Family Research,
https://doi.org/10.1007/978-3-030-56452-0_12

Globalization and human migration have drastically reshaped the world's social and cultural landscape. Canada and the United States have been the receiving destinations for many immigrants and their families. Specifically, one out of five Canadians, and one out of eight Americans are foreign-born (World Bank, 2020). When we trace the place of origin, the United States is home to the largest (13%) proportion of the global immigrants from Asia; and Canada is home to approximately 3% of this global immigration flow (United Nations, 2017). Changes and sometimes challenges occur at this nexus where cultural traditions meet host society influences.

Our chapter examines some of the key issues that impact families of Asian origin in Canada and the United States, which differ considerably in terms of their sociopolitical history and immigration policies. We recognize the diversity within and between Asian-origin families relating to their nationalities, ethnic backgrounds, cultural traditions, socioeconomic status, and immigration history. We use the terms *Asian descent*, *Asian ancestry*, and *Asian origin* interchangeably to describe all individuals who originated from Asia, regardless of citizenship and resident status in their respective North American context. This chapter covers four key topics, including: (1) acculturation and intergenerational relationship, (2) aging, (3) racism, discrimination, and stereotype, and (4) domestic violence. We then conclude with some remarks about future directions.

Acculturation and Intergenerational Relationship

Individual immigrants and their families must adapt to a different social, cultural, and economic environment upon arrival. This adaptation is called acculturation, which is the process whereby the values, attitudes, behaviors, and relationships of individuals from one culture are modified as a result of contact with a different culture (Berry, 2005). Acculturation is a common phenomenon in immigrant families and is influenced by many factors, such as age, length of residence, educational levels, existence of relatives or ethnocultural contacts in the host country, and differences between the native and host culture (Costigan & Dokis, 2006; Londhe, 2015; Ying & Han, 2007).

A variety of acculturation strategies or statuses exist (Berry, 2005). Not all members within the same family or families within the same ethnic group adopt the same strategy. Asian children generally embrace host cultural values and behaviors much quicker than do parents and other elders in the family (Gautam, Mawn, & Beehler, 2018). Family members' views of parental authority and familial expectations may also differ. Asian parents do not oppose their children's adaptation of the host society; however, they also want their children to retain their cultural traditions and native language (Kwak & Berry, 2001).

Regardless of ethnic group membership, acculturative differences between family members seemed to affect the intergenerational relationship (Dinh & Nguyen, 2006) and may contribute to more intrafamily conflicts (Farver, Narang, & Bhadha, 2002). In qualitative interviews with first-generation Chinese adolescents in the

United States, Qin, Way, and Mukherjee (2008) identified themes relating to alienation and estrangement in the family due to cultural and generational clashes, language barriers, and lack of time and communication between parents and their children. These themes were echoed in another study with South Asian women in Canada, where participants also identified intergenerational conflict, specifically the alienation and distancing that occurred within the family (Samuel, 2009).

Intergenerational and intercultural conflicts seemed to vary by groups. Kwak and Berry (2001) found that generational differences were greatest among East-Indian parents and their children compared to those of Korean and Vietnamese ethnic backgrounds. Moreover, Chung (2001) found that Japanese American youths in her study reported the lowest level of intergenerational conflict, and female participants reported higher levels of intergenerational conflicts in the area of dating and marriage (e.g., when to begin dating, whom to date/marry). Acculturated Vietnamese American female youths also reported more arguments with and criticism from their parents (Vu & Rook, 2013).

Not all acculturative differences or acculturation gaps were problematic (Lim, Yeh, Liang, Lau, & McCabe, 2009). For instance, Kim, Chen, Wang, Shen, and Orozco-Lapray (2013) found that the gap in American cultural orientation between parents and youths had more negative effects than the gap in their cultural heritage. The authors explained that immigrant parents who were not as acculturated to American culture may not know how to support their children's development in the new context, which then contributed to negative youth outcomes. It may also be the case that acculturative differences magnified pre-existing conflicts in the family prior to or after arrival in the host society. This was supported by research conducted by Hwang and colleagues, who proposed a framework called Acculturative Family Distancing (AFD) to understand the effects of acculturative differences in families (Hwang, 2006; Hwang & Wood, 2009). The framework included differences in cultural values and beliefs in the family and took into account the breakdown in communication that occurs between family members as a result of those differences. Hwang and Wood (2009) found that AFD predicted elevated levels of family conflict.

Acculturation, typified by change, is dependent on time; however, existing acculturation studies were mostly cross-sectional in nature (Chung, 2001; Hwang & Wood, 2009; Vu & Rook, 2013), making it challenging to determine whether conflicts occurred prior to or as a result of acculturative differences. To date, only a few studies have investigated the effects of acculturation longitudinally (Juang, Syed, Cookston, Wang, & Kim, 2012; Murray et al., 2014; Nguyen, Kim, Weiss, Ngo, & Lau, 2018). For example, Juang et al. (2012) found that acculturation conflicts between Chinese American adolescents and their parents were stable during middle- to late- adolescence. Although acculturation and everyday conflicts were distinct from each other, they were also strongly correlated, supporting the idea that acculturative differences between Asian immigrant parents and their children worsened everyday issues (e.g., arguments over dating and social activities).

Two additional studies explored the temporal order between acculturation discrepancies and intergenerational conflicts. First, Ying and Han (2007) found that acculturative differences between Southeast Asian American youth and their parents during early adolescence predicted more intergenerational conflicts three years later, which adversely affected the youths' mental health by exacerbating depressive symptoms. Nguyen et al. (2018) reported that acculturation conflicts between Vietnamese American adolescents and their parents at baseline increased family strain three months later, which further increased acculturation conflicts six months later. These studies provided preliminary evidence that acculturation and family conflicts had an iterative effect on each other.

However, the factors that assisted in alleviating the negative effect of intergenerational and intercultural conflicts remain unclear. Some studies indicated that acculturation conflicts between Asian immigrant parents and their children change for the better through maturation. For instance, about one-third of the Korean American college students in Kang, Okazaki, Abelmann, Kim-Prieto, and Lan's (2010) study reported that they had conflicts with their parents growing up, but they gained an understanding and appreciation of their parents' struggles upon reaching emerging adulthood.

Other factors that sparked the change for the emerging adults in the study were religious beliefs and spirituality (Kang et al., 2010), which had also been found among Chinese immigrant parents and their adult children (Chen Feng, Knudson-Martin, & Nelson, 2015). Ponder (2018) proposed that religion, specifically the Christian church, played an important role in strengthening family relationships. It helped to bridge the generational and cultural divides between first-generation immigrant parents and their second-generation children through a process called mentalization, where each generation attempts to understand each other by understanding their inner intentions, feelings, and beliefs. However, research in this area is relatively new and remains unexplored.

Other than maturation, Li (2014) also found that attitudinal familism, characterized by the feeling and perception of putting family interests over self-interest, buffered the negative impact of intergenerational conflicts on Asian American youths' mental health outcome. On the part of the family, parental warmth (Costigan & Dokis, 2006; Lim et al., 2009) and nurturance (Zhai, 2017) also mitigated the detrimental effects of acculturative differences.

It is unclear whether these factors can be incorporated into an intervention with Asian immigrant families facing severe acculturation and intergenerational challenges. The literature in this area is unsubstantial. One intervention that specifically addressed these acculturation challenges was developed by Ying (1999, 2009) called the Strengthening Intergenerational/ Intercultural Ties in Immigrant Families (SITIF). It was geared towards Chinese immigrant parents and consisted of eight 2-hour sessions, with topics ranging from learning about cultural differences, child and adolescence development, effective parenting practices, and coping with stress. Ying (1999, 2009) found that SITIF increased parental efficacy and improved intergenerational relationships among Chinese immigrant parents and their children. Efforts to develop additional programs and services to assist Asian-origin families in dealing with stressful acculturation conflicts are much needed.

Aging in Asian-Origin Families

Currently, the number of Asian older adults is increasing both in the United States and Canada (Kuo, Chong, & Joseph, 2008). This population faced unique challenges in the context of migration. Qualitative research with older Asian Indian immigrants in the United States, for example, highlighted experiences of loneliness and separation from their social and cultural networks from their country of origin (Tummala-Narra, Sundaram, & Sathasivam-Rueckert, 2013). Older immigrants also had difficulty navigating and adapting to the host society, such as learning a new language, learning how to drive, and/or using different services (Gautam et al., 2018). Many feared of being alone and losing their independence as they progressed into old age and did not want to be a burden to their adult children.

Older adults tried to reciprocate and contribute to the family by helping to care for their grandchildren. One study found that about a third of Chinese American grandparents provided care for their grandchildren (Tang, Xu, Chi, & Dong, 2016). Most grandparent caregivers were grandmothers (Kataoka-Yahiro, 2010). Caregivers spent an average of 12 hours to 49 hours each week engaging in caregiving activities (Kataoka-Yahiro, 2010; Tang et al., 2016). Many grandparents were satisfied with their caregiving role, but some experienced caregiving-related stress (Tummala-Narra et al., 2013). Specifically,12% of the Chinese grandparent caregivers in Tang et al.'s (2016) study reported some caregiving burden, and 10% perceived negative effects of caregiving.

Quantitative studies have linked negative aging experiences to elevated levels of psychological distress among Asian older adults (Sorkin, Nguyen, & Ngo-Metzger, 2011), particularly geriatric depression. According to a recent literature review of research in North America, rates of depression ranged from 15% in Filipino older adults to 64% in Vietnamese older adults (Kuo et al., 2008; Mui & Kang, 2006). Recency of arrival, lack of language competency, lower acculturation to the host culture, and lower health status strongly and consistently predicted depression among Asian elders (Kou et al., 2015). While demographic factors accounted for only 6% of the variance in depression, life and acculturative stress explained 36% percent of the variance in depression among Asian older adults (Mui & Kang, 2006).

Related to acculturative challenges, migratory grief may also heighten geriatric depression among Asian older adults. Migratory grief is the sense of loss and emotional distress associated with migration, including feeling that things were better in one's homeland, missing one's homeland, and feeling like a stranger in the host country (Casado & Leung, 2001). In a study with Chinese older adults, Casado and Leung (2001) found that, although years in the United States and English proficiency significantly predicted depression among the participants (12% of the variance), migratory grief accounted for over 41% of the variance in depression. Together, life and acculturative stressors may increase depression through decreasing the older adults' sense of control (Jang, Kim, & Chiriboga, 2006) and reducing their social connectedness (Kim et al., 2015). These are important factors to consider in professional practices with Asian older adult populations.

Various factors have been found to protect older adults from the deleterious effects of aging and acculturative stress. For example, older Asian Indian immigrants in the United States, who had a strong sense of mastery and control over their own lives and who frequently participated in religious activities, had fewer negative effects (Diwan, Jonnalagadda, & Balaswamy, 2004). Korean American older adults who felt more socially connected and more acculturated also reported more positive views of aging (Kim, Jang, & Chiriboga, 2012). When it comes to the social connections of older adults, the quality of the interactions, particularly with children, protected older adults from depression rather than the quantity or frequency (Kuo et al., 2008). And although marital status and language proficiency mitigated geriatric depression among Southeast Asian older adults, disaggregated analyses showed some ethnic differences (Kim et al., 2015). Specifically, social connectedness was a protective factor for Vietnamese older adults and English proficiency was a protective factor for Laotian elders. Therefore, future research needs to pay attention to these group differences.

For those caring for the elderly, the burden and stress of caregiving had also been documented. Caregiving work within Asian-origin families tended to be highly gendered, with the majority of caregivers being female, who were wives, daughters, or daughters-in-law (Lai, 2007). Although information was lacking, one study indicated about 20% of family caregivers of older Chinese adults in Canada reported experiencing at least some caregiving burden (Lai, 2010). Korean caregivers also described struggles to make a living in the United States and the lack of time to provide adequate care for their aging parents (Han, Choi, Kim, Lee, & Kim, 2008). Filipino and Chinese women in California (USA) caring for an elderly parent discussed the need to fulfil their filial obligations, cultural conflicts with their elderly parents, and role strain (e.g., spouse, grandparenting, work; Jones, Zhang, Jaceldo-Siegl, & Meleis, 2002).

Caregiving responsibilities took a physical and psychological toll on the caregivers, such as increasing the risk of depression (Lai, 2009). Some primary caregivers also described the lack of appreciation from other family members, who may even harshly criticize the way they provide care, yet did little to contribute (Han et al., 2008). Additionally, spouse caregivers seemed to be more likely to experience stress resulting from elder caregiving, possibly due to limited language skills, lower income, and personal health challenges (Casado & Sacco, 2012). Unfortunately, Asian caregivers were less likely to use formal services compared to caregivers from other racial groups due to various barriers (Pinquart & Sörensen, 2005).

At the personal level, there was a sense of pride as well as hesitation when it comes to inviting outside service providers into their private lives (Li, 2004). Caregivers also expressed a lack of information about the care recipients' condition and how to provide adequate care, along with a lack of culturally appropriate and adequate alternative to home care (Han et al., 2008). Extended care was often expensive and not affordable (Jones et al., 2002). Those who attempted to seek formal services reported that what they needed were either not available or the system was too complex for them to navigate (Li, 2004). Therefore, seeking formal services was seen as a last resort (Jones et al., 2002). To cope, the caregivers utilize their family resources, such as seeking spousal assistance and sibling responsibility sharing, as well as relying on their inner strength, commitment, endurance, and personal sacrifice. Some also leaned on their spirituality for support. Albeit the challenges, caregivers discussed positive outcomes of their caregiving role, mainly how the experience fostered their personal growth and inner strengths (Jones et al., 2002).

The stress related to elder caregiving could possibly escalate into elder maltreatment. A study of Chinese older adults in Canada identified a 4.5% prevalence of maltreatment (Lai, 2011), while those in the United States found around 15% (Dong, Chen, Fulmer, & Simon, 2014). In most cases, spouses (40.2%) and adult children (30%) were the main perpetrators (Lai, 2011). Qualitative study with Chinese older adults in Chicago (USA) revealed that caregiver neglect was the most prevalent form of elder maltreatment, with financial exploitation and physical abused being less common (Dong, Chang, Wong, Wong, & Simon, 2011). However, Asian older adults explained that psychological mistreatment, such as scolding, verbal attacks, and insults were the most intolerable.

Certain factors increased the risk of elder maltreatment. Lower educational levels, lack of religious beliefs and social support, and length of residence in Canada have been found to be risk factors for maltreatment towards Chinese older adults (Lai, 2011). Elders who reported family relationships characterized by high emotional closeness but also high family conflict (unobligated ambivalent), as well as those with low intergenerational engagement (detached), were at the highest risk for elder maltreatment (Li, Guo, Stensland, Silverstein, & Dong, 2019). Elder maltreatment had been linked to poorer quality of life (Dong et al., 2014) and greater suicidal ideation, especially among older women (Dong et al., 2016). Asian older adults generally lacked understanding of available resources to address elder maltreatment and how to seek help. Some also mentioned the fear of losing face due to being abused by a family member, which prevented help-seeking (Dong et al., 2011).

Racism, Discrimination, and Stereotype

Some of the more difficult to label and eliminate issues relate to racism, discrimination, and prejudice. This section discusses both historical and contemporary examples of larger institutional practices as well as personal examples of racism and discrimination that individuals of Asian origin experienced. We also examine how these negative experiences affect their health and outcomes.

Many critical immigration legislations targeting Asian immigrants were passed in the 1880s in the United States and Canada. For example, the United States enacted the Chinese Exclusion Act in 1882, banning immigration from China, and in 1907–1908, similar restrictions were placed on Japanese and Korean immigrants through the Gentlemen's Agreement (DIVA, 2009–2012). The Canadian parliament also passed similar legislations, banning or limiting immigration from certain regions of Asia. For example, in 1885, it passed the Chinese Immigration Act, placing a heavy head tax on Chinese immigrants to deter or limit immigration from

China (Canadian Museum of Immigration, 2017; DHR, 2017). Canada added an amendment to their Immigration Act in 1908, called the *continuous journey regulation*, which allowed only immigrants who made a continuous journey from their country of origin into Canada. This regulation was in response to increase anti-Asian sentiments, aiming to restrict immigration from Japan and India, because there were no continuous routes from these countries directly to Canada (DHR, 2017).

Asians in North America were also denied the rights to citizenship, suffrage, and due process under the law (Zia, 2000). In 1923 in *United States v. Bhagat Singh Thind*, the Supreme Court ruled that Asian Indians were ineligible for citizenship (Gee, Spencer, Chen, & Takeuchi, 2007). In Canada, citizenship and voting rights were restricted based on race. Canadians of East Indian, Chinese, and Japanese origin were not allowed to obtain citizenship or the right to vote until 1947 (DHR, 2017). Although some Asian ethnic groups, such as those of Japanese, Chinese, and Korean ancestry have been in North America for many generations, they were still considered foreigners.

Reports from Statistics Canada (2016, 2017) showed that 30% to 40% of Canadians of Asian origin reported experiences of discrimination or unfair treatment due to their race, ethnicity, religion, language, or accent. Similarly, a study of Southeast Asian refugees resettled in Canada revealed that over a third (40%) reported experiencing some form of subtle discrimination, such as being looked down upon, being treated unfairly, and hearing insulting remarks (Beiser, Noh, Hou, Kaspar, & Rummens, 2001). Approximately 10% experienced overt forms of discrimination, such as threats, racial graffiti on personal property, or physical abuse. Similarly, according to the 2016 Collaborative Multiracial Post-Election Survey in the United States, 44% of Asians have experienced discrimination (Do & Wong, 2017). These rates were higher for Koreans (61%) and lower for Asian Indians (31%). Similarly, those who were born outside of the United States tend to experience more discrimination.

Major events in North America also heightened the levels of racism and discrimination experienced by various ethnic and religious groups within the Asian community. After the terrorist attack on September 11, 2001 in the United States, Muslims and Sikhs, many of whom were of South Asian ancestry, were targeted and sometimes physically assaulted due to various physical markers, such as wearing a turban or head covering and having an uncut beard (Ahluwalia, 2011). According to the United States Department of Justice (2015), the prevalence of hate crimes against Sikh, Muslims, and South Asian Americans have skyrocketed after 9/11, reaching over 800 incidents. Many more hate crimes go unreported.

Racial discrimination negatively affects the physical and mental health of Asian Americans and Asian Canadians. The United States Surgeon General noted that racial discrimination was a risk factor for mental disorders and other psychological issues (USA DHHS, 2000). Perceived discrimination had been found to predict depression among Korean immigrants in Canada (Noh & Kaspar, 2003) and increased the risk for depressive and anxiety disorder in Vietnamese, Filipino, Chinese, Asian Indians, Japanese, Korean and Pacific Islanders in the United States (Gee, Delva, & Takeuchi, 2007). Racial discrimination also impaired physical health by increasing the risk of chronic illnesses, such as cardiovascular, respiratory, and pain conditions (Gee et al., 2007), even after controlling for demographic characteristics, such as age, sex, education, family income, nativity status (Yoo, Gee, & Takeuchi, 2009). Additionally, unfair treatment related to discrimination was linked to increased prescription and illicit drug use, as well as alcohol dependency in Filipino Americans (Gee, Delva, & Takeuchi, 2007).

Related to racism and discrimination is the emergence of bullying and peer victimization among youths. Asian American youths reported greater peer discrimination, through physical and verbal attacks and social exclusion, than their peers from other racial/ ethnic groups (Cooc & Gee, 2014; Fisher, Wallace, & Fenton, 2000). In a sample of diverse high school students, 84% of East Asian and 73% of South Asian students reported that they had been called racially insulting names by someone their own age (Fisher et al., 2000). These rates were similar to those found by Wang, La Salle, Wu, Do, and Sullivan (2018). Although the researchers did not specifically ask about racially motivated discrimination, they found that about 64% of the Asian American middle school students reported traditional victimization by a peer, and about 25% faced victimization online (Wang et al., 2018). Asian males faced greater risk of racial harassment from peers than Asian females (Cooc & Gee, 2014), and those from first- and second-generation (Peguero, 2009) were more likely to be victimized. In a study of first-generation Chinese adolescents in Boston and New York (USA), adolescents described experiences of discrimination and harassment from peers due to the recency of their immigration status, not being able to speak English well, and the model minority myth (Qin et al., 2008). To the last reason, Chinese youth recounted incidents of peer resentment towards their academic performance and teachers' positive perceptions of Asian students.

Racial/ethnic discrimination from peers seemed to have more deleterious effects on Asian-origin youths than those from other ethnic minority backgrounds (Rivas-Drake, Hughes, & Way, 2008). Specifically, Asian students reported higher distress related to peer discrimination than their white, Latino, and African American counterparts, with East Asians experiencing the highest levels of distress (Fisher et al., 2000). Peer discrimination related to more internalizing symptoms (e.g., depression, low self-esteem; Greene, Way, & Pahl, 2006; Wang et al., 2018) and externalizing symptoms (e.g., somatization, substance use; Juang & Alvarez, 2010).

Discrimination and racism towards individuals of Asian descent is difficult to address, because there is a general perception that this community does not face such problems. Data from the 2016 Collaborative Multiracial Post-Election Survey showed that even though 22% of White persons believed that there was "a lot" of discrimination towards white individuals, only 9% believed that there was "a lot" of discrimination towards Asians (Do & Wong, 2017). This may be due to the "model minority model" myth, where individuals of Asian ancestry were perceived to be successful and had few problems (Kawai, 2005). The perception of success may lead people to believe that Asians face relatively little to no racism or discrimination.

In addition to being viewed as a model minority, individuals of Asian ancestry also faced the perpetual foreigner stereotype, where they were seen as outsiders or foreigners, regardless of their place of birth or length of time in the host country (Huynh, Devos, & Smalarz, 2011). This stereotype may be due to their physical features. In an experiment in the United States, Cheryan and Monin (2005) found that white college students rated pictures of Asian faces as "less American" than those of blacks and Hispanics. In terms of their experiences, Asian American college students were five times more likely than whites, and 3.4 times more likely than blacks, to report being perceived as a foreigner. Researchers have shown that being perceived as a perpetual foreigner was a type of micro-aggression that was particularly damaging, because it invalidated and denied an individual's identity and sense of belonging (Cheryan & Monin, 2005). Awareness of the perpetual foreigner stereotype predicted lower self-esteem, more depressive symptoms, and more anxiety symptoms (Do, Wang, & Atwal, 2019), as well as lower life satisfaction (Huynh et al., 2011). These effects were significant even after accounting for reported levels of perceived discrimination (Huynh et al., 2011). Overall, these studies showed that even subtle forms of racism had a major impact of Asian's well-being and adjustment.

Attention has been dedicated to identifying protective factors and strategies to address peer discrimination among youths. For example, in a study of over 1000 high school students (14% were Asians), Bellmore, Nishina, You, and Ma (2012) found that positive peer, teacher, and school interracial climate were associated with lower levels of peer ethnic discrimination across time. Positive school interracial climate was particularly protective against peer discrimination for Asian students. Wang et al. (2018) also found that having a positive school climate buffered the negative effects of face-to-face and cyber victimization on suicidal thoughts and behaviors among Asian American students. Researchers had only begun to examine family-related protective factors. Family cohesion protected youth from the negative effects of ethnic/ racial discrimination by reducing anxiety (Juang & Alvarez, 2010), and parental involvement mitigated the adverse effects of face-to-face victimization on suicidal thoughts and behaviors, especially for Asian American girls (Wang et al., 2018). Much still can be done in researching pathways of protection and resilience to address racism, discrimination, and stereotyping among individuals and families of Asian background.

Domestic Violence

Accumulated stress and strain resulting from immigration may escalate into violence within the home. In this section, we review the literature on two broad categories of domestic violence: intimate partner violence (IPV) and child maltreatment. With each category, we examine the prevalence, risk factors, as well as the associated outcomes and related interventions. When appropriate, we also discuss gaps that can be addressed in future research.

There is a sizable body of research on IPV in Canada (see Okeke-Ihejirika et al., 2018) and the United States, particularly violence towards South Asian women (Choksi, Desai, & Adamali, 2010; Dasgupta, 2000). This was consistent with both countries' focus on developing programs and policies to address domestic violence (Abraham & Tastsoglou, 2016); however, national-level data on the prevalence of IPV among Asian population remained scarce. Some sources showed rates ranging from 10% to 25% among Chinese immigrants and 25% to 40% among South Asian immigrants in the United States (Midlarsky, Venkataramani-Kothari, & Plante, 2006; Silverman, 2002). Similar rates were found among a community sample of South Asian women in Canada (19%; Madden, Scott, Sholapur, & Bhandari, 2016).

The high prevalence of IPV within Asian immigrant communities may be due to personal, familial, social, as well as cultural factors (Lee & Hadeed, 2009). One such factor may be the strong patriarchal beliefs (Bhuyan, Mell, Senturia, Sullivan, & Shiu-Thornton, 2005). For example, Yoshioka, DiNoia, and Ullah (2001) found that high proportions of Vietnamese immigrants in the United States endorsed beliefs in male privilege, such as *a man is the ruler of his home* (60%) and *a husband should have the right to discipline his wife* (54%). They were also more likely to endorse wife beating for situation-specific reasons, such as *infidelity* (54%) or *nagging too much* (46%). Immigration-related factors, such as legal status, lack of transportation and limited language proficiency, may increase violence in the home (Midlarsky et al., 2006). Structural factors, including racism and a lack of culturally sensitive services and interventions in both Canada and the United States, may prevent victims from reporting or seeking help (Erez & Hartley, 2003; Miedema & Wachholz, 2000). Interviews with Cambodian immigrant women also revealed traditional beliefs about enduring the abuse as part of one's karma (Bhuyan et al., 2005). Asian immigrant women were reluctant to leave an abusive marriage or to seek help for domestic violence, because of the cultural and social stigma of divorce and familial and economic pressure to stay married (Midlarsky et al., 2006).

Qualitative work detailed the coping process among victims of domestic violence. Research with South Asian immigrant women in both Canada (Ahmad, Rai, Petrovic, Erickson, & Stewart, 2013) and the United States (Bhandari, 2018) described their personal willpower in deciding to leave an abusive situation, motivated by the desire to promote the well-being of their children and facilitated by the support of family and friends, both in the host country and back home in their country of origin. Their personal faith and structural support from professional services (e.g., housing, language classes, and immigration advice), as well as continual support from family and friends helped the women through the difficult transition.

More research is needed, especially studies using nationally representative samples both in Canada and the United States. As with the other topic areas, there is a continual need to disaggregate data among Asian ethnic groups (Chung, 2001). Although the majority of domestic violence was perpetuated by men, a few studies highlighted incidence of domestic violence with male victims (Kim & Emery, 2003). Due to strong patriarchal beliefs, these individuals may face greater resistance in reporting the abuse or seeking help (Cheung, Leung, & Tsui, 2009). IPV and domestic violence typically occurs within the couple relationship, but some studies revealed abuse committed by in-laws (Bhuyan et al., 2005; Raj, Livramento, Santana, et al., 2006). Additional research is needed to examine the experience of men in abusive situations and violence perpetuated by other members within the family.

IPV also comes in many different forms, including physical, verbal, psychological, and sexual abuse. To date, most of the research focuses on physical abuse. More studies are needed to explore other types of violence. One severe form is honor killings, which is "premeditated killings of family members, primarily women, who are thought to have brought shame or dishonour to their family by engaging in certain behaviors considered unacceptable" (Muhammad, 2010, p. 4). These killings are often planned in advance, the victims have been warned to change their behaviors, and multiple family members, including fathers, mothers, siblings, and other relative, are involved either in the killing or in covering up the act (Chesler, 2009).

Honor killing is a highly controversial topic. Many scholars are still debating whether the word "honor" is appropriate to be included in the label and if categorizing it as a form of domestic violence diluted the seriousness of the crime (Chesler, 2009; Terman, 2010). Honor killings, in Canada and the United States in particular, highlight the intersection between acculturative stress and domestic violence. The "dishonoring" acts, as the families see them, often involved "Westernized" behaviors that contradict their cultural and religious heritage, such as refusing to wear a head cover and wanting to lead an independent life (e.g., pursuing college, driving a car, seeking a divorce; Chesler, 2009, 2010; Muhammad, 2010). The family of the victim may feel judged by the community if they do not take action to punish the family member(s) who violated social norms to cleanse the shame and restore their honor (Muhammad, 2010).

More studies are needed to assess the extent to which honor killings are practiced. In 2000, the State of the World Population report estimated that approximately 5000 such killings occurred each year worldwide (UNFPA, 2000). The number of cases were much smaller in Canada and the United States (Chesler, 2010). However, there are currently no official estimates as these crimes are not tracked in either country. We also need to understand the experiences of the family members, but this topic is shrouded in secrecy, and families often do not want to put more focus on the shameful event. Therefore, it may be difficult to dig deeper into this phenomenon or explore their perspectives.

Related to IPV is child maltreatment. Available data suggested that child maltreatment tended to be lower among Asian Canadians and Asian Americans compared to other racial, ethnic or visible minority groups (DHHS et al., 2020; Lee, Rha, & Fallon, 2014). The national rate of child maltreatment in the United States was approximately 9 out of every 1000 children each year, but the rate for Asian children was only 2 out of every 1000 (DHHS et al., 2020s). However, if we look at the prevalence among Pacific Islanders, it was much higher than Asian alone and more comparable to the national average, at 9 out of every 1000 children (DHHS et al., 2020). Additionally, in a diverse sample of Asian/ Pacific Islander families in Washington state, the highest percentages of child maltreatment were among Vietnamese and Cambodian children (14.4% and 13.6% respectively; Pelczarski & Kemp, 2006).

Despite the existing differences, one clear trend was the high rates of physical abuse across sub-groups (Chang, Rhee, & Weaver, 2006; Rhee, Chang, Berthold, & Mar, 2012), ranging from about 37% to 67% (Lee et al., 2014; Lee, Fuller-Thomson, Fallon, Trocmé, & Black, 2017). These rates were substantially higher than other racial/ ethnic groups (Lee et al., 2014; Lee et al., 2017). Physical abuse involved behaviors such as hitting a child with an object, slapping a child, shaking, pushing, or grabbing a child. Using data from the Canadian Incidence Study of Reported Child Abuse and Neglect (CIS-2003), Lee et al. (2014) reported that of the 2703 cases involving East and Southeast Asian families, over a quarter of them resulted in physical harm to the child. An earlier study with Korean immigrant families in the United States found that more than half of the cases were of moderate to high severity, and over a third involved persistent abuse (Chang et al., 2006).

Child maltreatment within Asian families shared some similar, as well as some unique contributing factors. Zhai and Gao (2009) developed a useful explanatory framework to understand the mechanisms of both risk and protection against child maltreatment. The framework included three factors, including Asian cultural customs and childrearing practices, immigration experiences and minority status, and attitudes and practices of social service professionals. To the first factor, Asian cultures often emphasize parental authority and tend to be more accepting of physical punishment as a form of discipline. This was consistent with Lee et al.'s (2014) finding that approximately 76% of the physical abuse cases in Canada resulted from "harsh discipline." This rate was significantly higher than cases involving non-Asian children (49%).

The second factor related to acculturative and minority stress that Asian families experienced in their respective host societies. Surveys of Vietnamese immigrant families indicated that perpetrators of child abuse were more likely to have been in the United States for a shorter length of time (Rhee et al., 2012), and interviews with South Asian immigrant parents in Canada found that, in addition to parent-teen disciplinary issues, the majority of the families were involved with the child welfare system due to family conflicts resulting from acculturative and intergenerational conflicts (Maiter & Stalker, 2011). The last factor dealt with service providers' and professional's lack of knowledge and understanding of child maltreatment among Asian families. Although child protection workers that Lee et al. (2017) interviewed recognized physical abuse as the most salient type of maltreatment Asian children experienced, they believed that most were of low severity. They saw the need to engage with families in a more flexible, open, and culturally respectful way, but most acknowledged that they lacked an understanding of the needs of these families and that there were limited early interventions and culturally appropriate services. These sentiments were echoed by South Asian parents involved with child welfare services (Maiter & Stalker, 2011). The parents highlighted some positive experiences with workers, but many were also disappointed with the lack of interactions and the high turn-over of workers, which caused confusions and service interruptions. Parents also felt that many of the workers were unaware of the needs of their family and were culturally insensitive and unresponsive.

Although research continues to show that Asian families were less likely to report child maltreatment and less likely to seek help, those who were involved with child protective services expressed a desire to resolve their family problems (Maiter & Stalker, 2011). For example, South Asian parents in Maiter and Stalker's (2011) study acknowledged that they lacked an understanding of the child welfare system but described their experiences reaching out to their family physician, their therapist, and even the school system for help. Some also looked for resources through the local phone book, and when these resources were non-existent, they created their own support group to offer help to others going through similar situations.

Researchers have remarked that studies of child maltreatment within the Asian population in both Canada and the United States need further development (Behl, Crouch, May, Valente, & Crouch, 2001; Zhai & Gao, 2009). Lower rates of child maltreatment could be due to the presence of existing factors within the Asian community that helped to protect children from maltreatment; however, it could also indicate a problem with underreporting. For example, although research suggested that sexual abuse was low in Asian families (Futa, Hsu, & Hansen, 2001; Lee et al., 2014), one retrospective study with Filipina and South Asian women found that as high as 28% of the participants reported childhood sexual abuse (Kamimura, Nourian, Assasnik, Nourian, & Franchek-Roa, 2020). An additional study with over 8000 college students in Minnesota (USA) found that Asian/Pacific Islanders were more likely to experience sexual abuse during childhood than their white peers (Sieben, Lust, Ainslee, Renner, & Nguyen, 2019). What was more striking was the elevated risk of sexual abuse for Asian males compared to white males. These findings supported the notion that sexual abuse is a highly stigmatized and taboo topic within the Asian community, and people may be unwilling to report or discuss it (Futa et al., 2001). Available data further suggested that school and law enforcement were the two most common referral sources for child maltreatment (Chang et al., 2006), and that the family seemed more accepting of referrals from the latter source (Maiter & Stalker, 2011). Fostering partnerships between these two systems could help to increase awareness and address child maltreatment and other types of violence in the home.

Exploring both IPV and child maltreatment comprehensively, we need to sample family members who are bystanders to understand how they view domestic violence. This is critical, because as many as 27% of Asian adults had witnessed parental marital violence as a child (Yoshioka et al., 2001), and 15% to 23% of child maltreatment cases involved exposure to parental or domestic violence (Chang et al., 2006; Maiter & Stalker, 2011). Research with a nationally representative sample in the United States (4.2% Asian/ Native Hawaiian/Pacific Islanders) found that individuals who experienced maltreatment and who witnessed IPV in the home as a child were more likely to experience personal IPV as adults (Afifi, Mota, Sareen, & MacMillan, 2017). Therefore, further studies should examine the effect of witnessing domestic violence on the development of Asian children and youth from immigrant families, especially on their long-term outcomes and adjustments. Finally, the development of culturally sensitive and effective prevention and interventions to address IPV and child maltreatment in Asian families are warranted. Both parents and service providers agreed that a strength-based and family-centered approach is critical, calling attention to the need for training and professional development in cultural sensitivity and humility (Kwok & Tam, 2009; Lee et al., 2017).

Conclusions

The frontier of research on Asian-origin families is expanding, as researchers become more aware of existing and emerging challenges that minority families faced, as well as their strengths and resilience. In this chapter we touched on some of these topics, including acculturation and intergenerational relationships; aging; racism, discrimination, and stereotype; and domestic violence. The process of migration, adaptation, and adjustment created unique dynamics within the family and transformed how family members relate to each other. Asian families also faced unique challenges at the later part of the life course concerning caregiving and aging issues. This all occurred within the larger context of structural and institutional barriers, such as racism and discrimination. The accumulated stressors may exacerbate family tension and conflicts, increasing violence in the home.

One clear pattern in the research is the need to sample or examine specific Asian ethnic groups. As the Asian pan-ethnic label continues to grow to include other ethnicities, such as Pacific Islanders, the literature also needs to keep pace with the changes. In summarizing research covering the four major topics, very few empirical studies sampled Pacific Islanders. To promote the development of research with different communities, one possible strategy is to recruit and train researchers from these various backgrounds. They will most likely have access to the population of interest and will have a deeper understanding of issues that are in need to explore further.

Moreover, longitudinal designs will expand current understanding of how various immigration processes affect family life, such as acculturation, integrational relationships, and aging. The studies summarized in this chapter included a few that utilized a longitudinal framework. These studies showed some contrary results as well as some novel findings pertaining to Asian-origin families. Additionally, there were topics that have been underexplored or underdeveloped in research with Asian-origin families. For instance, taboo topics, such as "honor killing" and elder abuse need further attention. Finally, collaborations between Canadian and American researchers should be explored to conduct comparative research highlighting similarities and differences between various Asian communities in these two nations.

The research summarized in this chapter described the varied challenges that Asian families face; however, it also highlighted positive coping strategies and strengths of individuals and family systems. It is important, especially for practitioners, to know how families maintain nurturing and supportive relationships through the family's life course and in time of crisis. Our review highlights a clear need for the development of prevention and intervention efforts to assist Asian-origin families in addressing various challenges they encounter throughout the life course, as well as culturally relevant services targeting Asian families in both Canada and the United States. In particular, family scholars are calling for a specific focus on how culture not only provides a context for understanding differences in family life, but how it could also promote coping and adjustment (Chun, Moos, & Cronkite, 2006). For instance, researchers could examine cultural and social institutions (e.g., churches, social groups) that provide support and facilitate successful outcomes. Therefore, it necessitates an ecological perspective to understand Asian-origin families to provide them support to adapt and adjust to living in the United States and in Canada.

References

Abraham, M., & Tastsoglou, E. (2016). Addressing domestic violence in Canada and the United States: The uneasy co-habitation of women and the state. *Current Sociology Monograph, 64*, 568–585. https://doi.org/10.1177/0011392116639221

Afifi, T. O., Mota, N., Sareen, J., & MacMillan, H. L. (2017). The relationships between harsh physical punishment and child maltreatment in childhood and intimate partner violence in adulthood. *BMC Public Health, 17*, 493–503. https://doi.org/10.1186/s12889-017-4359-8

Ahluwalia, M. K. (2011). Holding my breath: The experience of being Sikh after 9/11. *Traumatology, 17*, 41–46. https://doi.org/10.1177/1534765611421962

Ahmad, F., Rai, N., Petrovic, B., Erickson, P. E., & Stewart, D. E. (2013). Resilience and resources among South Asian immigrant women as survivors of partner violence. *Journal of Immigrant Minority Health, 15*, 1057–1064. https://doi.org/10.1007/s10903-013-9836-2

Behl, L. E., Crouch, J. L., May, P. F., Valente, A. L., & Crouch, J. L. (2001). Ethnicity in child maltreatment research: A content analysis. *Child Maltreatment, 6*, 143–147.

Beiser, M., Noh, S., Hou, F., Kaspar, V., & Rummens, J. (2001). Southeast Asian refugees' perceptions of racial discrimination in Canada. *Canadian Ethnic Studies, 33*(1), 46–70.

Bellmore, A., Nishina, A., You, J., & Ma, T. (2012). School context protective factors against peer ethnic discrimination across the high school years. *American Journal of Community Psychology, 49*, 98–111. https://doi.org/10.1007/s10464-011-9443-0

Berry, J. W. (2005). Acculturation: Living successfully in two cultures. *International Journal of Intercultural Relations, 29*, 697–712. https://doi.org/10.1016/j.ijintrel.2005.07.013

Bhandari, S. (2018). South Asian women's coping strategies in the face of domestic violence in the United States. *Health Care for Women International, 39*, 220–242. https://doi.org/10.1080/07399332.2017.1385615

Bhuyan, R., Mell, M., Senturia, K., Sullivan, M., & Shiu-Thornton, S. (2005). "Women must endure according to their karma": Cambodian immigrant women talk about domestic violence. *Journal of Interpersonal Violence, 20*, 902–921.

Canadian Museum of Immigration. (2017). *The Chinese Immigration Act, 1885*. http://www.pier21.ca/research/immigration-history/the-chinese-immigration-act-1885

Casado, B. L., & Leung, P. (2001). Migratory grief and depression among elderly Chinese American immigrants. *Journal of Gerontological Social Work, 36*, 5–26. https://doi.org/10.1300/J083v36n01_02

Casado, B. L., & Sacco, P. (2012). Correlates of caregiver burden among family caregivers of older Korean Americans. *Journals of Gerontology: Series B, 67*, 331–336. https://doi.org/10.1093/geronb/gbr115

Chang, J., Rhee, S., & Weaver, D. (2006). Characteristics of child abuse in immigrant Korean families and correlates of placement decisions. *Child Abuse & Neglect, 30*, 881–891.

Chen Feng, J., Knudson-Martin, C., & Nelson, T. (2015). Intergenerational tension, connectedness, and separateness in the lived experience of first and second generation Chinese American Christians. *Contemporary Family Therapy, 37*, 153–164. https://doi.org/10.1007/s10591-015-9335-9

Cheryan, S., & Monin, B. (2005). Where are you really from?: Asian Americans and identity denial. *Journal of Personality & Social Psychology, 89*, 717–730. https://doi.org/10.1037/0022-3514.89.5.717

Chesler, P. (2009). Are honor killings simply domestic violence? *Middle East Quarterly, 16*, 61–69.

Chesler, P. (2010). Worldwide trends in honor killings. *Middle East Quarterly, 17*, 3–11.

Cheung, M., Leung, P., & Tsui, V. (2009). Asian male domestic violence victims: Services exclusive for men. *Journal of Family Violence, 24*, 447–462. https://doi.org/10.1007/s10896-009-9240-9

Choksi, R., Desai, S., & Adamali, A. (2010). Overview of domestic violence in the South Asian community in Canada: Prevalence, issues, and some recommendations. In J. Fong (Ed.), *Out of the shadows: Woman abuse in ethnic, immigrant, and aboriginal communities* (pp. 147–170). Women's Press Toronto.

Chun, C. A., Moos, R. H., & Cronkite, R. C. (2006). Culture: A fundamental context for the stress and coping paradigm. In P. T. P. Wong & L. C. J. Wong (Eds.), *Handbook of multicultural perspectives on stress and coping* (pp. 29–53). Springer.

Chung, R. H. G. (2001). Gender, ethnicity, and acculturation in intergenerational conflict of Asian American college students. *Cultural Diversity & Ethnic Minority Psychology, 7*, 376–386. https://doi.org/10.1037//1099-9809.7.4.376

Cooc, N., & Gee, K. A. (2014). National trends in school victimization among Asian American adolescents. *Journal of Adolescence, 37*, 839–849. https://doi.org/10.1016/j.adolescence.2014.05.002

Costigan, C. L., & Dokis, D. P. (2006). Similarities and differences in acculturation among mothers, fathers, and children in immigrant Chinese families. *Journal of Cross-Cultural Psychology, 37*, 723–741. https://doi.org/10.1177/0022022106292080

Dasgupta, S. D. (2000). Charting the course: An overview of domestic violence in the South Asian community in the United States. *Journal of Social Distress & the Homeless, 9*, 173–185. https://doi.org/10.1023/A:1009403917198

Diversity and Human Rights. (DHR, 2017). *Racism against Asian Canadians*. https://www.uoguelph.ca/diversity-human-rights/book-page/racism-against-asian-canadians

Dinh, K. T., & Nguyen, H. H. (2006). The effects of acculturative variables on Asian American parent-child relationships. *Journal of Social & Personal Relationships, 23*, 407–426. https://doi.org/10.1177/0265407506064207

DIVA. (2009–2012). *Gentlemen's Agreement of 1907*. https://diva.sfsu.edu/collections/ga1907

Diwan, S., Jonnalagadda, S. S., & Balaswamy, S. (2004). Resources predicting positive and negative affect during the experience of stress: A study of older Asian Indian immigrants in the United States. *The Gerontologist, 44*, 605–614. https://doi.org/10.1093/geront/44.5.605

Do, K. A., Wang, C., & Atwal, K. (2019). Peer victimization and the perpetual foreigner stereotype on Sikh American adolescents' mental health outcomes: The moderating effects of coping and behavioral enculturation. *Asian American Journal of Psychology, 10*, 131–140. https://doi.org/10.1037/aap0000132

Do, K. A. & Wong, J. (2017). *Discrimination among Asian Americans*. Connect! https://www.aast.umd.edu/wp-content/uploads/2016/08/Connect-Newsletter-Issue2_Fall-2017.pdf

Dong, X. Q., Chang, E.-S., Wong, E., Wong, B., & Simon, M. A. (2011). How do U.S. Chinese older adults view elder maltreatment? Findings from a community-based participatory research study. *Journal of Aging & Health, 23*, 289–312. https://doi.org/10.1177/0898264310385931

Dong, X. Q., Chen, R., Fulmer, T., & Simon, M. A. (2014). Prevalence and correlates of elder mistreatment in a community-dwelling population of U.S. Chinese older adults. *Journal of Aging & Health, 26*, 1209–1224. https://doi.org/10.1177/0898264314531617

Dong, X. Q., Chen, R., Wu, B., Zhang, N. J., Mui, A. C. Y. -S, .Chi, I. (2016). Association between elder mistreatment and suicidal ideation among community-dwelling Chinese older adults in the U.S.A. *Gerontology, 62,* 71–80. https://doi.org/10.1159/000437420

Erez, E., & Hartley, C. C. (2003). Battered immigrant women and the legal system: A therapeutic jurisprudence perspective. *Western Criminology Review, 4,* 155–169.

Farver, J. A. M., Narang, S. K., & Bhadha, B. R. (2002). East meets West: Ethnic identity, acculturation, and conflict in Asian Indian families. *Journal of Family Psychology, 16,* 338–350. https://doi.org/10.1037//0893-3200.16.3.338

Fisher, C. B., Wallace, S. A., & Fenton, R. E. (2000). Discrimination distress during adolescence. *Journal of Youth and Adolescence, 29,* 679–695. https://doi.org/10.1023/A:1026455906512

Futa, K. T., Hsu, E., & Hansen, D. J. (2001). Child sexual abuse in Asian American families: An examination of cultural factors that influence prevalence, identification, and treatment. *Clinical Psychology: Science and Practice, 8,* 189–209.

Gautam, R., Mawn, B., & Beehler, S. (2018). Bhutanese older adult refugees recently resettled in the United States: A better life with a little sorrow. *Journal of Transcultural Nursing, 29,* 165–171. https://doi.org/10.1177/1043659617696975

Gee, G. C., Delva, J., & Takeuchi, D. T. (2007). Relationships between self-reported unfair treatment and prescription medication use, illicit drug use, and alcohol dependence among Filipino Americans. *American Journal of Public Health, 97,* 933–940.

Gee, G. C., Spencer, M. S., Chen, J., & Takeuchi, D. (2007). A nationwide survey of discrimination and chronic health conditions among Asian Americans. *American Journal of Public Health, 97,* 1275–1282.

Greene, M. L., Way, N., & Pahl, K. (2006). Trajectories of perceived adult and peer discrimination among Black, Latino, and Asian American adolescents: Patterns and psychological correlates. *Developmental Psychology, 42,* 218–238.

Han, H., Choi, Y. J., Kim, M. T., Lee, J. E., & Kim, K. B. (2008). Experiences and challenges of informal caregiving for Korean immigrants. *Journal of Advanced Nursing, 63,* 517–526.

Huynh, Q., Devos, T., & Smalarz, L. (2011). Perpetual foreigner in one's own land: Potential implications for identity and psychological adjustment. *Journal of Social & Clinical Psychology, 30,* 133–162. https://doi.org/10.1521/jscp.2011.30.2.133

Hwang, W. (2006). Acculturative family distancing: Theory, research, and clinical practice. *Psychotherapy: Theory, Research, Practice, Training, 43,* 397–409.

Hwang, W.-C., & Wood, J. J. (2009). Acculturative family distancing: Links with self-reported symptomatology among Asian Americans and Latinos. *Child Psychiatry & Human Development, 40,* 123–138. https://doi.org/10.1007/s10578-008-0115-8

Jang, Y., Kim, G., & Chiriboga, D. A. (2006). Correlates of sense of control among older Korean-American immigrants: Financial status, physical health constraints, and environmental challenges. *International Journal of Aging & Human Development, 36,* 173–186. https://doi.org/10.2190/9QMQ-TG4A-1LDC-CNRR

Jones, R. S., Zhang, X. E., Jaceldo-Siegl, K. Y., & Meleis, A. I. (2002). Caregiving between two cultures: An integrative experience. *Journal of Transcultural Nursing, 13,* 202–209.

Juang, L. P., & Alvarez, A. A. (2010). Discrimination and adjustment among Chinese American adolescents: Family conflict and family cohesion as vulnerability and protective factors. *American Journal of Public Health, 100,* 2403–2409. https://doi.org/10.2105/AJPH.2009.185959

Juang, L. P., Syed, M., Cookston, J. T., Wang, Y., & Kim, S. Y. (2012). Acculturation-based and every family conflict in Chinese American families. *New Directions for Child & Adolescent Development, 2012,* 13–34. https://doi.org/10.1002/cd.20002

Kamimura, A., Nourian, M. M., Assasnik, N., Nourian, K., & Franchek-Roa, K. (2020). Childhood abuse and intimate partner violence victimization among Filipina and South Asian women in the United States. *Women's Health Report, 1.* https://doi.org/10.1089/whr.2019.0001

Kang, H., Okazaki, S., Abelmann, N., Kim-Prieto, C., & Lan, S. (2010). Redeeming immigrant parents: How Korean American emerging adults reinterpret their childhood. *Journal of Adolescent Research, 25,* 441–464. https://doi.org/10.1177/0743558410361371

Kataoka-Yahiro, M. R. (2010). Filipino American grandparent caregivers' roles, acculturation, and perceived health status. *Journal of Cultural Diversity, 17*, 24–33.

Kawai, Y. (2005). Stereotyping Asian-Americans: The dialectic of the model minority and the yellow peril. *Howard Journal of Communications, 16*, 109–130. https://doi.org/10.1080/10646170590948974

Kim, G., Jang, Y., & Chiriboga, D. A. (2012). Personal views about aging among Korean American older adults: The role of physical health, social network, and acculturation. *Journal of Cross-Cultural Gerontology, 27*, 139–148. https://doi.org/10.1007/s10823-012-9165-2

Kim, J. Y., & Emery, C. (2003). Marital power, conflict, norm consensus, and marital violence in a nationally representative sample of Korean couples. *Journal of Interpersonal Violence, 18*, 197–219. https://doi.org/10.1177/0886260502238735

Kim, S. Y., Chen, Q., Wang, Y., Shen, Y., & Orozco-Lapray, D. (2013). Longitudinal linkages among parent-child acculturation discrepancy, parenting, parent-child sense of alienation, and adolescent adjustment in Chinese immigrant families. *Developmental Psychology, 49*, 900–912. https://doi.org/10.1037/a0029169

Kim, T., Nguyen, E. T., Yuen, E. J., Nguyen, T., Sorn, R., & Nguyen, G. T. (2015). Differential role of social connectedness in geriatric depression among Southeast Asian ethnic groups. *Progress in Community Health Partnerships, 9*, 483–493. https://doi.org/10.1353/cpr.2015.0075

Kuo, B. C. H., Chong, V., & Joseph, J. (2008). Depression and its psychosocial correlates among older Asian immigrants in North America: A critical review of two decades' research. *Journal of Aging & Health, 20*, 615–652. https://doi.org/10.1177/0898264308321001

Kwak, K., & Berry, J. W. (2001). Intergenerational differences in acculturation among Asian families in Canada: A comparison of Vietnamese, Korean, and East-Indian groups. *International Journal of Psychology, 36*, 152–162. https://doi.org/10.1080/00207590042000119

Kwok, S.-M., & Tam, D. M. Y. (2009). Child abuse in Chinese families in Canada: Implications for child protection practice. *International Social Work, 48*, 341–348. https://doi.org/10.1177/0020872805051736

Lai, D. W. L. (2007). Cultural predictors of caregiving burden of Chinese-Canadian family caregivers. *Canadian Journal of Aging, 26*, 133–148. https://doi.org/10.3138/cja.26.suppl1.133

Lai, D. W. L. (2009). From burden to depressive symptoms: The case of Chinese-Canadian family caregivers for the elderly. *Social Work in Health Care, 48*, 432–449. https://doi.org/10.1080/00981380802591759

Lai, D. W. L. (2010). Filial piety, caregiving appraisal, and caregiving burden. *Research on Aging, 32*, 200–223. https://doi.org/10.1177/0164027509351475

Lai, D. W. L. (2011). Abuse and neglect experienced by aging Chinese in Canada. *Journal of Elder Abuse & Neglect, 23*, 326–347. https://doi.org/10.1080/08946566.2011.584047

Lee, B., Fuller-Thomson, E., Fallon, B., Trocmé, N., & Black, T. (2017). Asian-Canadian children and families involved in the child welfare system in Canada: A mixed methods study. *Child Abuse & Neglect, 70*, 342–355. https://doi.org/10.1016/j.chiabu.2017.06.022

Lee, B., Rha, W., & Fallon, B. (2014). Physical abuse among Asian families in the Canadian child welfare system. *Journal of Aggression, Maltreatment, & Trauma, 23*, 532–551. https://doi.org/10.1080/10926771.2014.904462

Lee, Y., & Hadeed, L. (2009). Intimate partner violence among Asian immigrant communities: Health/mental health consequences, help-seeking behaviors, and service utilization. *Trauma, Violence, & Abuse, 12*, 143–170.

Li, H. (2004). Barriers to and unmet needs for supportive services: Experiences of Asian-American caregivers. *Journal of Cross-Cultural Gerontology, 19*, 241–260. https://doi.org/10.1023/B:JCCG.0000034221.07028.9a

Li, M., Guo, M., Stensland, M., Silverstein, M., & Dong, X. Q. (2019). Typology of family relationship and elder mistreatment in a U.S. Chinese population. *Journal of the American Geriatrics Society, 67*. https://doi.org/10.1111/jgs.15892

Li, Y. (2014). Intergenerational conflict, attitudinal familism, and depressive symptoms among Asian and Hispanic adolescents in immigrant families: A latent variable interaction analysis. *Journal of Social Service Research, 40*, 80–96. https://doi.org/10.1080/01488376.2013.845128

Lim, S.-L., Yeh, M., Liang, J., Lau, A. S., & McCabe, K. (2009). Acculturation gap, intergenerational conflict, parenting style, and youth distress in immigrant Chinese American families. *Marriage & Family Review, 45*, 84–106. https://doi.org/10.1080/01494920802537530

Londhe, R. (2015). Acculturation of Asian Indian parents: Relationship with parent and child characteristics. *Early Childhood Development & Care, 185*, 528–537. https://doi.org/10.1080/03004430.2014.939650

Madden, K., Scott, T., Sholapur, N., & Bhandari, M. (2016). Prevalence of intimate partner violence among South Asian women living in southern Ontario. *Journal of Immigrant Minority Health, 18*, 913–920. https://doi.org/10.1007/s10903-015-0333-7

Maiter, S., & Stalker, C. (2011). South Asian immigrants' experience of child protection services: Are we recognizing strengths and resilience? *Child & Family Social Work, 16*, 138–148. https://doi.org/10.1111/j.1365-2206.2010.00721.x

Midlarsky, E., Venkataramani-Kothari, A., & Plante, M. (2006). Domestic violence in the Chinese and South Asian immigrant communities. *Annals of New York Academy of Science, 1087*, 279–300. https://doi.org/10.1196/annals.1385.003

Miedema, B., & Wachholz, S. (2000). Risk, fear, harm: Immigrant women's perception of the 'policing solution' to woman abuse. *Crime, Law and Social Change, 34*, 301–317.

Muhammad, A. A. (2010). Preliminary examination of so-called "honour Killings" in Canada. Report presented to the Family, Children and Youth Section of the Department of Justice Canada. http://www.justice.gc.ca/eng/rp-pr/cj-jp/fv-vf/hk-ch/toc-tdm.html

Mui, A. C., & Kang, S.-Y. (2006). Acculturation stress and depression among Asian immigrant elders. *Social Work, 51*, 243–255. https://doi.org/10.1093/sw/51.3.243

Murray, K. E., Klonoff, E. A., Garcini, L. M., Ullman, J. B., Wall, T. L., & Myers, M. G. (2014). Assessing acculturation over time: A four-year prospective study of Asian American young adults. *Asian American Journal of Psychology, 5*, 252–261. https://doi.org/10.1037/a0034908

Nguyen, D. J., Kim, J. J., Weiss, B., Ngo, V., & Lau, A. S. (2018). Prospective relations between parent-adolescent acculturation conflict and mental health symptoms among Vietnamese American adolescents. *Cultural Diversity & Ethnic Minority Psychology, 24*, 151–161. https://doi.org/10.1037/cdp0000157

Noh, S., & Kaspar, V. (2003). Perceived discrimination and depression: Moderating effects of coping, acculturation, and ethnic support. *American Journal of Public Health, 93*, 232–238.

Okeke-Ihejirika, P., Yohani, S., Muster, J., Ndem, A., Chambers, T., & Pow, V. (2018). A scoping review of intimate partner violence in Canada's immigrant communities. *Trauma, Violence, & Abuse.* https://doi.org/10.1177/1524838018789156

Peguero, A. A. (2009). Victimizing the children of immigrants: Latino and Asian American student victimization. *Youth & Society, 41*, 186–208. https://doi.org/10.1177/0044118X09333646

Pelczarski, Y., & Kemp, S. P. (2006). Patterns of child maltreatment referrals among Asian and Pacific Islander families. *Child Welfare, 85*(1), 5–31.

Pinquart, M., & Sörensen, S. (2005). Ethnic differences in stressors, resources, and psychological outcomes of family caregiving: A meta-analysis. *The Gerontologist, 45*, 90–106. https://doi.org/10.1093/geront/45.1.90

Ponder, L. S. (2018). Intergenerational and personal connectedness: Held together in Christian faith. *Journal of Psychology & Theology, 46*, 133–139. https://doi.org/10.1177/0091647118767989

Qin, D. B., Way, N., & Mukherjee, P. (2008). The other side of the model minority story: The familial and peer challenges faced by Chinese American adolescents. *Youth & Society, 39*, 480–506. https://doi.org/10.1177/0044118X08314233

Raj, A., Livramento, K. N., Santana, M. C., et al. (2006). Victims of intimate partner violence more likely to report abuse from in-laws. *Violence Against Women, 12*, 936–949.

Rhee, S., Chang, J., Berthold, S. M., & Mar, G. (2012). Child maltreatment among immigrant Vietnamese families: Characteristics and implications for practice. *Child and Adolescent Social Work Journal, 29*, 85–101. https://doi.org/10.1007/s10560-011-0253-x

Rivas-Drake, D., Hughes, D., & Way, N. (2008). A closer look at peer discrimination, ethnic identity, and psychological well-being among urban Chinese American sixth graders. *Journal of Youth & Adolescence, 37*, 12–21. https://doi.org/10.1007/s10964-007-9227-x

Samuel, E. (2009). Acculturative stress: South Asian immigrant women's experiences in Canada's Atlantic provinces. *Journal for Immigrant & Refugee Studies, 7*, 16–34. https://doi.org/10.1080/15562940802687207

Sieben, A., Lust, K., Ainslee, C., Renner, L. M., & Nguyen, R. H. N. (2019). Race and sex differences in adverse childhood experiences among Asian/ Pacific Islander college students. *Journal of American College Health*. https://doi.org/10.1080/07448481.2019.1677671

Silverman, J. A. (2002). Intimate partner violence against South Asian women in greater Boston. *Journal of the American Medical Women's Association, 57*, 111–114.

Sorkin, D. H., Nguyen, H., & Ngo-Metzger, Q. (2011). Assessing the mental health needs and barriers to care among a diverse sample of Asian American older adults. *Journal of General Internal Medicine, 26*, 595–602. https://doi.org/10.1007/s11606-010-1612-6

Statistics Canada (2016). *Visible minority, economic family income decile group, generation status, age, and sex for the population in private households of Canada, provinces and territories, census metropolitan areas and census agglomerations, 2016 Census – 25% sample data*. https://www12.statcan.gc.ca/census-recensement/2016/dp-pd/dt-td/Rp-eng.cfm?TABID=2&LANG=E&APATH=3&DETAIL=0&DIM=0& FL=A&FREE=0&GC=0&GK=0&GRP=1&PID=111826&PRID=10&PTYPE=109445&S=0&SHOWALL=0&SUB=0&Temporal=2017&THEME=120&VID=0&VNAMEE=&VNAMEF=

Statistics Canada. (2017). *Ethnic diversity and immigration*. https://www150.statcan.gc.ca/n1/pub/11-402-x/2011000/chap/imm/imm-eng.htm

Tang, F., Xu, L., Chi, I., & Dong, X. Q. (2016). Psychological well-being of older Chinese-American grandparents caring for grandchildren. *Journal of the American Geriatrics Society, 64*, 2356–2361. https://doi.org/10.1111/jgs.14455

Terman, R. L. (2010). To specify or single out: Should we use the term 'honor killing'? Muslim *World. Journal of Human Rights, 7*, 1–39. https://doi.org/10.2202/1554-4419.1162

Tummala-Narra, P., Sundaram, S., & Sathasivam-Rueckert, N. (2013). Voices of older Asian Indian immigrants: Mental health implications. *Professional Psychology, Research, & Practice, 44*, 1–10. https://doi.org/10.1037/a0027809

United Nations. (2017). *International migrant stock: 2017*. The UN's Department of Economic and Social Affairs: https://www.un.org/en/development/desa/population/migration/data/estimates2017/estimates17.asp

United Nations Population Fund (UNFPA). (2000). *State of the World Population 2000*. https://www.unfpa.org/publications/state-world-population-2000

United States Department of Health & Human Services (DDHS), Administration for Children and Families, Administration on children, Youth and Families, Child's Bureau (2020). *Child Maltreatment 2018*. https://www.acf.hhs.gov/sites/default/files/cb/cm2018.pdf#page=31

United States Department of Justice. (2015). *Combatting post-9/11 discriminatory backlash*. https://www.justice.gov/crt/combating-post-911-discriminatory-backlash-6

Vu, H. Q., & Rook, K. S. (2013). Acculturation and intergenerational relationships in Vietnamese American families: The role of gender. *Asian American Journal of Psychology, 4*, 227–234. https://doi.org/10.1037/a0029750

Wang, C., La Salle, T., Wu, C., Do, K. A., & Sullivan, K. (2018). School climate and parental involvement as moderators for victimization and suicidal thoughts and behaviors of Asian American middle school students. *Asian American Journal of Psychology, 9*, 296–307. https://doi.org/10.1037/aap0000138

World Bank. (2020). *International migrant stock (% of population) – Canada, United States*. https://data.worldbank.org/indicator/SM.POP.TOTL.ZS?locations=CA-US

Ying, Y. (1999). Strengthening intergenerational/intercultural ties in migrant families: A new intervention for parents. *Journal of Community Psychology, 27*, 89–96.

Ying, Y. W. (2009). Strengthening Intergenerational/Intercultural Ties in Immigrant Families (SITIF): A parenting intervention to bridge the Chinese American intergenerational acculturation gap. In N. H. Trinh, Y. C. Rho, F. G. Lu, & K. M. Sanders (Eds.), *Handbook of mental health and acculturation in Asian American families. Current clinical psychiatry*. Humana Press.

Ying, Y.-W., & Han, M. (2007). The longitudinal effects of intergenerational gap in acculturation on conflict and mental health in Southeast Asian American adolescents. *American Journal of Orthopsychiatry, 77*, 61–66. https://doi.org/10.1037/0002-9432.77.1.61

Yoo, H. C., Gee, G. C., & Takeuchi, D. (2009). Discrimination and health among Asian American immigrants: Disentangling racial from language discrimination. *Social Science & Medicine, 68*, 726–732.

Yoshioka, M. R., DiNoia, J., & Ullah, K. (2001). Attitudes toward marital violence: An examination of four Asian communities. *Violence Against Women, 7*, 900–926.

Zhai, F. (2017). Cultural orientation, parental nurturance, and parent-child conflict among Asian American parents in New York City. *Children & Youth Services Review, 76*, 1–9. https://doi.org/10.1016/j.childyouth.2017.02.026

Zhai, F., & Gao, Q. (2009). Child maltreatment among Asian Americans: Characteristics and explanatory framework. *Child Maltreatment, 14*, 207–224. https://doi.org/10.1177/1077559508326286

Zia, H. (2000). *Asian American dreams: The emergence of an American people* (1st ed.). Farrar, Straus and Giroux.

Chapter 13
Providing Therapy with Asian Immigrant Families: A Review of Prominent Issues and Treatment Considerations

Daniel Kaplin, Denise Farrelly, Kristen Parente, and Florette Cohen

Abstract In this chapter, we address several common family-related issues, which could necessitate seeking mental health treatment. A vignette is used as a framework for understanding four core stressors and clinical issues, which immigrants, refugees, and asylum-seekers experience. We also provide the reader with a 15-item assessment instrument, which can be used to augment traditional clinical interviews. This instrument focuses on acculturative, isolative, resettlement, traumatic stress, and resiliency factors, which serve to help immigrant families adjust to their new experiences in the United States and Canada. The following family-based clinical issues are discussed: (a) acculturative stress, (b) anti-immigration rhetoric, (c) differences in the experiences of refugees and asylum seekers relative to orderly migration, (d) stereotypes, (e) war-based conflict, (f) mental health stigma, (g) intimate partner violence, (h) physical punishment, (i) and other forms of abuse, neglect, and maltreatment. The chapter concludes with several therapeutic interventions, which have been found to be effective at addressing the unique needs of an individual, couple, or family.

Keywords Acculturative Stress · Asian Families · Family Violence · Trauma Informed Therapy · Couples Therapy · Family Therapy

D. Kaplin (✉)
St. Francis College, Brooklyn, NY, USA
e-mail: dkaplin@sfc.edu

D. Farrelly
Kingsborough Community College, Brooklyn, NY, USA
e-mail: Denise.Farrelly@kbcc.cuny.edu

K. Parente
Kean University, Union, NJ, USA

F. Cohen
The College of Staten Island, Staten Island, NY, USA
e-mail: Florette.Cohen@csi.cuny.edu

S. S. Chuang et al. (eds.), *Asian Families in Canada and the United States*, Advances in Immigrant Family Research,
https://doi.org/10.1007/978-3-030-56452-0_13

Immigrant and refugee families face adverse experiences emanating from multiple sources. Beginning with persecution within their country of origin, during the migration process, and within their re-settled countries, these individuals are more prone to experience traumatic, acculturative, isolative, and resettlement stress relative to U.S. born individuals (Abdi, 2018). Moreover, due to their exposure to violence and persecution, refugees have marked increases in mental health concerns relative to non-refugees (Betancourt et al., 2017).

To address these issues, we review common clinical concerns of immigrants, refugees, and asylum-seekers that come from West, South, and East Asia. Specifically, we focus on the four-core stressors immigrant and refugee families experience as a framework to understand migratory stress (Abdi, 2018). In relation to each of the core stressors, we provide a potentially useful screening instrument to guide the clinical assessment process with immigrant, refugee, and asylum-seeking families. We conclude by presenting several individual, couples, and family therapy interventions, which have been found to be effective with Asian immigrant family populations.

We preface our remarks by noting that because of the dynamic nature of culture, ongoing learning is recommended to ensure that clinicians have the most current understanding of culture and the variability within a given group (Chu, 2007; Tseng, 2004). Moreover, the general principles presented in this chapter do not absolve a clinician from careful assessment of the family unit to identify the unique risk factors they might be experiencing. To model this process, we offer a case vignette and discuss several treatment concerns for the individual, her parents, and the larger family unit. Because many chapters in this volume focus on traditional immigration processes, we have elected to draw more attention to Asian families who are forced to migrate based on war, persecution, violence, etc. The vignette presented below highlights how the principles discussed in this chapter can be applied in a West Asian, Syrian, refugee family.

Fatimah's Story

Fatimah[1] is a 14-year-old refugee who migrated to the United States with her family to escape the Syrian Civil War. Her parents came from the Bab al-Nasr neighborhood of Aleppo. Prior to the civil war, her father, Karam, worked as a shopkeeper and was a well-respected member of the local community. His wife, Amira, cared for Fatimah and her three younger siblings. Fatimah reported being a very happy child before the conflict.

[1] It should be noted that this vignette is not based on an actual client, but draws upon the first author's work as a clinical psychologist and experience working with immigrant and refugee families.

However, Fatimah said things changed for her, her parents, and her younger siblings when the bombings began. Fatimah recalls hearing bombings and fighting. This mental imagery continues to torment her. She reported having vivid dreams about her time in Syria, difficulty with fireworks and loud noises, and struggles with discussing some of the details of events she witnessed. The increase in violence, collapsing infrastructure, and threats to the family's safety resulted in Karam and Amira looking for refuge.

In 2014, the family was temporarily resettled in the Azraq Refugee Camp. While Fatimah was only nine at the time, she remembered feeling anxious about the loss of friends, belongings, and leaving her homeland behind. She reported experiencing a deep sadness that negatively impacted her perception of her experience in Jordan. Fatimah's father also became despondent because of his loss of ability to support and protect his family. He, like many refugees in Jordan, was prohibited from working during this time. Recognizing that their resettlement in Jordan was only a temporary solution for the family, Karam, Amira, Fatimah, and her younger siblings began to prepare for a more permanent move to the United States.

Working with a large non-governmental organization, the family was able to obtain clearance to be resettled in the United States. Fatimah noted changes in her father's character. The pain, loss, and psychological torment that occurred during their migratory journey altered how he related to the family. Karam, a kind-hearted and generous husband and father, became angrier and began speaking to the family in harsher tones. Although she notes that Karam never engaged in intimate partner violence or any other forms of abuse, his change in character would scare her.

In early 2016, the family settled in a major U.S. city with a strong Muslim population. More recently, the family has expressed concerns about a change in the political climate in America. The family received slurs because of their traditional mode of dress. For example, Fatimah reported being ridiculed for wearing a hijab while riding public transportation. Amira also noted that she sometimes would receive a glare from others in the supermarket. These negative expressions bring some of the pain about being Muslim in America to the surface.

Since migrating to the United States, there has also been some positive change for the family. Karam reflected on his gratitude to be able to actively express his faith in a safe environment. Fatimah is currently enrolled in a school that focuses on providing high-quality educational experiences to new arrivals. The school and neighborhood also serve as safe havens for the family. Karam was able to secure employment working for a ride-sharing company, Amira expressed joy in being able to raise her children, and Fatimah has blossomed in school. She has developed proficiency in the English language and has taken interest in helping raise her younger siblings. Fatimah has been asked to serve as a translator for her parents at doctors' appointments and with their legal counsel. As a result, she has developed an interest in becoming a pre-med student as she prepares for college.

Acculturative Stress

As immigrants and refugees wrestle with their competing cultures, they can struggle to develop a bicultural (Berry, 1997) or tricultural identity (Ferguson, Iturbide, & Gordon, 2014). As families try to reconcile these competing values, they can develop acculturative stress, which has a profound impact on their sense of self and psychological well-being. West Asian immigrants, in particular, face higher levels of acculturative stress than members of other regions of the world (Alhasanat-Khalil et al., 2018). This increase in acculturative stress is likely due to an anti-Arab sentiment that was sparked after the terror attacks on September 11, 2001. Alhasanat-Khalil et al. (2018) noted that acculturative stress is linked to poorer social support and, in women, an increased risk of post-partum depression.

This is especially pronounced for Muslim-Americans of West Asian descent, who have experienced anti-immigrant rhetoric, which has threatened their self-perception and has impacted the perception about what constitutes being American (Abu-Ras, Suárez, & Abu-Bader, 2018). Specifically, Muslim Americans reported higher rates of perceived religious discrimination and stress. These experiences predisposed West Asian Muslim immigrants and refugees towards developing a *marginalized identity*, which refers to a person who feels disconnected from their culture of origin, but both rejects and is rejected by the new culture (Berry, 1997). See Kaplin and Gielen (2020) for a summary of how various identity development models shape one's self-perception in adolescence.

South Asian immigrants also reported experiencing high levels of acculturative stress (Akram-Pall & Moodley, 2016). In their study, Akram-Pall and Moodley (2016) interviewed 13 South Asian Muslim immigrants who lived in Toronto. They found that acculturative stress was linked to depression. Similarly, in a study of Pakistani American immigrants, researchers found that first-generation parents often struggle with adjustment more than their children (Khaleque, Malik, & Rohner, 2015). Khaleque et al. also found that while Pakistani parents and children both showed considerable identification with their culture of origin, there was significantly more identification among parents than their children. These findings reflect a generational divide in the acculturation process.

Acculturative stress impacts the adjustment of East Asian immigrants as they navigate multiple worlds (Berry, 1997; Ho & Gielen, 2016). Ho and Gielen (2016) examined how Chinese American adolescents and young adults navigated their multicultural identities. They reflected on the delicate balance East Asian families encountered as they navigated potential deviations in family and gender roles, emotional expression, body image ideals, etc. Thus, in East Asian families, this acculturative stress was linked to anxiety, depression, and interpersonal problems (Qi, Wang, Pincus, & Wu, 2018).

Implications for Clinicians

Acculturative stress has a profound impact on immigrants' and refugees' sense of self (Akram-Pall & Moodley, 2016; Alhasanat-Khalil et al., 2018). Because of the ubiquitous nature of acculturative stress among Asian immigrants, it is essential for clinicians to screen the client and their families to determine whether conflicts related to differences in acculturation and marginalized identity exist. As seen in Table 13.1, Questions 1–4 of our assessment are designed to detect potential intergenerational distress, family and role-related distress, and challenges Asian immigrants face due to linguistic barriers. When doing a clinical assessment, clinicians can gain rich information about the family dynamics by inquiring about their premigratory, migratory, and post-migratory processes. Moreover, because of the multifaceted and complex nature of identity, it would be insufficient for a clinician to approach their clinical interview without exploring these factors.

Table 13.1 Screening Instrument for Immigrant and Refugee Individuals

Topic/Question
Acculturative Stress
1. How has your identity as a mother/daughter or father/son been impacted by your move to (insert country)?
2. In coming to (insert country), have you experienced any conflict related to adjusting to your new environment?
3. How have you and your family had to adapt your culture?
4. Have you experienced any cultural or linguistic barriers? How do you address these challenges?
Isolative Stress
5. How do you feel you have been received by the (insert country) society?
6. Have you experienced any forms of discrimination or isolation from your peers?
7. Did/do you experience other aspects of persecution or marginalization as a function of being an immigrant, refugee, or asylum-seeker and possessing another minority status?
Resettlement Stress
8. How have your experiences been post-settlement?
9. Have you experienced any challenges related to housing, employment, finances, health care, or transportation as a function of your move?
10. How has your relationship with your family back home been impacted by your resettlement?
Traumatic Stress
11. What factors resulted in your decision to relocate to (insert country)?
12. Did you experience any war, persecution, or displacement from your home?
13. Did you experience any family/community-based violence?
Resilience
14. What are some of your personal sources of strength that help you in your adjustment process?
15. What family/community-based resources have you utilized to that help you cope with the differences in culture?

Note. The first author of this chapter owns the rights to the questionnaire presented in this chapter

Application to Fatimah's Story

Fatimah and her family were navigating several acculturative stress factors. More specifically, Fatimah's father struggled with adjusting to the new realities in the United States. Once a successful business owner, he was unable to work during his refugee experience, and remained unsettled with the political climate in the United States. Using Berry's (1997) framework, Karam and Amira tended to romanticize pre-war Syria and felt less comfortable in the United States resulting in a separation-based identity. However, Fatimah and her younger siblings appeared to be able to integrate their Syrian and American identities, resulting in less distress than that of her parents. Using Ferguson et al.'s (2014) model, clinicians can further examine multiple identities competing within the host country against one another and how they relate to cultural values from one's country of origin.

Stereotypes and Discrimination

Asian immigrant families also experience stereotyping, prejudice, and discriminatory behaviors. One such stereotype, "the model minority," suggests that Asian Americans are more successful than other racial minority groups because of values emphasizing hard work, achievement, and belief in the "American dream" (Atkin, Yoo, Jager, & Yeh, 2018). However, the model minority stereotype is not applied universally within and across Asian groups.

West Asians have been portrayed as a "model minority" some times and at other times as a "problem minority" (Naber, 2012). Naber noted that West Asians who migrated to the United States in the 1950s and 1970s reported having a traditional experience with migration, emphasizing positive experiences. Yet, more recently, geopolitics impacted the view of immigrants from Arab-and Muslim-majority countries in a way that West Asian immigrants started to become viewed as a "problem minority" rather than a "model minority" group (Naber, 2012).

Similarly, South Asians experience mixed messages where, at times, they are viewed as a model minority; whereas, at other times, they are viewed as a threat (Ahluwalia, 2013; Mudambi, 2019). In her study, Ahluwalia (2013) reported Sikh Americans experienced threats to their civil liberties in the wake of the September 11, 2001 attacks. She noted that religious and ethnic minorities from South Asia were more vulnerable to discrimination and profiling, merely based on their appearance. This racial profiling resulted in South Asians experiencing violence from public safety personnel, higher than normal forensic examinations, and arrests (South Asian Americans Leading Together [SAALT], 2014). Profiling at points of entry into the United States, even with legitimate documents, or when air-traveling have become increasingly difficult (SAALT, 2014).

Moreover, after the tragedy on September 11, 2001, Sikhs were violently attacked, which led to injuries and deaths (Ahluwalia & Pellettiere, 2010). In one study, South Asian school children were subjected to physical and verbal abuse by their schoolmates just because of their skin tone and the appearance of being Muslim (Bajaj, Ghaffar-Kucher, & Desai, 2016). In an attempt to address this problem, Bajaj and colleagues proposed a six-module program to define the problem of xenophobia, increase empathy, and develop allies among schoolchildren who are part of the majority culture.

East Asians are also subjected to the model minority stereotype. In one study, the researchers found that White students, who adopted the model minority stereotype, were more inclined to adopt prejudicial attitudes towards Asian Americans (Parks & Yoo, 2016). Greater endorsement of the model minority stereotype and prejudicial attitudes towards Asian Americans were mediated by a greater endorsement of colorblind attitudes by White participants. Many Asian Americans internalized the model minority stereotype (Atkin et al., 2018). In one study, researchers found that the pressure to perform in the classroom resulted in significant psychological distress, such as anxiety, depression, and suicide (Phosaly, Olympia, & Goldman, 2019).

Implications for Clinicians

Clinicians should be aware of the paradoxical attitudes ("model minority" and "problem minority") experienced by members of the West and South Asian community. Unlike East Asians, who more commonly experienced the model minority stereotype, West and South Asians tended to face discriminatory practices and violence often based on people conflating brown skin with being Muslim. These marginalizing experiences could create a sense of isolative stress for immigrant families. Clinicians should screen how a person was received by their host country, whether they have experienced discrimination, marginalization, or isolation as a function of their move. These are reflected in Questions 5–7 of our screening instrument (See Table 13.1).

Application to Fatimah's Story

Similar to Naber (2012) and Ahluwalia (2013) findings, Fatimah and her family were treated as a "problem minority" and experienced post-September 11 profiling merely based on their mode of dress. These actions made the family feel less welcomed and were indicators of potential isolative stress. However, consistent with Beitin and Allen (2005), the family's faith could have played a buffering effect against isolative stress many immigrants and refugees face.

Resettlement Stress

Moving to a new environment can be challenging. More specifically, resettlement stress can be tied to a new arrival experiencing financial difficulties, housing or employment concerns, lack of community support, and reduced access to healthcare (Kaplin, Parente, & Santacroce, 2019). Resettlement stress is especially challenging for those refugees and asylum-seekers, who experienced forced migration. For example, McNeely and Morland (2016) noted that many Syrian new arrivals to the United States struggled to obtain work, housing, transportation, medical support, and psychological services were associated with their migratory experience. McNeely and Morland stressed that the Office of Refugee Resettlement (ORR) can be a valuable resource in connecting refugees with services and help refugees reach their potential in America in their first year of arrival.

South Asian refugees also experience resettlement stress. For example, Tamil refugees, resettled in Canada, experienced many pre-and-post resettlement stressors, which predisposed them to PTSD (Beiser, Simich, Pandalangat, Nowakowski, & Tian, 2011). Tamil refugees reported struggles with their finances, employment, and trauma. However, social support from the community appeared to have a buffering effect against trauma.

Similarly, resettlement stress is a challenge for refugees from East Asia. For example, in a study using Karen refugees from Myanmar who were resettled in the United States, researchers found that these individuals struggled to find employment, affordable housing, enrolling their children in school, and accessing primary health care (McCleary, 2017). As can be seen, resettlement stress cuts to the core of basic areas of existence and should be the priority of treatment. When these basic needs are met, clinicians can redirect their focus to other areas of psychological distress.

Implications for Clinicians

Even after immigrants and refugees resettle in the United States and Canada, they can struggle to have their basic housing, occupational, educational and health needs met. Thus, when working with Asian immigrant, refugee, and asylum-seeking families, it is helpful to inquire about potential resettlement stressors that can impact the functioning of the families. Moreover, based on the responses given, clinicians might help the family interface with social services agencies to fill this void. Questions 8–10 in Table 13.1 of our screening instrument assess the presence or absence of resettlement stressors.

Application to Fatimah's Story

This is another example of why individualized assessment is necessary. Unlike McNeely and Morland's (2016) findings, Fatimah and her family appeared to navigate the resettlement process fairly well. The family secured work, housing, transportation, medical care, and psychological services. However, one concern was noted. Consistent with studies on language brokering (Kaplin & Gielen, 2020; Shen, Kim, & Benner, 2019), many children experience stress related to being a language broker for their parents. Fatimah took upon herself to become the language broker within the family structure, which could result in some level of distress related to the family's resettlement.

Traumatic Stress

Refugees are at greater risk for traumatic stress than U.S. born individuals (Betancourt et al., 2017). According to the Pew Research Center (2019), nearly one out of every two refugees came from the Middle East. However, the U.S. admission rates of West and South Asian refugees were considerably lower compared to other admitting countries throughout the world (Pew Research Center, 2019). Only 40% of refugees admitted to the United States came from West or South Asia combined (DHS Office of Immigration Statistics, 2019). Instead, refugees in the U.S. more commonly hailed from Africa, East Asia, Latin America/Caribbean, and European nations (DHS Office of Immigration Statistics, 2019). The consequence of not admitting refugees is that they either remain under fear and persecution in their country of origin longer or they might have a prolonged migratory process. In both cases, this results in an increased risk for traumatic exposure.

Abi-Hashem (2011) found that West Asian immigrants and refugees experience high levels of exposure to war, violence, and displacement. In a study using West African and Middle Eastern refugee women, researchers found that these traumatic experiences sometimes resulted in the development of post-traumatic stress disorder (Schubert & Punamäki, 2016). West Asian refugees and asylum-seekers also experienced psychological distress (Alhasanat-Khalil et al., 2018) and health deficits (Nasseri & Moulton, 2011). Those individuals who identified with multiple vulnerable populations (e.g., sexual minorities) reported even higher rates of post-traumatic stress when fleeing from West Asia (Alessi, Kahn, & Chatterji, 2016). Yet, refugees and asylum seekers were less likely to receive psychological services, and these detrimental effects can linger for many years (Kallakorpi, Haatainen, & Kankkunen, 2019).

Similarly, Beiser, Goodwill, Albanese, McShane, and Kanthasamy (2015) conducted a study exploring the mental health of Tamil refugees from Sri Lanka living in Canada. They found that Tamil refugees, who experienced pre-migration adversity, had more difficulty with post-migratory integration. Thus, understanding the clients' migratory processes is an essential part of working with Asian immigrants, refugees, and asylum-seeking families.

Implications for Clinicians

The United Nations High Commissioner for Refugees (2019) notes that Syria (West Asia), Afghanistan (South Asia), and Myanmar (Southeast Asia) represent three of the five largest worldwide refugee communities. Immigrants, refugees, and asylum seekers from West and South Asia tend to experience traumatic stress at disproportionately higher rates relative to other parts of the world (Abi-Hashem, 2011; Beiser et al., 2015). Thus, it could be useful for clinicians to explore the motivation for migration, whether the family experienced war, persecution, or displacement, and if they experienced community-based violence. Questions 11–12 (Table 13.1) of our screening instrument address these issues.

Application to Fatimah's Story

Fatimah and her family experienced many pre-flight traumatic experiences. These experiences certainly shaped the family's mental health. Fatimah recounted bombings and fighting, which resulted in her reliving these experiences through flashbacks and nightmares. Her father also had a change in demeanor as a function of his preflight and migratory experiences, indicating the presence of traumatic stress. Outside of the war-based conflict, Fatimah did not note any other family or community-based violence.

Family and Relational Issues

Intimate Partner Violence

The West Asian family has higher rates of intimate partner violence (IPV) relative to western communities (Hawcroft et al., 2019). In their meta-analysis of 41 studies, spanning 10 West Asian countries and over 19,000 participants, they found that the lifetime exposure to either physical, emotional, or sexual-based IPV was 73.3% (Hawcroft et al., 2019), which is significantly higher than U.S. estimates (Smith et al., 2018). Haj-Yahia (2000) reported that violence towards women has been linked to reduced family support and interdependence, family reputation, women's inferiority and male supremacy, and breaches in family cohesion. Haj-Yahia (2003) also noted that perpetrators are likely to justify their actions and blame their wives for causing the abuse. This defensiveness among perpetrators of IPV makes treatment especially complicated when working with West Asian couples.

Perceptions of what constitutes IPV differ between U.S. and Asian cultures (Midlarsky, Venkataramani, & Plante, 2006). South Asian women who endorse honor beliefs (e.g., disrespecting one's husband), patriarchal attitudes, exposure to IPV as a child, a need for control, victim-blaming, financial control, need for family cohesion, divorce stigma, and substance abuse are at increased risk for IPV (Mitra, 2013; Rai & Choi, 2018). Many victims of IPV suffer in silence due to sociocultural and legal factors (Mitra, 2013).

Traditional female gender roles become more flexible as they acculturate to their host country (Kim, LaRoche, & Tomiuk, 2004). This could result in relational conflict and increase the risk for IPV (Cheung & Choi, 2016). For example, South Korean (and other East Asian) immigrants who experienced IPV were less likely to seek support through interventions, less likely to speak to friends about their experiences, and more likely to minimize the seriousness of their abuse (Shim & Nelson-Becker, 2009).

Marriage Related Practices

Arranged marriages are fairly commonplace, even by South Asians living in the diaspora (Aguiar, 2018). Support for arranged marriages diminished from the first generation to the second generation, which places a strain on South Asian immigrant families (Samuel, 2010). Another critical problem facing South Asian immigrants is child marriage. Seth et al. (2018) noted the powerful influences of patriarchy, coercion, and social norms on child marriages.

A final marriage related concern surrounds dowries, which increase the risk of abuse. Several South Asian countries have created laws to ban child marriages (Ghosh, 2011; Nasreen, Ali, & Shah, 2018) and dowries (Cheema, Abbas, & Khan, 2018), but they persist despite these laws. These practices are not without consequence. Child marriage practices increase the risk of psychological distress (Khan et al., 2018). The practices of arranged marriages, child marriages, and dowries all place women at greater risk of IPV (Kidman, 2017; Sabri, Simonet, & Campbell, 2018).

The risk of physical and sexual violence is amplified when one migrates to a country based on marriage, also referred to as *marriage migration* or *immigrant wives* (Chiu, 2017). Chiu analyzed the experiences of 15 women who moved from Mainland China to Hong Kong. She found that even though Hong Kong is part of China, there was an increase in IPV among those who moved to Hong Kong. Chiu notes that some women in East Asian culture are expected to follow their husband where he resides (*patrilocality*). Leaving one's location of origin creates the potential for social isolation, powerlessness, and victimization. Moreover, in some of these communities, it becomes difficult to return to their family of origin, which creates a sense of entrapment. Similar to Chiu's (2017) findings, South Asian marriage migrants to the United States were at increased risk for IPV (Chaudhuri, Morash, & Yingling, 2014)

Implications for Clinicians

As noted earlier, attitudes towards IPV vary between U.S. and Asian communities (Midlarsky et al., 2006). Violence can come at the hands of family members, handlers who help families migrate, and the general community. With South and East Asian immigrants, clinicians can probe whether IPV occurred as a function of marriage migration. Thus, asking West, South, and East Asian immigrants about their experience with violence during the migratory process could help identify any possible forms of traumatic stress. Finally, when a clinician works with South Asian immigrant families, it is important to explore if the family had an arranged or child marriage, provided a dowry, and determine whether any undue psychological distress resulted from these practices. Question 13 (Table 13.1) of our screening instrument assesses traumatic stress related to family or community-based violence.

Application to Fatimah's Story

Karam and Amira maintained traditional gender roles. He assumed the role of the breadwinner and she assumed the caregiver role. There was no indication that Amira was a child bride, had an arranged marriage, or experienced any other risk factor noted above that would predispose the couple towards IPV. In fact, Fatimah described her father as "a kind-hearted and generous husband…" Thus, although we noted earlier that there are higher rates of intimate partner violence among individuals coming from West Asian families (Hawcroft et al., 2019), there was no indication of intimate partner violence between Karam and Amira. There could be a discussion pertaining to effective communication for the couple, as will be discussed below.

Child Related Issues

Child Abuse, Neglect, and Maltreatment

A second example of family-based violence is that West Asian immigrants and refugees reported problems related to child abuse, neglect and maltreatment (Fayyad, Diab, Yousef, Farhat, & Karam, 2017). Abuse has been linked to lower self-esteem, anxiety, depression, and reduced quality of life (Al-Fayez, Ohaeri, & Gado, 2012). One notable challenge when dealing with sexual abuse in the Arab community is there tends to be more of a focus on blaming the victim rather than punishing the perpetrator (Abu Baker & Dwairy, 2003).

Physical punishment is fairly accepted within South Asian communities (Irfan, 2008). In India, females tended to report experiencing physical and emotional abuse more frequently than males (Valsala, Devanathan, & Kuttappan, 2018). Although it occurs at less frequent rates, sexual abuse does occur within the South Asian community (Choudhry et al., 2018). For South Asian individuals, child abuse adversely affects one's self-esteem (Valsala et al., 2018) and increases the risk for depression, suicidal ideations and attempts (Nijhara, Bhatia, & Unnikrishnan, 2018).

Misbehavior is often met with corporal punishment in East Asian families (Barry, Bernard, & Beitel, 2009). Nevertheless, attitudes towards corporal punishment vary by country (Son, Lee, Ahn, & Doan, 2017). In their study, Son et al. (2017) examined the views of corporal punishment between the United States, South Korean, and Japanese mothers. They found that American mothers were more likely to view corporal punishment as child abuse, followed by South Korean, and then Japanese mothers.

Implications for Clinicians

Child abuse, neglect, and maltreatment are fairly common in Asian families (Danawi & Hasbini, 2015; Son et al., 2017). Question 13 (see Table 13.1) of our screening instrument also has the capacity to probe violence towards children. Because laws regarding child abuse in the United States and Canada differ from those in West Asia, clinicians might review the local and national child protection laws requiring one to report suspected abuse, neglect, or maltreatment with immigrant families. Moreover, the clinician might discuss the adverse impact of abuse, neglect, and maltreatment on the psychological development of the child.

Application to Fatimah's Story

Al-Fayez et al. (2012) noted that abuse was linked to lower self-esteem, anxiety, depression, and reduced quality of life. While Fatimah noted her father began speaking in harsher tones, there were no indicators of child abuse, neglect, or maltreatment. This bodes well for Fatimah and her siblings.

Resilience

Resilience refers to the capacity to adapt or adjust to adversity or challenges following periods of significant risk or adversity (Masten, 2014). Julca (2011) stated that immigrants' vulnerability and resilience depend on several factors. The first dimension is the level of skilled labor one does. A second related dimension is a given sphere of influence (e.g., family, local community, national, and international community). Each domain has vulnerability and resilience factors. Resilience can come from within the person who experienced a given stressor, familial support, or community resources.

Ahmad, Rai, Petrovic, Erickson, and Stewart (2013) examined the role of resiliency and social support in helping South Asian survivors of IPV adapt post-trauma. These authors conducted 11 in-depth interviews with South Asian women who originated from India or Pakistan. Women who chose to address their experience with IPV tended to have more support, draw on their personal resolve, communal/social support, and professional assistance. These resiliency factors helped women leave threatening situations.

Yeh, Pituc, Kim, and Atkins (2008) conducted focused interviews with 10 groups of Chinese immigrant youth to explore barriers, resiliency, and social support factors. These authors reflected on several barriers that Chinese immigrants experience, which included language, finances, prejudice, and so forth. However, they note that resiliency is also linked to several of the barriers. These authors suggested ways to develop social support for these individuals as a way to buffer against the aforementioned stressors.

Beitin and Allen (2005) conducted a series of in-depth interviews with Arab American couples to explore the challenges and methods for coping with the experiences surrounding the September 11, 2001 attacks. These authors found that their "history, culture, traditions, and beliefs proved valuable when facing adversity" (Beitin & Allen, 2005, p. 266). While this study was limited in its sample size and composition, it is illustrative of the role resiliency can play in coping for West Asian immigrant families.

Implications for Clinicians

As noted above, immigrants, refugees, and asylum-seekers are susceptible to mental health concerns at differing degrees. These mental health concerns can be reduced when the person possesses internal, familial, community, and governmental support. Thus, clinicians should explore the presence or absence of these resiliency factors, which are included in Questions 14–15 of our screening instrument below.

Application to Fatimah's Story

Fatimah and her family have overcome so much adversity. Their ability to adjust to a new environment and recover quickly from adversity points to their resiliency. The family's connection to their faith and community serve as noteworthy social support factors. Lastly, the lack of commonly held clinical problems bodes well for family adjustment.

Treatment Considerations

In the final section of our chapter, we reflect on several treatment modalities that can be used to work with Asian immigrant families. However, it is essential to recognize that Asian immigrant families report higher rates of mental health stigma, which must be addressed as part of the treatment process (Karasz et al., 2019; Zolezzi, Alamri, Shaar, & Rainkie, 2018). Mental health stigma is reduced when practitioners provide their clients with information about the origins and impact of mental illness (Rastogi et al., 2014; Sewilam et al., 2015). Below, we present several interventions to address the trauma, relational and family-based issues that immigrant and refugee families might face.

Trauma-Based Interventions

To address potential trauma related to abuse, victimization, or as a function of refugee status, there are several useful interventions. Trauma-Focused Cognitive Behavioral Therapy (TF-CBT) is effective when working with refugees and asylum-seekers (Nosè et al., 2017). The goal is to help children and their families cope with their trauma through "PRACTICE," which is a mnemonic for psychoeducation and parenting skills, relaxation, affective expression, cognitive processing, trauma narrative development, in vivo mastery, conjoint parent-child sessions, and enhancing future safety (Cohen, Mannarino, & Deblinger, 2006).

Child-centered play therapy (CCPT) is effective when working with immigrant children. Its four components include structuring, reflective listening, fantasy play, and limit setting. This model assumes that children have an inherent tendency towards growth. In one study, researchers found that allowing children to play freely allowed them to share their inner experiences and move towards self-expression (Cook-Cottone, Kane, & Anderson, 2015).

Psychodynamic psychotherapies have also demonstrated effectiveness when working with individuals who experienced trauma (Ainslie, Tummala-Narra, Harlem, Barbanel, & Ruth, 2013). These authors noted that immigrants experience a sense of loss and cultural mourning, identity concerns and being racialized, pre-and-post migration trauma, and intergenerational conflict. As such, these experiences tend to be the focus of psychodynamic therapies.

Trauma-Systems Therapy for Refugees (TST-R) takes a multi-tier approach that focuses on strengthening support at each system level (Benson, Abdi, Miller, & Heidi Ellis, 2018; Kaplin et al., 2019). These authors take an ecological systems approach to treating trauma that includes the individual, their families, the community, and the larger society. Further research is needed to demonstrate the applicability and generalizability of TST-R to diverse communities (Kaplin et al., 2019).

Couples Therapy

In systemic-constructivist couples therapy (SCCT) interventions, the therapist engages partners in reflexive processing of both their own (intrapersonal) and their partner's ways of construing (interpersonal), and the reciprocity between these two (Ahmad & Reid, 2016; Reid, Doell, Dalton, & Ahmad, 2008). A core change mechanism of SCCT, couple identity (or "we-ness"), connotes the ability for thinking and experiencing relationally. Using a Canadian sample, these authors suggested that SCCT can be useful when helping Indian, Pakistani, Bangladeshi, and Sri Lankan couples work towards interdependence (Ahmad & Reid, 2016).

When addressing violence, feminist therapy can be used to address the needs of survivors of abuse (Kallivayalil, 2007). In this study, the researcher interviewed clinicians who worked with South Asian survivors of IPV. She found that it was important to address patriarchy and culturally specific concerns facing South Asian women. Kallivayalil (2007) noted that the most essential feature of intervention was empowerment. For the perpetrators of violence, it is essential that they learn to accept responsibility for their actions and their impact on their partner and family (Thandi, 2012).

Family Therapy

Family therapy can be useful in addressing acculturative stress factors. Contextual therapy works to synthesize individual, existential, interpersonal systemic, and intergenerational challenges individuals and families experience (Le Goff, 2001). Dutta (2014) found contextual family therapy can help South Asian immigrant family members reconcile their differences in tradition.

Larsen, Kim-Goh, and Nguyen (2008) reviewed the impact of Asian family values that impact Asian American immigrants' experience with child abuse, neglect, and maltreatment. These authors offered guidelines for preventing child violence. Finally, these authors provided a culturally sensitive approach to family therapy to address the needs of Asian immigrant families who engage in child abuse, neglect and maltreatment.

In this section of the chapter, we introduced several trauma-focused, individual, couples, and family-based therapy models that can potentially be used to address the needs of West, South, and East Asian immigrant families. While we would have liked to review several other approaches to treatment, we were limited in space. Thus, this chapter should serve as a selected sampling of the existing research on this matter. We have made every attempt to specify the populations used in each study to avoid overstating the utility of a given intervention.

Application to Fatimah's Story

Based on the family's overarching cultural value system, Fatimah and her family are vulnerable to mental health stigma (Zolezzi et al., 2018). See Sewilam et al. (2015) for ways to reduce stigma in West Asian families. Fatimah might benefit from trauma-focused cognitive behavioral therapy (Nosè et al., 2017) or a multi-modal intervention like trauma-systems therapy for refugees (Benson et al., 2018). To address some of the relational conflict, systemic-constructivist couples therapy could be useful to help Karam and Amira develop a stronger couple identity (Ahmad & Reid, 2016). In doing so, Karam might be able to communicate more effectively with Amira and the rest of the family.

Conclusions

Fatimah's family tended to be more collectivistic, had an emphasis on family cohesion, strong honor beliefs, and defined family and gender roles. In this chapter, we reflected on four core stressors and common clinical issues that occur in Asian immigrant and refugee families. We also explored several clinical issues immigrant families' experience, which were tied to acculturative, isolative, resettlement, and traumatic stress. Afterward, we reflected on the role of resiliency in buffering against these stressors. Interwoven in each section above, we presented common clinical issues facing immigrant and refugee families. See Table 13.2 for a summary. We also offered the reader several potential interventions that show promise when treating Asian immigrants, refugees, and asylum-seekers.

Table 13.2 Clinical Issues

Factor	West Asian Families	South Asian Families	East Asian Families
Acculturative Stress	Present	Present	Present
Anti-Immigration Rhetoric	Common	Common	Uncommon
Refugee Applications	Common	Common	Uncommon
Stereotyping	Terrorism and Model Minority Myth	Terrorism and Model Minority Myth	Model Minority Myth
War Based Conflict in Country of Origin	Very Common	Uncommon	Uncommon
Mental Health Stigma	Present	Present	Present
Intimate Partner Violence (IPV)	Common	Common	Common
Physical Punishment	Accepted Practice	Accepted Practice	Accepted Practice
Other forms of Abuse, Neglect, and Maltreatment	At-Risk	At-Risk	At-Risk

This chapter should serve as a general guide related to common family-related issues and treatment considerations for West, South and East Asian immigrants. We want to impress upon the reader the importance of assessing each client's cultural identity to avoid overgeneralization and stereotyping of Asian immigrant, refugee, and asylum-seeking families. Moreover, even when using a general framework, careful assessment is essential as no group is a monolith and overgeneralization can minimize the unique challenges of the individual and their family. To create a deeper context to some of the experiences of West Asian refugee families, we included a clinical case vignette. That served as a springboard of analysis.

A second unique element of our chapter is that we offered a 15-item questionnaire to allow the clinician to assess the four core stressors and resiliency factors that immigrant and refugee families can experience. These questions can be adapted to the experiences of the client, as needed. They are also designed to be semi-structured and should naturally lead to follow-up questions.

References

Abdi, S. M. (2018). Mental health of migrant children. *Oxford Research Encyclopedia of Global Public Health*. https://doi.org/10.1093/acrefore/9780190632366.013.12

Abi-Hashem, N. (2011). Working with Middle Eastern immigrant families. In A. Zagelbaum & J. Carlson (Eds.), *Working with immigrant families: A practical guide for counselors* (pp. 151–180). Routledge.

Abu Baker, K., & Dwairy, M. (2003). Cultural norms versus state law in treating incest: A suggested model for Arab families. *Child Abuse & Neglect, 27*(1), 109–123. https://doi.org/10.1016/s0145-2134(02)00505-7

Abu-Ras, W., Suárez, Z. E., & Abu-Bader, S. (2018). Muslim Americans' safety and well-being in the wake of Trump: A public health and social justice crisis. *American Journal of Orthopsychiatry, 88*(5), 503–515. https://doi.org/10.1037/ort0000321

Aguiar, M. (2018). *Arranging marriage: Conjugal Agency in the South Asian Diaspora*. University of Minnesota Press.

Ahluwalia, M. K. (2013). "What's under there?" the questioning of civil rights for Sikh men. *Journal for Social Action in Counseling & Psychology, 5*(1), 50–58. https://doi.org/10.33043/JSACP.5.1.50-58

Ahluwalia, M. K., & Pellettiere, L. (2010). Sikh men post-9/11: Misidentification, discrimination, and coping. *Asian American Journal of Psychology, 1*(4), 303–314. https://doi.org/10.1037/a0022156

Ahmad, F., Rai, N., Petrovic, B., Erickson, P. E., & Stewart, D. E. (2013). Resilience and resources among South Asian immigrant women as survivors of partner violence. *Journal of Immigrant and Minority Health, 15*(6), 1057–1064. https://doi.org/10.1007/s10903-013-9836-2

Ahmad, S., & Reid, D. W. (2016). Enhancing the relationship adjustment of South Asian Canadian couples using a systemic-constructivist approach to couple therapy. *Journal of Marital & Family Therapy, 42*(4), 615–629. https://doi.org/10.1111/jmft.12161

Ainslie, R. C., Tummala-Narra, P., Harlem, A., Barbanel, L., & Ruth, R. (2013). Contemporary psychoanalytic views on the experience of immigration. *Psychoanalytic Psychology, 30*(4), 663–679. https://doi.org/10.1037/a0034588

Akram-Pall, S., & Moodley, R. (2016). "Loss and fear": Acculturation stresses leading to depression in South Asian Muslim immigrants in Toronto. *Canadian Journal of Counselling and Psychotherapy, 50*(3), 137–155. https://cjc-rcc.ucalgary.ca/article/view/61055

Alessi, E. J., Kahn, S., & Chatterji, S. (2016). 'The darkest times of my life': Recollections of child abuse among forced migrants persecuted because of their sexual orientation and gender identity. *Child Abuse & Neglect, 51*, 93–105. https://doi.org/10.1016/j.chiabu.2015.10.030

Al-Fayez, G., Ohaeri, J., & Gado, O. (2012). Prevalence of physical, psychological, and sexual abuse among a nationwide sample of Arab high school students: Association with family characteristics, anxiety, depression, self-esteem, and quality of life. *Social Psychiatry & Psychiatric Epidemiology, 47*(1), 53–66. https://doi.org/10.1007/s00127-010-0311-2

Alhasanat-Khalil, D., Fry-McComish, J., Dayton, C., Benkert, R., Yarandi, H., & Giurgescu, C. (2018). Acculturative stress and lack of social support predict postpartum depression among U.S. immigrant women of Arabic descent. *Archives of Psychiatric Nursing, 32*(4), 530–535. https://doi.org/10.1016/j.apnu.2018.02.005

Atkin, A. L., Yoo, H. C., Jager, J., & Yeh, C. J. (2018). Internalization of the model minority myth, school racial composition, and psychological distress among Asian American adolescents. *Asian American Journal of Psychology, 9*(2), 108–116. https://doi.org/10.1037/aap0000096

Bajaj, M., Ghaffar-Kucher, A., & Desai, K. (2016). Brown bodies and xenophobic bullying in US schools: Critical analysis and strategies for action. *Harvard Educational Review, 86*(4), 481–505. https://doi.org/10.17763/1943-5045-86.4.481

Barry, D. T., Bernard, M. J., & Beitel, M. (2009). East Asian child-rearing attitudes: An exploration of cultural, demographic and self-disclosure factors among US immigrants. *International Journal of Psychology, 44*(5), 342–350. https://doi.org/10.1080/00207590802236258

Beiser, M., Goodwill, A. M., Albanese, P., McShane, K., & Kanthasamy, P. (2015). Predictors of the integration of Sri Lankan Tamil refugees in Canada: Pre-migration adversity, mental health, personal attributes, and post-migration experience. *International Journal of Migration, Health & Social Care, 11*(1), 29–44. https://doi.org/10.1108/ijmhsc-02-2014-0008

Beiser, M., Simich, L., Pandalangat, N., Nowakowski, M., & Tian, F. (2011). Stresses of passage, balms of resettlement, and posttraumatic stress disorder among Sri Lankan Tamils in Canada. *Canadian Journal of Psychiatry, 56*(6), 333–340. https://doi.org/10.1177/070674371105600604

Beitin, B. K., & Allen, K. R. (2005). Resilience in Arab American couples after September 11, 2001: A systems perspective. *Journal of Marital and Family Therapy, 31*(3), 251–267. https://doi.org/10.1111/j.1752-0606.2005.tb01567.x

Benson, M. A., Abdi, S. M., Miller, A. B., & Heidi Ellis, B. (2018). Trauma systems therapy for refugee children and families. In *Mental health of refugee and conflict-affected populations* (pp. 243–259). Springer.

Berry, J. W. (1997). Immigration, acculturation, and adaptation. *Applied Psychology: An International Review, 46*(1), 5–34. https://doi.org/10.1111/j.1464-0597.1997.tb01087.x

Betancourt, T. S., Newnham, E. A., Birman, D., Lee, R., Ellis, B. H., & Layne, C. M. (2017). Comparing trauma exposure, mental health needs, and service utilization across clinical samples of refugee, immigrant, and U.S.-origin children. *Journal of Traumatic Stress, 30*(3), 209–218. https://doi.org/10.1002/jts.22186

Chaudhuri, S., Morash, M., & Yingling, J. (2014). Marriage migration, patriarchal bargains, and wife abuse: A study of South Asian women. *Violence Against Women, 20*(2), 141–161. https://doi.org/10.1177/1077801214521326

Cheema, S. A., Abbas, M. Z., & Khan, A. U. (2018). Contribution of the Lahore High Court in the development of Islamic family law in Pakistan. *Journal of International Law & Islamic Law, 14*(1), 1–24. https://doi.org/10.2139/ssrn.3056579

Cheung, A. K. L., & Choi, S. Y. P. (2016). Non-traditional wives with traditional husbands. *Violence Against Women, 22*(14), 1704–1724. https://doi.org/10.1177/1077801216632615

Chiu, T. Y. (2017). Marriage migration as a multifaceted system: The intersectionality of intimate partner violence in cross-border marriages. *Violence Against Women, 23*(11), 1293–1313. https://doi.org/10.1177/1077801216659940

Choudhry, V., Dayal, R., Pillai, D., Kalokhe, A. S., Beier, K., & Patel, V. (2018). Child sexual abuse in India: A systematic review. *PLoS One, 13*(10), e0205086. https://doi.org/10.1371/journal.pone.0205086

Chu, B. C. (2007). Considering culture one client at a time: Maximizing the cultural exchange. *Pragmatic Case Studies in Psychotherapy, 3*(3), 34–43. https://doi.org/10.14713/pcsp.v3i3.90
Cohen, J. A., Mannarino, A. P., & Deblinger, E. (2006). *Treating trauma and traumatic grief in children and adolescents*. Guilford Press.
Cook-Cottone, C. P., Kane, L. S., & Anderson, L. M. (2015). *The elements of counseling children and adolescents*. Springer.
Danawi, H., & Hasbini, T. (2015). A review of fatherhood related issues in the country of Lebanon. *International Journal of Childbirth Education, 30*(2), 62–66.
DHS Office of Immigration Statistics. (2019). *Annual flow chart – refugees and asylees: 2017*. https://www.dhs.gov/sites/default/files/publications/Refugees_Asylees_2017.pdf
Dutta, D. (2014). "Paribar ka palan" ('watching over our family'): The application of contextual therapy for Indian immigrant families. *Journal of Systemic Therapies, 33*(4), 47–61. https://doi.org/10.1521/jsyt.2014.33.4.47
Fayyad, J., Diab, J., Yousef, N., Farhat, C., & Karam, E. G. (2017). Non-war related childhood adversities in the Arab world: A review. *Arab Journal of Psychiatry, 28*(1), 26–35. https://doi.org/10.12816/0036879
Ferguson, G. M., Iturbide, M. I., & Gordon, B. P. (2014). Tridimensional (3D) acculturation: Ethnic identity and psychological functioning of tricultural Jamaican immigrants. *International Perspectives in Psychology: Research, Practice, Consultation, 3*(4), 238–251. https://doi.org/10.1037/ipp0000019
Ghosh, B. (2011). Child marriage, society and the law: A study in a rural context in West Bengal, India. *International Journal of Law, Policy & the Family, 25*(2), 199–219. https://doi.org/10.1093/lawfam/ebr002
Haj-Yahia, M. M. (2000). Wife abuse and battering in the sociocultural context of Arab Society. *Family Process, 39*(2), 237–255. https://doi.org/10.1111/j.1545-5300.2000.39207.x
Haj-Yahia, M. M. (2003). Beliefs about wife beating among Arab men from Israel: The influence of their patriarchal ideology. *Journal of Family Violence, 18*(4), 193–206. https://doi.org/10.1023/A:1024012229984
Hawcroft, C., Hughes, R., Shaheen, A., Usta, J., Elkadi, H., Dalton, T., … Feder, G. (2019). Prevalence and health outcomes of domestic violence amongst clinical populations in Arab countries: A systematic review and meta-analysis. *BMC Public Health, 19*(1). https://doi.org/10.1186/s12889-019-6619-2
Ho, J., & Gielen, U. P. (2016). Chinese American adolescents and emerging adults in New York City: Striving for a place in the sun. In U. P. Gielen & J. L. Roopnarine (Eds.), *Childhood and adolescence: Cross-cultural perspectives and applications* (2nd ed., pp. 347–376). Praeger/ABC-CLIO.
Irfan, S. (2008). Childrearing practices among South Asian Muslims in Britain: The cultural context of physical punishment. *Journal of Muslim Minority Affairs, 28*(1), 147–161. https://doi.org/10.1080/13602000802011192
Julca, A. (2011). Multidimensional re-creation of vulnerabilities and potential for resilience in international migration. *International Migration, 49*, e30–e49. https://doi.org/10.1111/j.1468-2435.2010.00634.x
Kallakorpi, S., Haatainen, K., & Kankkunen, P. (2019). Psychiatric nursing care experiences of immigrant patients: A focused ethnographic study. *International Journal of Mental Health Nursing, 28*(1), 117–127. https://doi.org/10.1111/inm.12500
Kallivayalil, D. (2007). Feminist therapy: Its use and implications for South Asian immigrant survivors of domestic violence. *Women & Therapy, 30*(3/4), 109–127. https://doi.org/10.1300/J015v30n03_09
Kaplin, D., & Gielen, U. P. (2020). Cross-cultural perspectives on working with adolescents. In E. Congress & M. J. Gonzalez (Eds.), *Multicultural perspectives in working with families: A handbook for the helping professions* (pp. 137–152). Springer.

Kaplin, D., Parente, K., & Santacroce, F. A. (2019). A review of the use of trauma systems therapy to treat refugee children, adolescents, and families. *Journal of Infant, Child, and Adolescent Psychotherapy, 18*(4), 417–431. https://doi.org/10.1080/15289168.2019.1687220

Karasz, A., Gany, F., Escobar, J., Flores, C., Prasad, L., Inman, A., ... Diwan, S. (2019). Mental health and stress among South Asians. *Journal of Immigrant & Minority Health, 21*(1), 7–14. https://doi.org/10.1007/s10903-016-0501-4

Khaleque, A., Malik, F., & Rohner, R. P. (2015). Differential acculturation among Pakistani American immigrant parents and children. *Psychological Studies, 60*(4), 407–411. https://doi.org/10.1007/s12646-015-0337-3

Khan, R., Saleem, S., & Lowe, M. (2018), "Honour"-based violence in a British South Asian community. *Safer Communities, 17*, 11–21. https://doi.org/10.1108/SC-02-2017-0007

Kidman, R. (2017). Child marriage and intimate partner violence: A comparative study of 34 countries. *International Journal of Epidemiology, 46*(2), 662–675. https://doi.org/10.1093/ije/dyw225

Kim, C., LaRoche, M., & Tomiuk, M. A. (2004). The Chinese in Canada: A study in ethnic change with emphasis on gender roles. *The Journal of Social Psychology, 144*(1), 5–29. https://doi.org/10.3200/SOCP.144.1.5-29

Larsen, S., Kim-Goh, M., & Nguyen, T. D. (2008). Asian American immigrant families and child abuse: Cultural considerations. *Journal of Systemic Therapies, 27*(1), 16–29. https://doi.org/10.1521/jsyt.2008.27.1.16

Le Goff, J. F. (2001). Fundamentals of theory and practice revisited: Boszormenyi-Nagy and contextual therapy: An overview. *Australian and New Zealand Journal of Family Therapy, 22*(3), 147–157. https://doi.org/10.1002/j.1467-8438.2001.tb00469.x

Masten, A. S. (2014). *Ordinary magic: Resilience in development*. Guilford Press.

McCleary, J. S. (2017). The impact of resettlement on Karen refugee family relationships: A qualitative exploration. *Child & Family Social Work, 22*(4), 1464–1471. https://doi.org/10.1111/cfs.12368

McNeely, C. A., & Morland, L. (2016). The health of the newest Americans: How US public health systems can support Syrian refugees. *American Journal of Public Health, 106*(1), 13–15. https://doi.org/10.2105/AJPH.2015.302975

Midlarsky, E., Venkataramani, K. A., & Plante, M. (2006). Domestic violence in the Chinese and South Asian immigrant communities. *Annals of the New York Academy of Sciences, 1087*(1), 279–300. https://doi.org/10.1196/annals.1385.003

Mitra, N. (2013). Intimate violence, family, and femininity: Women's narratives on their construction of violence and self. *Violence Against Women, 19*(10), 1282–1301. https://doi.org/10.1177/1077801213506287

Mudambi, A. (2019). South Asian American discourses: Engaging the yellow peril-model minority dialectic. *Howard Journal of Communications, 30*(3), 284–298. https://doi.org/10.1080/10646175.2018.1491431

Naber, N. (2012). From model minority to problem minority. In N. Naber's (Ed.), *Arab America: Gender, cultural politics, and activism* (pp. 25–62). NYU Press.

Nasreen, S., Ali, A., & Shah, N. A. (2018). Child marriage: Changing trends in Pakistan. *New Horizons, 12*(1), 85–98. https://doi.org/10.2.9270/NH.12.2(18).06

Nasseri, K., & Moulton, L. (2011). Patterns of death in the first and second generation immigrants from selected Middle Eastern countries in California. *Journal of Immigrant & Minority Health, 13*(2), 361–370. https://doi.org/10.1007/s10903-009-9270-7

Nijhara, K., Bhatia, S., & Unnikrishnan, B. (2018). Corporal punishment in children and its implications on mental health. *Indian Journal of Pediatrics, 85*(5), 405. https://doi.org/10.1007/s12098-017-2525-8

Nosè, M., Ballette, F., Bighelli, I., Turrini, G., Purgato, M., Tol, W., ... Barbui, C. (2017). Psychosocial interventions for post-traumatic stress disorder in refugees and asylum seekers resettled in high-income countries: Systematic review and meta-analysis. *PLoS One, 12*(2), 1–16. https://doi.org/10.1371/journal.pone.0171030

Parks, S. J., & Yoo, H. C. (2016). Does endorsement of the model minority myth relate to anti-Asian sentiments among White college students? The role of a color-blind racial attitude. *Asian American Journal of Psychology, 7*(4), 287–294. https://doi.org/10.1037/aap0000056

Pew Research Center. (2019). Canada now leads the world in refugee resettlement, surpassing the U.S. https://www.pewresearch.org/fact-tank/2019/06/19/canada-now-leads-the-world-in-refugee-resettlement-surpassing-the-u-s/

Phosaly, L., Olympia, D., & Goldman, S. (2019). Educational and psychological risk factors for South Korean children and adolescents. *International Journal of School & Educational Psychology, 7*(2), 113–122. https://doi.org/10.1080/21683603.2019.1578709

Qi, W., Wang, K. T., Pincus, A. L., & Wu, L. Z. (2018). Interpersonal problems and acculturative stress over time among Chinese international students from mainland China and Taiwan. *Asian American Journal of Psychology, 9*(3), 237–246. https://doi.org/10.1037/aap0000119

Rai, A., & Choi, Y. J. (2018). Socio-cultural risk factors impacting domestic violence among South Asian immigrant women: A scoping review. *Aggression and Violent Behavior, 38*, 76–85. https://doi.org/10.1016/j.avb.2017.12.001

Rastogi, P., Khushalani, S., Dhawan, S., Goga, J., Hemanth, N., Kosi, R., … Rao, V. (2014). Understanding clinician perception of common presentations in South Asians seeking mental health treatment and determining barriers and facilitators to treatment. *Asian Journal of Psychiatry, 7*, 15–21. https://doi.org/10.1016/j.ajp.2013.09.005

Reid, D. W., Doell, F. K., Dalton, E. J., & Ahmad, S. (2008). Systemic-constructivist couple therapy (SCCT): Description of approach, theoretical advances, and published longitudinal evidence. *Psychotherapy: Theory, Research, Practice, Training, 45*(4), 477–490. https://doi.org/10.1037/a0014334

Sabri, B., Simonet, M., & Campbell, J. C. (2018). Risk and protective factors of intimate partner violence among South Asian immigrant women and perceived need for services. *Cultural Diversity & Ethnic Minority Psychology, 24*(3), 442–452. https://doi.org/10.1037/cdp0000189

Samuel, L. (2010). Mating, dating and marriage: Intergenerational cultural retention and the construction of diasporic identities among South Asian immigrants in Canada. *Journal of Intercultural Studies, 31*(1), 95–110. https://doi.org/10.1080/07256860903477712

Schubert, C. C., & Punamäki, R.-L. (2016). Posttraumatic nightmares of traumatized refugees: Dream work integrating cultural values. *Dreaming, 26*(1), 10–28. https://doi.org/10.1037/drm0000021

Seth, R., Bose, V., Qaiyum, Y., Chandrashekhar, R., Kansal, S., Taneja, I., & Seth, T. (2018). Social determinants of child marriage in rural India. *Ochsner Journal, 18*(4), 390–394. https://doi.org/10.31486/toj.18.0104

Sewilam, A. M., Watson, A. M. M., Kassem, A. M., Clifton, S., McDonald, M. C., Lipski, R., … Nimgaonkar, V. L. (2015). Suggested avenues to reduce the stigma of mental illness in the Middle East. *International Journal of Social Psychiatry, 61*(2), 111–120. https://doi.org/10.1177/0020764014537234

Shen, Y., Kim, S. Y., & Benner, A. D. (2019). Burdened or efficacious? Subgroups of Chinese American language brokers, predictors, and long-term outcomes. *Journal of Youth & Adolescence, 48*(1), 154–169. https://doi.org/10.1007/s10964-018-0916-4

Shim, W., & Nelson-Becker, H. (2009). Korean older intimate partner violence survivors in North America: Cultural considerations and practice recommendations. *Journal of Women & Aging, 21*(3), 213–228. https://doi.org/10.1080/08952840903054773

Smith, S. G., Zhang, X., Basile, K. C., Merrick, M. T., Wang, J., Kresnow, M., & Chen, J. (2018). *The National Intimate Partner and Sexual Violence Survey (NISVS): 2015 data brief – updated release*. Atlanta, GA: National Center for Injury Prevention and Control, Centers for Disease Control and Prevention.

Son, H., Lee, Y. A., Ahn, D. H., & Doan, S. N. (2017). Maternal understanding of child discipline and maltreatment in the United States, South Korea, and Japan. *Children & Youth Services Review, 82*, 444–454. https://doi.org/10.1016/j.childyouth.2017.10.015

South Asian Americans Leading Together. (2014). Under suspicion, under attack: Xenophobic political rhetoric and hate violence against South Asian, Muslim, Sikh, Hindu, Middle Eastern, and Arab Communities in the United States. http://saalt.org/wp-content/uploads/2013/06/SAALT_report_full_links1.pdf

Thandi, G. (2012). Working with South Asian male perpetrators of intimate partner violence in British Columbia, Canada. *Probation Journal, 59*(3), 219–234. https://doi.org/10.1177/0264550512448451

Tseng, W. (2004). Culture and psychotherapy: Asian perspectives. *Journal of Mental Health, 13*(2), 151–161. https://doi.org/10.1080/09638230410001669282

United Nations High Commissioner for Refugees. (2019). *Global trends: Forced displacement in 2018*. https://www.unhcr.org/5d08d7ee7.pdf

Valsala, P., Devanathan, S., & Kuttappan, S. M. (2018). Association of family challenges with self-esteem and perceived social support among Indian adolescents. *Child & Adolescent Social Work Journal, 35*(6), 625–637. https://doi.org/10.1007/s10560-018-0553-5

Yeh, C. J., Pituc, S. T., Kim, A. B., & Atkins, M. (2008). Poverty, loss, and resilience: The story of Chinese immigrant youth. *Journal of Counseling Psychology, 55*(1), 34–48. https://doi.org/10.1037/0022-0167.55.1.34

Zolezzi, M., Alamri, M., Shaar, S., & Rainkie, D. (2018). Stigma associated with mental illness and its treatment in the Arab culture: A systematic review. *International Journal of Social Psychiatry, 64*(6), 597–609. https://doi.org/10.1177/0020764018789200

Part VI
Methodology Considerations

Chapter 14
Critically Assessing the Methodological Challenges of Exploring Chinese Immigrant Fathers

Susan S. Chuang, Xuan Li, Ching-Yu Huang, and Yang Hu

Abstract Immigrant Chinese fathers remain severely under-researched despite their sizable and growing presence in host countries around the world and the recent progress in research on immigrant and ethnic minority fathers. In this chapter, we review the major themes and methods used in existing studies involving immigrant Chinese fathers and explore reasons behind immigrant Chinese fathers' low visibility in the fatherhood scholarship. While the demographic under-representation of immigrant Chinese families may be a possible reason, stereotypical assumptions about immigrant or ethnic minority fathers and particularly Chinese men may have contributed to the neglect of immigrant Chinese fathers. Specifically, these stereotypical assumptions include that immigrant Chinese fathers are well-integrated immigrants who successfully fulfill essential paternal responsibilities of co-residence and provision, as typically defined by the white mainstream fatherhood ideal. A focus on immigrant Chinese fathers would considerably enrich the fatherhood scholarship, especially when the fathers' parenting experiences, beliefs, practices, and influences are examined through a critical ecological approach.

Keywords Immigrant parents · Fatherhood · Father involvement · Parenting · Acculturation · Chinese · Methodology

S. S. Chuang (✉)
University of Guelph, Guelph, ON, Canada
e-mail: schuang@uoguelph.ca

X. Li
New York University Shanghai, Shanghai, China
e-mail: xuanli@nyu.edu

C.-Y. Huang
Keele University, Keele, UK
e-mail: c.s.huang@keele.ac.uk

Y. Hu
Lancaster University, Lancaster, UK
e-mail: yang.hu@lancaster.ac.uk

S. S. Chuang et al. (eds.), *Asian Families in Canada and the United States*, Advances in Immigrant Family Research,
https://doi.org/10.1007/978-3-030-56452-0_14

Although fathering scholarship has gained considerable attention since it began in the 1970s (see Lamb, 2010; Parke & Cookston, 2019), it has not been until the turn of the twenty-first century that researchers have paid explicit attention to ethnic and cultural diversity of fathers, fathering, and fatherhood around the globe, especially in multi-ethnic developed countries (Chuang & Tamis-LeMonda, 2013; Chuang & Moreno, 2008; Inhorn et al., 2014; Shwalb, Shwalb, & Lamb, 2013). The knowledge about these fathers will not only generate evidence that informs policy and practice that serve diverse families and communities but also reflect on and revise existing theories and assumptions about the fathers' roles in childrearing and family functioning across different stages of family cycles and individual lifespan (Garcia Coll & Pachter, 2002).

Unfortunately, immigrant Chinese fathers are much less visible in this burgeoning field despite their longstanding, substantial, and rapidly expanding global presence as immigrants and members of ethnic minority communities (Poston & Wong, 2016; Xiang, 2016). Thus, this review explores possible reasons behind the disproportionate invisibility of Chinese fathers and discusses how the study of immigrant Chinese fathers can enrich the fatherhood scholarship in significant ways. Specifically, we begin with a brief review of research on immigrant Chinese fathers, with attention to major themes and methodological characteristics of existing empirical studies. We then propose two potential reasons that underlie the invisibility of immigrant Chinese fathers. Finally, we discuss several conceptual limitations in the existing scholarship on immigrant Chinese fathers and suggest methodological avenues to advance future research in contributing to the scholarship on fathers, fathering, and fatherhood.

The Under-Researched Immigrant Chinese Fathers

The Chinese as immigrants are a sizable and diverse group with a long history of mass emigration (see Chuang et al., this volume). There are over 40.3 million overseas Chinese living outside of major Chinese societies As of 2011, the number of Chinese immigrants has grown at accelerating rates since the 1990s (Poston & Wong, 2016; Xiang, 2016). Beyond neighboring Asian countries that have been popular destinations, Chinese immigrants constitute one of the largest ethnic minority groups in major international migration destinations. For example, Chinese ethnics – including different generations of Chinese immigrants – comprise 5.1% of the Canadian population (Statistics Canada, 2017), 5.6% of the Australian population (Australian Bureau of Statistics, 2017) and 4.9% of the population in New Zealand (Stats New Zealand, 2019). They also represent 1.3% of the population in the United States (U.S. Census Bureau, 2018), 0.7% of the British population (Racial Disparity Unit, 2020), 0.5% of the Italian population (Istat, 2014), and approximately 0.4% to 8.3% of the French population (Latham & Wu, 2013). Although there are no official statistics on the number of fathers among overseas Chinese worldwide, the centrality of childbearing in Chinese masculinity ideals means there is good reason to expect that many of the men are actual or aspiring parents (Greenhalgh, 2014).

Given the sizable flows of Chinese immigrants around the globe and the proliferation of publications that explicitly focused on fathering in immigrant and ethnic minority families (e.g., see Chuang & Moreno, 2008; Cabrera & Tamis-LeMonda, 2013; Lamb, 2010; Shwalb et al., 2013), it would be expected that the attention to fathers in immigrant Chinese families would receive considerable attention. Unfortunately, there has been minimal attention to this particular group. As of June 2020, we conducted a thorough literature search on peer-reviewed journal articles and book chapters in the ProQuest database (which is selected for its comprehensive coverage of multidisciplinary scholarship and diverse formats of scholarly work) with keyword combinations such as "immigrant/minority," "father," "parent," and "Chinese/ Taiwanese /Hong Kong/Macau/Singapore/East Asian/ Asian," complemented by manual review of reference lists. Articles and chapters that were included met one of the following criteria: (a) focused on immigrant Chinese fathering or parenting; (b) immigrant Chinese fathers were informants of the study, regardless of the topic of the study; and (c) informants such as children and youth discussed their relationships with their parents and/or fathers. The search only yielded 55 empirically-based publications (see Table 14.1 for overview). Such a dearth is very surprising against the backdrop of an explosion of studies on immigrant Chinese families since the 2010s (see special issues and edited volumes such as Chan, 2013; Chuang & Costigan, 2018; Juang et al., 2013; Russell et al., 2010), which primarily focused on mothers. Research on ethnic minority or immigrant Chinese mothers spans a wider range of topics and they far outnumbered that of their male counterparts. For example, Liu and colleagues (2009) drew on data from a similar number of immigrant Chinese fathers and mothers, but the paternal data were excluded in further analysis out of the statistical reason that the father-related predictors did not show the expected association with child outcomes, but little conceptual justification was provided.

Themes of Existing Studies

Before we delve into the details and critiques of existing studies, it is important to stress that fathering/fatherhood has been its own separate field of scholarship and is often separate from the more generic research on parenting, family studies, and child development. Thus, studies on fathering/fatherhood often have distinctive foci, such as parental involvement in childcare, which is a central theme in fathering research but a relatively less dominant topic among studies on mothers. Of the 55 publications, four major themes or key topics emerged: (1) fathering, father involvement; (2) parenting practices and beliefs; (3) acculturation and immigration-related issues; and (4) academic and school-related topics. The fifth category was "other" which focused on a variety of other topics. While many of the studies include various themes (e.g., parenting practices and ethnic identity; Su & Costigan, 2009), we

Table 14.1 Summaries of the Immigrant Samples in Empirically-Based Publications With or About Immigrant Chinese Fathers by Key Themes

Key Themes/Author(s) and Year	Location	Place of Origin	Informants	Method(s)
Fathering, Father Involvement (8 articles)				
Capps, Bronte-Tinkew, and Horowitz (2010)	US	Chinese-origin[a]	Fathers	Survey
Chuang and Su (2008)	Canada	China	Fathers	Interviews, time diaries
Chuang & Zhu (2013, 2018)	Canada	China	Fathers	Time diaries
Ji and Koblinsky[a] (2009)	US	China mixed[b]	Parents[c]	Interviews
Tasopoulos-Chan, Smetana, and Yau (2009)	US	Chinese-origin	Children[d]	Survey
Waters (2010)	Canada	China mixed	Fathers	Interviews
Parenting Practices and Beliefs (18 articles)				
* Chao and Kaeochinda (2010)	US	Chinese-origin	Children	Survey
Chen, Sun, and Yu (2017)	US	China	Parents	Survey
Chuang and Su (2009a, 2009b)	Canada	China	Parents	Survey
Crockett, Veed, and Russell (2010)	US	China	Children	Survey
* Fung and Lau (2010)	US	Chinese-origin	Children, parents	Survey
Huntsinger and Jose (2009)	US	Mixed[e]	Children, parents, teachers	Survey, interviews, observations
Hsu (1996)	US	Chinese-origin	Parents	Observations
* Jose, Huntsinger, Huntsinger, and Liaw (2000)	US	China	Parents, teachers	Survey, interviews, observations
* Juang, Syed, and Takagi (2007); Li, Zhou, and Hou (2015)	US	Chinese-origin	Parents	Survey
Lin and Fu (1990)	US	Taiwan	Parents	Survey
Mao, Bottorff, Oliffe, Sarbit, and Kelly (2015)	Canada	Chinese-origin	Fathers	Interviews
* Miconi, Moscardino, Altoè, and Salcuni (2019)	Italy	China	Children, parents	Survey
* Padmawidjaja and Chao (2010)	US	Mixed	Children	Survey
* Russell, Chu, Crockett, and Doan (2010)	US	Chinese-origin	Children	Interviews
Su and Costigan (2009)	Canada	China mixed	Children, parents	Survey
Yuwen and Chen (2013)	US	China mixed	Children	Focus groups
Acculturation and Related Issues (23 articles)				

(continued)

Table 14.1 (continued)

Key Themes/Author(s) and Year	Location	Place of Origin	Informants	Method(s)
Chance, Costigan, and Leadbeater (2013)	Canada	China mixed	Parents	Survey
Costigan and Su (2004)	Canada	Mixed	Children, parents	Survey
Costigan and Dokis (2006a)	Canada	Chinese-origin	Children, parents	Survey
Costigan and Dokis (2006b)	Canada	China mixed	Parents	Survey
Costigan and Koryzma (2011); Costigan & Su (2008)	Canada	Mixed	Parents	Survey
Costigan, Lehr, and Miao (2016)	Canada	China mixed	Children, parents	Survey
Crane, Ngai, Larson, and Hafen Jr. (2005)	Canada, US	Mixed	Children, parents	Survey
Dinh and Nguyen (2006)	US	Mixed	Children, parents	Survey
Guo (2014)	New Zealand	China mixed	Children, parents	Interviews
Kim, Chen, Li, Huang, and Moon (2009), Kim et al. (2013); * Wang, Kim, Anderson, Chen, and Yan (2012)	US	China mixed	Children, parents	Survey
Klein[a] (2008)	US	China	Fathers	Interviews, observations
Koh, Shao, and Wang (2009)	US	Mixed	Children, parents	Written essays
* Lau (2010)	US	Mixed	Parents	Survey, interviews
* Li and Li (2017)	US	Mixed	Parents	Survey, focus groups
* Lieber, Nihira, and Mink (2004)	US	China mixed	Parents	Survey, interviews
Miao, Costigan, and MacDonald (2018); Rasmi and Costigan (2018)	Canada	China mixed	Children, parents	Survey
Qin (2009)	US	China mixed	Children, parents	Interviews
Shen, Kim, and Wang (2016); Weaver and Kim (2008)	US	Chinese-origin	Children, parents	Survey
* Tsai-Chae and Nagata (2008)	US	Mixed	Children	Survey
Academic and School-Related Issues (4 articles)				
* Huntsinger, Jose, Larson, Balsink Krieg, and Shaligram (2000)	US	Chinese-origin	Children, parents, teachers	Survey, math test, interviews, observations
* Huntsinger, Jose, and Larson (1998)	US	Chinese-origin	Children, parents, teachers	Time diaries, survey, math tests, interviews

(continued)

Table 14.1 (continued)

Key Themes/Author(s) and Year	Location	Place of Origin	Informants	Method(s)
Kim & Kulkarni (2009)	US	Mixed	Fathers	Survey
* Zhang, Keown, and Farruggia (2014)	New Zealand	Chinese-origin	Parents	Survey
Other Topics (2 articles)				
Kushner et al. (2017)	Canada	Chinese-origin	Parents	Interview
* Russell, Chu, Crockett, and Doan (2010)	US	Chinese-origin	Children	focus groups

*Note.** Studies do not distinguish between mothers and fathers
[a]Chinese-origin includes participants who self-identified as "Chinese" with no information about place of birth/specific Chinese heritage
[b]China mixed includes participants from Mainland China, Hong Kong, Taiwan, or Macau
[c]Parents include both mothers and fathers
[d]Children includes participants of various developmental age ranges from middle childhood to emerging adulthood
[e]Mixed includes participants from "East Asian" countries which may not necessarily be specified

coded for the overarching/primary theme such as the key purpose of the study, or if the primary theme was "other," we coded these themes if they were related to the four themes (see Table 14.1).

Fathering and Father Involvement

Although the fathering field has gained its own prominence as a separate field of study, to date, only eight studies explicitly investigated fathering and father involvement, with three studies conducted by the same research team (i.e., that of the first author; see Table 14.1 for listing of studies). This set of studies provided quantitative and qualitative descriptions of Chinese fathers' involvement in childrearing (e.g., Capps et al., 2010; Chuang, Moreno, & Su, 2013; Ji & Koblinsky, 2009), often underpinned by Lamb et al.'s (1987) tri-dimensional father involvement model (i.e., engagement, accessibility, and responsibility) that continues to lead the fathering field. For example, Chuang and Su (2008) used time-diary data involving fathers to recount two, 24-hour days (workday, non-workday) to document Chinese (from Mainland China) and Chinese-Canadian fathers' time investment in their young children's care. Compared to a few studies that have used time diaries (e.g., see Lamb et al., 2004; Yeung et al., 2001), regardless of country, these Chinese and Chinese-Canadian fathers' levels of involvement with their children were similar to fathers' times in other ethnic groups. In Klein's (2008) study, middle-class immigrant Chinese fathers with school-age children self-reported having actively engaged in their children's education by helping them cultivate good learning habits, although their counterparts from a lower social-class background were less able to do so (Ji & Koblinsky, 2009). It is interesting to note that these studies are fairly recent, with the earliest study published in 2008, three decades after the proposal of the Lamb et al.'s model (see Table 14.1).

Parenting Practices and Beliefs

Among the 55 studies, 18 studies have either included fathers as informants (13 studies) or the informants focused on parenting and parent-child relationships issues (5 studies). Generally, these studies explored various aspects of parenting such as parenting styles/practices (e.g., warmth, acceptance, control), parenting efficacy, parental goals and values (see Table 14.1). Unfortunately, four of the studies combined mothers' and fathers' ratings (Fung & Lau, 2010; Jose et al., 2000; Juang et al., 2007; Miconi et al., 2019) and three studies focused on youths' discussion of their relationships with their parents and parenting issues, without distinguishing between mothers and fathers (Chao & Kaeochinda, 2010; Padmawidjaja & Chao, 2010; Russell et al., 2010).

Although these studies have provided valuable preliminary insights into the parenting ideals and practices of immigrant Chinese fathers, few have examined more closely and systematically the individual, family, or contextual processes involved in fathering. Only a few exceptions have examined the couple relationship and co-parenting practices of immigrant Chinese fathers (see Chuang & Su, 2008; and X. Li et al., 2015, for exceptions). Only two studies assessed the fathers' own physical or mental health outcomes over the life course (Kushner et al., 2017; Mao et al., 2015). There has also been a surprisingly lack of gender sensitivity in the conceptualization of immigrant Chinese fathers. Although many studies have included fathers in the sample and contrasted the parenting experiences and practices of immigrant Chinese fathers and mothers (Costigan & Dokis, 2006a; Kim et al., 2009; Lin & Fu, 1990; Qin, 2009), these studies include little *a priori* theorization of immigrant Chinese fathers as gendered social actors beyond evoking the "strict father, warm mother" adage or the breadwinner-caregiver binary.

Acculturation and Immigration-Related Issues

One of the most commonly explored topics among immigrant families is acculturation and immigration-related issues. Immigrant Chinese families are no exception, and these studies composed of the largest proportion of research on Chinese fathers (23 out of the 55 studies). These studies were informative about the Chinese fathers' acculturation and adjustment experiences, shifting identities as new immigrants, discrepancies of acculturation with their children, which have yielded mix results. For example, Costigan and Dokis (2006a) compared immigrants' ethnic and cultural identification – particularly their endorsement of collectivist "Asian" versus independent values – between immigrant Chinese mothers and fathers in Canada. They found that these fathers identified more strongly with the Canadian culture than their female counterparts. Another study from the same team using a different sample, however, had reported that the level of acculturation is similar among Chinese fathers and mothers in Canada. These findings are consistent with the findings of Shen, Kim and Wang (2016) in the study of immigrant Chinese families in the U.S..

Academic and School-Related Issues

Finally, four studies explored academics and school-related issues in terms of teaching methods, educational attitudes (Huntsinger et al., 1998; Huntsinger et al., 2000), parental involvement in school (Zhang et al., 2014), and fathers' socioeconomic status and its link to their children's socio-economic status (Kim & Kulkarni, 2009). However, all these studies, except Kim and Kulkarni's (2009) study, combined mothers' and fathers' responses and thus, limiting the insights into fathers' contributions to their children's academic lives.

In addition, two studies were placed under the "other" theme, including Kushner et al.'s (2017) study that focused on work-family balance and Russell et al.'s study (2010) that explored youths' views about their relationships with their parents. Unfortunately, the youths' perceptions of the quality of their relationships with their parents were not differentiated by parental gender (see Table 14.1).

Demographics of the Samples

To gain greater insights into the roles that immigrant Chinese fathers play in their families, it is important to critically review the demographics of the studies' sample. Selectivity of the demographics and characteristics of the sample can limit the relevance and cultural meaningfulness of the findings as well as its comparability to data from other populations. Among the 55 studies, we analyzed three aspects of their sample characteristics that may have significant implications for the interpretation of findings: (a) age of the targeted children; (b) informants' host countries; and (c) informants' birthplace.

Age of the Targeted Children

From a developmental perspective, it is important for researchers to examine fathering and father involvement over different developmental stages of their children's life courses (Parke & Cookston, 2019). As shown in Table 14.2, the studies have

Table 14.2 Demographic Details of or About Immigrant Chinese Fathers in Empirically-Based Studies

Category	*n*	Percentage
Publication Date		
Before 2000	3	5.4
2000–2009	24	42.9
2010–2019	29	51.8
Informants		
Only fathers	7	12.7
Similar fathers, mothers	10	18.2
Mostly mothers	8	14.6
Children only	8	14.6
Children, similar fathers, mothers	18	32.7
Children, mostly mothers	4	7.3
Age of targeted Children		
2 years or less	7	12.7
3–5 years	4	7.3
6–11 years	4	7.3
12–19 years	17	30.9
19+ years	3	5.5
Mixed	20	36.4
Participants' Birth Place		
Mainland China	10	18.9
Taiwan	1	1.8
China, incl. HK[a], TW[b], Macau	15	27.3
Chinese-origin	17	30.9
Mixed	12	21.8
Host Countries		
Canada	18	32.7
Italy	1	1.8
New Zealand	2	3.6
United States	34	60.0
Canada, United States	1	1.8
Methodology		
Survey	32	60.0
Focus groups	2	3.6
Interviews	8	14.6
Observations	1	1.8
Time diaries	2	3.6
Essay writings	1	1.8
Mixed	9	16.4
Father/Parent Construct		
Father	37	67.3
Parents combined	17	31.0
Father and combined	1	1.8

Note. Column percentages may not add up to 100% due to rounding

[a]Hong Kong

[b]Taiwan

focused on a wide range of developmental stages, from infancy to emerging adulthood. Interestingly, the "youth years" have led a blurring of age stages where 12 studies' targeted child ages to include both middle childhood (6–11 years) and adolescence (12–18 years). However, these two age stages may require different forms of father involvement and fathering. For example, a father may engage in physical play with their 10-year-old child whereas a father with his 17-year-old youth may engage in more in-depth conversations about future academic and work prospects. Thus, researchers should be cautious in their sampling strategies as parental roles and responsibilities do change by the child's developmental needs, especially when children increasingly become more autonomous and spend more time with their peers and in other non-family related activities. Other developmental characteristics of the child, such as gender, should also be taken into consideration, especially as children enter adolescence (McHale et al., 2003).

Informants' Host Countries

It is necessary for researchers to consider immigrant families' host countries in studies on immigrant Chinese fathers, as the host countries' broader social, cultural, historical contexts help define the families' ways of life and in turn, influence fathers' parenting beliefs and practices in these immigrant families. In 2008, Arnett conducted an extensive review of the psychological research on children and families and reported that the majority of studies were conducted in the U.S., primarily with families of European backgrounds, even though the U.S.'s population is less than 5% of the world's population. In line with this pattern, most (34) of the empirical investigations of immigrant Chinese fathers are found in the U.S., followed by Canada with 18 studies. However, a closer examination of the studies in Canada revealed that two research teams conducted 15 of the studies: Costigan and her colleagues conducted 10 studies—nine of which focused on acculturation and immigration issues, and Chuang and her colleagues conducted five studies with three studies explicitly focusing on fathering (see Table 14.2). One study that was conducted in both the U.S. and Canada (Crane et al., 2005). Apart from the exception of three studies in Italy and New Zealand, investigations of immigrant Chinese fathers do not exist in other countries with well-established Chinese diasporas, such as Australia and the United Kingdom.

Informants' Country of Origin

Even more critical to examine is the immigrant fathers' country of origin. As Chuang, Li, and Huang (in this volume) highlighted in their in-depth discussions on the nuanced heterogeneities among families from Mainland China, Hong Kong, and Taiwan, there is great diversity within and among them both as former residents of their respective home societies and as immigrants. Therefore, researchers should not treat families originating from Chinese societies as culturally homogenous and disregard their geolocations of origin. Regrettably, only 11 studies (10 with fathers from Mainland China, one with fathers from Taiwan) focused on immigrant Chinese fathers from one single geographic location and considered the unique socioeconomic, cultural, political, and social characteristics of the location.

While 15 studies included a mixture of immigrant fathers from Mainland China, Hong Kong, Macau, and Taiwan, without distinguishing or controlling for their country of origin, 29 studies described their immigrant Chinese sample in ambiguous ways. Some of these studies placed immigrant Chinese fathers under broad umbrella terms such as "Chinese-origin" (17 studies) or "other places" or "Southeast Asia." Even more broad, other researchers included families from very diverse countries such as Singapore, Korea, Vietnam, Southeast or East Asian which we termed as "mixed" (12 studies; see Table 14.2). Although these studies do provide general information about Chinese families, not taking account of country and local specific political, cultural and social ecologies (Bronfenbrenner & Morris, 2006; Hu & Scott, 2016) may over-generalize and over-simplify the complexities of immigrant fathers and their families. Consequently, any unique sub-ethnic distinctions and experiences are minimized and masked, making it impossible for researchers not only to compare across studies but also to better understand the family dynamics and functioning of immigrant Chinese fathers and their families.

Methodological Approaches

Sample recruitment and methodological strategies are key to the understanding of findings and the extent to which the results can inform scholars and practitioners about the conceptualization, development, and functionality of fathers in families. Beyond the sample characteristics, we also coded existing studies based on the characteristics of their conceptual and methodological design, in terms of the following aspects: (a) methods of data collection; and (b) fathers as informants or targeted parent, and specifically, whether father constructs were individualized or combined with mothers' constructs.

Methods of Data Collection

Existing research on immigrant Chinese fathers has been limited not only in quantity but also in its methodological diversity. Much of the scholarship on immigrant Chinese fathers is derived from a single methodology strategy of quantitative survey data (32 studies). Quantitative measures can provide systematic overviews of fathering practices in large populations, but surveys designed using constructs and measures developed based on western, middle-class families would inevitably impose cultural assumptions of child development, fathering, and family life onto non-western families. The other single methodological approaches included qualitative interviews (eight studies), focus groups (two studies), time diaries (two, 24-hour accounts of daily activities; two studies), observations (one study), and essay writings (one study).

Nine studies adopted a mixed methods approach, including eight studies that included interviews along with other methods (see Table 14.2). While the methodological strategy of using other sources of information other than quantitative survey and qualitative is promising, with some studies taking on a mixed methods approach, the current lack of methodological diversity may limit potential theoretical revisions and breakthroughs.

Fathers as Informants or Targeted Parent

Over the years, various family members have been used as informants in studies on family dynamics and functioning in immigrant Chinese families (Chuang & Su, 2008). Although fathers' perspectives have been increasingly included, mothers as informants have dominated the field (see Wical & Doherty, 2005). In our review, 47 of the 55 studies included fathers as informants. Although 28 studies had similar numbers of fathers and mothers, seven studies focused only on fathers.

Unfortunately, in 16 of the studies, parenting responses or youth discussions about their parents, merged fathers and mothers as parents, and the distinct insights into mothers and fathers were lost (see Table 14.2). Specifically, for 11 studies that recruited both mothers and fathers, researchers combined mothers' and fathers' responses. For example, Li and Li (2017) recruited 16 mothers and 6 fathers, thus, having insufficient fathers to explore issues of psychological well-being and acculturative stress by parents' gender. However, as Chuang and Su (2009a) reported, not exploring parents' views by gender (as well as the gender of their children) in a gendered society can hide or obscure how gender may influence parents' socialization practices and family functioning.

For five studies that recruited youths, youths discussed their issues with their parents, with no explicit distinction between mothers and fathers. For example, Russell, Chu, Crockett, and Doan's (2010) study explored youths' views about autonomy in relation to their parents, with no discussions about how each parent may have contributed to their autonomy development. However, some studies have investigated youths' views about their relationships with their mothers and fathers. Even youths' conceptions of "good" parent-youth relationship was found to differ by parents' gender. Specifically, in a study of Cuban American youth, they believed that a good relationship with mothers would include extensive involvement in their children's lives whereas for fathers, they would make important decisions and deal with disciplining (see Crockett et al., 2010). Thus, it was very unfortunate that the opportunity to better understand how gender, and more specifically, fathers, may have played a role in family dynamics and relationships were overlooked.

Immigrant Chinese Fathers are Under-Researched

Conceptual Exclusions

The dearth of research on immigrant Chinese fathers may be attributable to the assumed deficiency of immigrant fathers that has colored much of the research on immigrant and ethnic minority fathers. Immigrant Chinese fathers (and more broadly, immigrant East Asian fathers) and particularly the new arrivals, unlike other less privileged ethnic minorities, are characterized by hyper-selectivity, ethnic capital, and the "stereotype promise" (Chen & Hou, 2019; Liu-Farrer, 2016; Zhou & Lee, 2017). Many Chinese immigrants are in the upper end of the socioeconomic spectrum and are seen as the "model minority" who can achieve upward socio-economic mobility within a short period of time (Zhou & Lee, 2017). For instance, Chinese ethnics in the United States, especially the American-born, are more likely to have obtained undergraduate or graduate degrees than the white majority (Pew Research Center, 2017). Chinese Americans also have above-median income, although a not-insignificant fraction of first-generation Chinese immigrants still struggle in poverty (Echeverria-Estrada & Batalova, 2020).

These socioeconomic patterns are similarly noted in Canada and the United Kingdom (UK) (Racial Disparity Unit, 2020): In the UK, in particular, Chinese men have the highest median gross hourly wage among men from all ethnic groups (Office for National Statistics, 2019). In addition, immigrant Chinese American fathers were as likely, if not more likely, to be in two-parent households with children than white, African American, and Latino fathers. Chinese American families are also less likely to be single-parent families (Hernandez et al., 2008). A similar pattern is observed in Canada (Chui, Tran, & Flanders, 2005) and the UK (Racial Disparity Unit, 2020). Given that immigrant Chinese men have exceeded minimal thresholds of responsible fatherhood (i.e., provision and co-residence), they are assumed to be functional, acculturated, and qualified. As the fatherhood research agenda has been driven primarily by a deficit/negative narrative when exploring ethnic minority fathers (e.g., fatherlessness among Black fathers; Green et al., 2019), the fact that Chinese fathers do not fit neatly into the stereotypical model of deficiency seems to have implied that they would not need scholarly, public or policy scrutiny (Kao et al., 2018).

Yet, it is worth noting that Chinese fathers are not always the elite immigrants that they are stereotypically believed to be. Many new Chinese immigrants suffer from poverty and hardship on the new shore, and some reside in the host country without legal immigration status (Wu & Sheehan, 2011; Yoshikawa, 2011). Unlike Chinese immigrants in North America and the UK, most of whom migrated as higher education students, skilled professionals, and investors, and thus enjoy high socioeconomic status, Chinese immigrants have below-average household income in Australia and New Zealand (Australian Government Department of Home Affairs, 2019; Stats New Zealand, 2017). Many Chinese immigrants in France and Italy, who arrived in Europe as unskilled workers through co-ethnic networks, would start off from the low end of the socioeconomic ladder and struggle to achieve social and economic mobility beyond the ethnic enclave (Ceccagno, 2003; Latham & Wu, 2013). Immigrant Chinese fathers in these contexts are probably less resourceful parents than their non-immigrant counterparts. However, little research has been conducted on these fathers, perhaps because they were perceived to be an unlikely threat to host societies' public safety and order due to stereotypes about Chinese males being physically and socially unaggressive, which can, in turn, create stress and challenges for their parental roles. The diverse socio-economic positions of Chinese fathers also call for comparative attention to host-society heterogeneities, in addition to a call for attention to distinct countries of origin for immigrant Chinese fathers.

Methodological Hurdles

The low visibility of immigrant Chinese fathers in existing research undoubtedly has to do with a host of factors. First, the relatively small population size of the Chinese diaspora in many host countries and the recency of Chinese immigrant communities, compared to other larger, more established ethnic minority groups (Echeverria-Estrada & Batalova, 2020) make it more challenging for researchers to recruit Chinese families. Size and history of immigrant communities matter as smaller groups may be filtered out from large datasets during data analysis (e.g., Cabrera et al., 2011), and recent arrivals may not have been included in census and research datasets in a timely manner.

The small populations of immigrant Chinese fathers are further divided by the vastly heterogeneous subgroups under the umbrella term "Chinese" that have distinctive economic, cultural, linguistic, and immigration backgrounds and sometimes divergent ethnic identifications (Chuang et al., in this volume). Such divergence may have resulted in even smaller samples of immigrant Chinese fathers (Qin & Chang, 2012), thereby precluding nuanced statistical analysis of complex family processes and meaningful intra-cultural comparisons.

Moreover, existing measurement schemes, such as the categorization of race and ethnicity in many surveys and the United States census, have not only failed to capture intra-ethnic diversity of "Chinese" ethnicity but have also often aggregated Chinese ethnicities into the categories such as "Asians" and "Asians and Pacific Islanders." These broad terms for "Chinese" have also been adopted by many researchers (see Table 14.1).

Perhaps more relevant and pressing is the difficulties in engaging with the Chinese community, and building a trust relationship with them. While researchers may be able to locate the Chinese community, gaining access to the families is challenging as many organizations, such as Churches, do not allow "business" to occur. Thus, it becomes even more limiting for researchers to recruit immigrant Chinese fathers, as fathers are re-establishing themselves and their families family in a new country with limited resources and time.

Conclusions and Future Directions

It is important to study immigrant Chinese fathers, given the predicted expansion of this group in the foreseeable future. Specifically, demographic projections suggest that the Chinese emigration to developed countries is likely to continue to grow, especially through enrollment in higher education and employment, expanding an already substantial body of young immigrants of childbearing age (Li & Li, 2013; Xiang, 2016). Nearly half (47.2%) of the Chinese ethnics in the UK are between 18 and 34 years of age (Race Disparity Unit, 2019), and China remains the largest sending country of international students to the United States (Echeverria-Estrada & Batalova, 2020) and the UK (Cebolla-Boado, Hu, & Soysal, 2018). Therefore, we can reasonably expect the population of immigrant Chinese fathers to grow in both size and visibility.

Secondly, the challenges faced by immigrant Chinese fathers and their children and families have rarely been acknowledged and scrutinized in existing research. A few studies (e.g., Miao et al., 2018; Qin, 2009) have outlined the challenges that immigrant Chinese fathers share with minority and immigrant fathers of other ethnicities, such as economic pressure, downward social mobility, and parent-child conflicts. However, the fathering and resources specific to immigrant Chinese fathers and their families are yet to be fully explored. Insights into immigrant Chinese fathers can serve as a starting point for research not only on immigrant Chinese communities but also a model for rendering visibility to other understudied groups of immigrant fathers and their distinctive cultural traditions, immigration pathways, socio-economic, and cultural standing in their host countries.

More importantly, the unique cultural and sociodemographic characteristics of immigrant Chinese fathers can help generate ethno-theories and contribute to decolonizing existing white and middle-class centered assumptions about immigrant and ethnic minority fathers. Moreover, immigrant Chinese fathers can also be a valuable data source for the investigation and its consequences for fathers, children, and other family members given their presence in diverse social niches of host countries worldwide. Qualitative (e.g., interviews, structured or naturalistic observation, and ethnography) and mixed methods, as well as archival, textual, and visual data can complement the widely-used quantitative methods to capture the potential intra-ethnic diversity of Chinese immigrant fathers who are potentially stratified by their economic resources, human capital (e.g., education and skills) and migration trajectories (e.g., as skilled professional/talent, family migrants, or undocumented immigrants).

Chuang (2018) criticized that studies on Chinese families often resort to cultural stereotypes (e.g., the "strict father, warm mother" adage) without acknowledging the cross-cutting influences of social, economic, and political transformations in modern Chinese societies on parental and gender roles (Hu & Scott, 2016). Existing studies on immigrant Chinese fathers are often predicated on implicit essentialist beliefs about a coherent "Chineseness," as reflected in an over-reliance on cultural values from traditional China and sometimes inappropriate generalizations of empirical evidence from contemporary Chinese societies to immigrant populations. Thus far, critiques are mainly directed at the problematic application of traditional Chinese values to modern Chinese contexts (Chuang et al., 2018). Yet one should be cautious to infer the characteristics of the Chinese immigrant population from observations of their geolocations of origin, due to the highly selective nature of Chinese emigrants in socioeconomic and cultural terms (Xiang, 2016; Zhou & Lee, 2017). As Chinese fathers of distinct socioeconomic traits are selectively channeled to different migration destinations, the conceptualization of immigrant Chinese fathers needs to be carefully considered in relation to varying mechanisms of self- and context-imposed selection of Chinese ethnics into international migration.

Some limitations of this review should also be noted. This review is drawn on research on immigrant Chinese fathers in relatively affluent, white-majority western countries that are typical exemplars of Western, Educated, Industrialized, Rich, and Democratic ("WEIRD") societies (Henrich et al., 2010). These countries are chosen because they have been major immigration destinations and they represent cases where the Chinese fathers' ethnic minority status is supposed to be most visible, which contrasts with the fact that immigrant Chinese fathers remain largely invisible in the fathering and fatherhood literature in these countries. By contrast, the ethnic minority status of immigrant Chinese fathers, despite their large demographic representation, is less visible in countries in East Asia (e.g., Japan, Korea) and Southeast Asia (e.g., Singapore, Thailand, Malaysia, and Indonesia). The beliefs, practices, and influences of immigrant Chinese fathers in non-western contexts warrant separate investigations. Finally, our review focused on recent English-language publications, which means that the interpretations of our critiques should be limited to the English-language scholarship. We are aware, though, that non-Anglophone countries such as France and Italy also have large immigrant Chinese communities. Thus, there may be a body of literature on immigration and ethnic minority fathers, and we hope that our review can be enriched by future coverage of the multilingual literature.

A useful direction is to comparatively examine Chinese fathers in diverse host locations as Anglophone countries have usually been taken as the "default" context of migration and multiculturalism. Comparing immigrant Chinese fathers in Anglophone countries with their counterparts that settled in same-race (such as Japan, Korea, or Singapore; see Chan, 2013) and non-white-majority host countries (e.g., Central and South America) could help reveal how host-country characteristics (e.g., migration policy, demographic composition, or the dominant masculinity norms) may influence the adjustment of immigrant fathers and their fathering beliefs and practices. In this sense, Wong's (1985) early comparative research on the family life (including the fathers' role) of Chinese immigrants in New York, Lima, and Manila sets a good example, and some recent studies of Chinese immigrants in a cross-national context provides a helpful road map (Tan, 2013).

Overall, immigrant Chinese fathers are disproportionately underrepresented in the existing research on immigrant families, even though scholars have acknowledged the importance of fathers' contribution to their children's development and have demonstrated interests in immigrant Chinese families. Existing empirical studies on Chinese fathers have focused on their involvement in childcare, fathering practices, acculturative experiences, and roles in children's education. However, these studies are not only small in number but also fall short in conceptual depth and methodological diversity. Thus, future research that employs diverse methods, addresses intra-ethnic diversity, and investigates immigrant Chinese fathers in non-WEIRD contexts could make substantial contributions to the fatherhood scholarship.

References

Arnett, J. L. (2008). The neglected 95%: Why American psychology needs to become less American. *American Psychologist, 63*, 602–614. https://doi.org/10.1037/0003-066X.63.7.602

Australian Bureau of Statistics. (2017). *Cultural diversity in Australia: 2016 Census data summary.*https://www.abs.gov.au/ausstats/abs@.nsf/Lookup/bySubject/2071.0~2016~Main Features~Cultural Diversity Data Summary~30

Australian Government Department of Home Affairs, A. G. (2019). *China-born community information summary*. https://www.homeaffairs.gov.au/mca/files/2016-cis-china.PDF

Bronfenbrenner, U., & Morris, P. (2006). The bioecological model of human development. In W. Damon & R. M. Lerner (Eds.), *Handbook of child psychology* (6th ed., pp. 793–828). Wiley.

Cabrera, N. J., Hofferth, S. L., & Chae, S. (2011). Patterns and predictors of father–infant engagement across race/ethnic groups. *Early Childhood Research Quarterly, 26*(3), 365–375. https://doi.org/10.1016/j.ecresq.2011.01.001

Cabrera, N. J., & Tamis-LeMonda, C. S. (Eds.). (2013). Handbook of father involvement: Multidisciplinary perspectives (2nd ed.). Routledge.

Capps, R., Bronte-Tinkew, J., & Horowitz, A. (2010). Acculturation and father engagement with infants among Chinese-and Mexican-origin immigrant fathers. *Fathering: A Journal of Theory, Research & Practice about Men as Fathers, 8*(1), 61–92. https://doi.org/10.3149/fth.0801.61

Cebolla-Boado, H., Hu, Y., & Soysal, Y. N. (2018). Why study abroad?: Sorting of Chinese students across British universities. *British Journal of Sociology of Education, 39*(3), 365–380. https://doi.org/10.1080/01425692.2017.1349649

Ceccagno, A. (2003). New Chinese migrants in Italy. *International Migration, 41*(3), 187–213. https://doi.org/10.1111/1468-2435.00246

Chan, K. B. (Ed.). (2013). *International handbook of Chinese families*. New York, NY: Springer.

Chance, L. J., Costigan, C. L., & Leadbeater, B. J. (2013). Coparenting in immigrant Chinese Canadian families: The role of discrepancies in acculturation and expectations for adolescent assistance. *Journal of Family Psychology, 27*(6), 905–914. https://doi.org/10.1037/a0034909

Chao, R. K., & Kaeochinda, K. F. (2010). Parental sacrifice and acceptance as distinct dimensions of parental support among Chinese and Filipino American adolescents. In S. T. Russell, L. J. Crockett, & R. K. Chao (Eds.), *Asian American parenting and parent-adolescent relationships* (pp. 61–77). Springer. https://doi.org/10.1007/978-1-4419-5728-3_4

Chen, J. J., Sun, P., & Yu, Z. (2017). A comparative study on parenting of preschool children between the Chinese in China and Chinese immigrants in the United States. *Journal of Family Issues, 38*(9), 1262–1287. https://doi.org/10.1177/0192513X15619460

Chen, W.-H. & Hou, F. (2019). *Intergenerational education mobility and labour market outcomes: Variation among the second generation of immigrants in Canada*. https://www150.statcan.gc.ca/n1/en/catalogue/11F0019M2019006.

Chuang, S. S. (2018). The complexities of immigration and families: Theoretical perspectives and current issues. In B. H. Fiese, M. Celano, K. Deater-Deckard, E. N. Jouriles, & M. A. Whisman (Eds.), *Handbook of contemporary family psychology: Applications and broad impact offamily*

psychology (Vol. 2, pp. 437–455). American Psychological Association. https://psycnet.apa.org/fulltext/2018-59955-027.pdf
Chuang, S. S., & Moreno, R. P. (Eds.). (2008). On new shores: Understanding immigrant fathers in North America. Lexington Books.
Chuang, S. S., & Costigan, C. L. (Eds.). (2018). Parental roles and relationships in immigrant families: An international approach. Springer. https://doi.org/10.1007/978-3-319-71399-1
Chuang, S. S., Glozman, J., Green, D. S., & Rasmi, S. (2018). Parenting and family relationships in Chinese families: A critical ecological approach. *Journal of Family Theory & Review, 10*, 367–383. https://doi.org/10.1111/jftr.12257
Chuang, S. S., Li, X., & Huang, C.-Y. (in press). Chinese families from China, Hong Kong, and Taiwan. In S. S. Chuang, R. Moodley, U. Gielen, & S. Akram (Eds.), *Asian families in Canada and the United States: Implications for mental health and well-being*. Springer.
Chuang, S. S., Moreno, R. P., & Su, Y. (2013). Moving fathers from the "sidelines": Contemporary Chinese fathers in Canada and China. In K. B. Chan & N. C. Hung (Eds.), *International handbook of Chinese families* (pp. 343–357). Springer. https://doi.org/10.1007/978-1-4614-0266-4_21
Chuang, S. S., & Su, Y. (2008). Transcending Confucian teachings on fathering: A sign of the times or acculturation. In S. S. Chuang & R. P. Moreno (Eds.), *On new shores: Understanding immigrant fathers in North America* (pp. 129–150). Lexington Books.
Chuang, S. S., & Su, Y. (2009a). Do we see eye to eye? Chinese mothers' and fathers' parenting beliefs and values for toddlers in Canada and China. *Journal of Family Psychology, 23*(3), 331–341. https://doi.org/10.1037/a0016015
Chuang, S. S., & Su, Y. (2009b). Says who?: Decision-making and conflicts among Chinese-Canadian and Mainland Chinese parents of young children. *Sex Roles, 60*(7–8), 527–536. https://doi.org/10.1007/s11199-008-9537-9
Chuang, S. S., & Tamis-LeMonda, C. S. (Eds.). (2013). *Gender roles in immigrant families*. Springer.
Chuang, S. S., & Zhu, M. (2018). Where are you Daddy?: An exploration of father involvement in Chinese families in Canada and Mainland China. In S. S. Chuang & C. L. Costigan (Eds.), *Parental roles and relationships in immigrant families: An international approach* (pp. 11–30). Springer.
Chui, T., Tran, K., & Flanders, J. (2005). *Chinese Canadians: Enriching the cultural mosaic*. https://www150.statcan.gc.ca/n1/en/pub/11-008-x/2004004/article/7778-eng.pdf?st=Eflucu7o
Costigan, C., Lehr, S., & Miao, S. (2016). Beyond economics: Broadening perspectives on immigration to Canada. *Canadian Ethnic Studies, 48*(1), 19–44. https://doi.org/10.1353/ces.2016.0006
Costigan, C., & Su, T. F. (2008). Cultural predictors of the parenting cognitions of immigrant Chinese mothers and fathers in Canada. *International Journal of Behavioral Development, 32*(5), 432–442. https://doi.org/10.1177/0165025408093662
Costigan, C. L., & Dokis, D. P. (2006a). Similarities and differences in acculturation among mothers, fathers, and children in immigrant Chinese families. *Journal of Cross-Cultural Psychology, 37*(6), 723–741. https://doi.org/10.1177/0022022106292080
Costigan, C. L., & Dokis, D. P. (2006b). Relations between parent–child acculturation differences and adjustment within immigrant Chinese families. *Child Development, 77*(5), 1252–1267. https://doi.org/10.1111/j.1467-8624.2006.00932.x
Costigan, C. L., & Koryzma, C. M. (2011). Acculturation and adjustment among immigrant Chinese parents: Mediating role of parenting efficacy. *Journal of Counseling Psychology, 58*(2), 183–196. https://doi.org/10.1037/a0021696
Costigan, C. L., & Su, T. F. (2004). Orthogonal versus linear models of acculturation among immigrant Chinese Canadians: A comparison of mothers, fathers, and children. *International Journal of Behavioral Development, 28*(6), 518–527. https://doi.org/10.1080/01650250444000234
Crane, D. R., Ngai, S. W., Larson, J. H., & Hafen, M., Jr. (2005). The influence of family functioning and parent-adolescent acculturation on North American Chinese adolescent outcomes. *Family Relations, 54*(3), 400–410. https://doi.org/10.1111/j.1741-3729.2005.00326.x

Crockett, L. J., Brown, J. R., Iturbide, M. I., Russell, S. T., & Wilkinson-Lee, A. M. (2009). Conceptions of good parent-adolescent relationships among Cuban American teenagers. *Sex Roles, 60*, 575–587. https://doi-org.subzero.lib.uoguelph.ca/10.1007/s11199-008-9469-4

Crockett, L. J., Veed, G. J., & Russell, S. T. (2010). Do measures of parenting have the same meaning for European, Chinese, and Filipino American adolescents?: Tests of measurement equivalence. In S. Russell, L. Crockett, & R. Chao (Eds.), *Asian American parenting and parent-adolescent relationships* (pp. 17–35). Springer. https://doi.org/10.1007/978-1-4419-5728-3_2

Dinh, K. T., & Nguyen, H. H. (2006). The effects of acculturative variables on Asian American parent–child relationships. *Journal of Social and Personal Relationships, 23*(3), 407–426. https://doi.org/10.1177/0265407506064207

Echeverria-Estrada, C., & Batalova, J. (2020). *Chinese immigrants in the United States*. Migrationpolicy.Org. https://www.migrationpolicy.org/article/chinese-immigrants-united-states

Fung, J. J., & Lau, A. S. (2010). Factors associated with parent–child (dis)agreement on child behavior and parenting problems in Chinese immigrant families. *Journal of Clinical Child & Adolescent Psychology, 39*(3), 314–327. https://doi.org/10.1080/15374411003691693

Garcia Coll, C., & Pachter, L. M. (2002). Ethnic and minority parenting. In M. H. Bornstein (Ed.), *Handbook of parenting: Social conditions and applied parenting* (Vol. 4, pp. 1–20). Erlbaum.

Green, D. S., Chuang, S. S., Parke, R. D., & Este, D. C. (2019). Multidimensionality and complexities of fathering: A critical examination of Afro-Jamaican fathers' perspectives. *Sex Roles, 81*, 576–593. https://doi.org/10.1007/s11199-019-1012-2

Greenhalgh, S. (2014). "Bare sticks" and other dangers to the social body: Assembling fatherhood in China. In M. C. Inhorn, W. Chavkin, & J.-A. Navarro (Eds.), *Globalized fatherhood* (Vol. 27, pp. 359–381). Berghahn Books.

Guo, K. (2014). For a better life: The aspirations of Chinese immigrants in parenting. *Journal of Immigrant & Refugee Studies, 12*(3), 293–310. https://doi.org/10.1080/15562948.2013.843047

Henrich, J., Heine, S. J., & Norenzayan, A. (2010). Beyond WEIRD: Towards a broad-based behavioral science. *Behavioral and Brain Sciences, 33*, 111–135. https://doi.org/10.1017/S0140525X10000725

Hernandez, D. J., Denton, N. A., & McCartney, S. E. (2008). Immigrant fathers: A demographic portrait. In S. S. Chuang & R. P. Moreno (Eds.), *On new shores: Immigrant fathers in North America* (pp. 47–104). Lanham, MD: Lexington Books.

Hsu, K. (1996). Joint attention in a father-child-mother triad: A Chinese-American case study. *Issues in Applied Linguistics, 7*(1), 77–90.

Hu, Y., & Scott, J. (2016). Family and gender values in China: Generational, geographic, and gender differences. *Journal of Family Issues, 37*(9), 1267–1293. https://doi.org/10.1177/0192513X14528710

Huntsinger, C. S., & Jose, P. E. (2009). Relations among parental acceptance and control and children's social adjustment in Chinese American and European American families. *Journal of Family Psychology, 23*(3), 321–330. https://doi.org/10.1037/a0015812

Huntsinger, C. S., Jose, P. E., & Larson, S. L. (1998). Do parent practices to encourage academic competence influence the social adjustment of young European American and Chinese American children? *Developmental Psychology, 34*(4), 747–756. https://doi.org/10.1037/0012-1649.34.4.747

Huntsinger, C. S., Jose, P. E., Larson, S. L., Balsink Krieg, D., & Shaligram, C. (2000). Mathematics, vocabulary, and reading development in Chinese American and European American children over the primary school years. *Journal of Educational Psychology, 92*(4), 745–760. https://doi.org/10.1037/0022-0663.92.4.745

Inhorn, M. C., Chavkin, W., & Navarro, J.-A. (Eds.). (2014). *Globalized fatherhood* (Vol. 27). Berghahn Books.

Istat (2014). Cittadini non comunitari regolarmente soggiornanti anni 2013–2014 [Legally residing non-EU citizens in years 2013–2014]. https://www.istat.it/it/files//2014/08/CITTADINI-NON-COMUNITARI.pdf

Ji, C. S., & Koblinsky, S. A. (2009). Parent involvement in children's education: An exploratory study of urban, Chinese immigrant families. *Urban Education, 44*(6), 687–709. https://doi.org/10.1177/0042085908322706

Jose, P. E., Huntsinger, C. S., Huntsinger, P. R., & Liaw, F.-R. (2000). Parental values and practices relevant to young children's social development in Taiwan and the United States. *Journal of Cross-Cultural Psychology, 31*(6), 677–702. https://doi.org/10.1177/0022022100031006002

Juang, L. P., Qin, D. B., & Park, I. J. K. (2013). Deconstructing the myth of the "tiger mother": An introduction to the special issue on tiger parenting, Asian-heritage families, and child/adolescent well-being. *Asian American Journal of Psychology, 4*(1), 1. https://doi.org/10.1037/a0032136

Juang, L. P., Syed, M., & Takagi, M. (2007). Intergenerational discrepancies of parental control among Chinese American families: Links to family conflict and adolescent depressive symptoms. *Journal of Adolescence, 30*(6), 965–975. https://doi.org/10.1016/j.adolescence.2007.01.004

Kao, G., Balistreri, K. S., & Joyner, K. (2018). Asian American men in romantic dating markets. *Contexts*. https://doi.org/10.1177/1536504218812869

Kendal. W. A. (2018). U.S. family-based immigration policy. https://fas.org/sgp/crs/homesec/R43145.pdf

Kim, D. Y., & Kulkarni, V. S. (2009). The role of father's occupation on intergenerational educational and occupational mobility: The case of second-generation Chinese Americans in New York. *Sociological Forum, 24*, 104–134. https://doi.org/10.1111/j.1573-7861.2008.01088.x

Kim, S. Y., Chen, Q., Li, J., Huang, X., & Moon, U. J. (2009). Parent–child acculturation, parenting, and adolescent depressive symptoms in Chinese immigrant families. *Journal of Family Psychology, 23*(3), 426–437. https://doi.org/10.1037/a0016019

Kim, S. Y., Chen, Q., Wang, Y., Shen, Y., & Orozco-Lapray, D. (2013). Longitudinal linkages among parent-child acculturation discrepancy, parenting, parent-child sense of alienation, and adolescent adjustment in Chinese immigrant families. *Developmental Psychology, 49*, 900–912. https://doi.org/10.1037/a0029169

Klein, A. (2008). From Mao to Memphis: Chinese immigrant fathers' involvement with their children's education. *School Community Journal, 18*(2), 91–118.

Koh, J. B. K., Shao, Y., & Wang, Q. (2009). Father, mother and me: Parental value orientations and child self-identity in Asian American immigrants. *Sex Roles, 60*(7–8), 600–610. https://doi.org/10.1007/s11199-008-9550-z

Kushner, K. E., Sopcak, N., Breitkreuz, R., Pitre, N., Williamson, D. L., Rempel, G., … Letourneau, N. (2017). On shifting ground: First-time parents' ideal world of paid work and family time. *Community, Work & Family, 20*(2), 119–141. https://doi.org/10.1080/13668803.2015.1074546

Lamb, M. E., Pleck, J. H., Charnov, E. L., & Levine, J. A. (1987). A biosocial perspective on paternal behavior and involvement. In J. B. Lancaster, J. Atlman, & A. Rossi (Eds.), *Parenting across the lifespan: Biosocial dimensions* (pp. 11–42). Academic Press.

Lamb, M. E. (Ed.). (2010). *The role of the father in child development* (5th ed.). Wiley.

Lamb, M. E., Chuang, S. S., & Hwang, C. P. (2004). Internal reliability, temporal stability, and correlates of individual differences in paternal involvement: A 15-year longitudinal study in Sweden. In R. Day & M. E. Lamb (Eds.), *Conceptualizing and measuring father involvement* (pp. 129–148). Erlbaum.

Latham, K., & Wu, B. (2013). *Chinese immigration to the EU: New trends, dynamics, and implications.* https://www.chathamhouse.org/sites/default/files/public/Research/Asia/0313ecran_lathamwu.pdf

Lau, A. S. (2010). Physical discipline in Chinese American immigrant families: An adaptive culture perspective. *Cultural Diversity and Ethnic Minority Psychology, 16*(3), 313–322. https://doi.org/10.1037/a0018667

Li, C., & Li, H. (2017). Chinese immigrant parents' perspectives on psychological well-being, acculturative stress, and support: Implications for multicultural consultation. *Journal of Educational and Psychological Consultation, 27*(3), 245–270. https://doi.org/10.1080/10474412.2016.1275648

Li, P. S., & Li, E. X. (2013). The Chinese overseas population. In C.-B. Tan (Ed.), *Routledge handbook of the Chinese diaspora* (pp. 15–28). Routledge.

Li, X., Zhou, Q., & Hou, K. (2015). Marital conflict of Chinese American immigrant couples: A mediator of socioeconomic incorporation and children's behavioral problems. *Journal of Child and Family Studies, 24*(12), 3816–3826. https://doi.org/10.1007/s10826-015-0190-y

Lieber, E., Nihira, K., & Mink, I. T. (2004). Filial piety, modernization, and the challenges of raising children for Chinese immigrants: Quantitative and qualitative evidence. *Ethos, 32*(3), 324–347. https://doi.org/10.1525/eth.2004.32.3.324

Lin, C. Y. C., & Fu, V. R. (1990). A comparison of child-rearing practices among Chinese, immigrant Chinese, and Caucasian-American parents. *Child Development, 61*(2), 429–433. https://doi.org/10.1111/j.1467-8624.1990.tb02789.x

Liu, L. L., Lau, A. S., Chen, A. C.-C., Dinh, K. T., & Kim, S. Y. (2009). The influence of maternal acculturation, neighborhood disadvantage, and parenting on Chinese American adolescents' conduct problems: Testing the segmented assimilation hypothesis. *Journal of Youth and Adolescence, 38*(5), 691–702. https://doi.org/10.1007/s10964-008-9275-x

Liu-Farrer, G. (2016). Migration as class-based consumption: The emigration of the rich in contemporary China. *The China Quarterly, 226*, 499–518. https://doi.org/10.1017/S0305741016000333

Mao, A., Bottorff, J. L., Oliffe, J. L., Sarbit, G., & Kelly, M. T. (2015). A qualitative study of Chinese Canadian fathers' smoking behaviors: Intersecting cultures and masculinities. *BMC Public Health, 15*(1), 286–295. https://doi.org/10.1186/s12889-015-1646-0

McHale, S. M., Crouter, A. C., & Whiteman, S. D. (2003). The family contexts of gender development in childhood and adolescence. *Social Development, 12*(1), 125–148. https://doi.org/10.1111/1467-9507.00225

Miao, S. W., Costigan, C. L., & MacDonald, S. W. S. (2018). Spillover of stress to Chinese Canadian immigrants' parenting: Impact of acculturation and parent–child stressors. *Asian American Journal of Psychology, 9*(3), 190–199. https://doi.org/10.1037/aap0000105

Miconi, D., Moscardino, U., Altoè, G., & Salcuni, S. (2019). Parental supervision, executive functions, and emotional-behavioral problems in Chinese immigrant and Italian nonimmigrant early adolescents in Italy. *The Journal of Early Adolescence, 39*(8), 1177–1209. https://doi.org/10.1177/0272431618812157

Office for National Statistics, U. K. (2019). *Ethnicity pay gaps in Great Britain*. https://www.ons.gov.uk/employmentandlabourmarket/peopleinwork/earningsandworkinghours/articles/ethnicitypaygapsingreatbritain/2018

Padmawidjaja, I. A., & Chao, R. K. (2010). Parental beliefs and their relation to the parental practices of immigrant Chinese Americans and European Americans. In S. T. Russell, L. Crockett, & R. K. Chao (Eds.), *Asian American parenting and parent-adolescent relationships* (pp. 37–60). New York, NY: Springer. https://doi.org/10.1007/978-1-4419-5728-3_3

Parke, R. D., & Cookston, J. T. (2019). Fathers and families. In M. H. Bornstein (Ed.), *Handbook of parenting* (Vol. 3, 3rd ed., pp. 64–136). Routledge.

Pew Research Center. (2017). *Chinese in the U.S. fact sheet*. https://www.pewsocialtrends.org/fact-sheet/asian-americans-chinese-in-the-u-s/

Poston, D. L., & Wong, J. H. (2016). The Chinese diaspora: The current distribution of the overseas Chinese population. *Chinese Journal of Sociology, 2*(3), 348–373. https://doi.org/10.1177/2057150X16655077

Qin, D. B. (2009). Gendered processes of adaptation: Understanding parent–child relations in Chinese immigrant families. *Sex Roles, 60*(7–8), 467–481. https://doi.org/10.1007/s11199-008-9485-4

Qin, D. B., & Chang, T.-F. (2012). Asian American fathers. In N. J. Cabrera & C. S. Tamis-LeMonda (Ed.), *Handbook of father involvement: Multidisciplinary perspectives* (2nd ed.). Routledge. http://ebookcentral.proquest.com/lib/nyulibrary-ebooks/detail.action?docID=1092738

Racial Disparity Unit, U. K. (2020). *Chinese ethnic group: Facts and figures*. GOV.UK. https://www.gov.uk/government/publications/ethnicity-facts-and-figures-chinese-ethnic-group/chinese-ethnic-group-facts-and-figures

Rasmi, S., & Costigan, C. L. (2018). Comparing the acculturation goals of parents and adolescents in Chinese Canadian families. In S. S. Chuang & C. L. Costigan (Eds.), *Parental roles and relationships in immigrant families* (pp. 213–232). Springer. https://doi.org/10.1007/978-3-319-71399-1_12

Russell, S. T., Chu, J. Y., Crockett, L. J., & Doan, S. N. (2010). The meanings of parent-adolescent relationship quality among Chinese American and Filipino American adolescents. In S. T. Russell, L. Crockett, & R. K. Chao (Eds.), *Asian American parenting and parent-adolescent relationships* (pp. 79–100). Springer. https://doi.org/10.1007/978-1-4419-5728-3_5

Russell, S. T., Chu, J. Y., Crockett, L. J., & Lee, S. A. (2010). Interdependent independence: The meanings of autonomy among Chinese American and Filipino American adolescents. In S. T. Russell, L. Crockett, & R. K. Chao (Eds.), *Asian American parenting and parent-adolescent relationships* (pp. 101–116). Springer. https://doi.org/10.1007/978-1-4419-5728-3_6

Shen, Y., Kim, S. Y., & Wang, Y. (2016). Intergenerational transmission of educational attitudes in Chinese American families: Interplay of socioeconomic status and acculturation. *Child Development, 87*(5), 1601–1616. https://doi.org/10.1111/cdev.12545

Shwalb, D. W., Shwalb, B. J., & Lamb, M. E. (Eds.). (2013). *Fathers in cultural context*. Routledge.

Statistics Canada. (2017). *Distribution (in percentage) of immigrants living in Canada, by admission category and year of immigration, 2016*. https://www.statcan.gc.ca/eng/dai/btd/othervisuals/other007

Stats New Zealand. (2017). *2013 Census ethnic group profiles*. http://archive.stats.govt.nz/Census/2013-census/profile-and-summary-reports/ethnic-profiles.aspx

Stats New Zealand. (2019). *2018 Census totals by topic – national highlights (updated)*. https://www.stats.govt.nz/information-releases/2018-census-totals-by-topic-national-highlights-updated

Su, T. F., & Costigan, C. L. (2009). The development of children's ethnic identity in immigrant Chinese families in Canada: The role of parenting practices and children's perceptions of parental family obligation expectations. *The Journal of Early Adolescence, 29*(5), 638–663. https://doi.org/10.1177/0272431608325418

Tan, C.-B. (Ed.). (2013). *Routledge handbook of the Chinese diaspora*. London, UK/New York, NY: Routledge.

Tasopoulos-Chan, M., Smetana, J. G., & Yau, J. P. (2009). How much do I tell thee?: Strategies for managing information to parents among American adolescents from Chinese, Mexican, and European backgrounds. *Journal of Family Psychology, 23*(3), 364–374. https://doi.org/10.1037/a0015816

Tsai-Chae, A. H., & Nagata, D. K. (2008). Asian values and perceptions of intergenerational family conflict among Asian American students. *Cultural Diversity and Ethnic Minority Psychology, 14*(3), 205–214. https://doi.org/10.1037/1099-9809.14.3.205

U.S. Census Bureau. (2018). *ACS demographic and housing estimates*. https://data.census.gov/cedsci/table?q=people%20reporting%20ancestry&tid=ACSDP1Y2018.DP05&t=Ancestry&vintage=2018

Wang, Y., Kim, S. Y., Anderson, E. R., Chen, A. C. C., & Yan, N. (2012). Parent–child acculturation discrepancy, perceived parental knowledge, peer deviance, and adolescent delinquency in Chinese immigrant families. *Journal of Youth and Adolescence, 41*(7), 907–919. https://doi.org/10.1007/s10964-011-9705-z

Waters, J. L. (2010). Becoming a father, missing a wife: Chinese transnational families and the male experience of lone parenting in Canada. *Population, Space and Place, 16*(1), 63–74. https://doi.org/10.1002/psp.578

Weaver, S. R., & Kim, S. Y. (2008). A person-centered approach to studying the linkages among parent–child differences in cultural orientation, supportive parenting, and adolescent depressive symptoms in Chinese American families. *Journal of Youth and Adolescence, 37*(1), 36–49. https://doi.org/10.1007/s10964-007-9221-3

Wical, K. A., & Doherty, W. J. (2005). How reliable are fathers' reports of involvement with their children?: A methodological report. *Fathering, 3*(1), 81–92.

Wong, B. P. (1985). Family, kinship, and ethnic identity of the Chinese in New York City, with comparative remarks on the Chinese in Lima, Peru and Manila, Philippines. *Journal of Comparative Family Studies, 16*(2), 231–254. https://doi.org/10.3138/jcfs.16.2.231

Wu, B., & Sheehan, J. (2011). Globalization and vulnerability of Chinese migrant workers in Italy: Empirical evidence on working conditions and their consequences. *Journal of Contemporary China, 20*(68), 135–152. https://doi.org/10.1080/10670564.2011.520852

Xiang, B. (2016). *Emigration trends and policies in China: Movement of the wealthy and highly skilled*. Migration Policy Institute.

Yeung, W.-J., Sandberg, J. F., Davis-Kean, P. E., & Hofferth, S. L. (2001). Children's time with fathers in intact families. *Journal of Marriage and the Family, 63*(1), 136–154.

Yoshikawa, H. (2011). *Immigrants raising citizens: Undocumented parents and their children*. Russell Sage Foundation. http://ebookcentral.proquest.com/lib/nyulibrary-ebooks/detail.action?docID=4386933

Yuwen, W., & Chen, A. C. C. (2013). Chinese American adolescents: Perceived parenting styles and adolescents' psychosocial health. *International Nursing Review, 60*(2), 236–243. https://doi.org/10.1111/inr.12002

Zhang, Q., Keown, L., & Farruggia, S. (2014). Involvement in preschools: Comparing Chinese immigrant and non-Chinese parents in New Zealand. *International Research in Early Childhood Education, 5*(1), 64–82. http://search.proquest.com/docview/1941333035/

Zhou, M., & Lee, J. (2017). Hyper-selectivity and the remaking of culture: Understanding the Asian American achievement paradox. *Asian American Journal of Psychology, 8*(1), 7–15. https://doi.org/10.1037/aap0000069

Index

S. S. Chuang et al. (eds.), *Asian Families in Canada and the United States*, Advances in Immigrant Family Research,
https://doi.org/10.1007/978-3-030-56452-0

J

Q

R

S

The manufacturer's authorised representative in the EU is Springer Nature Customer Service Centre GmbH, Europaplatz 3, 69115 Heidelberg, Germany. If you have any concerns regarding our products, please contact ProductSafety@springernature.com

Printed and bound by CPI Group (UK) Ltd, Croydon, CR0 4YY
30/09/2026
02225296-0013